COPYRIGHT AND FREE SPEECH

COPYRIGHT AND FREE SPEECH

COMPARATIVE AND INTERNATIONAL ANALYSES

Edited by

JONATHAN GRIFFITHS

and

UMA SUTHERSANEN

OXFORD

UNIVERSITY PRESS

OXFORD

UNIVERSITY PRESS

Great Clarendon Street, Oxford OX2 6DP

Oxford University Press is a department of the University of Oxford.
It furthers the University's objective of excellence in research, scholarship,
and education by publishing worldwide in

Oxford New York

Auckland Cape Town Dar es Salaam Hong Kong Karachi
Kuala Lumpur Madrid Melbourne Mexico City Nairobi
New Delhi Shanghai Taipei Toronto

With offices in

Argentina Austria Brazil Chile Czech Republic France Greece
Guatemala Hungary Italy Japan South Korea Poland Portugal
Singapore Switzerland Thailand Turkey Ukraine Vietnam

Published in the United States
by Oxford University Press Inc., New York

British Library Cataloguing in Publication Data

Data available

Library of Congress Cataloging in Publication Data

Data available

ISBN 0–19–927604–8   978–0–19–927604–2

3 5 7 9 10 8 6 4

Typeset by RefineCatch Limited, Bungay, Suffolk
Printed in Great Britain
on acid-free paper by
Biddles Ltd., King's Lynn

FOREWORD

Although we use the word 'right' in the phrases 'intellectual property right'[1] and 'the right of free speech', it is used in a quite different sense in the two cases. An IPR is essentially negative and private. It is negative in that it entitles its owner to stop other people doing things, an entitlement which will, if necessary, be enforced by the courts. And it is private because it is vested in a private owner, generally, an individual (real or corporate). The 'right of free speech' on the other hand is neutral or positive. Traditionally, under the common law, I suppose the 'right' rested essentially on the absence of any law, public or private, forbidding the conduct concerned—all that is not expressly forbidden is permitted. But in many countries the law now goes further—providing some sort of positive right of free speech. Such a law may, and indeed is intended to, come into conflict with any other law which is a law suppressing free speech: the First Amendment is an old example and Article 10 of the European Convention on Human Rights, given fresh life in this country by incorporation into domestic law, is more recent.

Legislatures have, of course, in various ways, sought to temper IPRs so that they did not interfere, or interfere too much, with free expression. Hence, for instance, 'fair use' exceptions to copyright. But the exercise has not been entirely successful. Often, for instance, parody (particularly for commercial purposes) has been stopped. I came across a good example when I was still a law student. *Cleopatra* starring Richard Burton and Elizabeth Taylor had been widely advertised by a poster depicting Burton as Mark Anthony standing imposingly by a chaise longue adorned by Taylor. The Carry On team made *Carry on Cleo* starring Sid James and Barbara Windsor. Its poster was a spoof copy of the *Cleopatra* poster, substituting a grinning Sid James for Burton and a saucy winking Windsor for Taylor. An interlocutory

---

[1] Here I include not only conventional IPRs—patents, designs, trade marks, and particularly copyright, but also what may fairly be called, for present purposes, 'extended IPRs' by which I mean things like the torts of defamation or malicious falsehood and the action for breach of confidence. The *Naomi Campbell* case was about enforceability-or-no of a sort of IPR.

injunction was granted, on the basis of copyright.[2] Ridiculous, but probably right.[3]

Courts, also, have sometimes developed rules to temper interference with free expression. I suppose the best example of this is the rule that an interim injunction will not be granted to restrain an alleged defamation or malicious falsehood where the defendant intends to justify. But there are limits to what courts can do, when faced with an IPR—a *property right*. Hence the importance of a countervailing positive right of free expression. Once such a right can be brought into play, then the court must weigh competing rights—a task which gives more room to favour free expression than merely trimming an IPR or its enforcement.

This book is a magnificent survey of the conflict between IPRs, particularly copyright, and free expression. Jonathan Griffiths and Uma Suthersanen of Queen Mary, University of London are to be congratulated on organizing the Seminar which inspired it and on bringing together this collection of essays.

The Rt Hon Sir Robin Jacob
The Royal Courts of Justice
October 2004

---

[2] I do not know whether the case was reported—it probably was, in *The Times*, otherwise I would not have known about it.

[3] There is a direct parallel with the famous Warner Bros Legal Department–Groucho Marx correspondence about *Casablanca* and *A Night in Casablanca* ('I am sure the average movie fan could learn in time to distinguish between Ingrid Bergman and Harpo. I don't know whether I could but I'd sure like to try'). The difference is that Warner Bros had no IPR to hang their hat on.

ACKNOWLEDGEMENTS

We would like to thank a number of organizations and people for their help in supporting the conference upon which this volume is based. Clifford Chance LLP was extremely generous in providing the conference venue, catering, and organizational support. Particular thanks are due to Vanessa Marsland and Jane Ramsell. The Intellectual Property Institute gave valuable marketing and administrative support. Sir Robin Jacob and Professor Fiona Macmillan gave their time to chair sessions at the conference.

The conference was partly funded by the Queen Mary Intellectual Property Research Institute and by the Department of Law at Queen Mary. Thanks also to Michael Blakeney, John Cahir, Alison Firth, Joey Johnson, Spyros Maniatis, Adrian Sterling, and Guido Westkamp for their assistance before and during the conference.

We would also like to thank: Graham Dutfield, for his invaluable assistance in reading several of the chapters and undertaking editorial work while Uma went off to have a baby; Brian Tutt, for patiently reading three versions of his wife's chapter; Chris Rycroft and Katarina Wihlborg for steering this volume firmly into print; Ali, Isaac, and Sam for their patience, and Oliver Kailash Tutt, for providing a sense of perspective in life.

CONTENTS — SUMMARY

III THE DIGITAL WORLD

CONTENTS

9. Not Such a 'Timid Thing': The UK's Integrity Right and Freedom of Expression

III THE DIGITAL WORLD

14. First Amendment Speech and the Digital Millennium
Copyright Act: A Proper Marriage

LIST OF CONTRIBUTORS

Professor Eric Barendt Professor of Media Law, Faculty of Laws, University College London
Eric Barendt is the Goodman Professor of Media Law, teaching media law, constitutional law, and civil liberties. He writes in the area of media law, including broadcasting law, and on freedom of speech and is published widely. He was the General Editor of the *Yearbook of Copyright and Media Law*, published by Oxford University Press from 1995 to 2002. He was Vice-Dean of the Faculty from 1998–2000, and was a Fellow and Tutor at St Catherine's College, Oxford from 1971–1990.

Mr Robert Burrell Reader in Law, University of Queensland
Robert Burrell is Reader in Law at the University of Queensland, and Associate Director of the Australian Centre for Intellectual Property in Agriculture. He worked previously at the Australian National University and at King's College London. He has published widely on intellectual property, is the co-author (with A. Coleman) of *Copyright Exceptions: the Digital Impact* (Cambridge: CUP, 2005), and is sub-editor and co-author of the 14th edition of *Copinger and Skone James on Copyright*.

Professor Thomas Dreier Institut für Informationsrecht, Zentrum für angewandte Rechtswissenschaft (ZAR), Universität Karlsruhe
Thomas Dreier, Dr iur (Munich), MCJ (NYU), is Professor of Law at the University of Karlsruhe, Germany, where he is the Director of the Institute for Information Law. He was also a Global Visiting Professor of Law at the New York University, School of Law. Before joining the University of Karlsruhe, Professor Dreier worked at the Max Planck Institute for Foreign and International Patent, Copyright, and Competition Law, Munich, Germany (1983–1999). He is Vice-President of the Association Littéraire et Artistique Internationale (ALAI) and Vice-Chairman of ALAI's German national group as well as a member of the Advisory Panel on Intellectual Property of the Steering Committee of the Mass Media of the Council of Europe. Professor Dreier also acts as Executive Secretary of the German Computer Law Society (Deutsche Gesellschaft für Recht und Informatik, DGRI).

Professor Gerald Dworkin Emeritus Professor, King's College, University of London

Professor Gerald Dworkin is Emeritus Professor of Law, King's College, University of London, and was the Herchel Smith Professor at Queen Mary, University of London. His teaching and research interests cover all aspects of international, European, and national intellectual property law. He is a member of many intellectual property committees, including: Chairman of the British Copyright Council, the UK representative on EC Commission's Academic Committee on Copyright Law; member and immediate past Chairman of the British Literary and Artistic Copyright Association (BLACA); council member of the UK Intellectual Property Institute (IPI) and a member of the UK Law Society Sub-Committee on Intellectual Property.

Mr Kevin Garnett, QC Joint Head of Hogarth Chambers, London

Kevin Garnett has practised extensively in this field and is the Senior Editor of *Copinger and Skone James on Copyright*, one of the leading practitioners' texts in this field. He sits as a Deputy High Court Judge and is a Recorder. He is a co-author of a new work on moral rights and is the author of a variety of articles in the Intellectual Property and Media fields. He is an associate fellow of the Society of Advanced Legal Studies and a member of the Executive Committee of the British Library and Artistic Copyright Association (BLACA). He is a Bencher of Lincoln's Inn. As from 1st February 2005, he will be a legal member of the Boards of Appeal at the European Patent Office Munich.

Professor Ysolde Gendreau Professor, Faculté de droit, Université de Montréal

Ysolde Gendreau has also taught at McGill University, Université de Paris II, Université de Nantes, Université de Strasbourg III, Université de Lyon 2, University of Victoria, University of San Diego, and Monash University. She is currently President of the *Association for the Advancement of Teaching and Research in Intellectual Property* (ATRIP) and an associate member of the International Academy of Comparative Law.

Professor Wendy J Gordon Professor of Law and Paul J Liacos Scholar in Law, Boston University School of Law

Wendy Gordon's scholarship employs economics, philosophy and common-law analogues to investigate how the law should address the generation and circulation of beneficial products, particularly works of culture and information. With Richard Watt she co-edited *The Economics of Copyright* (2003), and her many articles include 'An Inquiry into the Merits of Copyright' (*Stanford Law Review*), 'A Property Right in Self-Expression' (*Yale Law Journal*), 'Fair Use as Market Failure' (*Columbia Law Review*), 'Render Copyright Unto Caesar' (*U of Chicago Law Review*), and 'On Owning Information' (*Virginia Law Review*). She also authored the *Oxford Handbook on Legal Studies* chapter on 'Intellectual Property'. She has served as Visiting Senior Research Fellow for Oxford's St. John's College, as a Fulbright Scholar, as an American Law & Economics Association Area Organizer for Intellectual Property (IP), and as Chair of the IP Section of the Association of American Law Schools. Her editorial board service includes the new *Review of Economic Research on Copyright Issues*.

Mr Jonathan Griffiths Senior Lecturer, Department of Law, Queen Mary, University of London
Jonathan Griffiths has written widely in the fields of copyright and information law. He is a solicitor and is co-author of *Blackstone's Guide to the Freedom of Information Act 2000* (2nd edn, Oxford: OUP, 2004).

The Rt Hon Lord Justice Jacob Court of Appeal of England and Wales
Sir Robin Jacob was appointed to the Bench in October 1993 and was Senior Judge of the Patents Court from 1995 to 1997. He was Supervising Chancery Judge for Birmingham, Bristol, and Cardiff from 1997 to 2001. He was appointed to the Court of Appeal in October 2003. Prior to his appointment as a judge he practised at the Patent Bar from 1967 and was appointed a QC in 1981.

Professor Fiona Macmillan School of Law, Birkbeck College, University of London
Fiona Macmillan is Professor of Law at Birkbeck College, University of London. She has previously held academic positions at the University of New South Wales, Leicester University, the Institute of Advanced Legal Studies (University of London), and at Murdoch University. She was the inaugural Copyright Director of the Asia Pacific Intellectual Property Law Institute. Her areas of expertise are intellectual property law and corporate regulation. Fiona Macmillan has published extensively in the areas of intellectual property law, corporate regulation, and WTO law. She is the author of *WTO and the Environment* (Sweet and Maxwell, 2001) and is currently working on a

new monograph for Hart Publishing entitled *The World Trade Organization and Human Rights*.

Professor Neil Weinstock Netanel Professor, UCLA School of Law
Neil Weinstock Netanel teaches and writes in the areas of copyright, international intellectual property, and Internet governance. His most recent scholarship examines copyright in the digital environment and the conflict between copyright and free speech. Professor Netanel is a co-editor of *The Commodification of Information* (Kluwer Law International, 2003) and is currently completing a book entitled, *Copyright's Paradox: Property in Expression/Freedom of Expression*, to be published by Oxford University Press.

Professor Raymond T Nimmer Leonard Childs Professor of Law, Law Center, University of Houston
Raymond Nimmer is Leonard Childs Professor of Law at the University of Houston Law Center and Co-Director of the University of Houston Institute for Intellectual Property and Information Law.

Professor Jeremy Phillips Visiting Professorial Fellow, Queen Mary Intellectual Property Research Institute; Visiting Professor, UCL, Universities of Alicante and Bournemouth; Intellectual Property Consultant, Slaughter and May (London)
Professor Phillips joined the Queen Mary Intellectual Property Research Institute in 2003. He has been Intellectual Property Consultant to London-based solicitors Slaughter and May since 1994 and is the Founder-Editor of Sweet & Maxwell's *European Trade Mark Reports* and *European Copyright and Design Reports*. Professor Phillips previously held posts at Trinity College Dublin and the University of Durham. The author of numerous books and articles on intellectual property, Professor Phillips is Consultant Editor of the *Butterworths Intellectual Property Law Handbook* and the *Butterworths E-commerce and Information Technology Law Handbook* as well as Editor of the *Information Technology Law Reports* (Lawtext Publications). He is also co-author (with Alison Firth) of *Introduction to Intellectual Property Law* (4th edn, Butterworths, 2002).

Mr James Stellios Lecturer, Faculty of Law, Australian National University
James Stellios is a Lecturer at the Australian National University Faculty of Law. Prior to joining the Faculty in July 2001, he spent a number of years working for the Federal Attorney-General's Department in Australia, princi-

pally in the area of constitutional litigation. Immediately prior to joining the Faculty, he was Counsel Assisting the Solicitor-General of Australia. He writes and teaches in the areas of constitutional law and public and private international law. He is a co-author of the Australian supplement to DJ Harris' *Cases and Materials on International Law*, and is currently working on a monograph on the constitutional role of juries.

Professor Alain Strowel Covington & Burling, Brussels, and Facultés universitaires Saint-Louis
Alain serves as a professor at the Saint-Louis University (Brussels), the University of Liège and the Catholic University of Brussels-Leuven, where he mainly teaches copyright and design law. A member of the Brussels Bar since 1988, Professor Strowel graduated in law (1983) and obtained a PhD in law (1992) from the University of Louvain-la-Neuve. In addition, he obtained graduate degrees in economics (1984) and philosophy (1985). Prior to joining Covington & Burling in 2001, he worked in the Brussels IP section of the Dutch firm NautaDutilh. He has written numerous articles, and books including *Droit d'auteur et copyright* (LGDJ and Bruylant, 1993), *Of Authors and Origins* (Clarendon Press, 1994), and *Droit d'auteur et numérique: logiciels, bases de données, multimédia* (Bruylant, 2001).

Professor (Dr) Mira T Sundara Rajan Assistant Professor of Law, The University of British Columbia, Vancouver
Professor Sundara Rajan is The University of British Columbia's nominee for a Canada Research Chair in Intellectual Property Law. She holds a DPhil in Copyright Law from the Oxford Intellectual Property Research Centre, St Peter's College, Oxford University. Her book, *Copyright and Creative Freedom*, will be forthcoming in 2005 from Routledge. She has published extensively on Intellectual Property matters, and has taught and consulted in the UK, the EU, Russia, India, and Australia, as well as Canada and the United States of America.

Dr Uma Suthersanen Senior Lecturer, Queen Mary Intellectual Property Research Institute, University of London
Dr Suthersanen was appointed Lecturer in Intellectual Property Law at Queen Mary in October 1998, and Senior Lecturer in 2002. She is an Executive Committee Member of the Association Littéraire et Artistique Internationale, Executive Committee Member of the British Literary and Artistic Copyright Association, and a Committee Member of the Legal

Advisory Committee of the British Computer Society. She is a joint General Editor, along with Michael Blakeney, of the Queen Mary Studies on Intellectual Property Series and the Assistant Editor of the European Copyright and Design Reports. Her publications include *Design Law in Europe* (Sweet & Maxwell, 2000), *Copyright: World Law and Practice* (with Morag Macdonald, Sweet & Maxwell, 2004), and *Global Intellectual Property Law* (with G Dutfield and S Maniatis, Edward Elgar, 2005).

Professor François Tulkens Saint-Louis University, Brussels
François Tulken was admitted to the Brussels Bar in 1986. He is a professor at the Facultés universitaires Saint-Louis where he lectures on constitutional law and environmental law and is in charge of exercises in the field of contemporary legal thinking. He is the Assistant-Secretary of the law journal *Journal des Tribunaux*, a member of the Board of Editors of the *Revue belge de droit constitutionnel* and *Revue Aménagement–Environnement*. He is also the editor and author of several publications, particularly in the field of constitutional law and administrative law, urban development law and environmental law, as well as media law.

TABLES OF CASES

European Commission of Human Rights

European Court of Human Rights

European Court of Justice

TABLES OF NATIONAL PRIMARY AND SECONDARY LEGISLATION

Finland

France

Germany

Ireland

TABLE OF INTERNATIONAL INSTRUMENTS

LIST OF ABBREVIATIONS

CDPA	Copyright, Designs and Patents Act 1988
CTEA	Copyright Term Extension Act of 1998
DeCSS	Decrypted Content Scrambling System
DMCA	Digital Millennium Copyright Act
ECHR	European Convention on Human Rights
GATT	General Agreement on Tariffs and Trade
ICCPR	International Covenant on Civil and Political Rights
ICESCR	International Covenant on Economic, Social, and Cultural Rights
NGO	Non-Governmental Organization
OECD	Organization for Economic Cooperation and Development
TPM	Technological Protection Measure
TRIPs	World Trade Organization Agreement on Trade-Related Aspects of Intellectual Property Rights
UDHR	Universal Declaration of Human Rights
WIPO	World Intellectual Property Organization
WTO	World Trade Organization

1

INTRODUCTION

Jonathan Griffiths and Uma Suthersanen

Copyright allows right-holders to restrict access to a wide range of forms of **1.01** expression, including works of literature, paintings, and music. At the same time, it serves as an 'engine of free expression'[1] by providing shelter for independent creation. It has the potential both to promote and to restrict free speech. Until the mid-1990s, this tension between copyright and free speech was relatively unexplored. Indeed, until recently, it was widely assumed within the 'copyright community' that the two rights had nothing to do with one another. However, recent developments in copyright law, coupled with an increased appreciation of the effect of fundamental rights in the sphere of private law, have altered this assumption. In numerous jurisdictions, courts have been faced with disputes raising fundamental questions concerning copyright and free speech. Academic interest in the subject has rapidly increased

In March 2003, a gathering of international experts, chaired by Lord Justice **1.02** Jacob, met at the London offices of the law firm Clifford Chance LLP in order to examine these developments. The seminar was held under the auspices of Queen Mary, University of London. This volume is based upon a selection of papers presented at this event, expanded and updated to take

---

[1] *Harper & Row Publishers v Nation Enterprises* 471 US 539, 558 (1985).

account of subsequent developments. It also includes a number of additional contributions commissioned following the conference.

A. Mapping the Conflict

1.03 The first section of this collection provides theoretical or contextual perspectives on the tension between free speech and copyright. From the refreshing perspective of the public lawyer, Eric Barendt explains how potential conflict between human rights and intellectual property arises in this context. He employs classical justifications for free speech to argue that copyright law is not immune from free speech scrutiny. His historical survey of UK and US case law reveals how copyright law has ignored fundamental features of developed free speech doctrine. Judicial responsibility for upholding the constitutional rights of both the public and the speaker has been abdicated through over-reliance on a number of principles within copyright law: the idea–expression dichotomy; the assumption that copyright is an engine of free expression coupled with the assumption that copyright infringers have no free speech rights; the presence of the fair use and fair dealing defences; and the preference for property rights over free speech rights. This is particularly dangerous in the case of parody, satire, and appropriation art, or when the infringement reproduces information or images of political or social importance. Barendt concludes by making tentative suggestions as to how an appropriate accommodation between the two conflicting interests can be made. He argues that it is important to recognize the artificiality of the property interest protected under copyright law—to understand that copyright is closer to confidential information than to land.

1.04 Fiona Macmillan's chapter offers further insight into Barendt's argument that free speech principles remain relevant even though copyright interests are generally employed by private actors. She argues that copyright has become an important vehicle for the exercise of private control over speech. This constraint on speech is particularly worrying for Macmillan because she views the copyright system as an edifice upon which private power over cultural output is created and maintained. Copyright goods are viewed as tradeable commodities having economic value, rather than as expressions of human creativity and communication. The consequence of this commodification of creativity is that copyright ownership in the media and entertainment sector has been concentrated in the hands of six to ten communications companies who produce, own, and distribute the bulk of cultural and informational output. Macmillan warns of the danger of surrendering control of the 'cultural and intellectual commons' to private and unaccountable interests.

Wendy Gordon also argues that copyright law ought to offer shelter to those **1.05** who use copyright works for the purpose of criticism and dissent. However, she considers the matter from a different perspective. She explains why the traditional reasons offered for the existence of copyright protection—both those based on maximizing social welfare and those based upon conceptions of 'authors' rights'—converge to support user freedoms in certain circumstances. This conclusion is justified by common law analogies—from the laws of restitution and torts.

Uma Suthersanen's account of the public interest stems from her contextual- **1.06** izing international copyright law as an international human rights issue. She too acknowledges that both statute and case law reveal that national courts are unwilling to recognize the intrinsic link between copyright and human rights. This problem may be due to the fact that human rights jurisprudence, including free speech, is still seen as territorial in nature. Could the relationship between copyright and free speech be strengthened if human rights, such as the right to freedom of expression and information, were explicitly recognized within the intellectual property agreement framework? It is proposed that a balance between free speech and copyright can be found by adopting a holistic approach to copyright justifications. She argues that, if a concern for human rights were to be incorporated within international copyright law, it would address the particular dilemma faced by national courts in overriding legislative intent.

B. National and International Perspectives

In the second part of this collection, the contributors analyse various aspects **1.07** of the relationship between copyright and free speech in different national and international contexts. Neil Netanel examines the relationship within the law of the USA. In supporting arguments raised in the first section of the volume, he suggests that First Amendment values have made insufficient impact within copyright law. He offers a critical analysis of the US Supreme Court's landmark decision in *Eldred v Ashcroft*.[2] His argument that copyright should be subject to greater external First Amendment scrutiny is supported by a forensic rebuttal of the conclusions drawn by the Supreme Court in that case. He concludes by considering whether *Eldred* leaves any scope for First Amendment intervention within US copyright law. In this respect, he suggests that the approach of the courts to the defence of fair use is vital and recommends a more lenient and liberal application of the fair use defence, a shift of the burden of proof in certain circumstances, and compulsory licensing for reasonable use of a work.

1.08 From the perspective of a UK copyright lawyer, Gerald Dworkin traces an overview of the relationship between copyright and the public interest and the way in which principles of free speech have entered the copyright equation. In doing so, he asks a series of significant questions of fundamental relevance: can defences extrinsic to copyright law be employed to deny the copyright owner a remedy? Does the USA's defence of fair use allow for more free speech than the United Kingdom's defence of fair dealing? Is there a conflict between the defence of fair use and the United Kingdom's international obligations? Can all these issues be resolved by tweaking remedies rather than changing substantive law? Kevin Garnett's chapter examines the impact of the Human Rights Act 1998 on UK copyright law. He analyses the consequences of the important judgment of the Court of Appeal in *Ashdown v Telegraph Group Ltd*[3] and considers how a number of significant pre-Human Rights Act copyright decisions would be likely to be decided under the law as it now stands. Still within a UK context, Jonathan Griffiths's chapter focuses upon the integrity right introduced under the Copyright, Designs and Patents Act 1988. He argues that, while widely derided as ineffective, this right represents a potential threat to the freedom of expression. He suggests that this threat can be minimized through the application of a common law defence and the restrictive interpretation of the scope of the right.

1.09 Ysolde Gendreau demonstrates the particularity of the Canadian legal position, in which federal copyright law must be interpreted in accordance with not only the federal Charter of Rights and Freedoms but also the

---

[2] 537 US 186 (2003).   [3] [2002] Ch 149, CA.

provincial Charters. Her focus is upon the Quebec Charter of Human Rights and Freedoms. As Gendreau explains, both Charters have been invoked in copyright litigation. Interestingly, however, litigants have had greater success in relying upon protected rights other than the right of freedom of expression contained within the Charters.

The structure of rights protection in Australia is unusual in that, by contrast **1.10** with the USA, the United Kingdom, and Canada, it rests entirely upon a judicially implied freedom of political communication. Robert Burrell and James Stellios therefore focus upon the effect of Australian copyright law upon communication with a political content. Even within this relatively narrow compass, they argue that there is a potential conflict between copyright and free speech. They make this point by reference to a series of case studies and conclude by recommending rejection of UK authority on the scope of the fair dealing defences decisions and adoption of a more expansive reconsideration of the equivalent Australian provisions.

Alain Strowel and François Tulkens demonstrate that the civil law perspective **1.11** has certain surprises for common lawyers. Freedom of expression and information are guaranteed by the constitutional provisions of the EU Treaty, by the constitutions of the Member States, and by the European Convention on Human Rights. Moreover, several European countries have developed case law on the relationship with which this volume is concerned. Nevertheless, despite the ancient lineage of both authors' rights and free speech in many civil law jurisdictions, Strowel and Tulkens suggest that there has been considerable difficulty in reconciling both strands of the law. Their analysis is based primarily on the jurisprudence of the European Court of Human Rights and on national tribunals, particularly those of France. They also trace parameters within which a balance between copyright and freedom of expression may be maintained, suggesting that two different types of balances may be required—one for situations in which copyright prohibits derivative forms of expression, and another for those situations where copyright rules are content-neutral but nevertheless restrain access to works.

Mira Sundara Rajan offers a tantalizing glimpse of a quite different approach **1.12** to the relationship between copyright law and ideas of freedom of speech or expression. She suggests that strong protection for creators is an essential component of these freedoms. In support of this suggestion, she provides a detailed historical analysis of the way in which copyright law has evolved and been employed in the Soviet Union and Russia. She argues that the socialist and post-socialist experience of copyright can provide interesting lessons of general application.

C. The Digital World

1.13 The impact of technological developments upon copyright law are considered briefly in a number of the contributions to the two sections of this collection outlined above. However, it is in the final section that these developments are subjected to particular analysis. It is sometimes claimed that increased use of technological and legal tools, such as encryption methods and contractual provisions, in the digital environment presents new and formidable challenges to free speech interests. As a result of the introduction of anti-circumvention provisions under the Digital Millennium Copyright Act (DMCA), this concern has been especially marked in the USA. Raymond Nimmer offers a detailed and comprehensive analysis of the DMCA's anti-circumvention provisions and of the judicial response to First Amendment challenges to these provisions. Contrary to the views of 'rights restrictors', he argues that the DMCA encourages and supports First Amendment norms. He describes the DMCA as a rule-based regime which attempts to redress a reality created by modern copying and dissemination technology. He emphasizes that this technology has shifted the scales that once balanced copyright law, and that the DMCA merely seeks to restate the balance by restoring incentives to create.

1.14 In a European context, Thomas Dreier addresses this issue by tracing the relationship between contract, copyright, and free speech. He demonstrates how rights owners can now 'contract out of copyright' by employing contractual provisions to extend the ambit of protection beyond the default rules of copyright, and considers whether the law should permit contractual restrictions that 'eat into' the realm of socially significant copyright limitations. He expresses a wish that mounting criticism of a balance struck too favourably for copyright owners will contribute to the development of technology that is better capable of taking account of existing copyright limitations and exceptions.

1.15 Jeremy Phillips describes the parameters within which any assessment of the impact of Europe's *sui generis* database right upon human rights must be made. He argues that many of the consequences of the introduction of this right have not been fully appreciated because the interface between the database right and the fundamental freedom of expression can only be understood when considered alongside competition law and data protection.

D. Conclusion

As noted above, the potential conflict between copyright law and freedom **1.16** of speech can no longer be described as under-explored. The case reports and literature considered and referenced here provide ample evidence of academic and judicial interest. Nevertheless, it is hoped that this volume will not only provide readers with an understanding of the most significant arguments and authorities in this field, but will also offer a series of new and complementary perspectives. In particular, it is hoped that the inclusion of contributions from a range of different jurisdictions will ensure that the volume makes a valuable contribution to the literature. The contributions demonstrate that copyright and free speech cannot simply be 'balanced' in an unaccountable manner, but must be viewed in the detailed contexts of actionable legal rights.

If there is one conclusion that can be drawn from such a disparate set of **1.17** contributions, it may be that, while the tension between copyright and free speech has now undoubtedly been acknowledged, copyright law-makers have not yet fully recognized all the demands of free speech. Perhaps as a result of anxiety about the potentially disruptive effect of human rights thinking on commercial relationships, judges often appear to be primarily concerned to accommodate free speech norms with as little disruption to existing copyright principle as possible. Legislators appear to be entirely untroubled by free speech interests. In this climate, 'facial' attempts to force an accommodation between fundamental rights and copyright legislation seem to be doomed to failure. Many contributors suggest ways in which a more delicate accommodation of free speech interests could be made through use of flexible doctrines such as equity, fairness, and public interest, which are still to be found, under different names, in all the national and international copyright laws considered in this volume.

PART I

MAPPING THE CONFLICT

2

COPYRIGHT AND FREE SPEECH THEORY

Eric Barendt

A. Introduction

The relationship between freedom of speech and copyright protection has **2.01** increasingly attracted the attention of copyright lawyers.[1] They have become troubled by the impact on freedom of expression of the recent extension of

---

[1] See, eg, P Samuelson, 'Copyright, Commodification, and Censorship: Past as Prologue—but to what Future?' and PB Hugenholtz, 'Copyright and Freedom of Expression in Europe', in N Elkin-Koren and NW Netanel (eds), *The Commodification of Information* (The Hague: Kluwer, 2002), 63, 239; M Birnhack, 'The Copyright Law and Free Speech Affair: Making-up and Breaking-up' (2003) 43 Idea: J L & Technology 233; D Fewer, 'Constitutionalizing Copyright: Freedom of Expression and the Limits of Copyright in Canada' (1997) 55 U Toronto Faculty L Rev 175; P Drahos, 'Decentring Communication: The Dark Side of Intellectual Property', in T Campbell and W Sadurski (eds), *Freedom of Communication* (Aldershot: Dartmouth, 1994), 249.

the term of copyright in Europe and in the USA and by the expanding range of exclusive rights conferred by copyright. In contrast, the relationship has been more or less totally ignored by free speech theorists. This omission is very odd. The scope of other rights, notably the rights to reputation and privacy, has been significantly affected, and indeed curtailed, by free speech arguments accepted by the courts. Moreover, these developments were heralded, and have been welcomed, by free speech theorists. So, initial questions are why similar developments have not occurred in the case of copyright law and why jurists have not argued that copyright may significantly infringe the exercise of free speech, in some cases so disproportionately that the infringement should be held an unconstitutional interference with the right. Put shortly, are there any good reasons why copyright law should remain immune from free speech scrutiny?

2.02 Some conventional explanations for this immunity will be explored in section B of this chapter below. It will be shown that these explanations are inadequate to *justify* the present position, under which copyright escapes free speech scrutiny. In section C, it is argued that infringing works are at least entitled to fall within the *coverage* of a free speech (or expression) clause, even though in many instances the publication of a particular infringing work may properly be restrained by the rules of copyright law, so that it is not a *protected* exercise of the right to freedom of speech. There are positive reasons, drawn from the standard arguments for the special position of freedom of expression, for holding that infringing works are within the scope of the freedom. None of the argument in section C is particularly novel. What is perhaps more innovative is the exposition in section D of the way in which the courts' usual treatment of free speech arguments in the copyright context ignores some fundamental features of developed free speech doctrine and settled legal principle. The conclusion drawn is that copyright law certainly compromises free speech principles. Courts, and writers on freedom of speech as well as on copyright, should confront this clash of speech and property rights openly, and develop principles under which an appropriate accommodation of the two rights can be reached in concrete cases. Some tentative thoughts on this accommodation are offered in section E.

B. Conventional Explanations for the Copyright–Free Speech Divide

While the relationship of copyright and free speech has been explored in the **2.03** USA, until recently there has been relatively little discussion in legal writing in England.[2] The relationship has also been considered in a number of US cases. However, it is difficult to point to any worthwhile treatment by an English court, apart from the recent decision in *Ashdown v Telegraph Group Ltd*.[3] Inevitably, therefore, discussion in this section concentrates on arguments canvassed in US cases and legal writing. The question in that context is whether the rules of copyright laws may infringe freedom of speech, and if so, why they have survived any scrutiny under the First Amendment guarantee.

One argument might be that freedom of speech is protected only against **2.04** State infringement, and not against the limits imposed by private individuals or corporations. To take an obvious example, if a newspaper editor or book publisher declines to accept a feature article or book manuscript for publication, the author cannot complain that his or her free speech rights have been invaded. In the language of the US courts, there is no 'state action' which engages the First Amendment. Claims of copyright infringement are generally brought by private individuals and media corporations, and it may therefore be argued that there is no State action to bring freedom of speech into play. But that is a bad argument. Copyright is a right conferred by statute, interpreted and applied by the courts. Enforcement of copyright, therefore, inevitably involves State action. Moreover, US courts have not accepted this argument in the context of libel and privacy claims, which like copyright actions are brought by individuals on the basis of rights conferred by statute, or on the basis of the common law. Indeed, the State action argument was specifically rejected by the US Supreme Court in *New York Times v Sullivan*,[4] when it held that the common law of libel in Alabama

---

[2] Notable exceptions are the articles by FM Patfield, 'Towards a Reconciliation of Free Speech and Copyright', in EM Barendt et al, *The Yearbook of Media and Entertainment Law 1996* (Oxford: OUP, 1996), 199 and by J Griffiths, 'Copyright Law and Censorship: the Impact of the Human Rights Act 1998' (1999) Ybk Copyright & Media L 3.

[3] [2001] Ch 685; [2002] Ch 149, CA. This difference is not surprising, given that, until enactment of the Human Rights Act 1998 (HRA), it was difficult to argue that a UK statute should not be given effect because it infringed the exercise of the right to freedom of expression.

[4] 376 US 254, 265 (1964).

enjoyed no immunity from First Amendment scrutiny. So it would be impossible to put forward the State action point as an explanation, let alone a justification, for holding copyright law immune from free speech challenge.

2.05 We must, therefore, look elsewhere. It seems that US courts and commentators wholly ignored the conflict between copyright and free speech until the 1970s.[5] It is as if they occupied separate legal worlds. That is not the position now. The potential for conflict, at least in theory, is recognized. But courts, and commentators for the most part, accept that any conflict is reconciled within copyright law itself. Moreover, the US Constitution explicitly authorized Congress to 'promote the Progress of Science and useful Arts, by securing for limited Times to Authors and Inventors the exclusive Right to their respective Writings and Discoveries'.[6] It would be surprising, the argument goes, if legislation specifically authorized by the Constitution, and indeed enacted initially in 1790 shortly after its ratification, could be challenged on the basis of incompatibility with the First Amendment. After all, many of the same people were responsible for framing both the Constitution and, four years later, its first ten Amendments. This historical and constitutional case is buttressed by the argument that the very intention and effect of copyright law is to promote the production of literature and other works. In short, to use the familiar metaphor of O'Connor J in the leading US Supreme Court decision in this area, *Harper & Row Publishers v Nation Enterprises*, 'it should not be forgotten that the Framers intended copyright itself to be the engine of free expression.'[7]

2.06 Even if copyright law raises free speech concerns, it is said to meet them with two distinctive principles. The first of these is the idea–expression distinction. Copyright does not limit the dissemination of ideas or the spread of news and information, but only the use by others of the *expression* of the holder of copyright. Melville Nimmer, a distinguished writer on many areas of free speech law as well as a great copyright lawyer, contended that in this way First Amendment concerns were met by copyright legislation itself.[8]

---

[5] See M Birnhack, 'The Copyright Law and Free Speech Affair: Making-up and Breaking-up' (2003) 43 Idea: J L & Technology 247–51.

[6] US Constitution, Art I, s 8, cl 8 ('the copyright clause').

[7] 471 US 539, 558 (1985).

[8] M Nimmer, 'Does Copyright Abridge the First Amendment Guarantees of Free Speech and Press?' (1970) 17 UCLA L Rev 1180.

It will be seen that this conclusion is unsatisfactory.[9] Perhaps here it is pertinent to note that Nimmer himself did not think the distinction worked where the idea and the expression are inseparable, as in a news photograph. Reproduction of film of the assassination of President Kennedy or of the famous photograph of the My-Lai massacre in Vietnam was necessary in order to communicate the character of a news event.[10]

Secondly, it is said that copyright law recognizes free speech concerns **2.07** through the provision of 'fair use', or in the United Kingdom 'fair dealing', defences. This claim is accurate. But the question remains whether the statutory defences adequately satisfy the requirements of the constitutional right to freedom of speech (or expression). It has been questioned whether the fair dealing defence in the United Kingdom, as it has been interpreted by the courts, does justice to freedom of expression.[11] In any case, it is wrong for the courts to hold that the copyright statute *necessarily* safeguards freedom of speech, so no further consideration of the relationship of expression and copyright is required. That would be an abdication of their responsibility to determine the scope of constitutional rights, in this context the right to freedom of expression, and how far it is necessary to restrict its exercise to protect the right to copyright. The Court of Appeal in the *Ashdown* case, therefore, rightly held that the Convention right to freedom of expression may conflict with copyright, even though the statute itself sets out a number of fair dealing defences which give effect to that freedom.[12] It rejected the view of Sir Andrew Morritt V-C in the High Court that the 1988 copyright legislation made exhaustive provision for freedom of expression. However, the Court of Appeal suggested that conflicts between that freedom and copyright will only arise in 'rare circumstances'.[13] On that point, as the next section shows, it was wrong.

The conventional explanations for denial of the conflict may, at most, show **2.08** why courts, in the USA and elsewhere, have been reluctant to take freedom of speech/expression arguments seriously in the copyright context. But they

---

[9] See paras 2.21 and 2.22 below.

[10] M Nimmer, 'Does Copyright Abridge the First Amendment Guarantees of Free Speech and Press?' (1970) 17 UCLA L Rev 1198–9.

[11] See J Griffiths, 'Copyright Law and Censorship: the Impact of the Human Rights Act 1998' (1999) Ybk Copyright & Media L 15–20.

[12] [2002] Ch 149, CA, discussed further in para 2.18 below.

[13] Ibid, para 45.

do not begin to justify that reluctance. Except in terms of emergency, the US Supreme Court is normally unwilling to defer to legislative judgement concerning the limits of freedom of speech, and is even prepared to strike down statutes which are intended to promote that freedom's values.[14] In contrast, courts in the USA, including the US Supreme Court, are content to allow Congress a free hand to determine the scope and duration of copyright, as well as to delimit the defences which meet free speech concerns. Free speech principles are generally ignored or no weight is attached to them outside the terms of the copyright legislation itself.[15] That would not matter, of course, if we should conclude that copyright infringements fall outside the scope of freedom of speech, so that courts need not even consider a free speech argument. But that conclusion would be wrong, as the argument in the next section of this chapter will show.

C. Are Copyright Infringements *Covered* by Freedom of Speech?

2.09 The question considered here is whether copyright infringements are automatically excluded from protection by the First Amendment, by Article 10 of the ECHR, or by other relevant constitutional guarantees of freedom of speech/expression. In this context, it is important to observe the distinction drawn by Fred Schauer, a prominent free speech theorist, between the *coverage* and *protection* of a free speech clause.[16] Under the First Amendment, and other free speech provisions, most types of what a lay person would regard as 'speech' are covered by the provision, although the exercise of the speech right may be restricted, or even prohibited, if there is a very good reason for the imposition of that restraint. For example, defamatory allegations are treated in the USA, in Germany, and under the ECHR, as covered by the free speech/expression clause, though damages may be awarded to a defamed individual if the court concludes that free speech considerations do not, on the basis of developed legal principles, outweigh his

---

[14] This theme is developed in paras 2.26–2.28 below.

[15] A notable exception is the decision in *Campbell v Acuff Rose Music, Inc* 510 US 569 (1994), where the Court interpreted the 'fair use' defence generously to protect the parody of a rock ballad.

[16] F Schauer, *Free Speech: a Philosophical Enquiry* (Cambridge: CUP, 1982) 89–92.

or her interest in reputation.[17] In that event, it would be said that, although the defamatory remarks were covered by the constitutional guarantee of freedom of speech/expression, they were not on the facts protected. However, some types of speech are treated as not even covered by the free speech provision, so there is no further requirement for the State to justify their regulation before a court. Examples of speech which are not covered at all are perjury, bribes, the making of contractual promises, threats of violence in a face to face confrontation, and perhaps some extreme hard-core pornography. On the whole, the categories of excluded speech, not even covered by a free speech clause, have diminished, particularly in the USA. For instance, libel was brought within the coverage of the First Amendment in the historic ruling in *New York Times v Sullivan*, while other cases have established that neither professional nor commercial advertising is wholly excluded from its scope.[18]

The question is whether copyright infringement is, or more pertinently, **2.10** should be, totally excluded from the coverage of free speech. Should it be treated in the same way as, say, the offer of a bribe or the threat of violence? The scope of free speech depends on the reasons for which it is regarded as a valuable right, and given strong constitutional protection. To simplify complex arguments, bribes, perjury, and threats are excluded from coverage because there is no good reason, on any of the justifications for free speech guarantees, to think that they fall within it. A bribe, for example, does not contribute to public discourse or assert a proposition which may be true; nor is it easy to see it as enhancing the offeror's mental or other self-development. It does not merit cover under any of the three classic justifications for strong free speech protection: Mill's argument from truth, the role of public discourse in a liberal democracy, or the part played by speech in the development and fulfilment of individuals.[19] On these arguments, bribes, perjury,

---

[17] See *Gertz v Robert Welch Co* 418 US 323 (1974); *Böll* 54 BVerfGE 208 (1980); *Tammer v Estonia* (2003) 37 EHRR 43.

[18] *Virginia State Board of Pharmacy v Virginia Consumers Council* 425 US 748 (1964) (ban on advertising drug prices struck down); *Bates v State Bar of Arizona* 433 US 350 (1977) (ban on price advertising by lawyers struck down).

[19] See F Schauer, *Free Speech: a Philosophical Enquiry* (Cambridge: CUP, 1982) chs 2–5 and EM Barendt, *Freedom of Speech* (Oxford: OUP, 1987) 8–23 for discussion of these arguments for freedom of speech.

verbal threats, and contractual promises, fall outside the scope of free speech/
expression guarantees.

2.11 This, however, is not always the case with copyright infringement. If it were
so, copyright laws would not be expected to make any exceptions for free
speech, as they do with the provision of fair use or fair dealing defences. Some
infringements are regarded as worthy of protection because they contribute
to free discussion of, for example, the quality of a play or a work of art ('fair
dealing . . . for the purpose of criticism or review'[20]). Quite apart from these
legal rules, plainly some infringing works should be regarded as an exercise
of free speech rights, because the work is integral to the development of
its author or enhances our understanding of literature or the arts. This is
clearly the case with parodies, satire, and appropriation art, all of which may
use existing work and so may infringe copyright. Indeed, their effectiveness as
a parody or appropriation art depends on reproduction or adaptation of
significant parts of the earlier work, so copyright infringement is inevitable.[21]
It is therefore wrong to treat a parody as an infringement of copyright without considering the implications for the infringer's own freedom of speech as
an author or artist. Similar arguments may apply to the reproduction of
copyright photographs or letters in an infringing work. Such reproduction
should often be treated as covered by a freedom of speech clause, because it
may provide the public with valuable information and so contribute to public discourse.[22] In the absence of free speech arguments (or adequate statutory
fair use/dealing defences), rights-holders could use copyright to withhold
important information from the public to the impoverishment of political
debate.

2.12 The arguments for free speech guarantees do therefore suggest that at least
some infringing works are covered by the guarantee. The case is strongest
when the infringement is a work of satire, or a parody, or reproduces information or images of political or social importance.[23] In contrast, it is weak

---

[20] Copyright, Designs and Patents Act (CDPA) 1988, s 30(1).
[21] P Loughlan, 'Copyright Law, Free Speech, and Self-Fulfilment' (2002) 24 Sydney L Rev
427, 432–8.
[22] In UK copyright law, that argument is recognized by the defence of 'fair dealing . . . for
the purpose of reporting current events' (CDPA 1988, s 30(2)).
[23] See FM Patfield, 'Towards a Reconciliation of Free Speech and Copyright', in EM
Barendt et al, *The Yearbook of Media and Entertainment Law 1996* (Oxford: OUP, 1996),
199, 208–15.

or non-existent in straightforward commercial piracy, when the copier aims solely to exploit the artistic skills of others for his or her own financial advantage.[24] In those latter circumstances it is easy to persuade the court that there is no real free speech interest at stake, or alternatively that any free speech interest should be trumped by that of the rights-holder. However, it would be wrong to derive principles from this set of circumstances and apply them automatically to all instances of conflict between copyright and freedom of speech/expression. Indeed, since the latter right is constitutionally guaranteed, the onus should be on the rights-holder in every case to show why the copier is not entitled to the *protection* of the free speech clause or, in the terminology of the ECHR, to show that copyright law imposes necessary and proportionate restrictions on the exercise of the copier's freedom of expression. In many cases, it would in practice be easy to discharge that burden, but that would not necessarily be true where the copier claims that he is parodying the copyright work or giving the public information which would otherwise be impossible, or perhaps very expensive, to obtain owing to copyright restrictions. Moreover, whatever the practical implications, this enquiry would bring about a revolution in copyright–free speech law; it would in principle be for the rights-holder to show why his rights should be enforced, rather than for the infringer to show why she has a free speech/expression claim of such strength to trump copyright.

D. Four General Arguments of Free Speech Theory

From the perspective of free speech theory, much of the argument in the **2.13** preceding section was straightforward. It established that copyright infringement should not, as such, be excluded from the coverage of a free speech/expression clause. This section examines the application of four principles of freedom of speech, as they have been developed in the USA and (to some extent) under the European Convention on Human Rights in the context of copyright. The precise significance or weight of these principles varies according to the circumstances and, to that extent, their application may be controversial. But what is clear is that copyright law either ignores them or fails to do them justice. It has carved out an exception for copyright from

---

[24] See M Birnhack, 'The Copyright Law and Free Speech Affair: Making-up and Breaking-up' (2003) 43 Idea: J L & Technology 233, 252.

well-established free speech principles, which in other areas of law such as defamation and privacy are applied with little hesitation.

(1) Free speech confers rights on speakers as well as on recipients and the public

2.14 There is a vigorous debate among theorists whether free speech primarily protects the interests of speakers or of recipients, or indeed those of the general public. Put slightly differently, who may assert the right to freedom of expression? The answer may depend on the level at which the question is posed: is it concerned with the fundamental arguments of political philosophy for freedom of speech, or rather with specific legal issues concerning the scope of the right or its relationship with conflicting rights? That explains, perhaps, why Fred Schauer argues that abstract free speech arguments, notably the argument from truth and the argument about the significance of speech for democracy, emphasize the interests of society or the rights of members of the public to acquire ideas and information relevant to the development of an open democracy. However, he also says that the commitment to free speech entails the legal protection of *speakers*, who are usually more concerned to assert the uninhibited dissemination of ideas and information than are any particular recipients or members of the public. On that perspective, the entitlement of speakers derives from the underlying public interest in free communication.[25] Whether that argument is sound or not, most free speech claims in court, and certainly (virtually) all claims to freedom of the press and other media, are made by speakers rather than by listeners or viewers, although often their entitlement is supported by the argument that the public has an interest in receiving the information or ideas which they provide.[26]

2.15 These points explain why we are unconcerned whether the speaker's motive for his or her communication is primarily commercial or selfless. Even if we are unimpressed by a claim that the ideas represent the speaker's concern, say, for personal artistic development, he or she has generally something to gain, financially or in terms of creative reputation, from the exercise of free

---

[25] F Schauer, *Free Speech: a Philosophical Enquiry* (Cambridge: CUP, 1982) 105–6, 158–60.
[26] See EM Barendt, 'Interests in Freedom of Speech: Theory and Practice', in K Fan Sin (ed), *Legal Explorations: Essays in Honour of Michael Chesterman* (Sydney: Law Book Co, 2003), 175, for further discussion of these points.

speech rights. The speaker is, therefore, more likely to assert them than are the recipients of his or her speech. It is in the public interest, and in that of individual recipients, that speakers assert those rights when competing claims—to the protection of reputation or copyright—purport to limit them. It is therefore sensible for provisions such as Article 10 of the ECHR to guarantee a 'right to receive and *impart* information and ideas'.[27] To confine the right to claim freedom of expression to recipients would probably result in a failure to protect the right in practice.

Of course, the argument in the two preceding paragraphs assumed that the **2.16** primary theoretical argument for free speech is, as Schauer contends, that it enhances the interests of the public in receiving ideas and information. Some writers argue, contrary to this position, that freedom of speech should be valued irrespective of any interest of the potential audience or of the general public.[28] The primary justification for the freedom is that it is integral to the self-fulfilment of speakers, enabling them to formulate their ideas through expression and so to develop their personality. This argument is strongest in the case of literature, the arts, and academic work, where artistic and scientific freedom is essential to the flourishing of researchers, writers, and artists. It makes less sense in the case of commercial speech and advertising, where free speech claims are essentially based on the interests of consumers. Nevertheless, advertisers may be able to invoke a right to freedom of speech/ expression, because restrictions on their freedom would also curtail the freedom of consumers to acquire information, say, about the availability or prices of their products.

Copyright law assumes that copyright infringers have no free speech rights. **2.17** As Nimmer put it, an infringer who pirates the expression of others 'is not engaging in *self*-expression in any meaningful sense'.[29] But this misses two points. First, an infringer may nevertheless have a free speech right which is derived from the interest of the public in access to a work which the rights-holder may have chosen not to distribute, or perhaps only to have made available at a price which most people cannot afford. More importantly,

---

[27] Emphasis added.

[28] See, in particular, CE Baker, *Human Liberty and Freedom of Speech* (New York: OUP, 1989) ch 3 and RM Dworkin, 'Introduction', in RM Dworkin (ed), *The Philosophy of Law* (Oxford: OUP, 1977), 15.

[29] M Nimmer, 'Does Copyright Abridge the First Amendment Guarantees of Free Speech and Press?' (1970) 17 UCLA L Rev 1180, 1192.

Nimmer's conclusion does not do justice to the interests of satirists and appropriation artists who deliberately copy others' work in order to make important political or artistic points concerning, say, the clichéd character of the rights-holder's work. Nimmer assumed that a writer is only engaged in self-expression if she expresses her ideas in a form unique to her and does not borrow from others.[30]

2.18 These issues were considered by the Court of Appeal in the United Kingdom in the recent *Ashdown* case. The court held that, in exceptional circumstances, freedom of expression could conflict with the enforcement of copyright law. Paddy Ashdown, the former Leader of the Liberal Democratic Party, claimed infringement of copyright when the *Sunday Telegraph* printed substantial extracts from minutes he had kept of confidential discussions with the Prime Minister, Tony Blair, concerning political co-operation between the Labour government and the Liberal Democrats after the General Election of 1997. In addition to its (unsuccessful) argument that the publication amounted to fair dealing for the purpose of reporting current events, the newspaper argued that the right to freedom of expression, incorporated in UK law by the Human Rights Act 1998, limited the scope of copyright. In the Court of Appeal, Lord Phillips MR doubted whether freedom of expression generally 'extends to the freedom to convey ideas and information using the form of words devised by someone else'.[31] Nevertheless, he held that there might be a public interest that its members 'should be told the very words used by a person, notwithstanding that the author enjoys copyright in them'.[32] In this case, the newspaper's interest in publishing the minute was parasitic on the interest the public had in knowing details of the discussions between Blair and Ashdown, but Lord Phillips MR was wrong to imply that an infringer has no right to use others' words to communicate his ideas. His judgment ignored the argument that social critics, satirists, and political commentators have legitimate free speech interests of their own, which they may exercise by incorporating substantial extracts from the speeches of politicians and others on whose work they are commenting.[33]

---

[30] See P Loughlan, 'Copyright Law, Free Speech, and Self-Fulfilment' (2002) 24 Sydney L Rev 427, 432.

[31] [2002] Ch 149, para 31.   [32] Ibid, para 43.

[33] For a vigorous statement of this view, see J Waldron, 'From Authors to Copiers: Individual Rights and Social Values in Intellectual Property' (1993) 68 Chicago-Kent L Rev 840, 875–7.

The consequence of paying attention exclusively to the interests of readers, **2.19** and ignoring those of the writer or speaker, is shown in one of the very few cases to be considered in Strasbourg. In *De Geillustreerde Pers NV v Netherlands*,[34] the European Commission of Human Rights rejected a complaint by a commercial magazine publisher that the copyright held by broadcasting companies in their programme schedules interfered with its freedom of expression to list these schedules. The Commission considered that only the public's interest in access to the information was involved. That was satisfied through the provision of the schedules by the broadcasters. That latter point might be correct, though it would be contestable, say, if broadcasters were to charge exorbitant prices for their listings magazines. Moreover, the argument assumes that the commercial publisher had no free speech or free press interest of its own. It would clearly have had a strong interest of its own if it had used the schedules, for example, to make critical points about the quality of Dutch broadcasting. Quite apart from that point, it would surely have been better to conclude that the commercial publisher was exercising freedom of expression, but that, if it merely reproduced the listings compiled by the broadcasting companies, it was necessary to restrain exercise of that freedom in order to protect copyright.

An emphasis on the public utility of speech leaves the door open to the **2.20** argument that this utility is increased by the protection of intellectual property rights. That is what is meant by the 'engine of free expression' metaphor. Jeremy Waldron has persuasively argued that the standard perception of the copyright–free speech conflict presents copyright as a strong property right which, in some cases, has to be balanced against weak free speech arguments emphasizing the social interest in communication of information to the public.[35] That perspective implicitly denies that copyright infringers have rights as speakers, or for that matter, that members of the public have individual free speech rights to receive or listen to infringing copies. It may equally exaggerate the weight of copyright as a property right, which itself is established on the contestable proposition that strong intellectual property rights are always required to encourage the production

---

[34] 5178/71, (1976) 8 DR 5. See also *France 2 v France* 30262/92, discussed in PB Hugenholtz, 'Copyright and Freedom of Expression in Europe', in Dreyfuss et al (eds), *Expanding the Boundaries of Intellectual Property* (Oxford: OUP, 2001), 343, 359–60.

[35] J Waldron, 'From Authors to Copiers: Individual Rights and Social Values in Intellectual Property' (1993) 68 Chicago-Kent L Rev 840, 856–62.

of literary and other works, and so to promote the values of free expression. It is in fact much clearer that copyright laws violate the free speech rights of infringers (albeit that this can often be justified) than it is that the laws themselves promote the values which justify recognition of free speech rights.

(2) Freedom of speech concerns the form of speech as well as its contents

2.21 Freedom of speech means that the speaker determines the form in which propositions are put, as well as the intellectual content or subject matter of his or her discourse. The law improperly interferes with the exercise of that freedom if, for example, it proscribes the use of certain language on the ground that it is shocking or offensive.[36] This fundamental principle is exemplified in cases which allow publishers the freedom to use indecent language or display sexually explicit images, provided (in most jurisdictions) that the expression does not amount to hard-core pornography (which is not covered by the freedom of speech/expression clause at all). The European Court of Human Rights has developed a similar principle in defamation cases, recognizing that journalists have freedom under Article 10 of the ECHR to express their ideas in exaggerated or prejudiced terms, even though that may injure the self-esteem or standing of the persons criticized in their newspapers. Even more relevantly to the copyright context, it has held that a journalist had freedom under Article 10 to publish documents containing the tax assessments of the head of Peugeot in order to give credibility to a story about his salary. The journalist's conviction in the French courts for making unlawful use of tax documents was incompatible with the Convention.[37]

2.22 Copyright law departs from this fundamental free speech principle. It asserts that publishers are entitled to communicate an idea or provide information or news, provided that they do not use the words or expression of a rightsholder. This is the idea–expression dichotomy, which has already been referred to. Copyright law qualifies the principle that a speaker is entitled to choose how she formulates her arguments by proscribing the use of language and other material which have become the subject of intellectual property

---

[36] The classic authority is *Cohen v California* 403 US 15 (1971), where the Court held that the words, 'Fuck the Draft', on a jacket worn in a court-house corridor, were protected speech.
[37] *Fressoz and Roire v France* (2001) 31 EHRR 28.

rights.[38] To take one example from the USA, the Ninth Circuit Court of Appeals held that it was unnecessary to conjure up the Walt Disney characters in order to parody American life and society, and, therefore, there was no defence to an action for copyright infringement when those characters were depicted in adult comic books as figures in a free thinking, anarchistic counterculture.[39] However, that approach severely circumscribes the right of satirists to use familiar emblems, symbols, and characters to illustrate their critique. It is a real limitation on the manner of speech, if not its rational or intellectual contents.

(3) The speaker's motive does not generally matter

A speaker does not usually forfeit his or her right to free speech because it **2.23** is exercised largely or even entirely to make money. That result may at first glance run counter to the argument that freedom of speech is valued, and constitutionally guaranteed, because it is essential to, and an integral aspect of, individual self-fulfilment, or that it is essential for the discovery of truths of social importance. But again we should distinguish between the general arguments of political philosophy for an abstract right to freedom of speech and the considerations which determine whether the right should be recognized and protected in concrete litigation. In practice, it would be impossible for courts in each free speech case to scrutinize the motives of the speaker before determining whether his or her speech is protected. If the existence of a financial motive were to take speech outside the scope of the First Amendment or other constitutional provision, there would be few, if any, press freedom cases. Books, magazines, and newspapers are published, at least partly, to make money for their publishers. Further, as has been seen, there are other interests to consider. There is a freedom to receive information and ideas, and recipients are not generally troubled if the speaker has something to gain financially from publication. The point is that we protect freedom of speech as a constitutional right because there are some good arguments to justify that position, and then allow the right to be asserted by speakers, whatever their motives. Speech made for profit should be tolerated,

---

[38] Copyright law, of course, is not unique in this respect. Trade mark laws may create limited property rights in the use of words for marketing purposes. See *San Francisco Arts and Athletics Inc v US Olympic Committee* 483 US 522 (1987), discussed in para 2.31 below.

[39] *Walt Disney Productions v Air Pirates* 581 F 2d 751 (US Ct of Apps (9th Cir), 1978).

as must offensive speech, for otherwise the right to free speech would mean nothing.

2.24 But in copyright–free speech cases, courts sometimes emphasize the commercial motive of the copier as one reason for holding her liable for infringement of copyright. A good example of this is the leading decision of the Supreme Court in this area, *Harper & Row Publishers v Nation Enterprises*.[40] By a majority, it denied that the fair use defence covered the publication of substantial extracts from the unpublished memoirs of ex-President Ford. For the Court, O'Connor J stressed that the defendants intended to make a profit from supplanting the claimants' commercially valuable publication rights. This commercial purpose could not be regarded as a fair use for the purpose of the copyright statute.

2.25 The decision may be right as a matter of copyright law. But as Brennan J vigorously argued in dissent, it does not do justice to the free speech arguments. From that perspective, it is immaterial whether the copyright infringer acted purely or mainly for profit.[41] The point is that it was providing the public with material for robust political debate on President Ford's term of office, including his controversial decision to pardon President Nixon. That is not to say that *Harper & Row* was wrongly decided. The article in *The Nation* infringed copyright in material which was going to be published in the next few weeks. That fact being given, the free speech argument was relatively weak. It did not much matter whether the public read the memoirs a few weeks earlier than the scheduled publication date. But it might have mattered, if the memoirs were unlikely to be published for another year or so, and if they contained material which it was important to put to the public at an earlier time. In that event, the commercial motives of the copyright infringer should not weaken the argument for free speech protection.

(4) Scrutiny of legislation intended to promote speech

2.26 A distinctive feature of US jurisprudence is the courts' reluctance to accept that legislative restrictions on freedom of speech (or press freedom) should be

---

[40] 471 US 539 (1985).

[41] In a later parody case, the Court held that it was wrong to presume that commercial use was unfair, so that the 'fair use' defence could not be invoked: *Campbell v Acuff Rose Music Inc* 510 US 569 (1994).

upheld merely because the restrictions are intended to promote speech or to enhance equal opportunities for speech. Courts in the USA are distrustful of government intervention, fearing that it will distort the free market-place of ideas. Examples of this approach are the Supreme Court decisions striking down a state law providing for a right to reply to personal attacks in news-papers,[42] and invalidating provisions in a federal statute which were intended, through the imposition of limits on election expenditure, to enable lower income groups and candidates to contribute to political debate on a more equal footing with wealthy corporations and individuals.[43] Another example is the decision of the majority of the DC Circuit Court of Appeals to ac-cept the assessment of the Federal Communications Commission that the imposition of positive programme requirements on broadcasters to show programmes dealing with controversial local political issues infringed the First Amendment rights of the channels.[44] It was wrong, in its view, to interfere with the working of the free market, which could be relied on to ensure the transmission of some programmes of this character. In all these cases, the courts were unsympathetic to the argument that the intention and effect of the regulations was, overall, to promote the values underlying freedom of speech, by ensuring, for example, that the public was able to hear the views of the person attacked or to have access to serious programmes which private broadcasters might be unwilling to schedule for commercial reasons.

The approach in copyright litigation could not be more different. Courts **2.27** reject challenges to the enforcement of the copyright law, because it is regarded as an affirmative measure to promote the goals of freedom of speech. As the Fifth Circuit Court of Appeals put it, '[t]he judgment of the Constitution is that free expression is enriched by protecting the creations of authors from exploitation by others, and the Copyright Act is the con-gressional implementation of that judgment.'[45] The Supreme Court has recently expressed the same sentiment. In *Eldred v Ashcroft*, it rejected a challenge to the extension of the term of copyright from life plus fifty years to

---

[42] *Miami Herald v Tornillo* 418 US 241 (1974).

[43] *Buckley v Valeo* 424 US 1 (1976).

[44] *Syracuse Peace Council v FCC* 867 F 2d 654 (US Ct of Apps (DC Cir), 1989), cert denied 110 S Ct 717 (1990).

[45] *Dallas Cowboys Cheerleaders, Inc v Scoreboard Posters, Inc* 600 F 2d 1184 (US Ct of Apps (5th Cir), 1979) 1187.

life plus seventy years for published works with existing copyrights.[46] Part of the petitioners' argument was that the extension failed heightened judicial review under the First Amendment. The Court said such scrutiny was unnecessary on the familiar ground that copyright law itself contained 'built-in First Amendment accommodations'. Under the Constitution, the limited monopoly conferred by copyright was compatible with freedom of speech. Indeed, the very purpose of copyright 'is to *promote* the creation and publication of free expression'.[47] That is right. But it should not have given the legislation an immunity from First Amendment challenge, which was not accorded, for instance, to the right of reply statute which the Court had unanimously struck down as incompatible with the speech and press rights of newspapers.[48]

2.28 The approach of the Supreme Court in *Eldred*, as in *Harper & Row*, can only be explained in terms of its unwillingness to accept that copiers' free speech rights are engaged. In its view, freedom of speech does not extend to the right to make or use the speech of others. However, the argument advanced in section C above has already shown that this perspective is misconceived. Copyright infringement is covered by the First Amendment. If the Court had reached that conclusion, it is hard to believe that it would have been prepared to uphold copyright legislation merely because such legislation can be said to promote the values of freedom of speech. Not only is that approach, as already mentioned, inconsistent with that adopted in other areas of free speech law, but it may also itself be misconceived. It is in fact questionable whether copyright law, as it stands at present, does promote freedom of speech. Courts might ask, for example, how far authors and publishers need the range of rights conferred by copyright, or a term of protection as long as life plus seventy years, in order to encourage the production of literature and other works. Further, copyright law may promote the *production* of work, but equally clearly inhibits its *distribution*. These are complex issues. It is understandable that courts are reluctant to interfere with Congressional judgement. The point is that they have not shown the same reluctance in other contexts, notably in considering challenges to complex legislation

---

[46] 537 US 186, 154 L Ed 2d 683 (2003). The Court did, in principle, leave the door open to First Amendment challenge if Congress were to change the contours of copyright legislation. It is unclear what this means.

[47] Ibid 711 (emphasis of Ginsburg J for the Court).

[48] *Miami Herald v Tornillo* 418 US 241 (1974).

regulating election expenditure and contributions to political parties and candidates' campaigns. In this respect, as in the others considered in this section, courts have treated copyright as a special case, giving it 'talismanic immunity' from appropriate First Amendment scrutiny.[49]

E. Conclusion: Some Reflections on Balancing Free Speech and Copyright

We can conclude that freedom of speech (or expression) is certainly engaged **2.29** when actions are taken to enforce copyright. Moreover, the application of copyright laws compromises general free speech principles, at least as those principles have been developed in the USA. That does not mean, however, that in every case freedom of speech/expression should trump copyright. The freedom is not absolute.[50] The free speech rights of commercial pirates, who merely reproduce the copyright works of others for mass distribution, should be accorded little weight. That is the archetypal case of copyright infringement, but there are many others where free speech arguments are far from negligible. How should the law resolve the conflict between free speech and copyright then?

It is relevant in this context that copyright is a property right.[51] This **2.30** aspect of the right was emphasized by both Sir Andrew Morritt V-C and the Court of Appeal in the *Ashdown* case. The right to property is guaranteed by Article 1 of the First Protocol to the ECHR, so copyright is protected by the Convention.[52] The Vice-Chancellor held that the conflict between the two Convention rights was resolved by the copyright legislation. The 1988 Act determined how far it was necessary to restrict the exercise of freedom of expression in order to protect the copyrights of others, a permissible goal for

---

[49] The phrase 'talismanic immunity' is taken from Brennan J's judgment for the Court in *New York Times v Sullivan* (376 US 254, 269 (1964)), holding that libel was not entitled to immunity from the First Amendment.

[50] One possible explanation for denial of the conflict in the USA is that, in that jurisdiction, freedom of speech is given such strong protection that to bring copyright infringement within the scope of the First Amendment would require rights-holders to produce compelling reasons in justification of its restriction.

[51] CDPA 1988, s 1(1).

[52] See *Ashdown v Telegraph Group Ltd* [2001] Ch 685, para 8 (per Sir Andrew Morritt V-C).

restrictions under Article 10(2). He held that it would be wrong to consider freedom of expression arguments outside the context of the legislation. The Court of Appeal disagreed. As explained above in section B, it held that in some, albeit rare, circumstances, a defendant may argue that copyright laws infringe freedom of expression, even though the fair dealing or other specific defences provided by the Act itself do not apply.[53]

2.31 A good example of a conflict between free speech and property rights in the USA is provided by the Supreme Court ruling in *San Francisco Arts and Athletics Inc v US Olympic Committee*.[54] A provision in the federal Amateur Sports Act of 1978 conferred on the US Olympic Committee the right to prohibit the use of the word 'Olympic' and associated symbols for non-authorized commercial and promotional purposes.[55] By a majority of 7–2, the Court rejected the argument of the organizers of the Gay Olympics in San Francisco that they had a First Amendment right to use the prohibited words on promotional literature for their games. Powell J, for the majority, classified the Committee's exclusive rights as a limited property right, and held that this right could trump the freedom of the organizers to use the words. The organizers' literature was treated as commercial speech, entitled to less protection under the First Amendment than political discourse. However, Brennan J rightly protested in dissent that the legislation enabled restrictions to be placed on the organizers' choice of language. In effect, it permitted bans on the communication of an idea in the most effective form—in this case, the idea that the Gay Olympics are comparable to, and inspired by the same values as, the regular Games held every four years since the end of the nineteenth century. Copyright is not unique in showing a preference for property rights over free speech rights.[56]

2.32 It is indeed a striking feature of US jurisprudence that, in the context of First Amendment arguments, it gives much stronger protection to property

---

[53] Freedom of expression may be an example of a rule of law preventing the enforcement of copyright on the ground of 'public interest', as recognized by CDPA 1988, s 171(3).

[54] 483 US 522 (1987), and see the criticisms of RN Kravitz, 'Trade Marks, Speech, and the *Gay Olympics* Case' 69 Boston U L Rev 131 (1989).

[55] The Committee was not required to show that an unauthorized use would give rise to confusion to prohibit it, so its powers went beyond the normal confines of trade mark legislation.

[56] For a critical discussion of this preference, see DL Zimmerman, 'Information as Speech, Information as Goods: Some Thoughts on Marketplaces and the Bill of Rights' (1992) 33 William & Mary L Rev 665.

and commercial interests than it does to the rights to reputation and privacy. As already mentioned, free speech principles impose substantial constraints on the scope of libel actions. They have also significantly weakened the privacy tort, whether that takes the form of the public disclosure of private facts or of presenting the claimant in a false light.[57] In contrast, copyright and trade marks are well protected. Courts have also enforced the commercial rights of celebrities to market their attributes through publicity rights.[58] Treated as a type of property, these rights are more likely to prevail over free speech than are privacy rights.[59]

Should the characterization of copyright as property make so much dif- **2.33** ference when it is balanced against the right to freedom of speech? It may be helpful to compare this clash with another type of case where the conflict arises. Courts are usually reluctant to recognize free speech rights to use private property, such as a privately owned shopping centre or mall, to distribute leaflets or to hold meetings.[60] It could be argued that copyright infringements similarly involve the abuse of the property rights of private individuals, so free speech rights should be denied in those cases. But there are significant differences between the two situations. In the shopping centre cases, positive rights of access to land are claimed in order to make a speech or to demonstrate, in derogation of the owner's rights to exclude trespassers and determine the use to which his property is put. Recognition of the access right of speech may make it less easy for the owner to use his land for other purposes, whether commercial or recreational. Further, it is far from certain that, in this context, the exercise of freedom of speech is inhibited by State action. In contrast, copyright infringement less clearly impinges on the interests or freedom of the rights-holders, save for their reduced opportunity to make profits from royalty payments.[61] It is much easier to find State action, for copyright is dependent on legislation. Copyright, of course, is not

---

[57] See DA Anderson, 'The Failure of American Privacy Law', in B Markesinis (ed), *Protecting Privacy* (Oxford: OUP, 1999), 139, 157–9.

[58] Ibid 146–7.

[59] *Zacchini v Scripps-Howard Broadcasting Co* 433 US 562 (1977).

[60] See the leading US case, *Hudgens v NLRB* 424 US 551 (1972), and the recent decision of the European Court in *Appleby v UK* (2003) 37 EHRR 783, denying rights to use private shopping centres for speech against the owners' will.

[61] See the argument of J Waldron in 'From Authors to Copiers: Individual Rights and Social Values in Intellectual Property' 68 Chicago-Kent L Rev 840, 870–3.

a natural property right, but, it should be remembered, an artificial property right created to reward and promote creativity.

2.34 Different resolutions of the copyright–free speech conflict would probably be reached if copyright were treated as similar to confidential information rather than as belonging to the same legal category as land. There is a well recognized public interest defence to actions for breach of confidence in English law, which may be invoked whenever it is more important for the public to gain access to important information than it is to protect the confidential relationship. The US Supreme Court has held that the media have a First Amendment right to reveal the contents of secretly taped conversations involving the discussion of matters of public concern.[62] Yet a copyright claim brought in these circumstances would succeed, at least where the courts were disinclined to apply the free speech principles developed for confidentiality actions to preclude the enforcement of copyright. That happened in the Australian case, *Commonwealth of Australia v John Fairfax and Sons Ltd.*[63] In that case, the High Court dismissed the government's application for an injunction in breach of confidence to restrain the publication of documents concerning foreign affairs and defence policy, but allowed it in copyright. There is no apparent justification for this divergence, except that the label of 'property right' attaches to copyright, but does not to the protection of confidential information.

2.35 Opening up copyright to challenge on freedom of speech/expression grounds inevitably conjures up fears of commercial uncertainty for rights-holders and of endless litigation. Such fears were expressed by the courts in the *Ashdown* case. Judges, however, could surely develop principles on which it would be relatively easy to determine when freedom of speech arguments would be seriously considered and when, on the other hand, copyright would be regarded as a necessary and proportionate restriction on exercise of that freedom under the Human Rights Act. Freedom of expression challenges to the enforcement of copyright should only be sustained when copyright law is used to suppress the dissemination of information of real importance to the public or to stifle artistic creativity, parody, or satire, and moreover, when

---

[62] *Bartnicki v Vopper* 532 US 514 (2001).
[63] (1980) 147 CLR 39. See J Griffiths, 'Copyright Law and Censorship: the Impact of the Human Rights Act 1998' (1999) Ybk Copyright & Media L 3, 5–6 for criticism of this case.

the legislation itself does not provide adequate safeguards for that freedom. In other circumstances, most plainly those of commercial piracy, restriction of a thin right to freedom of expression is clearly necessary to protect copyright, whether or not it is characterized as a property right. The enforcement of some copyrights ought, however, to be successfully challenged. Commitment to freedom of expression, a fundamental human and political right, means that that prospect should be faced with equanimity.

3

COMMODIFICATION AND CULTURAL OWNERSHIP

Fiona Macmillan

A. Introduction

Copyright is not the first so-called private law right governing speech or **3.01** expression to be touched by the accusation that its operation may, in some respects, constitute a limit on freedom of speech. There is a relatively well-developed jurisprudence in which concepts of freedom of speech have operated in order to limit, for example, the rights to sue for defamation and breach of confidence. Freedom of speech issues have intruded into these areas as the result of a collision between these 'private rights' and matters of 'public interest or concern'. So in US defamation law, for example, the Constitutional protection of free speech has been invoked to limit the ability of 'public' figures to sue for defamation, on the basis that free expression on matters of public concern should not be chilled.[1] Similar considerations

---

[1] See *New York Times Co v Sullivan* 376 US 254 (1964).

motivated the decision in the United Kingdom that a municipal corporation should not be allowed to sue for defamation.[2] In relation to the right to sue for breach of confidence, it has long been clear that this right is forfeited when the discloser has acted in the public interest.[3] Particular latitude appears likely to be granted in cases concerning the public interest in speaking freely about the activities of government.[4]

3.02 In comparison, it is interesting to note that the case law governing the operation of copyright has been less concerned about freedom of speech issues. This is so despite the fact that copyright law grounds a system that might be argued to constitute extensive private control over speech. The key to copyright law's comparative inattention to countervailing concepts of free speech appears to be threefold. First, the role of copyright in stimulating expressive diversity is often considered to outweigh or nullify any negative effects on freedom of speech.[5] Secondly, there is a prevailing belief that copyright has internal mechanisms that are capable of dealing with freedom of speech issues, if they arise. Thirdly, the very fact that copyright enables the exercise of private, rather than governmental, control over speech means that the risks that copyright poses to free speech are underestimated or ignored. This chapter focuses on the third of these, but in doing so it attempts to demonstrate limitations inherent in the assumptions grounding the other two.

---

[2] *Derbyshire County Council v Times Newspapers Ltd* [1993] 2 WLR 449. See further F Patfield, 'Defamation, Freedom of Speech and Corporations' [1993] Juridical Rev 294.

[3] See, eg, *Gartside v Outram* (1856) 26 LJ Ch 113; *Hubbard v Vosper* [1972] 2 QB 84, CA; *Beloff v Pressdram* [1973] 1 All ER 241; *Woodward v Hutchins* [1977] 1 WLR 760, CA; *Francome v Mirror Group Newspapers Ltd* [1984] 1 WLR 892, CA; *Lion Laboratories v Evans* [1985] QB 526, CA.

[4] See *A-G v Jonathan Cape Ltd* [1976] QB 752; *Commonwealth of Australia v John Fairfax & Sons Ltd* (1980) 147 CLR 39; *AG (UK) v Heinemann Publishers Australia Pty Ltd and Wright* (1987) 10 NSWLR 86 and (1988) 77 ALR 449; *A-G (UK) v Wellington Newspapers Ltd* [1988] 1 NZLR 129; *A-G v Guardian Newspapers (No 2)* [1990] 1 AC 109. See further, M Blakeney, 'Protecting the Secrets of a Foreign Government: "Spycatcher" in Australia' (1988) 9 J Media L & Practice 13 and F Patfield, 'Spycatcher Worldwide: An Overview' [1989] 6 EIPR 201.

[5] See, eg, P Goldstein, *Copyright's Highway: From Gutenberg to the Celestial Jukebox* (New York: Hill & Wang, 1994) 228ff, especially 236. For a more nuanced approach to this proposition, see NW Netanel, 'Copyright and a Democratic Civil Society' (1996) 106 Yale L J 283, especially 347–64.

B. Freedom of Speech and Copyright

The right to free speech is typically framed as a right against the State or **3.03** against a public authority.[6] However, none of the major theories commonly advanced to justify the protection of free speech suggests that such a narrow approach is necessary. Each of the three major justificatory theories might be argued to focus on the importance of certain types of speech rather than on the identity of the person restraining such speech.[7] A brief consideration of these theories not only demonstrates this point, but also reveals a number of other considerations that are relevant to the question of the relationship between copyright and free speech.

The argument, generally credited to John Stuart Mill,[8] that freedom of **3.04** speech promotes truth appears to be founded on the notion that open public debate will aid the ascertainment of truth. It is unclear whether the importance of truth in this context is due to its character as a basic ethical value, its significance in securing social development, or both. Barendt suggests that the type of speech to which Mill's theory applies is probably of greatest relevance 'to discussion of political, moral, and social affairs'.[9] There is no obvious reason why only the State would be capable of wielding the type of power necessary to constrain such speech. Of course, the conclusion that private entities might wield this sort of power does not necessarily suggest that they would be able to do so using copyright. Copyright's famous idea–expression dichotomy means that copyright will only constrain speech that adopts substantially the same expression as the copyright work. However, it does not seem beyond the bounds of possibility that, in order to engage

---

[6] See, eg, E Barendt, *Freedom of Speech* (Oxford: OUP, 1987) 15: 'Freedom of speech is primarily a liberty against the state'.

[7] For a more comprehensive discussion of these theories in the context of the relationship with copyright law, see F Macmillan Patfield, 'Towards a Reconciliation of Free Speech and Copyright', in EM Barendt et al, *The Yearbook of Media and Entertainment Law* 1996 (Oxford: OUP, 1996), 199, especially 201–15.

[8] See E Barendt, *Freedom of Speech* (Oxford: OUP, 1987) 8, citing JS Mill, *On Liberty* (Everyman edn, 1972) ch 2. However, as Barendt points out, Mill was in this respect anticipated by John Milton: see Barendt, ibid 8, citing J Milton, *Areopagitica: A Speech for the Liberty of Unlicensed Printing* (1644) in *Prose Writings* (Everyman edn, 1958).

[9] Barendt, ibid 10, citing Mill, ibid 96.

in discussions about 'political, moral, and social affairs',[10] the expression adopted in certain materials might be as important to its impact as the idea behind it.[11] In such a situation, copyright constraints on the repetition of such expressions may well inhibit free speech. However, Mill's theory is open to criticism in ways that affect the question of the relationship between free speech theory and copyright. Aside from the issue of whether there is such a thing as truth, Mill's theory is open to the accusation that it overrates the value of free speech in discovering truth. If the value of free speech is overrated then its claim to override the interests protected by copyright is reduced commensurately.

3.05 A second major justificatory theory of the right to free speech is that it is 'an integral aspect of each individual's right to self development and fulfill-ment'[12] and is, therefore, a basic human right.[13] In comparison with Mill's argument, which appears to focus on the importance to society of freedom of speech, the argument based on the right to self-fulfilment seems to focus on its importance to the speaker. This nevertheless seems to suggest that, like Mill's argument (but for different reasons), this justification for protecting freedom of speech is particularly concerned with the expression of opinion.[14] Again, there is no clear reason why a restraint on the expression of an opinion would be any less to be condemned if it involved the exercise of private, rather than State, power. It may well be that to express an opinion on some matters requires the reproduction of copyright material in some circum-stances. However, reliance on this non-utilitarian justification for protecting freedom of speech is problematic in the copyright context. Where will the balance be drawn between the private right to speak and the private right to protect one's speech?

3.06 Part of the intuitive appeal of the third major justificatory theory is that, like Mill's theory, it focuses on the public importance of free speech. This theory argues that freedom of speech is essential to the preservation of

---

[10] Barendt, ibid 10.

[11] See F Macmillan Patfield, 'Towards a Reconciliation of Free Speech and Copyright', in EM Barendt et al, *The Yearbook of Media and Entertainment Law* 1996 (Oxford: OUP, 1996), 199, 208–19.

[12] E Barendt, *Freedom of Speech* (Oxford: OUP, 1987) 14.

[13] See, eg, R Dworkin, *Taking Rights Seriously* (London: Duckworth, 1977) 266ff.

[14] E Barendt, *Freedom of Speech* (Oxford: OUP, 1987) 17.

democracy.[15] It is also the most broad-based of the three theories, concerning itself with the interests of speaker and audience in both factual material and opinion. The concern of this theory with factual material as well as opinion expands the potential clash with copyright and its related rights.[16] Superficially, the theory based on democratic participation might be regarded as implying a particular concern with the ability of the State to constrain free speech about its activities. However, it is not too difficult to make the argument that the ability of citizens to participate in the democratic or political process can also be impeded by powerful so-called 'private' interests. Where the socio-economic power of such interests is significant, their power may be (at least) as relevant to constraining such participation as the power of the State. The phenomenon whereby private interests, especially media interests, seek to control the outcome of various political processes is well known. But other measures of control exercised by private interests may have a more insidious effect on the ability of individuals to participate in political processes.

Reliance on the democracy theory of free speech as a basis for challenging **3.07** the exercise of copyright in some circumstances might be thought to privilege the protection of certain types of speech. For example, it might be argued that speech that is overtly 'political' would have a special claim to free speech protection, whereas speech that is characterized as 'artistic', 'scholarly', or 'commercial' would have less or no claim to such protection. While this might constitute a basis for a workable interface between copyright law and free speech, it raises serious difficulties about how to define such categories of speech.[17] Further, it is based upon an implicit public–private divide in the nature of speech, which raises certain questions.[18] To what extent are things said to the public capable of being considered private? Is the personal, artistic, or commercial really not political? (Of course, the idea that artistic work

---

[15] See E Barendt, ibid, ch 1.

[16] See, eg, *BBC v Time Out* [1984] FSR 64. See also RM Gellman, 'Twin Evils: Government Copyright and Copyright-like Controls Over Government Information' (1995) 45 Syracuse L Rev 999 and F Macmillan Patfield, 'Towards a Reconciliation of Free Speech and Copyright', in EM Barendt et al, *The Yearbook of Media and Entertainment Law* 1996 (Oxford: OUP, 1996), 199, 204–5.

[17] See further Macmillan Patfield, ibid 208–15.

[18] On this topic generally, see SI Benn and GF Gaus, 'The Liberal Conception of the Public and the Private', in SI Benn and GF Gaus (eds), *Public and Private in Social Life* (New York: St Martin's Press, 1983).

cannot also be political is an absurdity.)[19] A strong argument can be made that any information in the hands of government has the potential to be politically significant (owing to the obvious socio-economic power wielded by government) and thus ought to be freely available.[20] It is this reasoning that lies behind the fact that the US government has no right to exercise copyright protection over government documents.[21] Perhaps, then, what makes speech 'political' is not only the nature of the speech, but also the nature of the entity attempting to control it? Where so-called 'private'[22] or non-State concentrations of power exercise significant socio-economic power,[23] their attempts to control expression through the use of copyright may be characterized as political, despite also being concerned with artistic, scholarly, or commercial speech. It is the contention of this chapter that the copyright system has provided an important part of the edifice upon which the creation and maintenance of a type of private power has been based. The chapter considers whether the significance of this power is such that

---

[19] See F Macmillan Patfield, 'Towards a Reconciliation of Free Speech and Copyright', in EM Barendt et al, *The Yearbook of Media and Entertainment Law* 1996 (Oxford: OUP, 1996), 199, 209. See also A Julius, *Transgressions: The Offences of Art* (Chicago: University of Chicago Press, 2002), especially ch III, in which subversive visual art is defined as falling into three dominant streams, one of which is visual art with a political agenda ('politically resistant art'), ibid 102.

[20] See RM Gellman, 'Twin Evils: Government Copyright and Copyright-like Controls Over Government Information' (1995) 45 Syracuse L Rev 999, 1019–23.

[21] 17 USC 105 (1988). Although, strangely, the relationship between this proscription and principles of free speech is unclear: see RM Gellman, ibid 999, 1001.

[22] There is, in fact, nothing private about entities the socio-economic power and influence of which exceed that of many nation states: see, eg, A Chayes, 'The Modern Corporation and the Rule of Law', in ES Mason (ed), *The Corporation in Modern Society* (Cambridge: Harvard University Press, 1959, reprinted 1980); S Bottomley, 'Taking Corporations Seriously: Some Considerations for Corporate Regulation' (1990) 19 Federal L Rev 203; A Wolfe, 'The Modern Corporation: Private Agent or Public Actor' (1993) 50 Washington & Lee L Rev 1673; F Macmillan Patfield, 'Challenges for Company Law', in F Macmillan Patfield (ed), *Perspectives on Company Law: 1* (London: Kluwer Law International, 1995); K Greenfield, 'From Rights to Regulation in Corporate Law', in F Macmillan Patfield (ed), *Perspectives on Company Law: 2* (London: Kluwer Law International, 1997). Further, the possibility that corporate bodies may be regarded as public figures for the purposes of US defamation law has long been recognized: see F Patfield, 'Defamation, Freedom of Speech and Corporations' [1993] Juridical Rev 294.

[23] See, eg, Chayes, ibid; P Selznick, *Law, Society and Industrial Justice* (New York: Russell Sage Foundation, 1969) ch 7; Greenfield, ibid; F Macmillan, 'Making Corporate Power Global' (1999) 5 Intl Trade L & Reg 3.

its exercise to constrain speech should be regarded as giving rise to freedom of speech concerns.

C. Copyright and Commodification

An arguable case[24] may be made for the proposition that copyright's rela-   **3.08** tionship to the concepts of creativity and culture, with which it is often rhetorically associated,[25] is most accurately viewed as an instrumental rather than a fundamental one.[26] A fundamental approach to cultural output would entail encouraging and protecting it on the basis that it has an intrinsic and non-economic value, not only as an expression of human creativity and autonomy, but also a means of communication within the larger cultural, social, and political domain. The instrumental approach that copyright has instead adopted focuses upon the realization of future economic value through the promotion of trade in the cultural output that comes within its purview. Thus, copyright deals with works in relation to which it subsists as products or commodities, the importance of which is reflected in their impact on trade rather than in any non-economic value they may enjoy. One of the best examples of this type of approach to copyright (and to intellectual property as a whole) arose in the context of the negotiation and conclusion of the WTO Agreement on Trade-Related Aspects of Intellectual Property Rights.

The conclusion of the TRIPs Agreement was, of course, driven by the USA.   **3.09** As Michael Blakeney has shown,[27] the USA used two tools, in particular, to drive the negotiations. First, it took on the burden of convincing the GATT Council that intellectual property rights were relevant to GATT. In

---

[24] See, eg, F Macmillan, 'Corporate Power and Copyright', in R Towse (ed), *Copyright and the Cultural Industries* (Cheltenham: Edward Elgar, 2002) and F Macmillan, 'The Cruel ©: Copyright and Film' [2002] EIPR 483.

[25] See further, J Waldron, 'From Authors to Copiers: Individual Rights and Social Values in Intellectual Property' (1993) 69 Chicago–Kent L Rev 841, 853.

[26] The fundamental/instrumental distinction drawn here is drawn from the World Commission of Culture and Development, *Our Creative Diversity* (2nd edn, UNESCO, 1996). For a further discussion and application of that distinction in the context of copyright, see F Macmillan, 'The Cruel ©: Copyright and Film' [2002] EIPR 483.

[27] M Blakeney, *Trade Related Aspects of Intellectual Property Rights* (London: Sweet & Maxwell, 1996) ch 1.

1983 and 1984, evidence was submitted to Congressional hearings by US trade associations on the economic loss that the members of those associations suffered internationally as a consequence of the non-enforcement or absence of intellectual property laws.[28] Amongst other things, evidence was presented at these hearings that the video industry was losing $6 billion annually.[29] The International Intellectual Property Alliance, representing American trade associations in the copyright-related industries, produced a study in 1985 estimating that non-enforcement or absence of copyright laws in Brazil, Egypt, Indonesia, Malaysia, Nigeria, the Philippines, the Republic of Korea, Singapore, Taiwan, and Thailand had caused annual losses of $1.3 billion to the US copyright industries.[30] The second tool used by the USA to drive the TRIPs process was the 1984 amendment to s 301 of the Trade Act of 1974 that made intellectual property protection explicitly actionable under s 301.[31] This was followed by the introduction in the Omnibus Trade and Competitiveness Act of 1988, of 'Special 301', enabling the US Trade Representative to put countries that failed to protect US intellectual property on a watch-list with a view to investigation and possible trade retaliation.[32] For those who would want to see copyright bolstering the fundamental rather than the instrumental role of culture, some comfort might be taken from the fact that the agreement refers to the trade-related aspects of intellectual property and thereby suggests that there may be some other aspects—but it is cold comfort. The truth is that, at least in the common law model of copyright law, we had already gone a long way down the instrumental–trade-related road before the USA did us the favour of bringing it all out into the open.

3.10 There are four interdependent aspects of copyright law that have been essential to the commodification process and to copyright's consequent instrumental approach to culture and creativity. The first and most basic tool

---

[28] *Possible Renewal of the Generalised System of Preferences: Hearing Before the Subcommittee on Trade of the US House of Rep Comm on Ways and Means*, 98th Cong 1st Sess (1983); and *Unfair Foreign Trade Practices, Stealing American Intellectual Property: Imitation is Not Flattery*, 98th Cong 2nd Sess (1984): both cited in Blakeney, ibid 2n.

[29] Blakeney, ibid 2.

[30] International Intellectual Property Alliance, *Piracy of US Counterfeited Works in Ten Selected Countries* (1985) 7, cited in Blakeney, ibid 2 and 2n.

[31] Blakeney, ibid 4.

[32] Ibid 5.

of commodification is the alienability of the copyright interest. A second significant aspect of copyright law making it an important tool of trade and investment is its duration. The long period of copyright protection increases the asset value of individual copyright interests.[33] Thirdly, the strong commercial distribution rights,[34] especially those which give the copyright holder control over imports and rental rights, have put copyright owners in a particularly strong market position, especially in the global context. Finally, the power of the owners of copyright in relation to all those wishing to use copyright material has hardly been undermined by a contraction of some of the most significant defences to copyright infringement. Of particular note in this respect are the repeated assaults on the cogency and practical utility of the fair use/dealing and public interest defences to copyright infringement.[35]

It may be possible to justify a degree of commodification by reference to the **3.11** need for creators to be remunerated in order to encourage them to create[36] and by reference to the need for cultural works to be disseminated in order to reap the benefits of their creation. This latter point would fit in with the argument that an important aspect of copyright is its communication role.[37] Whether some degree of commodification is essential to the integrity of copyright law or not, the point is that we have allowed the process of commodification to take over copyright without adequately considering the costs and consequences of this commodification.

---

[33] See R Towse, 'Copyright Risk and the Artist: An Economic Approach to Policy for Artists' (1999) 6 Cultural Policy 91, 98–9.

[34] See, esp, the TRIPs Agreement, Arts 11 and 14(4), which enshrine rental rights in relation to computer programs, films, and phonograms; WIPO Copyright Treaty 1996, Art 7; and WIPO Performances and Phonograms Treaty 1996, Arts 9 and 13.

[35] On the fair use/dealing defence, see paras 3.35–3.39 below. On the public interest defence, see paras 3.42–3.43 below.

[36] See, however, R Towse, *Creativity, Incentive and Reward: An Economic Analysis of Copyright and Culture in the Information Age* (Cheltenham: Edward Elgar, 2001), esp chs 6 and 8, in which it is argued that copyright generates little income for most creative artists. Nevertheless, Towse suggests that copyright is valuable to creative artists for reasons of status and control of their work.

[37] See W van Caenegem, 'Copyright, Communication and New Technologies' (1995) 23 Federal L Rev 322; and NW Netanel, 'Copyright and a Democratic Civil Society' (1996) 106 Yale L J 283.

D. Commodification and Private Power

(1) Global rights, global distribution, global dominance

3.12 One consequence of the commodification of creativity through copyright is the build-up of private power over cultural output.[38] The way in which the distribution rights attaching to copyright might be used by a multinational corporation to carve up the international market[39] is a small part of a much bigger story about the way in which commodification can lead to global domination of a market for cultural output. The capacity to achieve a position of global power is a combination of the international nature of intellectual property rights, the fact that many of the corporations owning the rights operate on a multinational level, and the fact that many of these media and entertainment corporations are conglomerates that display a high degree of horizontal integration by operating in a number of different areas of cultural output.[40] Most are also vertically integrated with a high degree of control over the entire distribution process.[41] The oligopolistic nature of the media and entertainment sector is accentuated through the prevailing pattern of horizontal and vertical mergers.

3.13 The fashion for horizontal and vertical mergers and acquisitions in the media and entertainment sector began in the 1970s. It seems that one force driving these mergers is the desire to increase the level of corporate ownership over copyright interests. As Smiers puts it: 'The best way to acquire rights on huge quantities of entertainment and other artistic materials is through

---

[38] See also, eg, R Bettig, *Copyrighting Culture: The Political Economy of Intellectual Property* (Boulder CO: Westview, 1996), esp ch 3; and R Towse, 'Copyright Risk and the Artist: An Economic Approach to Policy for Artists' (1999) 6 Cultural Policy 91.

[39] See further, F Macmillan, 'Copyright and Culture: A Perspective on Corporate Power' (1998) 10 Media & Arts L Rev 71.

[40] See also R Towse, 'Copyright Risk and the Artist: An Economic Approach to Policy for Artists' (1999) 6 Cultural Policy 91, 97–8.

[41] For further discussion of the way in which the filmed entertainment industry conforms to these industry features, see F Macmillan, 'The Cruel ©: Copyright and Film' [2002] EIPR 483.

mergers. Synergy is the rationale for media conglomerates snatching up as much copyrighted material as they can.'[42]

Such activity is not only stimulated by the significant asset value of copyright **3.14** interests,[43] it also reflects the strategic business concerns. Bettig describes mergers and acquisitions in the media and entertainment sector as 'a process of reorganization around core and related lines of business along with an effort to establish alliances across national boundaries with market dominant firms in other countries'.[44] This process has been reflected in the activities of media and entertainment corporations such as Viacom Inc (which owns Paramount Communications Inc), Time Warner Inc, News Corporation Ltd, The Disney Corporation, and Comcast Inc:[45] the activities of these corporations involve diversified lines of business including film and television production and distribution, international ownership of cinema chains, broadcasting, cable networks, and music and book publishing.[46] Beginning in the late 1980s, there has also been a trend on the part of corporations that were primarily engaged in the production of technology used in the distribution of media and entertainment content to merge with or acquire interests in corporations producing that content. So, for example, Sony Corporation acquired Columbia Pictures Entertainment in 1989; and Matsushita Electric Industrial Company acquired MCA, the parent company of Universal Pictures in 1991. The most significant recent example of this tendency towards the integration of corporations owning rights over content and distribution

---

[42] J Smiers, 'The Abolition of Copyrights: Better for Artists, Third World Countries and the Public Domain', in R Towse (ed), *Copyright and the Cultural Industries* (Cheltenham: Edward Elgar, 2002) 120. See also R Bettig, *Copyrighting Culture: The Political Economy of Intellectual Property* (Boulder CO: Westview, 1996) 40–2.

[43] For example, it was reported that Chrysalis, the music and broadcasting group raised £60 million against its music publishing catalogue, which comprised 50,000 copyrights valued for the purpose of the securitization at £150 million and generating a revenue stream of £8 million per year. See 'Chrysalis in £60m fundraising' *The Times*, 9 February 2001.

[44] R Bettig, *Copyrighting Culture: The Political Economy of Intellectual Property* (Boulder CO: Westview, 1996) 37.

[45] In February 2004, Comcast (in which Microsoft has a 7.4% holding) made a £35 billion hostile takeover bid for the Disney Corporation, after a merger proposition was rejected by the Disney board of directors. Some pundits suggest that this may mark the beginning of a period of more hostile activity in the media and entertainment sector. See E Warner, 'The spirit of Mickey must survive', *The Guardian*, 14 February 2004.

[46] For an example of this, see Bettig's description of the process of integration by Paramount Communications Inc: R Bettig, *Copyrighting Culture: The Political Economy of Intellectual Property* (Boulder CO: Westview, 1996) 37–8.

of filmed entertainment and those owning rights over the technology of distribution is the merger of AOL and Time Warner. Not only do these mergers increase the concentration of copyright ownership in the media and entertainment sector, they also place the ownership of the patent rights over the distribution technology in the same hands.[47] This process of concentration seems to be leading inexorably to the conclusion that 'a handful—six to ten vertically integrated communications companies—will soon produce, own and distribute the bulk of the culture and information circulating in the global marketplace.'[48]

3.15 An example of this type of concentration of corporate power, analysed by Anne Capling in 1996,[49] is the power that six[50] international entertainment corporations held over the Australian market for contemporary music. The companies in question were CBS (Sony), WEA (Time Warner), Polygram (NV Philips), EMI (Thorn EMI), BMG (Bertelmanns Music Group) and Festival (News Limited). All of these corporations operate as international conglomerates, some with substantial media interests, and between them they control seventy per cent of the world's recorded music market.[51] Furthermore, in Australia, they also have control of the distribution system— EMI and CBS do this by virtue of a joint venture, as do BMG and WEA; Polygram and Festival have subsidiaries that act as their distributors.[52] The specific copyright tool that they used to orchestrate their oligopoly was their control over the import of works to which they own the copyright.[53] The right to control parallel imports with respect to recorded music was removed from Australian copyright law in 1998.[54] However, this appears to have done little so far to alter patterns of control and distribution in the Australian recorded music market.

---

[47] Thus returning us, strangely enough, to the origins of the filmed entertainment industry, which grew out of a need to exploit patents over cinematograph technology. See further, eg, S Vaidhyanathan, *Copyrights and Copywrongs: The Rise of Intellectual Property and How it Threatens Creativity* (New York: New York University Press, 2001) 87–93.

[48] R Bettig, *Copyrighting Culture: The Political Economy of Intellectual Property* (Boulder CO: Westview, 1996) 38.

[49] A Capling, 'Gimme shelter!' *Arena Magazine*, February–March 1996, 21.

[50] Such is the process of merger and acquisition in this industry that the six are now four— and are likely soon to be three when the proposed merger between Sony and BMG takes place.

[51] A Capling, 'Gimme shelter!' *Arena Magazine*, February–March 1996, 21, 22.

[52] Ibid 21.

[53] Ibid.

[54] Copyright (Amendment) Act (No 2) (1998).

It seems that even without the right to control parallel imports, copyright has **3.16** been an essential tool in the orchestration of this type of global oligopoly because of the long period of control that it gives its owner over the distribution of content.[55] The market for filmed entertainment provides a particularly good example of this. In this market the copyright monopoly, allied with the vertical integration of the market, has allowed the major media and entertainment corporations to dominate not only the market for first-run cinema, but also the markets that have been created as a consequence of the development of new technologies for the distribution of filmed entertainment. That is, the same oligopolistic market structure controls the market for television feature films, cable transmission of films, videos, and (now) digital versatile disks (DVDs).[56] The video market, now being superseded by the market for DVDs, has been a particularly significant market for the major media and entertainment corporations. Bettig estimates that in the early 1990s the video market for sales and rentals accounted for 35 to 45 per cent of the global revenues of the filmed entertainment industry.[57] In 1992, six major filmed entertainment corporations accounted for 77 per cent of the total revenue of the North American video market. These were: Disney (21.3%), Warner Home Video (18.1%), FoxVideo (14.1%), Columbia Tri-Star Home Video (9.7%), Paramount (7.3%), and MCA/Universal Home Video (6.6%).[58] Making allowances for the processes of merger and acquisition that have characterized the media and entertainment sector, more or less the same major corporations dominate the video market in Europe.[59] For example, in 1987 the video-rental market in the United Kingdom was dominated by four US corporations: Warner (21.6%), CBS/Fox (18.5%), CIC Video handling distribution for MGM/UA, Universal, and Paramount (12.7%), and RCA/Columbia (11.6%). By 1992, CIC Video had increased its share of the rental market to 20 per cent. So far as the video-sale market in the United Kingdom was concerned, in 1992, Warner and Disney held approximately 50 per cent of this market between them. Other than Italy, in

---

[55] See R Towse, 'Copyright Risk and the Artist: An Economic Approach to Policy for Artists' (1999) 6 Cultural Policy 91.

[56] See R Bettig, *Copyrighting Culture: The Political Economy of Intellectual Property* (Boulder CO: Westview, 1996) 39–42.

[57] Ibid 40. According to one source, in 2002 video rentals accounted for 46.6% of studio revenues. See 'Net Pirates Turn Sites on Hollywood', *The Guardian*, 23 February 2002.

[58] R Bettig, *Copyrighting Culture: The Political Economy of Intellectual Property* (Boulder CO: Westview, 1996) 40.

[59] The source of the following material on the European video markets is Bettig, ibid 210–14.

which there was a significant market in pirated videos, the story is more or less the same in the rest of Europe. In Spain, for example, four of the US majors (RCA/Columbia, CBS/Fox, CIC and Warner), accounted for 70 per cent of the video market in 1990 and they managed to increase this dominance to 78 per cent by 1991. It is perhaps worth noting, finally, that the implementation of the obligations in the TRIPs Agreement is likely to have increased the market dominance of the major filmed entertainment corporations in countries where a significant portion of the video market was represented by the sale or rental of pirate videos.

(2) The role of technology

3.17 Technological developments tend to cause crises for the media and entertainment oligopolies by threatening their control over distribution. Copyright law, which is the key to the control of distribution, is intimately bound up with these technological developments because such developments raise questions about either the scope or the enforceability of copyright. Thus, the major music labels and music publishers leapt to the defence of their market control in a series of copyright cases in the USA directed at preventing the distribution of music on the Internet by the use of MP3 files. The upshot of at least some of these proceedings is that the major record labels have entered (or are negotiating to enter) into distribution arrangements with online music providers.[60]

3.18 Another controversy, which created alarm in the ranks of the filmed entertainment industry and saw the majors jumping to the defence of their distribution monopoly, was the release of the DeCSS (Decrypted Content Scrambling System) source code. This source code allows the copying of DVDs and their transmission via the Internet. Not only did the eight US majors of the filmed entertainment industry take an action against the publishers of sites that had disclosed the code, they also commenced proceedings against *Copyleft* for reprinting the code onto a T-shirt.[61] Of the three Internet site publishers pursued by the film industry majors, two negotiated consent decrees. The third, who goes by the underground name of Eric Corley,[62] had

---

[60] See further, F Macmillan, 'Corporate Power and Copyright', in R Towse (ed), *Copyright & the Cultural Industries* (Cheltenham: Edward Elgar, 2002) 108 and 108n.

[61] See *The Wizard*, 7 August 2000, <http://www.wizardfkap.com/page6.html> and <http://www.copyleft.net>.

[62] In homage to the character of the same name in George Orwell's, *Nineteen Eighty Four*.

published the code in his on-line journal, *2600: The Hacker Quarterly*, and chose to defend the case. On 17 August 2000, US District Court Judge Lewis Kaplan handed down a decision preventing *2600* from continuing to publish the DeCSS code on its website.[63] This decision, which may resonate in European jurisdictions as a result of Article 6 of the Copyright in the Information Society Directive, has now been affirmed on appeal.[64]

Judge Kaplan's original decision was based on a provision of the Digital **3.19** Millennium Copyright Act.[65] The Act, in s 1201(a)(1), prohibits the circumvention of technological measures controlling access to a copyright work. Section 1201(a)(2) prohibits a person, amongst other things, offering to the public or providing 'any technology, product, service, device, component or part thereof' that:

(a) is primarily designed for the purpose of circumventing a technological measure,

(b) has limited commercially significant purpose other than circumvention of a technological measure, or

(c) is marketed with personal knowledge of use in circumventing a technological measure.

Corley was held to have breached this section. This was despite the fact that **3.20** s 1201(c) of the Act provides that nothing in the section limits the rights of free speech for activities using consumer electronics, telecommunications, or computing products, nor the rights of fair use with respect to copyright works. Taking the matter of free speech first, there is a reasonable argument to be made that merely posting and linking the DeCSS code, as opposed to making use of it, is purely expressive. If this is so, then enjoining such behaviour raises serious free speech concerns. The US Court of Appeals for the Second Circuit accepted that the decryption code was constitutionally protected speech. However, it held that the right of the copyright holder to protect its property must be balanced against the right to free speech and that, as a result, the restraint imposed by the circumvention provisions of the Digital Copyright Millennium Act was not an undue restraint on speech.

So far as the issue of fair use/dealing is concerned, the consequences of **3.21** the case are also serious. The Court of Appeals noted that Corley was not

---

[63] *Universal City Studios, Inc v Shawn C Reimerdes* 111 F Supp 2d 294 (SDNY, 2000).

[64] *Universal City Studios, Inc v Corley* 273 F 3d 429 (US Ct of Apps (2nd Cir), 2001).

[65] Section 1201, Title 17 of the US Code.

claiming to have made a fair use of the copyright material. However, it did observe that fair use does not involve a right of access to copyright material 'in order to copy it by the fair user's preferred technique or in the format of the original'.[66] Overall, the Court of Appeals seems to have brushed aside the combined result of its determinations on the free speech and fair dealing issues. If the publication and use of the DeCSS code is not permitted it will not be possible to copy any part of a film on DVD. Consequently, the right to engage in a fair use/dealing with the film, for example, for criticism or review, is meaningless. Thus, the effect of this case is to strengthen considerably the rights of the filmed entertainment corporations over their output and fatally undermine the cogency of the fair use/dealing defence. The case does more than merely maintain the exclusive distribution rights of the majors.

3.22 Hot on the heels of the decision of the Court of Appeals in the DVD case was a case that explores the legitimacy of file-sharing software for the distribution of films over the Internet. The complaint in *Metro-Goldwyn-Mayer Studios Inc v Grokster Ltd*[67] was filed on behalf of the film studios making up the Motion Pictures Association of America (MPAA) in November 2001. It made up one part of two closely associated actions, the other filed as a class action on behalf of all music publishers represented by The Harry Fox Agency, against the same defendants in respect of the same activities. The activities complained of related to peer-to-peer file-sharing software provided by the defendants, which it is alleged amounted to 'a 21st century piratical bazaar where the unlawful exchange of protected materials takes place across the vast expanse of the Internet'[68] or 'a cybernetic Alice's Restaurant [where] the menu is our protected content'[69]—either way, a copyright infringement. The software in question, variously known as KaZaA, Grokster, or Morpheus (but referred to as Morpheus hereafter), could be downloaded by the user from the defendant's website. Having logged on to the defendant's server, the user was connected to a so-called 'supernode', a more powerful computer operated by another user. Search requests were sent to the supernode, which searched the computers of other users in the Morpheus network and

---

[66] *Universal City Studios, Inc v Corley* 273 F 3d 429 (US Ct of Apps (2nd Cir), 2001) 459.
[67] 259 F Supp 2d 1029 (CD Cal, 2003).
[68] Complaint in *MGM v Grokster*, para 1, see <http://www.eff.org/IP/P2P/NMPA_v_MusicCity/20011002_mgm_v_grokster_complaint.html>.
[69] Hearing Transcript in *MGM v Grokster*, 8, see <http://www.eff.org/IP/P2P/NMPA_v_MusicCity/20020304_mgm_hearing_transcript.html>.

compiled search results. The user then selected and downloaded the desired files directly from the other user.

The plaintiffs in the *Morpheus* case appeared to accept that the issue was not **3.23** about the software per se, but rather about the behaviour of the defendants in relation to the use of the software. That is, they argued that the defendants were 'knowingly and systematically, participating in, facilitating, materially contributing to, and encouraging'[70] infringing behaviour of the users. Concerns that the entertainment industry is attempting to use copyright law in a fashion that is anti-innovation should not, however, be allayed by this. The line between accepting the lawfulness of the program, but not of its distribution, is a rather blurry (if not completely meaningless) one. This is particularly so when there is a good argument to be made that distribution was the only thing the defendants had actually done. The defendants drew the attention of the users to their obligations under copyright law. Unlike the famous Napster program, the Morpheus program did not rely on a central server system to hold an index of all available files on the network. This was crucial to the decision of the Central District Court of California granting summary judgment to the defendants and denying it to the plaintiffs. This decision was affirmed by the US Court of Appeal for the Ninth Circuit, and the plaintiff studios have now petitioned the Supreme Court.[71] If the studios (and music publishers) are successful in this petition, we may not be a million miles away from the proposition that innovations in the use of the Internet have to be approved by the entertainment industry before the rest of us can enjoy them. Some may even think that the mere fact that the entertainment industry uses its deep pockets to take such overreaching actions in order to protect its distribution monopoly means that we are already there.

(3) The exponentiality of power

Despite the concern engendered by the new technologies, the general rule **3.24** appears to be that the position of power that is enjoyed by media and

---

[70] Complaint in *MGM v Grokster*, para 52, see <http://www.eff.org/IP/P2P/NMPA_v_MusicCity/20011002_mgm_v_grokster_complaint.html>.

[71] See *MGM v Grokster* (US Ct of Apps (9th Cir), 19 August 2004), <http://www.eff.org/IP/P2P/MGM_v_Grokster/20040819_mgm_v_grokster_decision.pdf> and *MGM v Grokster*, Petition for a Writ of Certiorari, US Sup Ct, 8 October 2004, <http://www.eff.org/IP/P2P/MGM_v_Grokster/20041008_Grokster_final_petition.pdf>.

entertainment corporations is self-reinforcing. By having such considerable power, they are able to acquire more. Put simply, this is a consequence of the interdependence in most Western economies between the public and private sectors.[72] This puts corporations in the position to demand of government that it take steps to protect their interests and thereby to reinforce their positions of private power.[73] It is important in this context not to forget that it was the US corporate sector that the US government was seeking to protect when it engaged in its various strategies to force the progress of the TRIPs Agreement. Not only has the US government protected the media and entertainment corporate sector, its actions have allowed the sector substantially to increase its stranglehold over international cultural output protected by copyright. The fact that the government is so willing to act in the interests of the corporate sector—even if for its own reasons—shows the power that the sector wields.[74] It has already been suggested in this chapter that the power of the private sector compares with that of government (if not exceeds it).[75] One significant difference is that the power of government, at least in democratic societies, is legitimated through accountability mechanisms such as elections and the rules of administrative law.[76] The private sector has a free hand to use power in a way that government can only dream about. This tends to suggest that the exercise of that power to constrain freedom of speech should not be regarded with equanimity.

E. Private Power and Freedom of Speech

3.25 This part of the chapter attempts to assess the ways in which the copyright-facilitated aggregation of private power might be argued to limit freedom of

---

[72] See further F Macmillan, 'If not this WTO, then what?' [2004] Intl Company & Commercial L Rev 75.

[73] Not to mention the fact that the economic power of the media and entertainment sector gives it deep enough pockets to fend for itself in problematic cases like *Universal City Studios, Inc v Corley* 273 F 3d 429 (US Ct of Apps (2nd Cir), 2001) and *MGM v Grokster* 259 F Supp 2d 1029 (CD Cal, 2003).

[74] Bettig argues that the copyright laws follow the logic of capital: R Bettig, *Copyrighting Culture: The Political Economy of Intellectual Property* (Boulder CO: Westview, 1996).

[75] See para 3.07 above.

[76] See further F Macmillan Patfield, 'Challenges for Company Law', in F Macmillan Patfield (ed), *Perspectives on Company Law: 1* (London: Kluwer Law International, 1995) 7–15.

speech unacceptably; freedom of speech is taken here to embrace both the freedom to speak and the freedom to access speech.[77] On the basis of the arguments at the beginning of this chapter,[78] a copyright-based limitation on speech is argued to be unacceptable where a powerful interest stifles speech that has a political purpose or effect, broadly defined. The following discussion considers two interrelated aspects of the way in which the patterns and structures of corporate dominance operate to constrict creative or expressive autonomy in ways that impact on the general shape of society and might, therefore, be described as broadly political. First, the following discussion considers the way in which the media and entertainment industry, in particular, controls the scope of cultural expression as a result of the combined effect of its structure and the exercise of its copyright power. Secondly, consideration is given to the way in which powerful private interests assert direct copyright control over the use of material that appears to be part of the commons.

(1) Control over the scope and nature of cultural expression

Let us return, first, to the example of the contemporary music industry and **3.26** the way it operates in Australia. According to Anne Capling, even though the then big six (now four) corporations control seventy per cent of the global market for music, they only release around twenty per cent of this music in Australia. Not only does this mean that these corporations act as a cultural filter, controlling what we can hear, it also means that the music offered for retail sale has 'about as much cultural diversity as a Macdonald's menu':[79]

> The domination by these global entertainment corporations of the Australian market facilitates the globalization of a mass culture of mediocrity in a number of ways. It ensures, for instance, the prevalence of the top sellers to the

---

[77] See paras 3.03–3.07 above.   [78] Ibid.

[79] A Capling, 'Gimme shelter!' *Arena Magazine*, February–March 1996, 22. The issue of release and promotion of recorded music is a big issue for many popular composers and performers. For example, popular music composer Michael Penn is quoted as saying: 'People disappear in this business not through drug abuse but because record companies sign them and then mess them around . . . They're very vengeful people. If you protest, like George Michael and Prince did, you're a whining rock star. In our case you're simply a loser . . . Epic put my album out but they won't spend a cent on promotion. The business is incredibly narrow now. The opportunities for flukes are zero. To escape this multinational hell, your only recourse is stuff like MP3', *Evening Standard*, London, 12 July 2000.

detriment of other less mainstream overseas music . . . Pop and rock account
for close to ninety per cent of the Australian music market and, with the
exception of a handful of Australian acts which have won an international
following, this market is overwhelmingly dominated by North American and
British artists.[80]

3.27 And, of course, Australia is hardly likely to be the only market where this
happens. The processes that produce cultural homogeneity and mediocrity
are global.[81] It is interesting, in this respect, to note that one of the arguments
that is made on behalf of the activities of MP3 Internet music file trading
services, such as Napster, is that they give exposure and airplay to smaller
artists and small independent labels.[82] If this is so, then it is a benefit likely
to be lost if the major labels gain a distribution grip over the online music
providers.

3.28 It is not just in the music industry that the corporate sector controls what
filters through to the rest of us. For example, the control over film distribution enjoyed by the major media and entertainment corporations means that
these corporations can control to some extent what films are made, what
films we can see, and our perception of what films there are for us to see. The
expense involved in film production and distribution mean that without
access to the deep pockets of the majors and their vertically integrated distribution networks, it is difficult, but not impossible, to finance independent
film-making and distribution. This, naturally, reduces the volume of independent film-making. The high degree of vertical integration that charac-
terizes the film industry, especially the ownership of cinema chains, means
that many independent films that *are* made find it difficult to make any
impact on the film-going public. This is mainly because we don't know they
exist. The control by the media and entertainment corporations of the films
that are made is also a consequence of their habit of buying the film rights
attached to the copyright in novels, plays, biographies, and so on. There is no
obligation on the film corporations to use these rights once they have
acquired them but, of course, no one else can do so without their permission.
Similarly, the film corporations may choose not to release certain films in
which they own the exclusive distribution rights, or only to release certain

---

[80] A Capling (n 79 above), 22.

[81] Cf A Moran, *Copycat TV: Globalisation, Program Formats and Cultural Identity* (Luton:
University of Luton Press, 1998).

[82] See, eg, n 79 above.

films in certain jurisdictions or through certain media. All these things mean that the media and entertainment corporations are acting as a cultural filter.[83]

A further example of this filtering function, if one is needed, is provided by **3.29** the publishing industry. The economic power of publishers has, in its wake, conferred a broader power on publishers to determine what sort of things we are likely to read. Richard Abel is eloquent on this topic:

> Book publishers decide which manuscripts to accept; form contracts dictate terms to all but best-selling authors; editors 'suggest' changes; and marketing departments decide price, distribution and promotion. Sometimes publishers go further ... The Japanese publisher Hayakawa withdrew a translation of *The Enigma of Japanese Power* because the Dutch author had written that the Burakumin Liberation League 'has developed a method of self-assertion through "denunciation" sessions with people and organizations it decides are guilty of discrimination'. Anticipating feminist criticism, Simon and Schuster cancelled publication of Bret Easton Ellis's *American Psycho* a month before it was to appear.[84]

There are a number of other examples of the same phenomenon in publish- **3.30** ing. It was reported that HarperCollins (UK), a member of the Murdoch Group, declined to publish former Hong Kong Governor Chris Patten's memoirs, in breach of contract, because the memoirs allegedly included commentary on the Beijing government that might threaten Murdoch's substantial business interests in China.[85] It has also been suggested that the takeover of the British publisher Fourth Estate by HarperCollins (UK) was in some way related to a biography of Rupert Murdoch contracted to be published by Fourth Estate. The biography was not published by Fourth Estate.[86] On the other hand, a development that may have the effect of breaking down some of the power of publishers is the advent of electronic self-publishing. It seems, however, that any inroads that this makes in the power of publishers will be confined to publications by the very few authors who command

---

[83] For further discussion of the issue of cultural filtering and homogenization in the film industry, see F Macmillan, 'The Cruel ©: Copyright and Film' [2002] EIPR 483, 488–9.

[84] R Abel, *Speech and Respect* (London: Sweet & Maxwell, 1994) 52 (footnote omitted). Ironically, in attempting to publish the monograph in which this passage appears, Abel himself was to feel the brunt of his publisher's attempt at censorship. He has subsequently defined this as an attempted exercise of private power to control speech. See R Abel, 'Public Freedom, Private Constraint' (1994) 21 J L & Society 374, 380.

[85] 'Londoner's Diary', *Evening Standard*, 11 July 2000.

[86] Ibid.

sufficient market power to dispense with the promotional services of the publishers.[87]

(2) Loss of the commons

3.31 So the media and entertainment industry controls and homogenizes what we get to see, hear, and read. In so doing, it is likely that it also controls the way we construct images of our society and ourselves.[88] The scope of this power is reinforced by the industry's assertion of control over the use of material assumed by most people to be in the intellectual commons. The irony is that the reason people assume such material to be in the commons is that the copyright owners have force-fed it to us as receivers of the mass culture disseminated by the mass media. The more powerful the copyright owner, the more dominant the cultural image, but the more likely that the copyright owner will seek to protect the cultural power of the image through copyright enforcement. The result is that, not only are individuals unable to use, develop, or reflect upon dominant cultural images, they are also unable to challenge them by subverting them.[89] This is certainly unlikely to reduce the power of those who own these images.

3.32 As an example of this type of concern, Waldron[90] refers to the case of *Walt Disney Prods v Air Pirates*.[91] In this case, the Walt Disney Corporation

---

[87] In 2000, Stephen King decided to bypass the electronic publishing division of his publishers, Simon & Schuster, by publishing his novel, *The Plant*, himself on the Internet. See 'King writes off the middleman', *Weekend Australian*, 22–3 July 2000. King later abandoned this project. See *Metro* (London), 30 November 2000.

[88] See further, eg, R Coombe, *The Cultural Life of Intellectual Properties* (Durham NC: Duke University Press, 1998) 100–29, which demonstrates how even the creation of alternative identities on the basis of class, sexuality, gender, and race is constrained and homogenized through the celebrity or star system.

[89] See also M Chon, 'Postmodern "Progress": Reconsidering the Copyright and Patent Power' (1993) 43 DePaul L Rev 97; DM Koenig, 'Joe Camel and the First Amendment: The Dark Side of Copyrighted and Trademark-Protected Icons' (1994) 11 Thomas M Cooley L Rev 803; F Macmillan Patfield, 'Towards a Reconciliation of Free Speech and Copyright', in EM Barendt et al, *The Yearbook of Media and Entertainment Law* 1996 (Oxford: OUP, 1996), 199, 219–22.

[90] J Waldron, 'From Authors to Copiers: Individual Rights and Social Values in Intellectual Property' (1993) 69 Chicago–Kent L Rev 841.

[91] 581 F 2d 751 (US Ct of Apps (9th Cir), 1978), *cert denied*, 439 US 1132 (1979). For other US case examples of the use of copyright to chill political speech, see NW Netanel, 'Copyright and a Democratic Civil Society' (1996) 106 Yale L J 283, 294.

successfully prevented the use of Disney characters in *Air Pirates* comic books. The comic books were said to depict the characters as 'active members of a free thinking, promiscuous, drug-ingesting counterculture'.[92] Note, however, that the copyright law upon which the case was based does not prevent this depiction only, it prevents their use altogether. Waldron comments:

> The whole point of the Mickey Mouse image is that it is thrust out into the cultural world to impinge on the consciousness of all of us. Its enormous popularity, consciously cultivated for decades by the Disney empire, means that it has become an instantly recognizable icon, in a real sense part of our lives. When Ralph Steadman paints the familiar mouse ears on a cartoon image of Ronald Reagan, or when someone on my faculty refers to some proposed syllabus as a 'Mickey Mouse' idea, they attest to the fact that this is not just property without boundaries on which we might accidentally encroach . . . but an artifact that has been deliberately set up as a more or less permanent feature of the environment all of us inhabit.[93]

Assuming that one is convinced by the argument that freedom of speech is **3.33** unjustifiably constrained when powerful corporate interests seek to prevent the reproduction of dominant cultural images for the purpose of commenting upon them, what is interesting about this case is the light that it casts on the inability of the idea–expression dichotomy to prevent a conflict between copyright and free speech. It seems likely that representational copyright works (photographs, films, drawings, paintings) are particularly likely to attract the claim that freedom of speech cannot be properly served by simply describing the idea behind the expression.[94] As Koenig notes, in relation to commercial icons:

> This uneasy compromise, limiting discussion to facts or ideas but not the method of expression, can result in a form of censorship when the copyrighted

---

[92] J Waldron, 'From Authors to Copiers: Individual Rights and Social Values in Intellectual Property' (1993) 69 Chicago–Kent L Rev 841, 842, quoting KW Wheelwright, 'Parody, Copyrights and the First Amendment' (1976) US Federal L Rev 564, 582.

[93] J Waldron, 'From Authors to Copiers: Individual Rights and Social Values in Intellectual Property' (1993) 69 Chicago–Kent L Rev 841, 883 (footnote omitted).

[94] See further M Nimmer, *Freedom of Speech* (1984), 2:05[C], 2–73, concerning photographs of the My Lai massacre; J Waldron, 'From Authors to Copiers: Individual Rights and Social Values in Intellectual Property' (1993) 69 Chicago–Kent L Rev 841, 858n, concerning the video film of two white Los Angeles policemen beating Rodney King, a black motorist; and F Macmillan Patfield, 'Towards a Reconciliation of Free Speech and Copyright', in EM Barendt et al, *The Yearbook of Media and Entertainment Law 1996* (Oxford: OUP, 1996) 216–19.

material uses attractive elements. Copyright law shields those attractive elements from the full brunt of discourse and criticism. Commercially unsavoury products cannot be effectively attacked when the best criticism depicts the creative attraction itself. Thus RJR Nabisco's creative cartoons which link tobacco smoking with the good lifestyle can only be attacked, according to the idea/expression distinction, by talking about the idea rather than using the very cartoon itself to counter the message . . . [T]he First Amendment has a role in its own right beyond the Copyright Act and . . . it is not sufficiently protected in the idea/expression dichotomy . . . [This] prevents the growth of counter-images in a post-modern society.[95]

3.34 While Mickey Mouse and other dominant cultural icons[96] might be characterized as a form of artistic and/or commercial speech, criticizing them through subversion is a form of political speech that directs itself to the very shape of society and to the power relations that form it.[97] One might have thought, therefore, that such speech merits particular protection under free speech theory. The alternative is to surrender control of what should be the cultural and intellectual commons to private and unaccountable interests.

(3) Copyright's answer?

3.35 Coombe describes this corporate control of culture as monological and, accordingly, as destroying the dialogical relationship between the individual and society:

Legal theorists who emphasize the cultural construction of self and world—the central importance of shared cultural symbols in defining us and the realities we recognize—need to consider the legal constitution of symbols and the extent to which 'we' can be said to 'share' them. I fear that most legal theorists concerned with dialogue objectify, rarefy, and idealize 'culture', abstracting 'it' from the material and political practices in which meaning is made. Culture is not embedded in abstract concepts that we internalize, but in the materiality of signs and texts over which we struggle and the imprint of those struggles in

---

[95] DM Koenig, 'Joe Camel and the First Amendment: The Dark Side of Copyrighted and Trademark-Protected Icons' (1994) 11 Thomas M Cooley L Rev 803, 813.

[96] These are often produced by the advertising industry. The power of some of these images and icons is demonstrated by a higher recognition rate among six year olds of the Camels' (cigarettes) 'Old Joe' cartoon character than of Mickey Mouse: R Abel, *Speech and Respect* (London: Sweet & Maxwell, 1994) 56–8.

[97] See also NW Netanel, 'Copyright and a Democratic Civil Society' (1996) 106 Yale L J 283, 350–1.

consciousness. This ongoing negotiation and struggle over meaning is the essence of dialogic practice. Many interpretations of intellectual property laws quash dialogue by affirming the power of corporate actors to monologically control meaning by appealing to an abstract concept of property. Laws of intellectual property privilege monologic forms against dialogic practice and create significant power differentials between social actors engaged in hegemonic struggle. If both subjective and objective realities are constituted culturally—through signifying forms to which we give meaning—then we must critically consider the relationship between law, culture, and the politics of commodifying cultural forms.[98]

If copyright has any hope of answering a criticism this cogent, it is through **3.36** the fair use/dealing defence. It is this aspect of copyright law that is apparently designed to permit some degree of resistance and critique.[99] Not only is the fair use/dealing defence a weak tool for this purpose, its credentials for safeguarding freedom of speech more generally are even poorer. The determination in *Rogers v Koons*[100] that the fair use defence only applies where the infringing work has used a copyright work for the purpose of criticizing that copyright work, rather than for the purpose of criticizing society in general, exposed a crucial flaw in the use of the defence as a tool of resistance and critique. So far as protecting a more general right of free speech is concerned, judges have been loath to connect the fair use/dealing defence to the protection of freedom of speech. Given the constitutional protection of free speech, this is perhaps a little more surprising in the USA than elsewhere. However, it seems that this judicial reluctance is a result of adherence to the notion that the idea–expression dichotomy addresses any free speech problems in copyright.[101] Optimists may argue that decisions on both sides of the Atlantic in cases like *Campbell v Acuff-Rose Music, Inc*[102] and *Time Warner Entertainments Company LP v Channel 4 Television Corporation plc*[103] repair or mitigate some of the damage that *Rogers v Koons* previously did to

---

[98] R Coombe, *The Cultural Life of Intellectual Properties* (Durham NC: Duke University Press, 1998) 86.

[99] See also J Gaines, *Contested Culture: The Image, the Voice and the Law* (Chapel Hill: University of North Carolina Press, 1991) 10.

[100] 751 F Supp 474 (SDNY, 1990), *aff'd*, 960 F 2d 301 (US Ct of Apps (2nd Cir), 1992), *cert denied*, 113 S Ct 365 (1992).

[101] See *Harper and Row Publishers, Inc v Nation Enterprises* 471 US 539, 556 (1985), quoting the US Ct of Apps (2nd Cir), 723 F 2d 195, 203 (1983). See also, NW Netanel, 'Copyright and a Democratic Civil Society' (1996) 106 Yale L J 283, 303.

[102] 510 US 569 (1994).

[103] [1994] EMLR 1.

the vitality of the fair use/dealing defence as a weapon for securing the right of critique. However, even if this is true, they give little comfort with respect to the protection of freedom of speech more generally.

3.37 The US Supreme Court decision in *Campbell v Acuff-Rose Music, Inc* has made it clear that parody should be regarded as being capable of falling within the fair use defence. It rejected the distinction between parody and social comment, which appears to have been crucial to the decision in *Rogers v Koons*. One of the issues in the case was whether parody that amounts to a commercial use of the original copyright work should be granted the benefit of the defence. While finding that commercial use would not necessarily preclude the application of the defence, the Supreme Court seemed to assume that parody for the purposes of commercial exploitation was the least convincing example of parody falling within the fair use defence. This might be regarded as suggesting that, at least under US law, parody and satire for political and artistic reasons would be regarded as more deserving cases for the application of this defence. However, the case shows little apprehension on the part of the judges that parody and satire may involve issues of free speech and therefore require some weighing up of the relative interests of copyright and free speech. The Supreme Court did not discuss the First Amendment. Rather, it appeared to regard itself as trapped in a world entirely bounded by the interests of the copyright system. Kennedy J, for example, said: '[i]f we allow any weak transformation to qualify as parody . . . we weaken the protection of copyright. And underprotection of copyright disserves the goals of copyright just as much as overprotection, by reducing the financial incentive to create.'[104] Koenig observes that the result of this analysis 'is that instead of leaving breathing room for the First Amendment, a copyright analysis leaves breathing room for copyright protection'.[105]

3.38 Rather than being concerned with the question of commercial speech, the United Kingdom case of *Time Warner Entertainments Company LP v Channel 4 Television Corporation plc* was concerned with broadly political speech. The Court of Appeal sustained the argument of Channel 4 Television that the use of extracts from the film *Clockwork Orange* as part of a documentary programme was a fair dealing for the purposes of criticism or review. The use

---

[104] 510 US 569 (1994) 586.

[105] DM Koenig, 'Joe Camel and the First Amendment: The Dark Side of Copyrighted and Trademark-Protected Icons' (1994) 11 Thomas M Cooley L Rev 803, 816.

of the film extracts was justified in order to make the point that the decision not to show the film in the United Kingdom because of its violent content was questionable in the light of other substantially more violent films subsequently exhibited. Not only does the case give some support to the right to engage in political speech by way of fair dealing, it also suggests that fair dealing may occur when the copyright work is used for the purpose of general social criticism rather than for the purpose of criticizing the copyright work. This determination gives some scope for protecting freedom of speech by using the fair dealing defence. However, the case is a very long way from suggesting that the fair dealing defence is intended or adapted for this purpose. Nor, in its result, does the case answer some of the concerns that have been aired in this chapter. For example, as required by authority, the Court of Appeal emphasized issues of proportionality, both in terms of the proportion of what was taken to the whole copyright work and the proportion of what was taken in relation to the work in which it was used. This type of approach might not be well-suited to dealing with the type of critiques that focus on icons, symbols, or other types of visual representations. The other problem with the proportionality approach is its inherent vagueness, which makes users of copyright works reluctant to rely on the fair use/dealing defence, especially where this involves taking on a large and powerful corporate interest. Such reluctance can only lead to an increase in the power of the copyright owner over the work.

Recent legislative developments concerning the application of the fair use/ **3.39** dealing defences in the digital context are also a cause for concern.[106] The pressures that gave rise to the WIPO Copyright Treaty of 1996 have spawned domestic and regional legislation that tips the copyright power balance even more strongly in favour of the commodifiers.[107] The legislation in question is designed to strengthen the position of copyright owners in the face of the perceived threat to copyright as a consequence of digitization and new forms of communication technology, such as the Internet. One of the ways in

---

[106] On the need for strong fair dealing exemptions in the digital environment, see W van Caenegem, 'Copyright, Communication and New Technologies' (1995) 23 Federal L Rev 322.

[107] See, eg, the Digital Millennium Copyright Act 1998, the Australian Copyright Amendment (Digital Agenda) Act 2000, and the European Parliament and Council Directive (2001/29) on the harmonization of certain aspects of copyright and related rights in the Information Society, [2001] OJ L1767/10.

which this legislation typically seeks to shore up the position of copyright holders is by removing or reducing the existence or practical utility of the fair dealing or fair use exemptions.[108] This point could hardly be better illustrated than by *Universal Studios v Corley*.[109]

F. And?

3.40 The foregoing is not so much an argument against copyright per se. Rather, it is an argument against what Netanel describes as 'the neoclassicist economic view of creative expression as a commodity and of copyright as a mechanism to further allocative efficiency'.[110] For the purposes of the current argument, it is accepted that a certain degree of copyright protection is necessary for the maintenance of free speech, perhaps because it is likely to encourage expressive autonomy and diversity, but at least because it is likely to encourage the widespread dissemination of such expressive autonomy and diversity; these in turn are prerequisites for the sort of vigorous public domain that is essential to maintaining a democratic political and social environment.[111] However, that vigorous public domain is as much threatened by the concentration in private hands of copyright ownership over cultural products as it would be if such ownership was concentrated in the hands of the State. In fact, an argument might even be made that concentration of such ownership in private hands is all the more dangerous because at least the State is accountable for the way it wields power. The private sector is, of course, accountable through market mechanisms. However, once media and entertainment corporations have acquired the ability to shape taste and demand through cultural filtering, and the ability to suppress critical speech about the process of taste-shaping, the market mechanism may work rather imperfectly.

---

[108] See further, eg, F Macmillan, 'Striking the Copyright Balance in the Digital Era' (1999) 10(12) International Company & Commercial L Rev 350; S Vaidhyanathan, *Copyrights and Copywrongs: The Rise of Intellectual Property and How it Threatens Creativity* (New York: New York University Press, 2001) ch 5.

[109] *Universal City Studios, Inc v Corley* 273 F 3d 429 (US Ct of Apps (2nd Cir), 2001).

[110] NW Netanel, 'Copyright and a Democratic Civil Society' (1996) 106 Yale L J 283, 364. See, eg, WJ Gordon, 'Assertive Modesty: An Economics of Intangibles' (1994) 94 Columbia L Rev 2579.

[111] For a full working out of this argument, see NW Netanel, 'Copyright and a Democratic Civil Society' (1996) 106 Yale L J 283.

Copyright's embrace of cultural domination, and its concomitant failure to **3.41** found a broad demotic culture, must be put down to the overwhelming influence of the notion that copyright is a tool to commodify creativity and capture all the future value of that creativity. This influence has been apparent in the progressive expansion of some of the pillars upon which the commodification process has been based. It has been argued above that the commodification process rests on four pillars of copyright law: assignability, duration, wide exclusive distribution rights, and the erosion of the fair use/dealing defence. While assignability of the copyright interest is essential to its commodification, it seems likely that the ability to procure assignments of copyright is largely a consequence of the market power of the would-be assignee. In any case, assignability has always been a feature of the common law landscape of copyright law.[112] Changes in the other aspects of copyright law implicated in the commodification process seem particularly likely to have contributed to the exponential increase in the power that the corporate sector wields over cultural output. Not only have the exclusive distribution rights been subject to relatively recent extension at the international level,[113] the duration of copyright has been considerably lengthened in, for example, the European Union countries and the USA.[114] The contraction of the fair use/dealing defence, which began early on when its focus shifted from what the defendant had added to the copyright work to what the defendant had taken,[115] and was not ameliorated by the confusing morass of case law that governed its application, has reached a critical stage as a result of developments in relation to digital copying.[116]

As long as copyright law continues along this path, it will continue to erode **3.42** the domain in which the right to free speech can be exercised. Valuable

---

[112] See further L Bently, 'Copyright and the Death of the Author in Literature and Law' (1994) 57 Modern L Rev 973, 980–1.

[113] See, esp, the TRIPs Agreement, Arts 11 and 14(4), which enshrine rental rights in relation to computer programs, films and phonograms; WIPO Copyright Treaty 1996, Art 7; and WIPO Performances and Phonograms Treaty 1996, Arts 9 and 13.

[114] See, respectively, Council Directive (EEC) 93/98 harmonizing the term of protection of copyright and certain related rights [1993] OJ L290/9 and the Copyright Term Extension Act 1998.

[115] See L Bently, 'Copyright and the Death of the Author in Literature and Law' (1994) 57 Modern L Rev 973, 979n, citing *Sayre v Moore* (1785) in *Cary v Longman* (1801) 1 East 358, 359n, 102 ER 138, 139n; *West v Francis* 5 B & Ald 737, 106 ER 1361; and *Bramwell v Halcomb* (1836) 2 My & Cr 737, 40 ER 1110, as examples of this transition.

[116] See paras 3.38–3.39 above.

suggestions have been made as to ways in which the commodification process might be limited, especially as it relates to duration[117] and to fair use/dealing,[118] while still preserving the integrity of copyright as a means of encouraging speech and the dissemination of that speech. The question is whether the tools of copyright alone can ever repair the damage that copyright itself has done to the public domain. Other solutions may need to be broached. One of these might be a resuscitated public interest defence to the exercise of copyright. As noted at the beginning of this chapter, there are precedents for the use of this defence in relation to other private law rights governing speech. In relation to copyright, however, developments in common law jurisdictions have raised questions about the vitality of the public interest defence. In Australia, for example, doubts about the existence of this defence to an action for copyright infringement are relatively long-standing.[119] The decision of the US Supreme Court in *Eldred v Ashcroft*[120] is eloquent testament to the fact that public interest will rarely, if ever, trump the proprietary interests of the copyright holder. In the United Kingdom, even before the decision of the English Court of Appeal in *Hyde Park v Yelland*,[121] which appeared to have killed off the defence in the United Kingdom, there was considerable evidence that the courts were unwilling to engage with the question of the relationship between copyright and the public interest.[122] However, the subsequent decision of the Court of Appeal in *Ashdown v Telegraph Group*[123] shows that the public interest defence may yet have a spark of life in the United Kingdom, although it is unclear whether this decision will have much, if any, application outside the overtly party political arena.

---

[117] See NW Netanel, 'Copyright and a Democratic Civil Society' (1996) 106 Yale L J 283, 366–71.

[118] Ibid 376–82.

[119] See Gummow J in *Corrs Pavey Whiting & Byrne v Collector of Customs for the State of Victoria* (1987) 10 Intellectual Property R 53, 70–7 and *Smith, Kline & French Laboratories (Australia) Ltd v Secretary, Department of Community Services & Health* (1990) 17 Intellectual Property R 545, 583.

[120] 537 US 186 (2003).

[121] [2001] Ch 143, CA. See further R Burrell, 'Defending the Public Interest' [2000] EIPR 394.

[122] See, eg, *Secretary of State for the Home Department v Central Broadcasting* [1993] EMLR 253 and *Beggars Banquet Records Ltd v Carlton Television* [1993] EMLR 349. See also, F Macmillan Patfield, 'Towards a Reconciliation of Free Speech and Copyright', in EM Barendt et al, *The Yearbook of Media and Entertainment Law 1996* (Oxford: OUP, 1996), 199, 223–5.

[123] [2002] Ch 149, CA.

Even legal recognition, in the form of a public interest defence, of the fact **3.43** that the exercise of the private copyright power may adversely affect the public interest in a vigorous public domain, may be insufficient to address the structural effects of private global concentrations of copyright power. To counter such structural effects, we need to think more broadly about the potential role of media and competition law at the international level.[124] The legal architecture of international corporate regulation also requires some rethinking. If we want to control the power of the corporate sector, we have to look for ways of making private power more publicly accountable. So far as the media and entertainment corporations are concerned, continued reliance on market mechanisms to achieve accountability does not seem justified in the light of their control over the domains of cultural production, construction, and deconstruction.

---

[124] See further, eg, the World Commission of Culture and Development, *Our Creative Diversity* (2nd edn, UNESCO, 1996), International Agenda, Action 5. In this context, the approval of the proposed Sony–BMG merger by the EU competition authorities is profoundly depressing, see O Eralp, 'Sony merger unsafe at any volume', *The Guardian*, 10 June 2004.

4

COPYRIGHT NORMS AND THE PROBLEM OF PRIVATE CENSORSHIP

*Wendy J Gordon**

Copyright policy must resolve intelligently the tension between upstream **4.01** and downstream creators, between incentives to create and incentives to use. Downstream authors who copy and transform others' images or words as an input to new creativity have obvious free speech concerns. So do simple copiers in those many instances where even non-creative copying is essential for expressing one's ideas or allegiances.

Part of the tension is economic. Because virtually every author needs access **4.02** to predecessor texts, a legislature that increases copyright protection for today's creators simultaneously increases tomorrow's costs of creation[1] or use. But the issue goes far beyond mere pricing and output.

---

* Copyright © 2005 Wendy J Gordon. I thank Gary Lawson, Mike Meurer, Neil Netanel, and Rebecca Tushnet for their comments, and Brandon Ress for his research assistance.

[1] WM Landes and RA Posner, 'An Economic Analysis of Copyright Law' (1989) 18 J Legal Studies 325–63.

4.03 All exclusive rights impose restraints on the behaviour of fellow citizens.[2] This is true not only of rights enforceable by injunction; the law typically enforces even rights to receive money, such as compulsory licence provisions,[3] by criminal sanctions and the courts' contempt power, leading at the extreme to imprisonment for users who refuse to pay. Therefore, like all privately-held rights, copyright empowers a private person[4] (including juridical persons such as corporations) to impose restraints on liberty.

4.04 Moreover, since copyright subsists in work of expression, it has great potential for restraining liberties of speech. In particular, copyright can empower a private party to censor criticism or ridicule to which his works might otherwise be subject, or to limit how copies of his work are used. Criticism often needs to replicate part of its target's content in order to illustrate for the audience the flaws perceived. If copyright is too strong, however, the law can strip the critic of his or her ability to reproduce crucial evidence.[5]

---

[2] For every exclusive right in the law, there is (definitionally) a corresponding duty. Persons subject to a duty are (definitionally) not at liberty to disregard it. See generally WN Hohfeld, *Fundamental Legal Conceptions as Applied in Judicial Reasoning and Other Legal Essays*, ed W Cook (1923); WN Hohfeld, 'Some Fundamental Legal Conceptions as Applied in Judicial Reasoning' (1913) 23 Yale L J 16.

[3] It is easy to overstate the differences between 'liability rule' protection (money only) and 'property rule' protection (injunctive power given to private owner). For the origins of the locution, see G Calabresi and AD Melamed, 'Property Rules, Liability Rules and Inalienability: One View of the Cathedral' (1972) 85 Harv L Rev 1089–128.

[4] Governments can also own copyrights under US law, except for works created by federal employees within the scope of their employment. 17 USC, s 105. Thus, for example, some cases involve copyright claims by local municipalities. This chapter focuses on private rather than governmental copyright owners. However of course a First Amendment defence should be available a fortiori when the plaintiff is a governmental entity.

[5] The courts in the US do sometimes recognize the importance of copyrighted work as 'evidence' in public debate. In *Nunez* the publicly debated question was whether the copyrighted photograph of a near-naked beauty queen should deprive her of her crown, and the media reproduction of the photograph was upheld as fair use. *Nunez v Caribbean Intern News Corp* 235 F 3d 18 CA 1 (Puerto Rico), 2000. Similarly, some courts seem to be sensitive to the way that created works, once integrated into the culture, can become facts of life with which the defendant and her audience need to engage. See *SunTrust Bank v Houghton Mifflin Co* 268 F 3d 1257 (11th Cir 2001) (reversing on fair use grounds a preliminary injunction against a novel parodying and criticizing the American classic *Gone With The Wind*). However, under most current interpretations of doctrine, such uses can be defeated if the other factors in the fair use calculus so indicate.

Evidence in public debate is, further, only a subset of a larger class: all those instances in which the copyrighted work is reproduced *because its existence as a fact* is what makes it important to the defendant.

Similarly, people need symbols and texts that they mutually recognize, and for copyright to deprive the public of the ability to use symbols in the contexts they prefer can distort their ability to inform and reform culture in which they live.[6] The question is how the law should reply to such attempts at private censorship.

In the USA, the federal Constitution empowers Congress 'To promote the **4.05** Progress of Science and useful Arts, by securing for limited Times to Authors and Inventors the exclusive Right to their respective Writings and Discoveries'.[7] The Constitution also, in its First Amendment, invalidates laws that restrain free speech.[8] The question then becomes how the Amendment limits either Congress's power to enact copyright legislation, or courts' interpretation and implementation of the legislation. If that Amendment is unavailable, then the focus needs to shift to what other protections the law contains for free speech. This chapter will address the First Amendment issue first, and then explore alternative avenues for shelter.

A. First Amendment Protection for Free Speech

In regard to First Amendment doctrine, three kinds of cases should be **4.06** roughly distinguished: cases using the First Amendment to challenge legislation in which Congress uses copyright to take sides in a religious or ideological dispute; cases using the First Amendment to challenge legislation in which Congress amends the copyright statute in a general way that nevertheless affects speech; and cases that do not raise facial challenges to copyright legislation, but rather seek to use the First Amendment against particular claims of copyright infringement. The term 'private censorship' applies to this last group of cases. In this last class, defendants either seek to assert an explicit First Amendment defence, or seek to persuade courts that they can avoid conflicts with the First Amendment only by interpreting existing

---

   [6] See generally Jack M Balkin, 'Digital Speech And Democratic Culture: A Theory Of Freedom Of Expression For The Information Society', 79 NYU L Rev 1 (2004); Rosemary Coombe, *The Cultural Life of Intellectual Properties: Authorship, Appropriation, and the Law* (Durham NC: Duke University Press, 1998).
   [7] US Const, Art I, s 8, cl 8.
   [8] 'Congress shall make no law . . . abridging the freedom of speech, or of the press', US Const Amendment I.

provisions of copyright law (such as the fair use doctrine or the non-ownable status of ideas and facts) in a broad, pro-liberty fashion.

4.07 Most obviously vulnerable to challenge on First Amendment grounds is legislation in the first group, namely, copyright laws through which the government seeks to favour one speaker or viewpoint over another. One such case (and they are rare) involved the writings of Mary Baker Eddy, founder of Christian Science. When a split in the Christian Science Church arose, the branch of the Church that owned copyright in Eddy's work asked Congress for private legislation to extend or restore Eddy's copyrights, as a means to prevent variant editions by believers who disagreed doctrinally with the majority group. 'Church witnesses supporting enactment of [the] Private Law . . . frankly admitted that their distress over variant editions was religiously motivated',[9] and Congress was persuaded to extend the copyrights by enacting the requested Private Law. The courts struck the Private Law down as unconstitutional, on the ground that Congress had 'lent the Church leadership the assistance vital to shaping the beliefs of lay worshipers'. To my knowledge, this is the only piece of copyright legislation struck down on First Amendment grounds, and even there the court based its decision on the Amendment's 'free establishment' clause rather than on the 'free speech' clause.[10]

4.08 A second class of cases involves challenges to generally oriented provisions of the copyright statute—provisions that do not take sides in ideological or religious controversies, but nevertheless have the potential to distort public communications and debate. The *Eldred* challenge to the Sonny Bono Act's extension of copyright term is one such case, and a key issue in such cases is the level of scrutiny to which the Court should subject the statutes at issue.[11]

4.09 The third class of cases, the area of 'private censorship', involves the desire of individual defendants to use free speech as a defence to a particular charge of copyright infringement, either explicitly or to give force to other

---

[9] *United Christian Scientists v Christian Science Board Of Directors, First Church Of Christ, Scientist* 829 F 2d 1152 (DC Cir 1987).

[10] Ibid. Note, however, that the opinion in passing mentions both 'speech and religious' issues, and it is hard to imagine that the court would have come out any differently had it rested explicitly and solely on free speech grounds.

[11] *Eldred v Ashcroft* 537 US 186 (2003). See the extensive discussion of *Eldred* in ch 6 below.

doctrines such as fair use. Explicit First Amendment defences have almost never been allowed, and even First Amendment influence is sometimes resisted;[12] ordinarily the courts act as if the traditional fair use doctrine and the dichotomy between ownable expression and non-ownable ideas and facts provided such sufficient shelter for free speech that the constitutional issue need not be reached. Yet many sad proofs exist that conventional doctrine fails in this regard.

One such case ironically parallels the Christian Science example. A splinter **4.10** church begun by former ministers in the Worldwide Church of God sought to reproduce an unexpurgated version of the writings penned by the founder of both churches. The writings at issue were protected by generally applicable copyright (rather than by a Private Act in which Congress took sides in the dispute). The majority church disapproved of the unexpurgated original, and had solely issued a revised edition. The court refused to shelter the dissidents' reproduction under fair use, not seeing that the defendants' use of the scriptures was essentially factual, as providing the dissidents' best evidence for proper belief.[13] In such cases, one person's exclusive right under copyright conflicts with—and is enforced over—another person's desire to write, paint, sing, proselytize, or otherwise 'speak' in ways that employ the symbols and expression of his culture.

This third class of cases is difficult in part because the First Amendment **4.11** prohibits *government* from abridging free speech, and copyright plaintiffs are not government actors. Although much American scholarship questions how sharp a divide really exists between 'private action' and 'state action', a divide between public and private still informs much jurisprudence: American lawyers usually think of the federal and state constitutions as

---

[12] Thus, Judge Posner writes:

'Copyright law and the principles of equitable relief are quite complicated enough without the superimposition of First Amendment case law on them; and we have been told recently by the Supreme Court not only that "copyright law contains built-in First Amendment accommodations" but also that, in any event, the First Amendment "bears less heavily when speakers assert the right to make other people's speeches." Eldred v. Ashcroft, 537 U.S. 186, 123 S.Ct. 769, 788–89, (2003). Or, we add, to copy, or enable the copying of, other people's music.'

In re: *Aimster Copyright Litigation* 334 F 3d 643 at 656 (7th Cir 2003). It is difficult, however, to know how to interpret his brief reference.
[13] *Worldwide Church of God v Philadelphia Church of God, Inc* 227 F 3d 1110 (9th Cir 2000).

having the task of reining in abuses of governmental power, and usually think of federal and state legislation as having the role of reining in abuse of private actors' wealth or strength. The notion of using the federal Constitution to rein in private actors' use of law fits uneasily in this scheme. Yet when a private person sues, he or she is using the government's own power.

4.12 Private rights to sue have sometimes been recognized as sufficiently governmental action that the First Amendment applies to them.[14] Thus, in defamation suits, Supreme Court case law allows newspaper reporters to draw on the First Amendment for shelter if they print false and injurious statements about a public official as a result of reasonable error.[15] Arguably a critic, historian, or other author who utilizes another's copyrighted expression for, for example, evidentiary purposes should be able to avail herself of similar free speech defences based in the First Amendment.

4.13 There are many reasons why the courts hold back from employing free speech analysis wholeheartedly in copyright cases. One contributing factor may be the interaction between the Supreme Court precedent on physical property and the familiar if controversial trope that treats copyright as 'property'[16]. Although some early US Supreme Court cases suggested that free speech could provide a defence to suits enforcing rights in land (as when a speaker sought access to the streets of a wholly-owned 'company town' to address its residents), for many years now the Court has been reluctant to recognize that property cases can implicate the First Amendment. Although that reluctance is probably ill-founded, it may play a role in the courts' reluctance to embrace the First Amendment wholeheartedly in copyright cases. There is ample

---

[14] Netanel points to helpful precedent in the areas such as trademark, right of publicity, intentional infliction of emotional distress. See para 6.08 below.

[15] *New York Times v Sullivan* 376 US 254 (1964) holds that the First and Fourteenth Amendments protect media false statements made about the official conduct of a public official, such that damages may be awarded only if 'actual malice' is shown. When the plaintiff shows that the media defendant published the statement in reckless disregard of its truth or falsity, that constitutes a sufficient showing of actual malice.

[16] Virtually any right can be characterized as 'property' if it involves a right to forbid, a liberty to do, and a power to transfer. Yet the concerns of *physical* property law are inapplicable to many of the rights in intangibles.

I can suggest some alternative labels for the 'property' nomenclature in copyright. One is 'transferable mini-monopoly', or the coined word, 'minopoly'. By 'mini' I mean to reflect that copyright is not a full monopoly: although copyright law prevents strangers from duplicating the copyrighted work, it is not necessarily accompanied by market power and does not prevent competition from similar but independently created works.

ground to distinguish physical property from copyright—for example, copyright governs behaviour in regard to *patterns*[17] rather than *things*; for another, the infringing act in copyright law need not harm the plaintiff in the least, unlike the typical invasion or taking of physical property—yet the 'property' locution is so well-embedded in copyright practice that judges may fear that recognizing a First Amendment defence to copyright could erode physical property rights.

Probably the most important factor is that American judges typically feel **4.14** that the First Amendment commits them to a neutrality that discourages them from making distinctions based on the content of particular speech.[18] The value of one position or another is supposed to evolve through public debate, not through governmental fiat. How then can judges evaluate if disallowing a particular copyright suit—to avoid imposing a burden on speech—would 'outweigh' the arguable loss of incentive, or the injury to the plaintiff's 'right to keep silent'? And if judges cannot weigh, would recognizing the First Amendment's applicability commit them to dismiss *any* copyright cause of action that has even the slightest impact on speech? The latter course would gut copyright, which is not a route the courts are willing to follow.

In the defamation area, accommodations have been found for these desires to **4.15** achieve neutrality while simultaneously protecting both free speech and the core of the private right of action. To accomplish this, the courts employ a mixture of devices, primarily tests of factual falsity and recklessness: if a reporter prints something false with reckless disregard as to whether the statement about a public official was true or not, a court can feel comfortable imposing damages on him. A reporter's proven recklessness serves as a proxy for the low value of his contribution to debate. In copyright, by contrast, no similar proxy has been identified that can serve to substitute for direct evaluation of the worth of speech.

These are some of the reasons why American courts vacillate when copyright **4.16** confronts the First Amendment. Not long ago a federal court held that 'copyrights are categorically immune from challenges under the First

---

[17] WJ Gordon, Chapter 28: Intellectual Property Law, in Peter Cane and Mark Tushnet (eds), *Oxford Handbook of Legal Studies* (Oxford: OUP, 2003) 617–46.
[18] This is one reason why European jurisdictions regulate 'hate speech' in ways that would be unthinkably direct for the USA.

Amendment'.[19] The US Supreme Court then repudiated that harsh ruling.[20] The High Court acknowledged implicitly that sometimes each of us *does* have a Constitutional right under the First Amendment to employ the copyrighted works of others.[21] However, the Court treated that right as 'second-class',[22] and upheld a copyright term extension without the kind of scrutiny that content-distorting legislation ordinarily receives. Wrote the Court, 'The First Amendment . . . bears less heavily when speakers assert the right to make other people's speeches.'[23] Many Americans hope that US copyright law will be written and applied in a way that safeguards the public's interest in free speech,[24] but the aspiration remains to be realized.

4.17 The question remains largely open elsewhere as well. Like the US Constitution, the Universal Declaration of Human Rights simultaneously recognizes both a right to own one's expression and a right of free speech. Thus, Article 27(2) provides support for patents and copyrights. It states that 'Everyone has the right to the protection of the moral and material interests resulting from any scientific, literary or artistic production of which he is the author.' Yet Article 19 states that 'Everyone has the right to freedom of opinion and expression' including 'freedom . . . to seek, receive and impart information and ideas'. Similarly, Article 27(1) states that 'Everyone has the right freely to participate in the cultural life of the community, to enjoy the arts and to share in scientific advancement and its benefits.'

4.18 Both copyright on the one hand, and cultural participation and free speech on the other, can serve goals of human flourishing. That both appear in the same documents is therefore unsurprising. But different means to the same abstract end can conflict with each other. Which clause governs in the case of a conflict? The Declaration does not say. In the USA, by contrast, it is clear

---

[19] *Eldred v Reno* 239 F 3d 372 at 376 (US Ct of Apps (DC Cir), 2001), reversed *sub nom Eldred v Ashcroft* 537 US 186 (2003).

[20] Wrote the Supreme Court, 'We recognize that the DC Circuit spoke too broadly when it declared copyrights "categorically immune from challenges under the First Amendment".' *Eldred v Ashcroft* 537 US at 789–90.

[21] Ibid.

[22] D McGowan, 'Why the First Amendment Cannot Dictate Copyright Policy' [2004] 65 U Pitt L R 281.

[23] 537 US at 789–90.

[24] Thus, the *Eldred* Court noted: '[I]t is appropriate to construe copyright's internal safeguards to accommodate First Amendment concerns'. Ibid at n 24. Although the Court's suggestion was essentially rebuffed in *Aimster Copyright Litigation* 334 F 3d 643 at 656 (7th Cir 2003), it may fare better in other contexts.

that free speech holds the trump card;[25] although, as mentioned, there is often a lack of clarity as to when and how (and even *if*) the trump may be exercised in copyright cases.

What besides the First Amendment could protect free speech in copyright **4.19** law? Copyright law contains specific exemptions that sometimes can serve the interest of free discussion. In the USA, for example, these include provisions for library photocopying[26] and the doctrines of 'first sale' or 'exhaustion' that allow for the circulation of used copies.[27]

Most nations also share some doctrines whose defining concepts are capable **4.20** of flexible interpretation, such as the rule that copyright ownership does not extend to 'facts'. However, these are of uncertain reliability. For example, except when considering issues of computer interoperability,[28] most US courts persist in refusing to see that copyrighted works that usually function as expression sometimes can also function as facts.[29] Thus, in the *Worldwide*

---

[25] The First Amendment *commands*—Congress 'shall make no law . . . abridging the freedom of speech, or of the press', US Const Amendment I—while the Constitution's copyright and patent clause merely *authorizes* Congress to enact copyright legislation, and does not command it. US Const Art I, cl. 8.

[26] 17 USC, s 108.

[27] Ibid, s 109.

[28] In computer cases US courts have come to recognize the importance of allowing factual uses: as when the factual dominance of a particular copyrighted computer program will make some copying necessary for the purpose of achieving interoperability. Thus, defendants prevailed in such cases as *Sega Enterprises Ltd v Accolade, Inc* 977 F 2d 1510 (9th Cir 1992) and *Lotus Development Corp v Borland Int'l, Inc* 49 F 3d 807 (1st Cir 1995), aff'd mem, 516 US 233 (1996) (4–4 decision). Also see *Computer Associates Int'l, Inc v Altai Inc* 982 F 2d 693, 710 (2nd Cir 1992) (copyright does not extend to features of the program 'dictated by efficiency or external factors').

[29] Some of this inability to see that our cultural landscape exists as a 'fact' is due to the all-or-nothing way in which the US statute frames the fact–expression dichotomy. Facts cannot be 'owned' and are placed outside the protectable scope of copyrightable subject matter, 17 USC s 102(b), but the harder question is how to handle works of expression that sometimes act as facts and sometimes do not.

Also important are Supreme Court dicta that posited a false dichotomy between works of authorship that are 'created,' and facts that are not 'created' but merely 'found'. See, eg, WJ Gordon, 'Reality as Artifact: From *Feist* to Fair Use' (1992) 55 L & Contemporary Problems 93–107 (arguing against the dicta of *Feist* that created works do indeed sometimes function as facts in the world, and arguing that special privileges should pertain in such cases). An analogy can be made to the way that the US law of evidence treats some statements as facts: US courts do not consider it 'hearsay' when witnesses quote statements made by third parties for a reason other than proving the truth of the matter asserted. Thus, when such a quotation is offered for the purpose of proving some *other* matter (such as the hearer's state of mind), the witness can repeat the statement made by another person without that 'copying' being hearsay.

Church of God case, mentioned earlier, worshipers wanted to rely upon what they considered the authoritative version of their scripture as their best and perhaps only evidence of correct belief. Yet in empowering the majority faction of the church to curtail this liberty, the court saw the non-ownership of facts as irrelevant.[30]

4.21 Other doctrines with some flexibility are the requirement that the plaintiff prove that the amount the defendant copied was 'substantial' enough to be wrongful, and the rule that 'expression' but not 'ideas' can be owned. But the elasticity of these concepts is limited, as is suggested below in the discussion on the idea–expression dichotomy.

4.22 A more fruitful avenue is the adoption of flexible, equitable doctrines (either as defences or as limitations on the copyright owner's prima facie rights) that allow explicit reference to the public interest. For example, nations with independent judiciaries should supplement the specific statutory exemptions with such defences as an expanded 'fair use'[31] and 'fair dealing' defence, or a

---

[30] *Worldwide Church of God v Philadelphia Church of God, Inc* 227 F 3d 1110 (9th Cir 2000) (enforcing the copyright owned by a dominant church group against the effort of a splinter group to reproduce the unexpurgated version of their founder's writings). The racist nature of the works the defendants wanted to reproduce may have played a role in the court's decision.

[31] A judicially developed doctrine that retains its flexibility, 'fair use' now appears in the copyright statute at 17 USC, s 107. That provision reads as follows:

§ 107. Limitations on exclusive rights: Fair use

Notwithstanding the provisions of sections 106 and 106A, the fair use of a copyrighted work, including such use by reproduction in copies or phonorecords or by any other means specified by that section, for purposes such as criticism, comment, news reporting, teaching (including multiple copies for classroom use), scholarship, or research, is not an infringement of copyright. In determining whether the use made of a work in any particular case is a fair use the factors to be considered shall include—

(1) the purpose and character of the use, including whether such use is of a commercial nature or is for nonprofit educational purposes;

(2) the nature of the copyrighted work;

(3) the amount and substantiality of the portion used in relation to the copyrighted work as a whole; and

(4) the effect of the use upon the potential market for or value of the copyrighted work.

The fact that a work is unpublished shall not itself bar a finding of fair use if such finding is made upon consideration of all the above factors.

Note that the statutory section on fair use singles out 'criticism and comment' as deserving of solicitude, and parody as a form of criticism has long been considered an important exercise of fair use.

'free speech' defence—that can allow individualized, case-by-case accommodation. Such defences are needed both in litigation involving traditional copyright infringement (roughly, 'copying' cases) and where a defendant is accused of bypassing encryption to reveal copyrighted material (roughly, 'access' cases). No nation has a fully available 'fair use' defence; even the USA disallows use of the defence in cases charging bypass of encryption devices,[32] and many US courts, even in copying cases implicating free speech issues, will refuse to employ the fair use defence in the face of strong substitutionary harm.

In the Aristotelian sense, equity is a means of correcting for the law's in-   **4.23** evitable over-inclusiveness.[33] The purpose and justification of such flexible doctrines is usually that they allow the judge or other decision maker 'to say what the legislator himself would have said had he been present, and would have put into his law if he had known'.[34] Free speech warrants the extra cost of individualized investigation.

For reasons explored earlier, the First Amendment is unlikely to yield immedi-   **4.24** ate payoff today. The remainder of the chapter will explore other doctrinal sources for sheltering free speech. In particular, it will suggest that the idea–expression dichotomy is problematic, but that the very norms that justify

---

The Supreme Court has indicated that, at least in cases of parody, a factor weighing in favour of a defendant receiving fair use treatment is a copyright owner's unwillingness to license an attack on its property. Where there is no licensing market, there may be an absence of harm from giving fair use. Thus the Court wrote:

> The market for potential derivative uses includes only those that creators of original works would in general develop or license others to develop. Yet the unlikelihood that creators of imaginative works will license critical reviews or lampoons of their own productions removes such uses from the very notion of a potential licensing market. *Campbell v Acuff-Rose Music, Inc*, 510 US 569 at 592 (1994).

For general discussion of fair use and an unwillingness of plaintiffs to license, see WJ Gordon, 'Fair Use as Market Failure: A Structural and Economic Analysis of the *Betamax* Case and its Predecessors' (1982) 82 Columbia L Rev 1600; also see WJ Gordon, 'Excuse and Justification in the Law of Fair Use: Transaction Costs Have Always Been Only *Part* of the Story' (2003) 13 J Copyright Society 149 (Fiftieth Anniversary Issue).

[32] Digital Millenium Copyright Act, codified as amended at 17 USC §§ 1201–5.

[33] Aristotle writes, 'When the law speaks universally, then, and a case arises on it which is not covered by the universal statement, then it is right, where the legislator fails us and has erred by over-simplicity, to correct the omission.' Aristotle, '10 Ethics', in D Ross trans, JL Ackrill and JO Urmson, *The Nicomachean Ethics* (Oxford: OUP, 1984), 133.

[34] Ibid.

copyright can be referenced as sources to flesh out flexible doctrines, such as fair use, in a way that furthers free speech goals.[35]

B. Is There Shelter for the Necessary Freedom to Borrow in the Idea–Expression Dichotomy?

4.25 A primary tool for accommodating the interests of new generations who wish to criticize their predecessors is the doctrine that while expression can be owned, ideas remain free for all to borrow. The doctrine, often known as the idea–expression dichotomy, is adopted by most copyright systems as a mode of keeping the social costs of the copyright monopoly low. Someone who wishes to quote, but is unable or unwilling to pay the requisite price, is entitled to restate the underlying idea in her own words. The dichotomy seeks to assure that the fundamental building blocks of creation can be used freely, with no need to seek out and bargain with the party who placed the idea in the stream of culture. But it is far from clear that courts today are using the doctrine to safeguard this necessary freedom with the requisite vigilance.

4.26 The line between 'ideas' and 'expression' is, not surprisingly, a hazy one, and should a new artist happen to cross the line, he will be guilty of creating an unauthorized derivative work. Further, sometimes ideas and expression are inextricably linked. Scholars such as Richard Lanham suggest that this is the rule rather than the exception; they view the purported independence of message from mode of expression as largely an illusion.[36] Thus, James Joyce's

---

[35] See WJ Gordon, 'Toward a Jurisprudence of Benefits: The Norms of Copyright and the Problem of Private Censorship', 57 U Chicago L Rev 1009–49 (review essay, 1990). Some of the material in Section B and following is indebted to that early essay.

[36] Richard Lanham, *Analyzing Prose* (2nd edn, Continuum International Publishing Group, 2003). Also see Stanley Fish, *Rhetoric*, in Frank Lentricchia and Thomas McLaughlin (eds), *Critical Terms For Literary Study* 203 (Chicago: U Chicago Press, 1990). On one occasion, even the US Supreme Court recognized this, although not in a copyright context. When a young man was arrested for displaying the words 'Fuck the Draft' in a public building, the Court ruled that the First Amendment freed him. The defendant could have found other words to express the idea, yet, as the Court noted, '[M]uch linguistic expression serves a dual communicative function: it conveys not only ideas capable of relatively precise, detached explication, but otherwise inexpressible emotions as well. In fact, words are often chosen as much for their emotive as their cognitive force. We cannot sanction the view that the Constitution, while solicitous of the cognitive content of individual speech has little or no regard for that emotive function which practically speaking, may often be the more important element of the overall message sought to be communicated.' *Cohen v California* 403 US 15, 26 (1971).

work deeply questioned 'copyright's notion that ideas and facts are anterior to their particular expressions, and thus separable';[37] he doubted ideas and facts could 'yield[] to paraphrase, transmissible without either disfigurement or infringement'.[38]

Yet, art sometimes requires the use of predecessors' work, whether the use is **4.27** hostile (as discussed by Harold Bloom)[39] or grateful (as discussed by Lewis Hyde).[40] The author of a new work is unlikely to obtain permission from a prior author if he wishes to criticize the prior work or use the prior author's material in a way that rejects or undercuts the meaning the predecessor meant to invest in her materials or symbols. It may be precisely the travesty that is most in the need of freedom.[41]

It is true that 'creative misprision' can often proceed without infringing a **4.28** prior work. But that is not always the case. For example, central to the post-modernist movement in art is commenting on existing culture, often by employing the specific icons and images others have popularized.[42] Whether the art at issue is a photo-collage showing the Statue of Liberty swimming for her freedom,[43] a retelling of Hamlet from the point of view of its minor characters,[44] or a collocation by Picasso that pastes copyrighted textiles onto

---

Such recognition is rare for copyright courts. And one can understand why: the more sensitively the courts recognize how restraining the copying of words can also restrain the substance of communication, the more the courts will need to develop a new jurisprudence if much is to be preserved of copyright. This development will hopefully occur, but has not yet.

[37] P K Saint-Amour, *The Copywrights: Intellectual Property and the Literary Imagination* (Cornell, 2003) 189 (discussing the 'Oxen of the Sun' episode in Joyce's *Ulysses*).

[38] Ibid.

[39] Harold Bloom, *The Anxiety of Influence: A Theory of Poetry* (2nd edn, Oxford: OUP, 1997).

[40] Lewis Hyde, *The Gift: Imagination and the Erotic Life of Property* (Vintage, 1983).

[41] Compare T Stoppard, *Travesties* (Grove Press, 1975) 85–7.

[42] 'The referent in post-Modern art is no longer 'nature,' but the closed system of fabricated signs that make up our environment.' John Carlin, 'Culture Vultures: Artistic Appropriation and Intellectual Property Law' (1988) 13 Columbia-VLA J L and the Arts 103, 111. Carlin argues that 'some arrangement needs to be developed whereby artists' traditional freedom to depict the environment in which they live and work is upheld' (ibid 140–1). The art form known as 'appropriation' makes an audience see pre-existing art in a new light or take a different stance towards it. Sometimes appropriation art involves making substantial changes in the pre-existing artwork; sometimes it does not. See generally, ibid.

[43] As in M Langenstein's 'Swimmer of Liberty,' pictured in Latman, Gorman, and Ginsburg, *Copyright for the Nineties* at 159. (Note I merely speculate about the reasons for Ms Liberty's dip).

[44] As in T Stoppard's *Rosencrantz and Guildenstern are Dead* (Grove Press, 1967).

canvas,[45] much art might not be created if consent were required from the person whose work is being commented on. More generally, an artist or speaker sometimes needs to use the expressions, symbols, and characters that represent what he is attempting to rebut, integrate, or criticize in order to make his point clearly. In American doctrine, 'fair use' gives its strongest shelter to transformative uses, but uses that simply take and use symbols created by others can also have profound free speech implications.[46] Thus, in holding that the State may not criminally prosecute someone for burning a flag in political protest,[47] even the US Supreme Court has recognized that it can be essential to self-expression to make hostile use of symbols originated by others.[48]

4.29 We are social creatures, and there are many symbols less noble than the flag that have a power over our minds. As the Court observed, 'Symbolism is a primitive but effective way of communicating ideas ... a short cut from mind to mind. Causes and nations ... and ... groups seek to knit the loyalty of their followings to a flag or banner, a color or design.'[49] Advertisers and entertainment conglomerates also seek to knit loyalty through the use of symbols. To free one's self or one's neighbours from an unquestioning loyalty, or simply to retain cultural vitality, it is sometimes necessary to use a

---

[45] The derivative work right, 17 USC section 106(2), has sometimes been extended to bar the reuse of legitimately puchased embodiments of a copyrighted work.

[46] For example, consider a dissenting church that wishes to distribute copies of a copyrighted 'scripture' that exactly duplicate the scripture's original form, but differ from the expurgated version preferred by the copyright holder. The free speech implications are clear, even though the dissenter wants to 'copy' rather than 'transform'. Nevertheless, in a case closely resembling this fact pattern, the copyright holder (the dominant portion of a divided church) was granted a judgment of copyright infringement against the dissenters. *Worldwide Church of God v Philadelphia Church of God, Inc* 227 F 3d 1110 (9th Cir 2000). The importance of non-transformative copying to free speech—and the sometimes inadequate shelter the fair use doctrine may provide it—is explored in Rebecca Tushnet, 'Copy This: How Fair Use Doctrine Harms Free Speech and How Copying Serves It',__Yale LJ__(Essay, forthcoming).

[47] *Texas v Johnson* 491 US 397 (1989).

[48] See *Texas v Johnson* 491 US 397 (1989). If anyone originated the flag design, it was Betsy Ross. But the Court has difficulty seeing the issue when it is presented in the context of a so-called intellectual property right. Thus, in *The San Francisco Arts & Athletics, Inc v United States Olympic Committee* 483 US 522 (1987), the Court held that the unauthorized use of the word 'Olympics' to promote the Gay Olympics, a non-profit athletic event, violated the US Olympic Committee's property right in the word.

[49] *Texas v Johnson* 491 US 397 at 405 (1989), quoting *West Virginia Bd of Ed v Barnette* 319 US 624, 632 (1943).

received symbol in an unexpected way, a way that the originators would not have wanted.[50] When the Disney organization successfully restrained a counter-cultural comic parody of Mickey Mouse that implicitly mocked both Disney and the suburban lifestyle legitimated in the Disney canon, one critic of the decision aptly commented: 'Prodigious success and its responsibilities and failures draws parody. That's how a culture defends itself. Especially from institutions so large that they lose track of where they stop and the world begins so that they try to exercise their internal model of control on outside activities.'[51]

How might these necessary freedoms be preserved? One answer is to apply **4.30** the First Amendment as a defence where appropriate in particular cases, but so far the courts are resistant to that approach for reasons already intimated. Another possibility is to look at the policies on which copyright itself is justified, and discover whether they contain natural 'limits' that would prevent their restraining important communicative activity. In prior work, I have argued that the public has a right to self-expression—a right to copy and adapt that can trump copyright in appropriate circumstances—based on the same justificatory claims that provide copyright's own normative foundations. Flexible doctrines such as fair use can and should take content from these norms.

C. Identifying Relevant Principles and Policies

There are at least two possible referents when searching for antecedents con- **4.31** sistent with giving hostile works some degree of freedom: copyright itself, viewed as an isolated set of doctrines, or copyright within the context of the law as a whole. Let us begin with the copyright law, canvassing briefly some of the available principles and policies. The chapter will then turn to cognate areas of law, restitution and tort.

Copyright in the USA has one dominant purpose, 'to further the progress of **4.32** Science and the Useful Arts', but many subsidiary purposes are intermittently recognized, such as maintaining equality among different classes of authors,

---

[50] See paras 3.31–3.34 above.

[51] S Brand, 'Dan O'Neill Defies US Supreme Court: A Really Truly Silly Moment in American Law' [Spring 1979] Coevolution Q 41.

or honoring a perceived moral claim that authors may have in their works.[52] It is not yet clear how the various policies should be ranked and weighted. This chapter will explore this mix of purposes and ways we might resolve the problem this mixture poses.

(1) Maximizing social welfare

4.33 There are many norms by which a property system might be judged or justified. One type of justification is instrumental and aggregative, producing legal rules dictated by a social welfare function aimed at maximizing some particular variable. In copyright, the three most salient candidates for maximization are dollars (economic value 'as measured by ... willingness to pay'),[53] utility, and the 'progress of science'.[54]

4.34 Each of these variables has its own definitional ambiguities and internal variations, but their major deficiencies and strengths are fairly clear and familiar. The chief advantage of economic inquiry is that dollars are measurable; the chief disadvantages are that it reflects existing distributions of wealth, ignores the non-monetizability of many values, and treats preferences as sovereign even when the preferences are perverse or mistaken.

4.35 The strength of utilitarianism is that it treats people as equals regardless of wealth. Yet utility, too, (in many hands) measures nothing but simple

---

[52] I speak here of moral entitlements underlying conventional copyright. There is also a doctrine known as 'moral rights' which protects, in particular, the 'integrity' of a piece of art. That right, too, should be limited by free speech defences. (See paras 9.01–9.60 below.) By giving the holders of an integrity right a protection against distortion, 'moral rights' doctrine gives them a power of manipulation. The integrity right allows an author to say 'This is my symbol, my character, my image: use it only as I want you to use it. If you think my use distorts a truth, you must find some way to address that problem without making direct use of my distortion.' In the USA, the integrity right is limited largely to *originals*. That is, an artist can stop someone from marking up or otherwise distorting his original canvas, 17 USC, s 106A, or even a limited number of signed copies, but mass reproduction is outside the scope of the integrity right. It is submitted that this is a good compromise: when there is only one instantiation of a work (like the original canvas), and a choice must inevitably be made between artist and critic, it makes sense to honour the former more. But when a work exists in multiple copies, the critic's desire to use *one copy* is backed by a stronger claim than the author's desire to eliminate criticism or mockery.

[53] See, generally, RA Posner, *Economic Analysis of Law 9* (Little, Brown, 3rd edn, 1986).

[54] See RS Brown, 'Eligibility For Copyright Protection' (1985) 70 Minnesota L Rev 579.

preference, and even when preference-satisfaction is a proper goal, utility is difficult or impossible to measure and to compare interpersonally.

The progress of 'science' (understood as 'knowledge') has the strength of **4.36** being, in the USA at least, the Constitutional explanation for copyright. Yet progress, too, is difficult to measure, and its use as a criterion poses an additional institutional difficulty: judges have been admonished by years of copyright jurisprudence to beware the inability of 'persons trained only to the law' in evaluating cultural worth.[55]

In seeking to maximize social welfare, moreover, each of these approaches **4.37** seems to suffer from another potential deficiency: paying insufficient attention to individuals. Under an aggregative inquiry, the interests of a person who has done nothing morally culpable can be improperly sacrificed in order to serve the 'greater good' (however measured).[56]

(2) Authors' rights

The authors' rights tradition contains two strands that are commonly **4.38** blended,[57] but that in copyright law play separate roles meriting individual

---

[55] *Bleistein v Donaldson Lithographing Co* 188 US 239, 251 (1903) (Holmes). The institutional problem persists even if the 'progress of science' criterion could be applied to types of work or the system as a whole, rather than to individual works. See *Mitchell Brothers Film Group v Cinema Adult Theater* 604 F 2d 852, 860 (5th Cir, 1979).

[56] See U LeGuin, *Those Who Walk Away from Omelas*, in *The Wind's Twelve Quarters* (Harper & Row, 1975) 224 (powerful allegory of a culture dependent on allowing harm to innocents). In practice, aggregative approaches may not lead to such extreme results. Mitchell Polinsky reminds us, for example, that persons whose interests are sacrificed in the pursuit of economic efficiency can be rewarded by transfer payments after the 'larger pie' has been created. AM Polinsky, *An Introduction to Law and Economics* (2nd edn, Little, Brown, 1983) 7–10, 119–27. Even without transfer payments, utilitarianism can yield significant protection for individual interests. For example, FI Michelman, in 'Property, Utility and Fairness: Comments on the Ethical Foundations of "Just Compensation" Law' (1967) 80 Harv L Rev 1165, 1224, examines the US constitutional requirement that 'just compensation' be paid for 'takings' of property. That requirement is open-ended, and judges can interpret it through both utilitarian and fairness approaches. Michelman shows that both utilitarian and fairness criteria yield significant protections for the existing property entitlements of individuals—with utility, surprisingly, sometimes protecting individuals from uncompensated State action in ways that a pure fairness approach might not.

[57] Although these strands are usually seen as non-aggregative, they are also often intertwined with aggregative instrumental arguments. See, eg, D Ladd, 'The Harm of the Concept of Harm in Copyright' (1983) 30 J Copyright Society USA 421, 425–6.

treatment.[58] One strand rests on the beneficial results that authors generate. It has to do with securing, for those who create works of value, reward for their 'just deserts'. It can be viewed in various ways: as a form of causation-based corrective justice,[59] (holding that the person who creates value should be paid for it, just as—arguably—those who generate harm should be made to compensate their victims);[60] as an offshoot of Lockean labour theory;[61] as a notion of fairness; as a sort of strict liability for benefits; or as a variant of the law of unjust enrichment. The key notion in this branch of the so-called 'authors' rights' or 'natural rights' tradition is the claim to deserve some reward, which might take the form of a claim to control.

4.39 The second 'authors' rights' strand has to do with an author's personal stake in what she has made. It too can be found in Locke,[62] though arguably only with some strain, and its defenders often make use of the work of Hegel and his interpreters.[63] Its proponents might emphasize that 'we have the feeling of our personality being in some inexplicable way extended to encompass the objects we own.'[64] If people experience such cathexis to ordinary items of

---

[58] For an interesting investigation of one form that the restitutionary and personality approaches might take, and comparisons between them, see J Hughes, 'The Philosophy of Intellectual Property' (1988) 77 Georgetown L J 287. See also, AC Yen, 'Restoring the Natural Law: Copyright as Labor and Possession' (1990) 51 Ohio State L J 491; WJ Gordon, 'An Inquiry Into The Merits Of Copyright: The Challenges Of Consistency, Consent, And Encouragement Theory', (1989) 41 Stanford L Rev 1343 at 1446–69; EC Hettinger, 'Justifying Intellectual Property' (1989) 18 Philosophy and Public Affairs 31; WJ Gordon, 'On Owning Information: Intellectual Property and the Restitutionary Impulse' (1992) 78 Virginia L Rev 149–281 and WJ Gordon, 'A Property Right in Self-Expression: Equality and Individualism in the Natural Law of Intellectual Property' (1993) 102 Yale L J 1533–609.

[59] See the discussion of corrective justice in WJ Gordon, 'On Owning Information: Intellectual Property and the Restitutionary Impulse' (1992) 78 Virginia L Rev 149–281 and the sources cited therein.

[60] Compare G Sher, *Desert* (Princeton, 1987) 69–90.

[61] See J Locke, *The Second Treatise of Government* (Bobbs-Merrill, 1952) ch 5. Also see WJ Gordon, 'A Property Right in Self-Expression: Equality and Individualism in the Natural Law of Intellectual Property' (1993) 102 Yale L J 1533 and J Hughes, 'The Philosophy of Intellectual Property' (1988) 77 Georgetown L J 287, 296–330.

[62] See, eg, K Olivecrona, 'Appropriation in the State of Nature: Locke on the Origin of Property' (1974) 35 J Historical Ideas 211; K Olivecrona, 'Locke's Theory of Appropriation' (1974) 24 Philosophical Q 220, 225.

[63] See J Hughes, 'The Philosophy of Intellectual Property' (1988) 77 Georgetown L J 287, 330–66 and MJ Radin, 'Property and Personhood' (1982) 34 Stanford L Rev 957.

[64] K Olivecrona, 'Appropriation in the State of Nature: Locke on the Origin of Property' (1974) 35 J Historical Ideas 211.

property, then how much closer, it is thought, must be the connection of the author to his creative works? Proponents of the 'personality view' might also argue that property contributes to 'self-actualization . . . personal expression . . . dignity and recognition as an individual person,'[65] and that control over one's intellectual products is a form of property uniquely suited to these ends.

Searching for a definitive ordering among these policies and principles, the **4.40** scholar founders. The courts' statements waver, and policies interpenetrate.[66] Given this ambiguous mix of policies, with instrumentalism dominant but not exclusive, how should the flexible doctrines be construed? One might handle suppression cases by assessing the underlying policy concerns implicated by each fact pattern and deciding, according to some calculus, whether enforcing the author's prima facie rights of control, or giving the hostile user the freedom to copy, best serves the relevant goals. But, as noted above, determining the relevant calculus to accommodate the various goals is, at this stage of copyright's development, a difficult matter. This is not a sign of copyright's immaturity as a discipline; virtually all legal doctrines contain a mix of policies competing for strength.[67]

Another way to handle the mix of policies is to minimize the conflict by **4.41** identifying some dominant purpose. Thus, one might identify providing economic incentives as the dominant purpose of copyright, and recommend that special consideration be given to users whenever the copyright owner's motivations differ from that approved motive. But such a simplification threatens to distort.

A third way of reconciling these diverse policies is to investigate whether **4.42** there is any result on which all relevant policies can converge. This possibility will now be considered.

---

[65] J Hughes, 'The Philosophy of Intellectual Property' (1988) 77 Georgetown L J 287, 330

[66] For an intriguing exploration and application of several alternative policies, see WW Fisher III, 'Reconstructing the Fair Use Doctrine' (1988) 101 Harv L Rev 1659.

[67] See, eg, AA Leff, 'Law And . . .' (1978) 87 Yale L J 989 (arguing that such mixes are inevitable).

D. Safeguarding Hostile Uses from Suppression:
A Search for Converging Policies

4.43 As mentioned, the two major strains in copyright are the economic or instrumental perspective, and the authors' rights perspective. This dual perspective parallels the configuration in property and tort law as a whole, where quandaries such as the suppression problem are sometimes analysed in terms of whether the individual holding an entitlement is a 'steward' entrusted with the resource solely for the social good that is likely to result from his productive use of it, or a 'sovereign' to be left unregulated in managing the resource.[68] Despite their potential for conflict, the sovereignty and stewardship models often generate results that converge.[69] It may be that copyright's various normative strands can be similarly reconciled in regard to particular issues. It will be suggested that in regard to at least some suppression issues—notably, those involving authors who have already made the copyrighted work part of the public debate or consciousness[70]—it may be possible to reach some consensus among the competing policies and principles, thus rendering it unnecessary to choose one dominant strand on which to rely. But such an analysis requires that one voyage some distance beyond the explicit words of the copyright statute.

---

[68] See LL Weinreb, 'Fair's Fair: A Comment on the Fair Use Doctrine' (1990) 103 Harv L Rev 1137, 1139–41 (implicitly addressing sovereignty and stewardship models).

[69] It is their convergence in the usual case that permits their continued coexistence as competing perspectives. For example, one way to serve the 'social good' is, arguably, to respect individual owners' investments in their property; compare FI Michelman, in 'Property, Utility and Fairness: Comments on the Ethical Foundations of "Just Compensation" Law' (1967) 80 Harv L Rev 1165 (utility arguments support paying compensation to owners disadvantaged by government activity in a fairly wide range of instances). Similarly, a way to serve the economic health of a society is, arguably, to honour owners' decisions as to how their property should be used. This latter argument is, at its extreme, Adam Smith's 'invisible hand' notion.

On the general notion of convergence, I am indebted to Randy Barnett.

[70] The arguments that follow apply most strongly to the enforcement of copyright in published works.

(1) The economics of suppression

It may seem odd to contend that second-guessing an owner's decision **4.44** whether or not to license or sell a resource can be consistent with neoclassical economics. That tradition stresses the sovereignty of individual decision-making. However, in the suppression context, there exist many well-recognized economic phenomena that should diminish our confidence that the owner's decisions will in fact tend toward the 'maximization of economic value' in any meaningful sense. Consider, for example, a historian who denies a hostile critic permission to quote fairly extensively from her book, or sets an extremely high price (say, $10,000) that she believes will be the amount lost in revenues if the critic's hostile review is published. Also assume that the review would be ineffective without the quotations. If the critic, who stands to make, say, $500 from the review, declines to purchase a licence but publishes the quotations nevertheless, and the historian sues, the following reasons counsel that the courts not assume that because the historian's price was higher than the critic's offer it would produce more 'value' to enjoin the unconsented use of the quotations rather than to allow distribution of the review.

First, the critic's fee is unlikely to represent all the value that publication of **4.45** the review will bring to the affected audience, in part because the market for such goods rarely if ever gives their sellers a price that captures the resulting surplus.[71] Thus, the buyer's likely maximum offer ($499) will probably understate significantly the actual value of the use in her hands.

Secondly, the historian's minimum price of $10,000 is likely to overstate **4.46** significantly the social value of the quotations remaining solely in the historian's hands, since much of that amount reflects mere pecuniary loss: if the review is published, many consumers of historical works will simply shift their purchases to other (perhaps better) historians, and there may be no net social loss at all. There may even be a social benefit if an inferior history is ignored and a better one supported by the reading public.

---

[71] See ML Katz, 'An Analysis of Cooperative Research and Development' (1986) 4 Rand J Economics 527, 527 (in the absence of price discrimination, a firm that invests in research and development 'will be unable to appropriate all of the surplus generated by the licensing of its R&D'). Whether the historian's similar inability would exceed the critic's would be an empirical question.

4.47 Thirdly, the historian's reputation and image are involved, and when such irreplaceable items are at stake the very ownership of an entitlement can crucially change one's market behaviour.[72] When goods as important and irreplaceable as life or reputation are on the table, the effect of the initial grant of entitlements is so strong that it may well determine where the resource rests in the final analysis: Persons are unlikely to sell what they own at any price;[73] yet if they have no legal entitlement to the thing at issue, their ability to buy it is limited by their available resources. In such cases, the results of consensual bargains cannot be relied upon to yield any independent information about 'value'.

4.48 Of course, the above discussion is quite summary. Nevertheless, it should suggest why the copyright owner's pursuit of a non-monetary interest could give an economically-oriented court special reason to inquire into the weight of the affected interests rather than simply deferring to the plaintiff's claim of right.

(2) Authors' rights and suppression

4.49 The authors' rights approach has, as mentioned, two principal lines of argument, one resting largely on the perceived appropriateness of rewarding valuable labour, the other on the perception that authors have a special personal attachment to their works. While, conceivably, either of these strands could be employed to argue that authors should be free to suppress others' unfriendly use of their work, such an argument does not inevitably follow from the arguments' terms. To the contrary, attention to questions of proper reward, or personal development and psychological cathexis, may better indicate that the power to suppress should not be given to artists.

4.50 Turning first to the restitutionary strain of argument, it appears to rest on the notion that a person should retain the benefits that he or she generates.

---

[72] For further discussion of the way that owning an entitlement can shift resource allocation, see for example, EJ Mishan, 'The Postwar Literature on Externalities: An Interpretive Essay' [1971] 9 J Economic Literature 1, 18–21 ('income' or 'welfare' effects illustrated arithmetically); see also AC Yen, 'Restoring the Natural Law: Copyright as Labor and Possession' 51 Ohio State L J 518–19.

[73] Compare RH Coase, 'Notes on the Problem of Social Cost' in RH Coase, *The Firm, the Market, and the Law* (U Chicago, 1988), 157, 170–4 (suggesting that the effects of owning an entitlement are unlikely to be significant in contexts not involving irreplaceable goods such as, in this context, reputation or self-esteem).

That notion in turn might be traced to any one of a number of arguments: a strict view of personal responsibility, perhaps, suggesting that every individual should keep the benefits she generates and pay for the harm she does; or perhaps a notion that the existing balance of goods among persons warrants respect as a prima facie matter, so that any unjustified taking of a benefit or imposition of a harm causes an imbalance or inequality that demands recompense. But these notions do not support an unqualified plaintiff's right.

Instead, they tend to be symmetrical;[74] they suggest that if 'pay for the benefits you receive from others' is a relevant principle, so is 'do no harm to others', or 'pay for the harm you do others'. If so, the author's right is limited by the very consideration that supports it.[75] An author under an obligation to refrain from harm is not at liberty to withdraw her work at will from the use of those whom it has affected. **4.51**

Another possible foundation for the restitutionary strain is the 'natural rights' argument is Lockean labour theory. Here, too, non-owners' rights against harm have an important role. A harm-based limitation on property rights is captured in Locke's theory by his famous 'enough and as good' proviso.[76] **4.52**

Locke argued that one who labours in the common to draw forth water from the lake or pick apples from the field is entitled to that to which his labour is joined. Modern debates have employed his theory to suggest that an artist who labours to give expression to ideas he draws from the public domain is similarly entitled.[77] But Locke thought the ownership entitlement could only **4.53**

---

[74] In fact, if there were an asymmetry, it would probably be to give defendants a stronger protection against harm than it would give plaintiffs a right to recapture benefits. See S Levmore, 'Explaining Restitution' (1985) 71 Virginia L Rev 625, 671–2 (suggesting that such an asymmetry exists in the common law).

[75] This is the key point explored in WJ Gordon, 'A Property Right in Self-Expression' (1993) 102 Yale L J 1533.

[76] See J Locke, *Second Treatise of Government*, ch 5 at para 26, 32. The condition that 'enough and as good' be left for others is commonly known as the 'proviso' or 'sufficiency condition'.

[77] This reliance sometimes extends to claims for a perpetual and unlimited copyright. Such a use of Locke is particularly inapt, given his expressed views on the pre-copyright Licensing Act. See Peter King, *The Life and Letters of John Locke* (London 1884) 202–09 (memorandum from 1693 in which Locke expresses inter alia the view that rights over copying should be limited in time).

arise where 'enough, and as good' was left for others.[78] If giving exclusive dominion to the labourer will leave others worse off than they would have been in his absence, then the proviso is not satisfied, and the labourer is not entitled to property rights in what he has taken.

4.54 The structure of this argument gives primacy to the harm principle, as it should, since it can be argued that Locke's affirmative argument also derives from a harm principle. To see this, consider Locke's primary argument for property.[79] Locke first argues that each of us has a property in his body and the labour of his body. Secondly, he posits that when one appropriates things from the common (picking apples, drawing water from the river) one joins one's labour to the things so taken. Thirdly, he posits that because labour is property, others have no right to what the labour is 'joined to'. Here he is implicitly building upon his earlier expressed notions of what it means to have 'property': it is an entitlement not to have something unjustifiably taken away or harmed.[80] It would harm the labourer to take the apples or water from him because doing so would take the labour he had joined to these items of sustenance as well.

4.55 Therefore, one who labours to draw forth objects from the common plenitude 'has a property' in the things so gathered, at least if there is 'enough, and as good' left for others, because others are under an obligation not to harm him by taking the things from him. In short, Locke's labour theory may depend upon a 'do no harm' rule, and acting upon the theory (with no additional justification) is problematic when doing so itself causes harm. Suppression can cause harm, both in the sense of injury, and in the sense of making someone worse off than if they had never encountered the suppressed text.

---

[78] See J Locke, *Second Treatise* ch 5 at para 26, 32; also see para 37 ('though men had a right to appropriate by their labour, each one to himself, as much of the things of Nature as he could use, yet this could not be much, nor to the prejudice of others, where the same plenty was still left, to those who would use the same industry').

[79] See ibid, and the discussion in WJ Gordon, 'A Property Right in Self-Expression' (1993) 102 Yale L J 1533. Given here is an interpretation of Locke's 'labour-joining' argument. Locke's *Second Treatise* also contains other arguments regarding, for example, the beneficial results of property ownership.

[80] See J Locke, *Second Treatise*, ch 5. The proviso that 'enough, and as good' be left for others constitutes an additional 'do no harm' principle. See also LC Becker, *Property Rights: Philosophic Foundations* (Routledge & Kegan Paul, 1977). Similarly, Locke's argument regarding waste suggests he saw nothing wrongful in taking property from someone to whom it had no value. J Locke, *Second Treatise*, ch 5 para 36–37. If so, Locke would seem to view a non-harmful taking as non-wrongful, at least in the state of nature.

Once a copyright owner has injected something into the common culture, its **4.56** audience may be unable to purge it from their memories. Having changed the community's culture, the author may actively be committing a harm if he then withdraws the work from the community when its new artists seek to integrate, assess, and respond to its influence. Perhaps, on balance, the first artist's work is still more valuable than not; if so, perhaps some payment is owed to that first artist even when a hostile or critical use is made of his work. But even if the restitutionary strain in 'natural rights' theory will justify complete control and injunctive relief in some circumstances, it will not do so here: neither an entitlement to capture the effects one creates, nor Lockean labour theory, supports a complete right of exclusion against those whom the property negatively affects.[81] Locke's property right works against those who are not 'industrious', those who merely desire to benefit from 'another's pains'.[82] The copyist who cares about the content of the work, either positively or negatively, is simply not the kind of trespasser Locke envisaged.[83]

What of the 'personality' theories? Clearly the artist who finds his work **4.57** attacked will not be happy about it. And yet a regard for emotional attachments or self-actualization does not point solely in the direction of suppression and the artist's interests; audiences, too, develop attachments to the symbols surrounding them, and for audiences, as for artists, use of the symbols may be essential to self-expression and to making an impression on

---

[81] For a fuller development of this theme, see WJ Gordon, 'A Property Right in Self-Expression' (1993) 102 Yale L J 1533; WJ Gordon, 'An Inquiry Into The Merits Of Copyright: The Challenges Of Consistency, Consent, And Encouragement Theory' (1989) 41 Stanford L Rev 1343 at 1460–5.

[82] It is the proviso that 'enough and as good' be left that helps Locke identify persons who have a duty to respect claims to own private property. Locke writes:

'God gave the world to men in common, but since He gave it them for their benefit and the greatest conveniencies of life they were capable to draw from it, it cannot be supposed He meant it should always remain common and uncultivated. He gave it to the use of the industrious and rational (and labour was to be his title to it); not to the fancy or covetousness of the quarrelsome and contentious. He that had as good left for his improvement as was already taken up needed not complain, ought not to meddle with what was already improved by another's labour; *if he did it is plain he desired the benefit of another's pains*, which he had no right to . . .' Locke, *Second Treatise*, ch 5, par 33 (emphasis added).

[83] Ibid. Also see WJ Gordon, 'Render Copyright Unto Caesar: On Taking Incentives Seriously' 71 U Chi L Rev 75 at 78–81 (using Locke to identify the defendants against whom copyright is most appropriately used) (2004).

the world around them.[84] When the defendant seeks to deface the only copy of the plaintiff's work, the plaintiff's interest should probably prevail. But when the plaintiff's work exists in myriads of copies, it is the critic's personal interest in producing her defaced, altered, or out-of-place copy—her 'moral right' to do so—that seems the greater and should prevail.[85]

(3) Reference to analogues in the common law

4.58 Yet, all this is at a fairly high level of generality, and debatable. To what other sources might one look to determine what a lawmaker should decide when faced with a claimed right to suppress? One possibility is to look to decision makers in analogous contexts. This leads us to the common law, particularly the area known as substantive restitution or 'unjust enrichment'.[86] This is the area of the common law most concerned with copyright's central issue: the question whether (and when) the law should impose non-contractual liability for benefits one person derives from another's efforts. Persons who wilfully take advantage of benefits made possible by others' efforts are sometimes required to pay for them.[87]

4.59 The restitution cases, however, are marked by a strong concern with preserving the defendant from an erosion of his autonomy,[88] and with preserving

---

[84] See J Waldron, *The Right to Private Property* (Oxford: OUP, 1988) 4, 343, 378–81 (arguing that the upshot of the Hegelian analysis is that, in Hegel's own words, 'everyone must have property').

[85] The US moral rights statute, 17 USC sec 106A, roughly follows this pattern. It applies only to works of visual art that exist in only one or a very few number of copies, 17 USC sec 101 (definitions) and 106A, and the moral rights are subject to fair use, 17 USC sec 107.

[86] I here mean to focus on restitution that provides the basis of a cause of action, rather than on restitution that serves simply as a remedy for the violation of rights provided by other doctrines.

[87] See WJ Gordon, *On Owning Information: Intellectual Property and the Restitutionary Impulse* (1992) 78 Virginia L Rev 149 (exploring the implications of restitution and unjust enrichment doctrine for issues concerning rights over data); WJ Gordon, 'Of Harms and Benefits: Torts, Restitution, and Intellectual Property' 21 J Legal Studies 449–82 (1992) (comparing the exceptions to the 'intermeddler' rule with doctrines in copyright).

[88] See GE Palmer, *The Law of Restitution* (Little, Brown, 1978) 359 ('long-standing judicial reluctance to encourage one person to intervene in the affairs of another by rewarding restitution of benefits thereby conferred.')

the defendant from harm. Thus, when the choice is between leaving a labourer unrewarded and causing a net harm to the defendant, frequently the labourer is left without recourse.[89] If the common law is any guide, then, authors might not be entitled to copyright's rewards in cases where copyright enforcement would leave the defendant suffering a net harm. If so, authors who attempt to use copyright law to suppress works unfavourable to them should not be completely free to do so.[90] Some concern for the users' autonomy and safety from harm—some concern with the audience's own moral rights—is necessary. Thus it is not merely the Lockean proviso that counsels giving some latitude to the user who is trying to recast for herself and others harmful symbols and text that have been thrust upon her.

The common law might also offer guidance to some of the other questions **4.60** canvassed above. A particularly useful source of analogy might be torts, which in many ways functions as the converse of intellectual property.[91] As a mirror provides a great deal of information through its reversed images, it may be that the literature of tort law, the civil branch of the law of harms, could contain significant wisdom applicable to the jurisprudence of benefits.

First, both copyright and torts can be interpreted as serving non- **4.61** instrumental ends. Thus, whether using terms of morality, fairness, or 'corrective justice', one can argue that an innocent victim injured by a harm-causer 'deserves' to be made whole and that the defendant 'ought' to pay. Similarly, it is often argued that a creative person 'deserves' to be paid for what he has brought to the world, and that the user of another's work 'ought' to give recompense for it.

---

[89] See S Levmore, 'Explaining Restitution' (1985) 71 Virginia L Rev 625, [77–8, 84] (law denies restitution where a non-bargained 'benefit' may not in fact make the recipient better off; even at a 'less-than-market' price the unsolicited benefit 'may be undesirable to a wealth-constrained' recipient); see generally WJ Gordon, 'On Owning Information: Intellectual Property and the Restitutionary Impulse' (1992) 78 Virginia L Rev 149.

[90] Of course, the desirability of avoiding harm expresses itself as a legal principle with weight in many other areas of the common law as well.

[91] See WJ Gordon, 'Copyright as Tort Law's Mirror Image: "Harms", "Benefits" and the Uses and Limits of Analogy' (2003) 34 McGeorge L Rev 533; WJ Gordon, 'Of Harms and Benefits: Torts, Restitution, and Intellectual Property' (1992) 21 J Legal Studies 449–82.

4.62 The question of what role should be played by a creator's claim to 'fair return' is largely unresolved in copyright. It is likely that there is some grain of truth in that much-invoked but little-analysed notion, 'the natural rights of an author', and only systematic analysis can separate that grain from the rhetoric of perpetual and all-encompassing claims that now clings to it. Perhaps the literature exploring notions of 'desert' and 'corrective justice' in torts, and in criminal law as well, could be of assistance here. In all nations, tort rights have limits; not all injuries are compensable.

4.63 Secondly, and perhaps more importantly, both copyright and torts serve a particular incentive function: they seek to 'internalize externalities'. That is, both copyright and torts seek to bring decisions' effects to bear on persons with power to affect how things are done. In torts, the primary person to be affected is the tortfeasor; he is ordinarily the 'cheapest cost avoider' and is discouraged from taking unnecessary risks with others' persons and possessions by the spectre of a suit imposing liability for harm caused. In copyright, the primary person to be affected is the creator; he is ordinarily the 'best benefit generator' and is to be encouraged to produce by being given a right to capture a portion of the benefits he creates.[92]

4.64 Thus, both doctrines aim at providing incentives. Conceivably, the lessons of one could be useful for the other. We might, for example, try viewing the creative user problem from the perspective of the tort doctrines that recognize that the person best able to effectuate desirable action is not always the person in the defendant's position. For example, consider accident law. If a pedestrian is 'contributorily' or 'comparatively' negligent by running in front of a car, that behaviour will eliminate or reduce any recovery that might be sought. The economic logic is familiar: when the pedestrian is better positioned than the driver to avoid an accident,[93] it is the pedestrian's behaviour the law should seek to change; one way to change that behaviour is to force pedestrians to bear some of their own costs if they choose to behave carelessly.

4.65 The formal lesson of the logic is also familiar: in every transaction there are two parties, and deciding how to 'internalize' costs between them is a choice

---

[92] Persons with the potential to create valuable works have rights over the use others make of their products; the benefits the authors create are brought home via licence or royalty fees, and productive behaviour is encouraged.

[93] See generally G Calabresi, *The Costs of Accidents: A Legal and Economic Analysis* (Yale, 1970) 134–40 ('cheapest cost avoider').

that should depend on context rather than on formal classifications such as plaintiff or defendant.[94] If all the harms that would not occur 'but for' the defendant's driving were internalized to that driver, others who might become involved might have an inadequate incentive to be careful.

The same lesson could be applied, just as simply, to copyright. If all the **4.66** benefits that could be traced to a first artist through a 'but for' test were internalized to her, no one else would have a monetary incentive to build upon her work. If a creative copyist is in a better position to contribute to the culture than is the first artist, then perhaps the law should take care to direct positive incentives to such persons by, for example, giving them shelter from infringement suits.[95] Tort tests of responsibility remind us that 'incentive' works both ways.

Similarly, tests of 'proximate cause' in tort tend to ask if the injury caused was **4.67** of the kind that made the defendant's act negligent. Courts in copyright cases should make a similar inquiry: they should ask if the plaintiff's motives for suit are of the kind that made the legislature provide copyright protection in the first instance. Motives to suppress were not those the legislature sought to further in the copyright law, and should not be effectuated through copyright suits.[96]

E. Conclusion

Copyright is not a self-executing concept. It must have limits to make sense. **4.68** An unlimited copyright would give an author a perpetual right to control

---

[94] See RH Coase, 'The Problem of Social Cost' (1960) 3 J L & Economics 1.

[95] Such shelter is especially needed when the new author is unable to purchase a licence, but is not limited to such cases. See sources cited immediately infra.

[96] See, eg, WJ Gordon, 'Fair Use as Market Failure', 82 Columbia L Rev 1600 at 1632 (1982) (arguing that fair use may be employed to defeat anti-dissemination motives); also see WJ Gordon, 'Excuse and Justification in the Law of Fair Use: Transaction Costs Have Always Been Only *Part* of the Story' (2003) 13 J Copyright Society 149 (arguing that fair use should be divided into two subcategories, excuse and justification; the excuse category involves factual obstructions like transaction costs, while the justification category involves occasions when the copyright owner asserts a right that is outside the proper normative scope of her control). Admittedly, many cases involve mixed motives. To examine the difficult questions they pose would take us beyond the scope of this chapter.

all the benefits that others draw from her work. Such a regime would cause paralysis.

4.69 In searching for the limits that can make sense of copyright, one can make reference to its dominant policies, namely, incentives and authors' rights. One can also explore analogies in other areas of law. All these investigations converge in reminding us that sometimes encouraging the copyright *defendant* rather than the copyright plaintiff can best serve copyright's goals. In particular, blind copyright enforcement is particularly unwise in cases where the copyright owner seeks to restrain a defendant who wishes to copy for purposes of criticizing or mocking the copyrighted work.

4.70 In some ways, this offers a distinctly American view. In our 'romance with the First Amendment',[97] Americans honour the iconoclastic dissenter and critic over the person whose feelings may be hurt or whose orthodoxy may be weakened. But even for nations with different priorities, equitable doctrines such as 'fair use' can provide great benefits to individuals and the societies to which they belong.

4.71 The same norms that give copyright its (contested) claim to legitimacy should simultaneously generate significant protections for free speech. Those protections may not be sufficient—they largely protect the public from harm from being unable to respond to existing works that have shaped their environment and their very selves, and free speech may demand more. Nevertheless, if recognized and incorporated into flexible doctrines such as fair use, these limits could ameliorate some of the unfortunate results caused by the American courts' reluctance to embrace fully the First Amendment's applicability to copyright.

---

[97] See Steven H Shiffrin, *The First Amendment, Democracy And Romance* (Princeton University Press, 1990).

5

TOWARDS AN INTERNATIONAL PUBLIC INTEREST RULE? HUMAN RIGHTS AND INTERNATIONAL COPYRIGHT LAW

Uma Suthersanen

A. Contextualizing Technology and Knowledge as a Human Rights Issue

5.01 Why discuss international copyright law in the context of international human rights regimes, and vice versa? Historically, both human rights and copyright were national concerns. Nevertheless, the need for an increased influence of international human rights policy within the international and national copyright regimes is undeniable for several reasons.

5.02 In the last decade, international legal regimes, such as the World Trade Organization (WTO) and the United Nations (UN) legal systems, have witnessed the contextualization of international intellectual property law as both trade and human rights issues. Not only has intellectual property law-making occurred in different UN fora, but intellectual property is recognized as being part of the human rights regime in several international instruments.[1] It is specifically referred to in the three primary international human rights instruments: the Universal Declaration of Human Rights (UDHR), the International Covenant on Civil and Political Rights (ICCPR), and the International Covenant on Economic, Social and Cultural Rights (ICESCR). There is, however, little reciprocal recognition of human rights values in international intellectual property instruments.

5.03 This lacuna is being criticized. The 2003 United Nations Development Programme report on the world trading system, for instance, acknowledges that the TRIPs Agreement has 'important human development implications for public health, technology and knowledge and biological resources'.[2] In relation to copyright protection, the report concludes that TRIPs raises the cost of copyright protected educational material and software. The report also cautions that technological protection measures make it possible for copyright owners to control and limit access to information. Other reports too have challenged the moral legitimacy of international intellectual property rights as manifested in the TRIPs Agreement.[3] One result of these challenges has been the 2001 Declaration on the TRIPs Agreement and Public Health, which responds to the claim by developing nations that they are unable to afford the patented pharmaceuticals needed to address the massive

---

[1] For doubts as to whether intellectual property rights are recognizable fundamental human rights, see HG Schermers, 'The International Protection of the Right of Property', in F Matscher and H Petzold (eds), *Protecting Human Rights: The European Dimension* (1988), 579; P Drahos, 'The Universality of Intellectual Property Rights: Origin & Development', in *Intellectual Property and Human Rights* (Geneva: WIPO/UNHCHR, 1998), 31.

[2] UNDP, *Making Global Trade Work for People* (Geneva: UNDP, 2003) 205, 214, <http://www.undp.org/dpa/publications/globaltrade.pdf>.

[3] UK Commission on Intellectual Property Rights, *Integrating Intellectual Property Rights and Development Policy* (London: CIPR, 2002) 5–6, <http://www.iprcommission.org/graphic/documents/final_report.htm>; IPRsonline, UNCTAD-ICTSD *Capacity Building Project on Intellectual Property Rights*, <http://www.iprsonline.org/unctadictsd/description.htm>; L Helfer, 'Regime Shifting: The Trips Agreement And New Dynamics Of International Intellectual Property Lawmaking' (2004) 29 Yale J Intl L 1, 3–5; UNDP Report on Human Rights and Human Development (2000), <http://hdr.undp.org/reports/global/2000/en/>.

HIV–AIDS crisis within their borders.[4] Indeed, the liberalization of markets and trade negotiations have made not only intellectual property rights, but also human rights, the centre of focus. Of particular interest within the 2001 Declaration is the reaffirmation of the principle of balanced intellectual property protection, and the notion that each provision of the TRIPs Agreement should be interpreted using customary rules of interpretation of public international law.[5] Secondly, this Declaration also highlights the movement of interests from private interests to public interest so as to address the perceived imbalance between rights owners and users.[6] Finally, the Declaration explicitly contextualizes intellectual property rights as a human rights issue.

Is it true that international intellectual property instruments, such as the **5.04** TRIPs Agreement or the more recent WIPO Copyright Treaties, ignore human rights obligations? It is arguable that certain provisions within key international copyright instruments can be construed as forming the basis of human rights concerns, and this is discussed below. Nevertheless, the implementation and interpretation of international intellectual property agreements into national legislation has been poor from a human rights perspective. First, most states do not expressly adopt the relevant fundamental freedoms into the copyright statute. Secondly, without clear legislative signals, national tribunals have been reluctant to curtail copyright protection on grounds of human rights arguments. Indeed, some national courts have not even been willing to recognize the intrinsic link between copyright and human rights. Recent decisions in the United Kingdom and USA indicate that national courts are reluctant to override Parliamentary or Congressional intent and derive their authority straight from an unrelated international agreement or convention. Indeed, the trans-Atlantic attitude appears to be that free speech and freedom of expression have no role to play in copyright law.[7] This problem has been exacerbated by the fact that human rights jurisprudence is still seen as being territorial in nature while many copyright obligations are viewed as being part of international law. Even

---

[4] Declaration on the TRIPs Agreement and Public Health, WTO Doha Ministerial Conference, 4th Sess, WTO Doc WT/MIN(01)/DEC/W/2 (14 November 2001).

[5] Ibid, para 5(a).

[6] Susan K Sell, 'TRIPs and the Access to Medicines Campaign' (2002) 20 Wisconsin Intl L J 481, 519.

[7] M Birnhack, 'Copyrighting Speech: A Trans-Atlantic View', in PLC Torremans (ed), *Copyright and Human Rights* (The Hague: Kluwer Law International, 2004), 37–42.

where courts have recognized the interrelationship between copyright and human rights legislation, there appears to be a bias towards the rights of the copyright owner as opposed to the rights of individual users.[8]

5.05 This chapter discusses the contextualization of intellectual property rights within a human rights framework. Incorporating a human rights concern into international copyright law would go some way towards addressing the particular dilemma faced by national courts in overriding legislative intent. Moreover, states should be made to ensure that national copyright legislation enshrines a balance between the rights of owners of property rights and those of members of the wider society. The final query is how should this recognition of a human rights ethos within intellectual property agreements be framed?

B. Justifying Copyright within an Economic–Human Rights Framework

5.06 A key issue is the balance between the rights of two disparate groups: the protection of creators' and entrepreneurial works by property rights and the protection of fundamental freedoms of individuals and groups within a society (such as the right to freedom of expression and information, and education). It is proposed that a link can be found between human rights and copyright by adopting a holistic approach to copyright justifications. Copyright law can be justified on various grounds.

(1) Utilitarian approach

5.07 The utilitarian or ontological approach is often espoused within the traditional economic rationale for the protection of intellectual property. This theory holds that knowledge is a public good—it is non-rival (use by one does not limit or leave less for the other to use) and non-excludable (one cannot practically exclude people from reproducing)—and its original costs of production are usually high.[9] If it is only regulated by the exigencies

---

[8] For the position in the US, see ch 6 below; in the UK, see ch 8 below; in Austria, see *Re Copyright In Translated Legal Document* [1999] ECC 131.

[9] OECD Report, *Competition Policy and Intellectual Property Rights* (Paris: OECD, 1989) 12; K Arrow, 'Welfare Economics and Inventive Activity', in NBER (ed), *The Rate and Direction of Inventive Activity*, (Princeton: Princeton University Press, 1962), 617–18.

of market forces, where non-excludability and non-rivalry can flourish, the result is free-riding or obtaining a benefit at no cost.[10] Dissemination of public goods is predicted to be lower than would be optimally efficient and the goods are likely to be underproduced.[11] This market failure can be corrected by either public ownership or State intervention, which can take various forms including State subsidies or temporary private property rights.

The economic rationale recognizes that intellectual property rights must **5.08** be curtailed. Thus, it is considered to be a 'wrong allocation' of rights to award intellectual property protection to ideas owing to the subsequent high transaction costs incurred either through licensing fees or attempting to create around basic ideas.[12] Sometimes, courts go further and cite general public interest grounds in denying copyright protection to works, especially where there is reason to believe that the property right can lead to the capture of certain modes of expression, which, although acceptable in the case of entertainment or cultural works, is economically unhealthy in relation to historical, industrial, or factual matter.[13] In such situations, the concern could be that there may only be one or a limited number of modes of expressing a textual or visual message effectively, and a similar or identical message cannot be efficiently conveyed without using substantially similar or identical words, symbols, or images. At the other end of the spectrum, where rights have been incorrectly allocated, there should be a realignment of rights.[14] Under most intellectual property laws, there are corrective mechanisms to reallocate resources, including intrinsic limitation devices such as fair use exceptions or compulsory licensing, or extrinsic ones such as competition law.

---

[10] H Demsetz, 'Toward a Theory of Property Rights' (1967) 57 American Economic Rev Proceedings 347, 348.

[11] WJ Gordon, 'An Inquiry into the Merits of Copyright: The Challenges of Consistency, Consent, and Encouragement Theory' (1989) 41 Stanford L Rev 1343, 1435–6.

[12] W Landes and R Posner, *The Economic Structure of Intellectual Property Law* (Cambridge/London: Harvard University Press, 2003) 91–7.

[13] For examples within UK copyright law, see *Ravenscroft v Herbert* [1980] RPC 193; *L B (Plastics) Ltd v Swish Products Ltd* [1979] RPC 551, 604–5; *Cramp (GA) & Sons Ltd v Smythson (Frank) Ltd* [1944] AC 329.

[14] H Demsetz, (n 10 above).

(2) Natural rights: individual values and property

5.09 A second means of justifying copyright law is the deontological or natural rights approach which proposes that the individual has a natural property right to the fruits of his labour. This approach is analogous to classical human rights obligations which are an intrinsic part of our civilization. Indeed, current international human rights law did not necessarily have its genesis within the UN Declaration of Human Rights but rather arose from early religious and philosophical thinking. The Bible, for example, contains examples of individual rights and duties: the injunction not to kill corresponds to the right to one's life; similarly, 'thou shalt not steal' implies a right to property. Later philosophers, such as Hobbes, Locke, and Rousseau,[15] recast the individual as being the beneficiary of the State's duty to secure his natural rights to life, liberty, *and* property.[16]

5.10 Traditional human rights analysis posits that there are three categories which reflect the 'three generations of rights movement', and copyright law can be rationalized within all three categories.[17] The first category, the body of classical (and individual) civil and political rights, is the traditional bastion developed by liberals during the Enlightenment, which guarantees the rights of the private individual such as the right to life, liberty, and

---

[15] T Hobbes, *The Leviathan* (1652); J Locke, *The Two Treatises* (1690); J-J Rousseau, *On the Geneva Manuscript* (1762).

[16] Many municipal laws adopted and reflected these natural rights sentiments including the (oft-forgotten) 1679 Habeas Corpus Act, the 1689 English Bill of Rights, the 1776 US Declaration of Independence, and the 1789 French Declaration of the Rights of Man and Citizen. One should note that the latter two instruments duly recognized the importance of property rights within the human rights framework.

[17] A popular alternative to this classical approach is the approach of Lukes who categorizes current rhetoric on human rights into five doctrines: (a) utilitarian approach which is measured in terms of utility, whatever this term denotes; (b) communitarian approach which views all individuals and subcommunities as being equally valid within the community; (c) proletarian approach which views human rights from a social class (ie communist) perspective; (d) libertarian approach whereby human rights is viewed in terms of market value and cost-benefit analysis, the right to property is prized and there is distrust of social and public support; (e) egalitarian approach where one person's well-being and freedom are regarded as just as valuable as any other's and the list of human rights is kept short by comprising basic civil and political rights, the rule of law and freedom of expression and association. S Lukes, 'Five Fables about Human Rights' (1993) 40 Dissent 427.

human dignity.[18] These rights have also always been advocated by the Western states as constituting the foundations of democracy. The rights of the creator or copyright owner are recognized readily under this category of rights. Under German law, for instance, the right to enjoyment of property is not the only basis of the copyright (or author's rights) regime; German courts have expressly accepted that the rights to human dignity and personal development also constitute the basis for author's rights. The latter derives from the Hegelian notion that author's rights are for the protection of the authorial personality.[19] The second generation of human rights are the newer social, economic, and cultural rights which were developed by socialists during the nineteenth century and oblige public authorities to take active measures. UK copyright law, which ordinarily tends towards a more economic-based reasoning, accepts that one basis of copyright law is the fundamental right to enjoyment of property.[20]

(3) Natural rights: collective values and 'intellectual' property

The last category of human rights within the traditional typology is known **5.11** as 'collective human rights'. Human rights principles do not stem solely from the individual's perspective. An over-emphasis on individual rights can undermine societal values, that is those values which can only be enjoyed collectively. Aristotle advocated a more communitarian approach in stressing that laws should be made for the common weal and good.[21] This trend was pursued by socialists in the mid-nineteenth century and resulted in more communitarian rights such as the rights to health and education, as well as

---

[18] JS Mill, '[I]t is the privilege and proper condition of a human being . . . to use and interpret experience in his own way . . . He who lets the world, or his own portion of it, choose his plan of life for him has no need of any other faculty than the ape-like one of imitation', *On Liberty* (1859) 70–1, 124–5; EJ Mitnick, 'Three Models Of Group-Differentiated Rights' (2004) 35 Columbia Human Rights L Rev 215, 232–4.

[19] G Hegel, *Philosophy of Right*, tr TM Knox, (Oxford: Clarendon Press, 1952) para 68. The intersection between moral rights and human rights is clearly seen in *Re Neo-Fascist Slant In Copyright Works*, where the German Regional Court of Appeal, held that an author's right was based on a mixture of fundamental constitutional principles as well as fundamental freedoms. Case 11 U 63/94, Oberlandesgericht (Regional Court of Appeal), (Frankfurt Am Main), 6 December 1994, [1996] ECC 375.

[20] *Ashdown v Telegraph Group Ltd* [2002] ECDR 32.

[21] Book II of Aristotle's *Politic*.

rights for creators of intellectual property.[22] In respect of copyright law, for instance, the positive rights accorded to the author engender negative rights to others. An adjacent twentieth-century phenomenon is the advocacy of human rights rhetoric by marginalized groups such as women, environmentalists, the Internet community, and ethnic groups. Property theory, surprisingly, adopts a similar view in that any allocation of rights must take into account the benefit and detriment caused to both parties in resolving a rights dispute. Consider this example: A's actions or rights will harm B. Should A be allowed to continue to inflict such harm on B, or should B, conversely, be allowed to harm A, by restraining A's actions or rights? A Hohfeldian restatement of this proposition is to recognize that the right of inventors/creators to exclude others from property brings about the correlative duty of society not to use the property or resource.[23]

5.12 This last set of rights usually reflects post-colonial demands to secure rights to collectives such as national minorities (or indigenous groups) or rights to development or self-determination.[24] Nevertheless, this category of rights also reminds us that the term 'human rights' should not refer merely to individualistic concerns but also to the protection of activities and relations that make individuals' lives more valuable since such rights straddle both private, individual interests and public, communitarian interests.[25] An example of this approach can be seen in respect of claims of indigenous peoples to the right of property. The concept of indigenous properties and territories is now deemed to cover 'the total environment of the areas which the peoples concerned occupy or otherwise use'. This concept of totality recognizes that indigenous resources include intellectual properties and that the rights thereof are of a collective character comprising a combination of possession, use, and management rights.[26]

---

[22] P-J Proudhon, *What is Property?* (1840); K Marx, *On the Jewish Question* (1843).

[23] EJ Mishan, 'Comment on Public Goods and Natural Liberty', in T Wilson and A Skinner (eds), *The Market and the State: Essays in Honour of Adam Smith* (Oxford: Clarendon Press, 1976), 287–91.

[24] J Morsink, *The Universal Declaration of Human Rights* (Philadelphia: University of Pennsylvania Press, 1999) ch 3, 210–12.

[25] S Lukes, 'Five Fables about Human Rights' (1993) 40 Dissent 427.

[26] S James Anaya, 'International Human Rights and Indigenous Peoples: the Move Toward the Multicultural State' (2004) 21 Arizona J Intl & Comparative L 13, at 38–9; and generally, G Dutfield and D Posey, *Beyond Intellectual Property: Toward Traditional Resource Rights for Indigenous Peoples* (Toronto: International Development Resource Centre, 1996); Draft Declaration on the Rights of Indigenous Peoples 1993.

It is clear that the above categorization of human rights is amorphous and **5.13**
indistinct. Thus, the right to freedom of expression and communication
protects both artistic expression and the communication of information—
this right lends itself to the interests of both the owners and users of copyright works. Rather than viewing copyright through this traditional human
rights typology, it may be more rewarding to abandon strict categorization
and adopt a more holistic approach in respect of international human rights.
This approach, which takes note of the proliferation of international human
rights treaties,[27] argues that not only are all rights of equal importance, but
they are also distinctly integrated.[28] This view also would incorporate both
individual values and collective values. Let us now see what values or interests
have to be taken into account.

C. Mapping our Values and Interests

(1) Interpretation rules

There are two types of interests that one should take account of: individual **5.14**
and collective. From the perspective of the individual, it is not only the
author's interests that one should recognize, but also the corporate interests
that lie behind many copyright works. From the perspective of the 'collective', one should note that societal values are of importance. This is in
accordance with the interpretative rules within human rights jurisprudence.
Thus, the European Court of Human Rights has adopted, inter alia,[29] the

---

[27] Besides the Universal Declaration of Human Rights, there are six other core human
rights treaties: (a) the Convention on the Elimination of Discrimination Against Women,
(b) the Convention on the Rights of the Child, (c) Convention on the Elimination of All
Forms of Racial Discrimination, (d) the Convention Against Torture and Other Cruel,
Inhuman or Degrading Treatment, (e) the International Covenant on Economic, Social and
Cultural Rights, and (f) the International Covenant on Civil and Political Rights.

[28] I Merali and V Oosterveld (eds), *Giving Meaning to Economic, Social and Cultural Rights*
(Philadelphia: University of Pennsylvania Press, 2001), especially chs 1 and 2.

[29] Other interpretative rules are (a) the principle of proportionality which recognizes that
restrictions to the exercise of fundamental rights, such as the right to freedom of expression,
are permissible if the legislative objective is sufficiently important to justify a limitation, and
if the measures used to impair the right are not unfair or arbitrary, and if the means used to
impair the freedom are no more than is necessary to accomplish the objective; and (b) the
purposive or teleological approach which takes account of 'present day conditions'; thus,
instead of operating a strict doctrine of precedent, the Strasbourg court has consciously

communitarian principle. This principle has been aptly summed up by Lord Steyn in *Brown (Margaret) v Stott*[30] where he observed:

> The fundamental rights of individuals are of supreme importance but those rights are not unlimited: we live in communities of individuals who also have rights. The direct lineage of this ancient idea is clear: the European Convention (1950) is the descendant of the Universal Declaration of Human Rights (1948) which in article 29 expressly recognised the duties of everyone to the community and the limitation on rights in order to secure and protect respect for the rights of others.

5.15 The communitarian rule, which is akin to a more holistic concept of human rights law, argues against positioning the individual subject as being fully independent of societal concerns, and against prioritizing the individual over the community.[31] The communitarian principle also underlines the fact that many of the fundamental freedoms guaranteed under human rights laws are not only qualified rights but also antithetical in character.

5.16 Nowhere is this more so than in the case of copyright and the right to freedom of expression. On the one hand, copyright is recognized as being part of the human rights regime in several international instruments,[32] including the Universal Declaration of Human Rights (UDHR).[33] Article 27(2) of the UDHR prescribes rights for 'moral and material interests resulting from any scientific, literary or artistic production'. The European Convention on Human Rights (ECHR), in contrast, has no equivalent provision in respect of intellectual property rights, though courts have accepted that there is a muted basis for copyright in Article 1, First Protocol, of the

---

operated 'a doctrine of evolutionary law' whereby the persuasiveness of the decision is inversely proportional to its maturity. *De Freitas v Permanent Secretary of Ministry of Agriculture, Fisheries, Lands and Housing* [1999] 1 AC 69, 80, affirmed in *R v Shayler* [2002] 2 WLR 754. Also see J Jowell, 'Beyond the Rule of Law: Towards Constitutional Judicial Review' [2000] PL 671; F Klug, 'The Human Rights Act: A "Third Way" or "Third Wave" Bill of Rights' [2001] 4 EHRLR 361, 366.

[30] *aka Brown v Procurator Fiscal (Dunfermline)* [2001] 2 WLR 817, 840.

[31] D Feldman, *Civil Liberties and Human Rights in England and Wales* (Oxford: OUP, 2002) 6–7.

[32] Cf P Drahos, 'The Universality of Intellectual Property Rights: Origins & Development', in WIPO (ed), *Intellectual Property and Human Rights* (Geneva: WIPO/OHCHR, 1998), 31.

[33] UDHR, Art 27. Also see International Covenant on Economic, Social and Cultural Rights (ICESCR), Art 15; UNESCO Recommendation on the Status of Scientific Researchers 1974, Arts 35–7.

ECHR, which promises peaceful enjoyment of 'possessions'.[34] On the other hand, all these instruments stress that the individual right to private property is balanced against the usage rights of the community. Article 27(1) of the UDHR stresses the communitarian rule by guaranteeing that everyone has the right 'freely to participate in the cultural life of the community, to enjoy the arts and to share in scientific advancement and its benefits',[35] while the property provision under the ECHR is qualified in that deprivation or third-party use of property is expressly allowed for 'public interest' or 'general interest' reasons.[36]

A similar sort of balance between conflicting interests can be read within **5.17** Article 10 of the ECHR. The first paragraph provides: 'Everyone has the right to freedom of expression. This right shall include freedom to hold opinions and to receive and impart information and ideas without inter-ference by public authority and regardless of frontiers. This article shall not prevent States from requiring the licensing of broadcasting, television or cinema enterprises.'

Once again, Lord Steyn offers a concise basis for the right: 'First, it promotes **5.18** the self-fulfilment of individuals in society. Secondly, in the famous words of Holmes J (echoing John Stuart Mill), "the best test of truth is the power of the thought to get itself accepted in the competition of the market." Thirdly, freedom of speech is the lifeblood of democracy. The free flow of information and ideas informs political debate.'[37]

Copyright clearly encroaches on the right to freedom of expression since the **5.19** property right inhibits one from copying the method of expression used by the copyright owner. Article 10(1) of the ECHR acts as a counterbalance to copyright in that it gives a court the basis for questioning the width of a property right where that right conflicts with the provision's general policy towards access to information and where such access is required to promote individual and societal well being. Conversely, Article 10(2) states:

---

[34] UNDP, *Making Global Trade Work for People* (Geneva: UNDP, 2003) 1377, <http://www.undp.org/dpa/publications/globaltrade.pdf>.

[35] Art 27(1), and also UNESCO's Declaration of Principles of International Cooperation, Art 1.

[36] ECHR, Art 1 to 1st Protocol.

[37] *R v Home Secretary, ex p Simms* [2000] 2 AC 115, 126.

The exercise of these freedoms, since it carries with it duties and responsibilities, may be subject to such formalities, conditions, restrictions or penalties as are prescribed by law and are necessary in a democratic society, in the interests of national security, territorial integrity or public safety, for the prevention of disorder or crime, for the protection of health or morals, for the protection of the reputation or rights of others, for preventing the disclosure of information received in confidence, or for maintaining the authority and impartiality of the judiciary.

5.20 Thus, the right to freedom of expression is curtailed by the need to 'protect the rights of others'. Irrespective of the status of the rights to property and freedom of expression as basic pre-conditions for an individual's self-fulfilment, these rights are *inter se* antithetical, and are qualified by further societal considerations. So, what are the communitarian interests that have to be taken into account?

(2) Human rights: from citizenry values to corporate values

5.21 The classical notion of human rights legislation firmly focuses on the regulation of the relationship between the individual citizen and the State within the national societal sphere. The emphasis lies on that individual's freedom vis-à-vis the State. The concepts of the 'individual' and 'society', however, have expanded so as to recognize that not only governmental agencies but also private corporations take an extremely active part in shaping international, and hence, national policies. Indeed, one human rights jurist goes so far as to argue that States are under pressure to hand over public responsibilities to private actors, who are often multinational corporations. The latter then sacrifice 'community interest' to the dictates of profit and are not bound directly by the existing human rights instruments.[38] From this perspective, it cannot be controversial to argue that an accepted tenet of human rights legislation is that all societal actors, including private multinational corporations, are subject to rules protecting human rights.

5.22 The Universal Declaration on Human Rights specifies that everyone has duties to the community. Its Preamble specifies that 'every organ of society . . . shall strive . . . to promote respect for these rights and . . . to secure their universal and effective recognition and observance.' It is arguable that

---

[38] P Alston, 'The Myopia of the Handmaidens: International Lawyers and Globalisation' (1997) 8 Eur J Intl L 435, 438.

corporations are 'organs of society' and, therefore, have an obligation under the Universal Declaration to respect human rights.[39] Justice, after all, concerns the proper distribution of benefits and duties across all persons in society, which should include legal as well as natural persons.[40] Moreover, the globalization effect emphasizes the diminished role of the State in being exclusively responsible in carving out legislation in many areas; indeed, the internationalization of human rights legislation has been occurring since the Second World War.[41] This phenomenon is repeated in the international copyright scene and the role of private enterprises is evident in the setting of norms of international copyright standards.[42]

(3) Copyright: from the 1886 author to the 1996 entrepreneur

Similarly, traditional justifications of modern copyright law invariably focus **5.23** on the right as conferred on and exercised by the individual, as opposed to the right being exercised by a corporation or exercised on behalf of the individual by a collecting society.[43] Each new expansion of copyright, be it the duration of protection or the nature of rights held by the creator, is often viewed by society as an additional weapon for the poor sole creator who must battle against the threat of piracy. It would be naïve, however, to think that the author is, and ever was, in sole control of national copyright developments. It would be foolish to imagine that he or she is in charge of international copyright law. It is true that the copyright regime confers exclusive and *individual* private rights on authors. One should note, nevertheless, that the 'author', in the wider Anglo-American usage of the term, includes both

---

[39] Applicability of human rights standards to private corporations is no new phenomenon—witness the development of labour law and social law. Moreover, ECHR case law has made clear that in many instances the State has a duty to see to it that fundamental rights standards are respected in third-party relationships; failure to do so may lead to the conclusion that the State has violated its obligations under the ECHR—*Lopez-Ostra*, ECHR 9 December 1994.

[40] J Rawls, *A Theory of Justice* (1971) 5–10.

[41] H Steiner and P Alston, *International Human Rights in Context: Law, Politics, Morals* (Oxford: OUP, 2000) 56–135.

[42] See F Macmillan's discussion on corporate power in ch 3 above.

[43] The 'individual' right perspective is generally evident both in the civil law personality-based and the common law economic-based copyright theories. See A Strowel, *Droit d'auteur et Copyright: Divergences et Convergences* (Brussels/Paris: Bruyland/LGDJ, 1993) para 75 et seq and M Rose, *Authors and Owners* (Cambridge/London: Harvard University Press, 1993) chs 3 and 8.

natural and legal persons. The major participants in the development of international copyright principles are not only governments and UN organizations, but also private corporations which are the major stakeholders in the intellectual property rights scene. Not only do corporations own the majority of intellectual property rights, they are also heavily involved in setting international intellectual property norms.[44]

5.24 The legal environment of copyright has been on the international agenda since the Berne Convention 1886. Although it remained largely a private law matter which regulated private property and reflected the national concerns of signatories, the Berne Convention was driven by authors and their collecting societies. Whilst the Berne Convention reflects national concerns, it is true to say that national laws, today, have become more influenced by international developments. The State's ability to shape its own legislations grows limited in light of the multitude of international instruments such as the 1994 TRIPs Agreement and the 1996 World Intellectual Property Organization (WIPO) Copyright Treaties.

5.25 This phenomenon of decreasing State and authorial influence is largely due to the increased role of international trade. Increased international trade or 'globalization' has been a two-edged sword. International trading has increased profits; however, the barter of information respects no geographical borders. Technological revolutions in mass production (especially the digitization of literary and musical works), coupled with the phenomenal growth of the consuming public, renders national laws on illicit copying useless. International trade has also enhanced the roles of multinational corporations *and* of non-governmental organizations (NGOs) in international policy making. Helfer, for example, employs public choice analysis to explain domestic and international intellectual property policy making.[45] He eschews

---

[44] The UNDP Report on trade confirms that the main beneficiaries of intellectual property protection are largely transnational corporations 'while the world's poorest people face higher prices and restrictions on access to new technologies and products'. UNDP, *Making Global Trade Work for People* (2003) 205, 207. Also see generally M Ryan, *Knowledge Diplomacy: Global Competition And The Politics Of Intellectual Property* (Washington: Brookings Institution Press, 1998).

[45] Public choice theory can be defined as the analysis of 'non-market decision making' which generates political outcomes. N Mercuro and S Medema, *Economics and the Law: From Posner to Post-Modernism* (Cambridge: Princeton University Press, 1997) 84; G Dutfield, *Intellectual Property Rights and the Life Science Industry* (Dartmouth: Ashgate, 2003) 32.

the purist perspective of public choice theory which regards the main players as being politicians and public servants, and opts for a broader view where one traces the ultimate sources of government decisions. Using this theory, he identifies trade officials from the USA and the EC as being the specific governmental and private actors who motivated the incorporation of intellectual property rights into the WTO, as manifested in the move from WIPO to GATT to TRIPs. If one goes behind the scenes, however, one notes that this strategy was adopted at the urging of American and European intellectual property industries, which were dissatisfied with the current state of play in international intellectual property law.[46]

(4) Developing an international balance: public interest

This is an important aspect of the nexus between international copyright law **5.26** and international human rights legislation and codes: societal values do not only mean authorial or creator values, from an individualistic perspective, but also encompass entrepreneurial values of exploitation. Moreover, these values should be balanced against collective, communitarian, or societal perspectives. This is invaluable in realizing that the rights to property which ensure copyright's basis, are there to be employed not only by authors, but by publishers, sound recording companies, film companies, and broadcasters. The latter groups comprise society just as much as do the individual creators. Moreover, the notion of the individual, either as a citizen or a creator, is a romantic and mythical figure—the average citizen rarely acts outside a group; the average creator rarely acts outside his collecting society or guild or trade union. As with all other groups, a certain level of critical mass is reached whereby the individuals within the group, rather in the manner of a Rousseauan pact, relinquish their will for the common weal.

However, as corporations become more heavily involved, and as their role **5.27** and influence grows, there is a need for copyright law to rethink seriously two interrelated issues: do corporate entities have corporate responsibility? If so, how should such responsibilities be incorporated into international copyright legislation?

---

[46] L Helfer, 'Regime Shifting: The Trips Agreement And New Dynamics Of International Intellectual Property Lawmaking' (2004) 29 Yale J Intl L 1, 19.

D. The 'Human Rights–Copyright–Public Interest' Nexus

(1) Corporate responsibility

5.28 Are private parties subject to human rights obligations? Do the international human rights instruments advocate corporate responsibility, thus recognizing that multinational corporations with considerable influence over international law should be recognized as States? The traditional view is that instruments like the Universal Declaration of Human Rights were drafted so as to place duties and obligations on sovereign States and their agents, rather than on private actors such as corporate entities. Increasingly however, international legal obligations and standards—including those protecting human rights— are being applied to other actors. Human rights obligations are being placed not only on groups of individuals but also on legal persons such as international financial institutions and companies.

5.29 Of course, individual company officers can be held liable under international law if responsible for violations of human rights. However, whilst crimes such as systematic or widespread policies of murder, slavery and trafficking, torture, or forced and arbitrary displacement of people are relatively easy to detect, any widespread and systematic policies to deter access to culture and information, or interferences with freedom of expression, may be less visible. Companies are already subject to many laws that regulate companies in relation to human rights: anti-discrimination laws, laws protecting unions and the right to organize, and laws punishing companies that commit environmental harm. The problem in an era of global economic integration is the degree to which such laws are found or enforced in different countries. This is very similar to the problem of international copyright laws.

5.30 There are two ways in which international instruments can directly impact upon corporate entities or groups representing individuals. First, States have a duty to protect human rights and in consequence must ensure that private actors, including companies, do not abuse them. This duty on States gives rise to indirect obligations on companies. Human rights are often viewed as advocating negative obligations (such as do not kill, do not interfere with privacy, do not suppress free speech), whereby violations of such rights are seen as being within the purview of the international community vis-à-vis the State and its agents. However, some of the rights and obligations within the international instruments can be viewed as obliging positive action, such as ensuring an adequate judicial system so as to ensure fair trials, and so on. It follows naturally that positive action to protect rights of individuals includes implementing specific legislation that prevents abuses emanating from private actors such as companies.

Should international law place direct legal obligations on companies, which **5.31** might be enforced internationally when States are unable or unwilling to take action themselves? The Preamble to the Universal Declaration of Human Rights states that 'every individual and *every organ of society* [emphasis added]' should promote respect for human rights. The International Labour Organization Tripartite Declaration of Principles Concerning Multinational Enterprises and Social Policy, 1977, also states that companies 'should respect the Universal Declaration of Human Rights and the corresponding International Covenants'. The OECD Guidelines for Multinational Enterprises (as revised in 2002) states that multinational enterprises should 'respect the human rights of those affected by their activities consistent with the host government's international legal obligations and commitments'.

(2) Copyright-related obligations under international instruments

One of the most urgent issues that is awaiting a definitive analysis is the **5.32** identification of the ways and means whereby States and other 'organs of society' (such as corporations, NGOs, and regional bodies) can ensure that the protection of intellectual property rights is consistent with the ethical norms as established by the existing corpus of international conventions and codes. There are four different facets in the interaction between fundamental freedoms and copyright law: property, freedom of expression, right to access culture, and right to access information. These facets can be recognized in different manners in the relevant major international conventions.[47]

The Preamble to the Universal Declaration on Human Rights 1948 reads **5.33** that 'freedom of speech and belief and freedom from fear and want has been proclaimed as the highest aspiration of the common people.' The Convention also doubly guarantees the right to the protection of intellectual

---

[47] See also Arts 35–7, UNESCO Recommendation on the Status of Scientific Researchers, 1974 (one specific aim of the Recommendation was to clarify the remit of Art 27, UDHR).

property rights and the right to share, inter alia, in scientific advancement and its benefits. Specifically, Article 27 of the UDHR sets out two provisions which stand at the two ends of the single continuum of intellectual production. On the one hand, Article 27(1) guarantees the usage rights of society by stressing communitarian values with the pronouncement that everyone has the right '*freely to participate in the cultural life of the community, to enjoy the arts and to share in scientific advancement and its benefits*'.[48] Article 19 complements this right by recognizing a right to freedom of opinion and expression, which includes the '*right to receive and impart information and ideas through any media and regardless of frontiers* [emphasis added].' On the other hand, Article 27(2) is even more clear in its intention in prescribing individual rights for '*moral and material interests resulting from any scientific, literary or artistic production* [emphasis added]', whilst Article 17(1) complements this right by according a general right of property.[49]

5.34 Property has been affirmed as an international human right. The Universal Declaration of Human Rights states, 'Everyone has the right to own property alone as well as in association with others,' and that '[n]o one shall be arbitrarily deprived of his property.' Similar prescriptions are repeated in Article 21 of the American Convention on Human Rights, Article XXIII of the American Declaration on the Rights and Duties of Man, the First Protocol of the European Convention for the Protection of Human Rights and Fundamental Freedoms, 20 March 1952 (ECHR)

5.35 Both the International Covenant on Civil and Political Rights (ICCPR) and the International Covenant on Economic, Social, and Cultural Rights (ICESCR) were adopted by the General Assembly of the United Nations on 16 December 1966. It is important to accept at the outset that economic, social, and cultural rights constitute fundamental human rights and are equally as important to democratic values within a society as civil and political rights. The division of the two sets of rights into two covenants reflects a divergence in political ideology rather than an intrinsic philosophical or legal

---

[48] Emphasis added. The suggestion of the communitarian ethos in Art 27(1) is further substantiated by Art 1 of UNESCO's Declaration of Principles of International Cooperation.
[49] Imre Szabó, *Cultural Rights* (Leiden: W Sijthoff, 1974) 45–6.

difference.[50] This divergence continues in the manner in which these two sets of rights are perceived as reflecting 'negative' rights and 'positive' rights. Civil and political rights are perceived as negative rights denoting a freedom from interference. Conversely, economic, social, and cultural rights, being positive rights to something, are perceived as requiring the distribution of resources by the State.

At a general level, the ICESCR recognizes that social and economic development is realized by improving methods of production, conservation, and distribution of resources through technical and scientific knowledge, and by developing efficient systems so as to achieve efficient development and utilization of resources (Article 11.2). Specifically, the Covenant guarantees protection of intellectual property rights as well as societal rights to enjoy the benefits of scientific progress, but also the need of States to achieve conservation, development, and diffusion of scientific research (Article 15). Thus, a balance is to be sought between protection and diffusion of arts and sciences. **5.36**

Whilst the ICCPR does not offer a positive basis for the protection of intellectual property rights, it does guarantee the protection of rights (especially moral rights) indirectly by insisting that there be no unlawful attacks on an individual's honour and reputation (Article 17). Moreover, although there is a strong guarantee to the right to freedom of expression, which again includes the right to receive and impart information and ideas, this right is curtailed by Article 19(2) which makes the right to freedom of expression and information conditional on respecting the rights or reputations of others which are prescribed by law and are necessary, and on protecting the national security or public order (ordre public), or of public health or morals. The problem is that the precise legal effect of these various declarations has not been conclusively determined. **5.37**

The Preamble to the UN Declaration on the Right to Development 1986 states that the notion of 'development' of a nation state is a comprehensive **5.38**

---

[50] Intriguingly, it was the Soviet states which championed economic, social, and cultural rights as manifesting socialist values whilst civil and political rights were promoted by Western states as the cornerstones for Western democratic ideals. C Puta-Chekwe and N Flood, 'From Division to Integration: Economic, Social and Cultural Rights as Basic Human Rights', in I Merali and V Oosterveld (eds), *Giving Meaning to Economic, Social and Cultural Rights* (Philadelphia: University of Pennsylvania Press, 2001) 39–51.

'economic, social, cultural and political process, which aims at the constant improvement of the well-being of the entire population and of all individuals on the basis of their active, free and meaningful participation in development and in the fair distribution of benefits resulting therefrom'. Generally the Declaration recognizes the right to development as an inalienable right including (a) the right to participate in and enjoy economic, social, cultural, and political development; (b) the right to full sovereignty over all natural wealth and resources (Article 1); (c) the right to formulate international development policies and laws which aim to ensure meaningful participation of all stakeholders in the fair distribution of benefits which, in turn, is underpinned by international co-operation (Articles 2, 4.2, and 10).

5.39 Can we learn from the efforts of indigenous peoples to institute respect for their intellectual properties as well as recognize the concept of common heritage of mankind? Interestingly, the Declaration also states that all human beings have a positive duty and responsibility for development, either as individuals or as collectives (Article 2). Should this also extend to corporations?

(3) Disparate copyright interests

5.40 The problem is that property rights tend to be pushed forward by social or cultural groups, whereas duties to respect such rights and the correlative right to freedom of expression tend to fall to groups of individuals who have no common identity or characteristic. We need first to recognize that rights are, at times, a means of recognizing and according social membership. An individual categorically excluded from, say, the right to express oneself freely, could hardly be considered a full member of the society in question. To a similar extent, an individual excluded from the class of persons granted authority to select a nation's lawmakers would be a stranger, or worse, a servant, in relation to that political community. In this way, membership in or exclusion from the class of persons deemed rights-bearers may powerfully affect an individual's social identity, and even their self-perception. Of course, in part for this reason, liberal democracies today view the exclusion of categories of persons from general rights on the basis of involuntary human characteristics as, for the most part, patently unjust.[51]

---

[51] EJ Mitnick, 'Three Models Of Group-Differentiated Rights' (2004) 35 Columbia Human Rights L Rev 215, at 218–19, 232–4.

One means of ensuring that all sectoral interests are taken into account is to **5.41** introduce an *international public interest rule* within international copyright law. It is clear that 'public interest' must be taken into account from the stance of UN human rights bodies who view the TRIPs Agreements as a threat to 'economic, social, and cultural rights'. Non-binding declarations and interpretive statements issued by human rights bodies emphasize the public's interest in access to new knowledge and innovations and assert that States must give primacy to human rights over TRIPs where the two sets of obligations conflict.[52] The scope of such a rule would be eventually mapped out by the national courts; however, the judiciary can perhaps be made to ensure that the rule accommodates the normative rules of interpreting human rights legislation. In today's world of international trade and other transnational transactions, including cyberspace transactions, corporations are imposing a body of rules that is free from idiosyncratic national differences. For the convenience of traders, a new type of *lex mercatoria* is emerging which emphasizes the use of (a) standard form contracts, usually drawn by trade associations to reflect the interests of traders in a particular commodity; (b) 'choice of forum' and 'choice of law' provisions; and (c) provisions for settlement of the dispute by arbitration or other non-curial means, ensuring that the formal institutions of States are not involved.[53]

(4) Extrinsic and intrinsic control

Should copyright legislation be reworded in terms of the social and ethical **5.42** responsibility of enterprises (including the media industries), much in the same way as is being demanded of patent legislation? Secondly, if it is argued that the copyright system is part of the fundamental freedoms, then should the related rights regime (including performances and phonogram recordings) be viewed as being part of the human rights framework as well? If so, who should the beneficiaries be? Both propositions should be answered in the affirmative. The incorporation of a human rights ethos into copyright or intellectual property instruments merely reflects an accepted practice called regime or forum shifting. Regime shifting occurs where states and

---

[52] L Helfer, 'Regime Shifting: The Trips Agreement And New Dynamics Of International Intellectual Property Lawmaking' (2004) 29 Yale J Intl L 1, 49 *et seq.*

[53] J Goldring, 'Consumer Protection, Globalisation and Democracy' (1998) 6 Cardozo J Intl & Comparative L 1, at 56.

NGOs attempt to alter the status quo ante by moving treaty negotiations, lawmaking initiatives, or standard-setting activities either from one international venue to another, or from a domestic venue to an international venue or vice versa.[54] Regime shifting can be intra-regime in that the shift occurs to another lawmaking venue situated within the same regime (for example, the WIPO-based Berne Convention vis-à-vis the UNESCO-based Universal Copyright Convention). Conversely, States and other actors can engage in inter-regime shifting by moving discourse into an entirely different regime. A clear example of this is the GATT–WTO regime which has moved away from a system of trade rules for goods to a regime which includes rules governing the protection of intellectual property, service industries, and health and safety measures. Moreover, WTO rules have had an impact also on other areas not subject to any specific WTO regulation, including environmental and human rights policy.[55]

5.43 There are two means of ensuring proper behaviour of corporations: extrinsic means and intrinsic means. One example of an extrinsic means is competition law. Hence the over-zealous exercise of copyright law should, theoretically, be countered by investigations by national competition authorities. However the multinational nature of corporations makes this difficult— witness for example, the Warner–AOL merger which called for co-operation of national institutions. A second means of extrinsic controls is voluntary codes of conduct—such codes publicly express their company's profile and become part of the company's identity.[56] There is, however, a limit to voluntarism in the absence of a legal framework. Finally, the international human rights declarations may have some impact as they can be cited by both courts and parties in national and international courts.

5.44 Extrinsic means can be important when one considers that the future of international copyright jurisprudence may emanate primarily from the interpretation of the TRIPs Agreement. A factor, thus, that should be borne in mind is that one of the main purposes of a dispute settlement is to clarify the provisions of the WTO agreements 'in accordance with customary rules of

---

[54] L Helfer, 'Regime Shifting: The Trips Agreement and New Dynamics of International Intellectual Property Lawmaking' (2004) 29 Yale J Intl L 1, 14.

[55] Notably, Art XX, GATT 1947, as incorporated in GATT 1994, Annex 1A, WTO Agreement.

[56] See D Petrasek, *Business and Human Rights: Towards Legal Accountability*, speech delivered on 23 January 2003, available on <http://www.amnesty.org>.

interpretation of public international law'.[57] Thus, it is not necessary that the human rights perspective be solely within the intellectual property rights treaty—it can also be considered by a TRIPs panel if it is part of the general principles of sovereign states or recognized custom. The problem, however, is determining to what extent rights to freedom of expression and information have become general principles within national law or internationally recognized custom. As one US court acknowledges, the current US copyright landscape has been changed by the 1996 WIPO Treaties.[58]

A much better means of ensuring that the balancing exercise which is advo- **5.45**
cated by the above instruments is undertaken both by international and national panels and by courts is to incorporate human rights responsibilities into international copyright agreements. Intrinsic measures entail analysing whether the existing limitations within international copyright law offer sufficient basis to argue that corporate responsibility is an inherent facet within these limitations. Or do we need to augment the existing limitations and exceptions to emphasize the accepted human right tenet that all rights are equal, and the court ultimately must balance the different sets of rights: creator rights and individual user rights? The minimum standards regime allows individual states to make their own interpretations and to allow for exceptions and limitations which fit with their national ideals of the encouragement of free expression, creation of further works, and cultural development. Such a regime arguably does not fit well with adjudication by a supranational trade body. Indeed, several commentators have argued that in the area of exceptions to copyright, and Article 13, national legislatures and courts should be accorded the highest degree of deference.[59]

Existing limitations within international copyright law fall within one large **5.46**
exception: the Berne Three-Step Test. The three conditions it contains—
certain special cases, no conflict with normal exploitation, and no unreasonable prejudice to legitimate interests—are often referred to as the three-step test. Since its genesis in the Berne Convention during the 1967 Stockholm

---

[57] Art 3.2, *Understanding on Rules and Procedures Governing the Settlement of Disputes*, WTO Agreement, Annexe 2.

[58] *Universal City Studios, Inc v Shawn C Reimerdes* 111 F Supp 2d 294 (SDNY, 2000); 273 F 3d 429 (US Ct of Apps (2nd Cir), 2001).

[59] NW Netanel, 'Asserting Copyright's Democratic Principles in the Global Arena' (1998) 51 Vanderbilt L Rev 217, at 296–308.

Revision, the test has appeared three further times: the 1994 TRIPs Agreement for all economic rights under the copyright regime; the WIPO Copyright Treaty; and the EC Directive for Copyright and Related Rights in the Information Society. The latter two are initiatives aimed at updating copyright law for the digital age; should the three-step test be updated for this same age? Should we augment the Berne Three-Step Test so that it reflects human rights, and thus ensuring that corporations who are the major rights holders in the new digital era, and who employ access-protection and copy-protection devices, as sanctioned under the WIPO Copyright Treaties, are subjected to some consideration of societal concerns as to freedom of expression and access to information? This would eliminate the trade bias, for instance, in the TRIPs Agreement. One jurist argues that it is imperative, owing to the strength of the WTO institution, to counter the trade bias with appropriate mechanisms so as to highlight other interests, such as environmental interests or labour rights interests, without undermining the strengths of the trading system.[60] Moreover, UN agencies have been calling for a more human rights sensitive approach to the TRIPs Agreement. The Chair of the Sub-Commission on the Promotion and Protection of Human Rights, for instance, adopted a resolution on 'Intellectual Property Rights and Human Rights' which stated that 'actual or potential conflicts exist between the implementation of the TRIPs Agreement and the realization of economic, social and cultural rights.'[61]

5.47 The areas of concern were primarily the patenting of life, erosion and control of cultural values, and the right to health. Indeed, the Sub-Commission called four different sets of actors (national governments, intergovernmental organizations, UN human rights bodies, and NGOs) to address the intersection of human rights and intellectual property, and especially asked national lawmakers to integrate 'human rights obligations and principles' into their activities, with a particular focus on the social function of intellectual property. The underlying principle of future lawmaking, the resolution argues, should be 'the primacy of human rights obligations over economic policies and agreements'.[62] UN human rights bodies have devoted

---

[60] A Guzman, 'Global Governance and the WTO' (2004) 45 Harv Intl L J 303, at 314.

[61] Res 2000/7, UN ESCOR Comm'n on Hum Rts, 52nd Sess, Provisional Agenda Item 4, at 1 and 2, UN Doc E/CN4/Sub2/2000/L20 (2000), available at <http://ap.ohchr.org/documents/E/SUBCOM/resolutions/E-CN_4-SUB_2-RES–2000–7.doc>.

[62] Ibid, para 3.

much attention to intellectual property issues in the past few years culminating in several results, including an analysis of TRIPs by the High Commissioner, which argues that intellectual property laws must promote the *public interest* in access to new knowledge and innovations and opposes the adoption of TRIPs-plus standards.[63] Moreover, the Committee on Economic, Social, and Cultural Rights (ICESCR Committee) asserted in its statement that intellectual property rights 'must be balanced with the right to take part in cultural life and to enjoy the benefits of scientific progress and its applications', and that both national and international intellectual property regimes must be consistent with the obligation of states which are parties to the ICESCR.[64]

(5) A public interest rule

There are several examples of public interest led provisions in the Berne **5.48**
Convention. Article 2(4), for example, allows member countries to give effect to their 'views of the public interest' by either excluding copyright protection or limiting it in the case of laws, administrative and legal orders, and other such texts.[65] Public interest also underlies the basis and interpretation of Article 2(8), which excludes protection from 'news of the day or to miscellaneous facts having the character of mere items of press information'. The broad interpretation of this provision is that the Berne Convention does embody the interests of freedom of information and expression; the more narrow public policy interpretation is that copyright should not extend to ideas, facts, and information per se.[66] Another example is Article 2*bis*(2), which allows member countries to limit the scope of copyright protection on certain types of speeches and lectures if 'such use is justified by the

---

[63] Report of the High Commissioner—The Impact of the Agreement on Trade-Related Aspects of Intellectual Property Rights on Human Rights, UN ESCOR Comm'n on Hum Rts, 52nd Sess, Provisional Agenda Item 4, paras 10–15, 27–58, UN Doc E/CN4/Sub2/2001/13 (2001).

[64] Substantive Issues Arising in the Implementation of the International Covenant on Economic, Social and Cultural Rights—Follow-Up to the Day of General Discussion on Article 15.1(c), Statement on Human Rights and Intellectual Property, UN ESCOR Comm on Econ, Soc, & Cultural Rts, 27th Sess, Agenda Item 4, paras 4, 11, UN Doc E/C12/2001/15 (2001).

[65] S Ricketson, *The Berne Convention for the Protection of Literary and Artistic Works: 1886–1986* (London: Queen Mary/Kluwer, 1987) paras 6.67 and 6.74.

[66] Ibid, para 6.73.

informatory purpose'. As Ricketson points out, the rationale of this provision is clearly a public interest one where reproduction or communication of a work is allowed if made with the purpose of informing the public. Article 2*bis*(2) is analogous to Article 10*bis*(2), the difference being that the latter provision applies to articles on 'current economic, political or religious topics and of broadcast works of the same character'. Moreover, Article 10*bis*(2) allows for a narrower exception as use of works is justified by its '*informatory purpose* [emphasis added]' but only for the purposes of reporting 'current events'.[67] This exception, made for the benefit of the press, again recognizes the fundamental importance of allowing usage of copyright works for the purposes of free flow of information, education, and research.[68]

5.49 The TRIPs Agreement similarly recognizes public policy objectives within its preamble. Moreover, Article 7 appears to allow courts to take into account 'social and economic welfare', whatever this may entail, and urges 'a balance of rights and obligations'; whilst Article 8 specifically states that members may, 'in formulating or amending their laws and regulations, adopt measures necessary to protect public health and nutrition, and to promote the public interest in sectors of vital importance to their socio-economic and techno-logical development, provided that such measures are consistent with the provisions of this Agreement'.

5.50 Another most promising international provision is Article 13 of the TRIPs Agreement, which sets out the three-step test as first adopted at the Stockholm Conference in relation to the Berne Convention. The TRIPs Agreement extends the three-step test to cover all exceptions to exclusive rights. Concern, however, can be expressed as to the meaning of 'normal exploitation of the work' and 'unreasonable prejudice'. The terms, as expressed in the Berne Convention, had vague interpretations. 'Normal exploitation' ultimately depended on the nature of the work and how national tribunals sought to define the term; while, the notion of 'unreasonable prejudice' appears to cover both absolute exceptions to the right, and compulsory licences, depending on the nature of the appropriation.[69]

5.51 How is an international rule forged? And if the principle is forged, what standard is employed? What denotes an international level of equity, law,

---

[67] S Ricketson (n 65 above), paras 9.39, 9.40.   [68] Ibid, para. 9.29
[69] Ibid, paras 9.7–9.8.

or justice? One means of determining this issue is to note that international legal norms are broadly grouped into five distinct categories, though a general principle of law can fall into more than one category:

(a) principles of municipal law recognized by civilized nations;
(b) general principles of law derived from the specific nature of the international community;
(c) principles intrinsic to the idea of law and basic to all legal systems;
(d) principles valid through all kinds of societies in relationships of hierarchy and co-ordination;
(e) principles of justice founded on the very nature of man as a rational and social being.[70]

The ideal place for the rule would be within the TRIPs Agreement since it **5.52** redrew the existing boundaries of international intellectual property law. It did this by (a) enhancing the substantive rules found in pre-TRIPs intellectual property law, (b) consolidating all relevant intellectual property rules within a single comprehensive international code, (c) obliging the entire WTO membership to invoke domestic intellectual property laws, and thus increasing the number of states offering intellectual property protection and, (d) providing, unlike previous intellectual property treaties and laws, enforcement provisions to safeguard against non-compliance with TRIPs.[71] Another reason for choosing the TRIPs Agreement is to engage in regime shifting not in relation to intellectual property rights, but in relation to human rights. Intellectual property standards are not affected by 'soft' intellectual property rules in international instruments which deal with biodiversity or human rights. Instead, a more substantive move would be to incorporate a human rights regime within an international intellectual property regime.[72] One need do nothing more than turn to the language of the 1996 WIPO Copyright Treaty to note that there is a ready made rule lying within the Preamble: 'a need to maintain a balance between rights of authors and the large public interest, particularly education, research and access to information'.

---

[70] O Schachter, *International Law in Theory and Practice* (1991) at 50.
[71] JH Reichman, *Universal Minimum Standards of Intellectual Property Protection Under the TRIPs Component of the WTO Agreement* (1995) 29 Intl L 345; L Helfer, 'Regime Shifting: The Trips Agreement And New Dynamics Of International Intellectual Property Lawmaking' (2004) 29 Yale J Intl L 1, at 23.
[72] L Helfer, ibid, at 58.

5.53 With regard to providing a new three-step rule, it is proposed that the present Article 13 of the TRIPs Agreement be extended as shown: Members shall confine limitations or exceptions to exclusive rights to certain special cases which do not conflict with a normal exploitation of the work and do not unreasonably prejudice the legitimate interests of the right holder, *taking note of the need to maintain a balance between the rights owners and the larger public interest.*

5.54 Surely this cannot be such a revolutionary proposal?

PART II

NATIONAL AND INTERNATIONAL PERSPECTIVES

6

COPYRIGHT AND THE FIRST AMENDMENT: WHAT *ELDRED* MISSES—AND PORTENDS

Neil Weinstock Netanel

A. Introduction

The First Amendment provides that 'Congress shall make no law . . . abridg- **6.01**
ing the freedom of speech.' Copyright law's potential for abridging speech
has long been recognized in US case law, legislation, and commentary.[1]

---

[1] Some of the cases are cited in note 3 below. Among an outpouring of recent commentary, see CE Baker, 'First Amendment Limits on Copyright' (2002) 55 Vanderbilt L Rev 891; Y Benkler, 'Free as the Air to Common Use: First Amendment Constraints on the Enclosure of the Public Domain' (1999) 74 New York U L Rev 354; MA Lemley and E Volokh, 'Freedom of Speech and Injunctions in Intellectual Property Cases' (1998) 48 Duke L J 147; L Lessig, 'Copyright's First Amendment' (2001) 48 UCLA L Rev 1057; NW Netanel, 'Locating Copyright Within the First Amendment Skein' (2001) 54 Stanford L Rev 1;

Because of copyright, speakers may be unable to convey their message effectively and audiences may be deprived of valuable expression.

6.02 That does not necessarily mean that the First Amendment places limits on copyright's application and scope. First Amendment doctrine is highly complex and First Amendment protections far more qualified than the Amendment's sweeping, absolute language suggests. In fact, the law imposes many speech burdens that do not give rise to any justiciable claim under the First Amendment.

6.03 Nevertheless, copyright law does implicate traditional First Amendment concerns. Accordingly, as argued in this chapter, where necessary to protect speech, courts should apply the First Amendment to cabin copyright holder prerogatives. At the very least, even if the First Amendment is not applied as an external constraint, Congress and the courts should interpret and develop copyright doctrine in line with First Amendment values.

6.04 The argument that copyright should be subject to external First Amendment constraint runs against prevailing precedent. Courts have almost never imposed First Amendment limitations on copyright, and most have summarily rejected First Amendment defences to copyright infringement claims.[2] Courts have recognized that copyright can abridge speech and thus that it raises First Amendment concerns. But in almost every instance, courts have assumed that First Amendment values are fully and adequately protected by

---

NW Netanel, 'Market Hierarchy and Copyright in Our System of Free Expression' (2000) 53 Vanderbilt L Rev 1879; J Rubenfeld, 'The Freedom of Imagination: Copyright's Constitutionality' (2002) 112 Yale L J 1; R Tushnet, 'Copy this Essay: How Fair Use Doctrine Harms Free Speech and How Copying Serves It' (2004) 109 Yale L J 101. Some scholars respond that the First Amendment does not limit copyright. For thoughtful commentary in that vein, see CL Eisgruber, 'Censorship, Copyright, and Free Speech: Some Tentative Skepticism About the Campaign to Impose First Amendment Restrictions on Copyright Law' (2003) 2 J Telecommunications & High Technology L 17; David McGowan, 'Why the First Amendment Cannot Dictate Copyright Policy' (2004) 65 U Pittsburgh L Rev 281.

[2] There are only two cases of which I am aware in which courts have ruled in favour of First Amendment defences to copyright enforcement without being subsequently vacated. Both are district court decisions. One was upheld on appeal on non-First Amendment grounds: *Triangle Publ'ns Inc v Knight-Ridder Newspapers Inc* 445 F Supp 875 (SD Fla, 1978), aff'd on other grounds, 626 F 2d 1171 (US Ct of Apps (5th Cir), 1980). The other is unreported: *Holliday v Cable News Network* New York L J, Jan 21, 1994 (CD Cal, 11 June 1993).

limitations on rights within copyright doctrine itself.[3] Some have even posited that 'copyrights are categorically immune from challenges under the First Amendment.'[4]

The courts are correct that, in principle, copyright's free speech burden could **6.05** be ameliorated by various safeguards within copyright law. But, as I have detailed elsewhere, copyright's much-touted internal free speech safety valves in fact fall far short of their promise.[5] As a result, copyright doctrine has proven inadequate to protect free speech. The notion that what remains of copyright's fair use privilege, idea–expression dichotomy, and limited term serve as an effective proxy for the First Amendment is judicial formalism at its worst. On paper, those doctrines stand for First Amendment values. In practice, they protect speech only against the most egregious incursions, and, even then, far from consistently.

As a result, First Amendment scrutiny is both warranted and, most probably, **6.06** necessary to restore an appropriate balance between copyright holder prerogatives and free speech. At the very least, the First Amendment should be applied to ensure that copyright's traditional free speech safety valves actually live up to their task.

---

[3] See, eg, *Harper & Row, Publishers Inc v Nation Enterprises* 471 US 539 (1985) 560 (explaining that First Amendment protections are 'already embodied in the Copyright Act's distinction between copyrightable expression and uncopyrightable facts and ideas'); *Roy Export Co v CBS Inc* 672 F 2d 1095 (US Ct of Apps (2nd Cir), 1982) 1099 ('No circuit that has considered the question . . . has ever held that the First Amendment provides a privilege in the copyright field distinct from the accommodation embodied in the "fair use" doctrine'); *Sid & Marty Krofft Television Prods Inc v McDonald's Corp* 562 F 2d 1157 (US Ct of Apps (9th Cir), 1977) 1170 (stating that an idea–expression dichotomy accommodates First Amendment concerns). Recent cases have followed the view that copyright requires no external First Amendment scrutiny. See, eg, *A&M Records Inc v Napster Inc* 239 F 3d 1004 (US Ct of Apps (9th Cir), 2001) 1028 ('We note that First Amendment concerns in copyright are allayed by the presence of the fair use doctrine'); *Worldwide Church of God v Phila Church of God Inc* 227 F 3d 1110 (US Ct of Apps (9th Cir), 2000); *LA Times v Free Republic* 54 USPQ 2d (BNA) 1453 (CD Cal, 2000); *Chi Sch Reform Bd of Trustees v Substance Inc* 79 F Supp 2d 919 (ND Ill, 2000); *Southco Inc v Kanebridge Corp* 53 USPQ 2d (BNA) 1490 (ED Pa, 2000); *Intellectual Reserve Inc v Utah Lighthouse Ministry Inc* 75 F Supp 2d 1290 (D Utah, 1999); *Eldred v Reno* 74 F Supp 2d 1 (DDC, 1999). But see *Universal City Studios Inc v Corley* 273 F 3d 429 (US Ct of Apps (2nd Cir), 2001) (applying First Amendment analysis to the anti-trafficking provisions of the Digital Millennium Copyright Act of 1998, but holding that the provisions survived First Amendment scrutiny).

[4] *Eldred* 239 F 3d 372, 375, *reh'g en banc denied, Eldred v Ashcroft* 255 F 3d 849 (US Ct of Apps (DC Cir), 2001).

[5] NW Netanel, 'Locating Copyright Within the First Amendment Skein' (2001) 54 Stanford L Rev 1.

6.07 Copyright's judicial exoneration does not only ignore the actual workings of copyright law and practice. It is also sharply out of step with the rest of First Amendment doctrine. During the very period that courts have trumpeted copyright's categorical immunity, they have subjected a wide array of other intellectual property and private causes of action to First Amendment scrutiny. Courts have brought the First Amendment to bear on the laws of trade marks, trade secrets, the right of publicity, defamation, the right of privacy, tortious interference with business relations, intentional infliction of emotional distress, a private right of action for damages caused by illegal wiretapping, and, in some instances, personal and real property.[6] Of course, First Amendment scrutiny does not always mean that the defendant's speech trumps the intellectual property or other private right. But, to avoid a potentially 'chilling effect' on valued speech, courts often place formidable barriers before individuals seeking to vindicate proprietary or personal rights.

6.08 What is more, in marked contrast to the judicial exoneration of copyright, courts do not ordinarily consider a body of law's internal free speech safeguards to obviate the need for First Amendment scrutiny. Courts have regularly applied First Amendment restrictions to other private rights, including intellectual property rights, that, like copyright, have built-in mechanisms designed to protect free speech interests. Even prior to First Amendment intervention, for instance, trade mark law generally denied trade mark owners the right to prevent the unauthorized use of their marks for news reporting, commentary, parody, and artistic expression.[7] Similarly,

---

[6] See, eg, *Bartnicki v Vopper* 532 US 514 (2001) (private right of action for damages under wiretapping laws); *Hustler Magazine Inc v Falwell* 485 US 46 (1988) (intentional infliction of emotional distress); *NAACP v Claiborne Hardware Co* 458 US 886 (1982) (tortious interference with a business); *Time Inc v Hill* 385 US 374 (1967) (right of privacy); *New York Times v Sullivan* 376 US 254 (1964) (libel); *Lloyd Corp v Tanner* 407 US 551 (1972) 567 (real property); *Westchester Media v PRI. USA Holdings Inc* 214 F 3d 658 (US Ct of Apps (5th Cir), 2000) (trade mark); *Cardtoons LC v Major League Baseball Players Ass'n* 95 F 3d 959 (US Ct of Apps (10th Cir), 1996) 971–6 (right of publicity); *Herceg v Hustler Magazine Inc* 814 F 2d 1017 (US Ct of Apps (5th Cir), 1987) (civil action for incitement); *DVD Copy Control Association Inc v Bunner* 4 Cal Rptr 3d 69 (Cal Sup Ct, 2003) (trade secrets); *Intel Corp v Hamidi* 1 Cal Rptr 3d 32 (Cal Sup Ct, 2003) 51 (trespass to chattel).

[7] Such uses are deemed not to cause consumer confusion and thus not to infringe. See *Cardtoons LC v Major League Baseball Players Ass'n* 95 F 3d 959 (US Ct of Apps (10th Cir), 1996) 970 (describing trade mark law's likelihood of confusion requirement as a built-in mechanism that serves to avoid First Amendment concerns). Likewise, the Federal Trademark Dilution Act of 1995 exempts from liability trade mark fair use, noncommercial uses, and 'all forms of news reporting and news commentary', 15 USC s 1125(c)(4)(A)–(C) (2001).

the right of publicity has long been subject to a privilege to use a person's name or likeness for the dissemination of news or as part of artistic expression.[8] Yet, despite these internal free speech protections, courts have subjected trade mark rights[9] and the right of publicity[10] to further, independent First Amendment constraints. Likewise, common law defamation[11] and right of privacy[12] were remoulded to conform with First Amendment strictures despite internal doctrine that already limited aggrieved persons' redress in order to protect free speech.

To be certain, the First Amendment has little, if anything, to say about judicial enforcement of private causes of action or even direct government regulation touching upon much of what we commonly consider 'speech'.[13]   **6.09**

---

[8] See *Rogers v Grimaldi* 875 F 2d 994 (US Ct of Apps (2nd Cir), 1989) 1003–5; *Finger v Omni Publ'ns Int'l, Ltd* 77 NYS 2d 138 (NY Sup Ct, 1990).

[9] See, eg, *Rogers v Grimaldi* 875 F 2d 994 (US Ct of Apps (2nd Cir), 1989) 998–9; *Westchester Media v PRL USA Holdings Inc* 214 F 3d 658 (US Ct of Apps (5th Cir), 2000) 671–3; *Cliffs Notes Inc v Bantam Doubleday Dell Publishing Group* 886 F 2d 490 (US Ct of Apps (2nd Cir), 1989) 495.

[10] See, eg, *Hoffman v Capital Cities/ABC Inc* 255 F 3d 1180 (US Ct of Apps (9th Cir), 2001); *Cardtoons LC v Major League Baseball Players Ass'n* 95 F 3d 959 (US Ct of Apps (10th Cir), 1996) 971–6; *Comedy III Prods Inc v Gary Saderup Inc* 25 Cal 4th 387 (Cal Ct App, 2001) 407.

[11] To further free speech interests, courts refused to enjoin libel at common law. See *Brandreth v Lance* 8 Paige Ch 24 (NY Ch, 1839) 26. Likewise, the law of libel has traditionally recognized a privilege for news dealers, bookstores, and libraries that transmit defamatory material published by others without knowing of its defamatory character. See *Restatement (Second) of Torts* § 581(1) (1977). Finally, while the expression of an opinion was potentially libelous at common law, the common law recognized a privilege of fair comment, involving expressions of opinion on matters of public concern. See *Restatement (Second) of Torts* § 566 cmt a (1977).
  In imposing the First Amendment, the Supreme Court held that that public figures who allege that they have been defamed must bear the burden of proving that the allegedly defamatory statement is indeed false and that the defendant acted knowingly or recklessly, not just negligently, in making the false statement: *New York Times v Sullivan* 376 US 254 (1964) 279–80. It also sharply restricted the imposition of strict liability and presumed or punitive damages even in actions for the defamation of non-public figures, at least those involving statements regarding matters of public concern. See *Gertz v Robert Welch Inc* 418 US 323 (1974) 347–50; *Dun & Bradstreet Inc v Greenmoss Builders Inc* 472 US 749 (1985) 759–60.

[12] The right of privacy is limited by a privilege to publicize newsworthy matters. See *Restatement (Second) of Torts* § 652D (1977). While that privilege arose as an internal limit, it is now recognized to have an overriding constitutional dimension. See *Virgil v Time Inc* 527 F 2d 1122 (US Ct of Apps (9th Cir), 1975) 1128–9; *Matthews v Wozencraft* 15 F 3d 432 (US Ct of Apps (5th Cir), 1994) 440.

[13] F Schauer, 'The Boundaries of the First Amendment: A Preliminary Exploration of Constitutional Salience' (2004) 117 Harv L Rev 1765.

Laws regulating the content of corporate proxy statements and prohibiting fraudulent misrepresentation and criminal conspiracy are but a few of many examples. But copyright law falls squarely within the realm of those types of speech-burdening regulations that generally do implicate the First Amendment.[14] In contrast to the regulation of general conduct and of forms of expression effectively deemed 'non-speech' for First Amendment purposes, copyright law's entire focus is on providing some speakers with the legal entitlement to restrict others' speech. And in doing so, copyright is heavily involved in the structuring and operation of traditional First Amendment media. Copyright law touches directly and consistently on literature, art, film, television broadcasts, photographs, political polemic, criticism, scholarship, and other expression lying at the core of First Amendment protection.

6.10 Courts' persistent immunization of copyright from First Amendment scrutiny is thus a striking anomaly. Their failure even to ask whether copyright's traditional safety valves are sufficient to pass First Amendment muster stands in sharp contrast to other closely analogous areas of First Amendment doctrine. At the very least, courts should, as they have in other areas, apply the First Amendment prophylactically to ensure that the enforcement of copyright holder rights does not chill valued speech. Courts understandably do not wish to interpret and apply First Amendment tests in every copyright infringement action. But, as with defamation, privacy, and other torts, they could refashion copyright doctrine to comport more consistently and rigorously with First Amendment requirements without having repeatedly to entertain First Amendment defences to copyright infringement claims.

B. The Supreme Court speaks: *Eldred v Ashcroft*

6.11 The most recent and conclusive statement on the relationship between copyright and the First Amendment is the Supreme Court's January 2003 decision in *Eldred v Ashcroft*.[15] In *Eldred*, the Court, by a seven to two majority, rejected a First Amendment challenge to the Sony Bono Copyright Term Extension Act of 1998. The *Eldred* majority conceded that lower courts have spoken too broadly when declaring copyrights categorically immune

---

[14] See NW Netanel, 'Locating Copyright Within the First Amendment Skein' (2001) 54 Stanford L Rev 1, 45–7.

[15] 537 US 186 (2003).

from First Amendment challenge. But in rejecting Eldred's challenge, the Court held that when 'Congress has not altered the traditional contours of copyright protection, further First Amendment scrutiny is unnecessary'.

By that ruling, the Supreme Court has perpetuated copyright's aberrant **6.12** treatment. *Eldred* did put to rest the sweeping (and ludicrous) suggestion that no Copyright Act provision could possibly run afoul of the First Amendment. (After all, what if Congress amended the Copyright Act to provide that only registered Republicans enjoy copyright protection?) But in holding that First Amendment scrutiny is unwarranted when 'Congress has not altered the traditional contours of copyright protection', the Court almost entirely closed the door on further First Amendment challenges to traditional copyright law.

The Court's explanation for its holding is no less disappointing than the **6.13** result. *Eldred* shows remarkably little understanding of, or appreciation for, the First Amendment values at stake in copyright's burdening of speech. And the majority's opinion gives further credence to lower court justifications for exonerating copyright from First Amendment review, some of them no less doctrinally and logically unsound than the broad statement that copyrights are categorically immune from First Amendment scrutiny.

At the same time, it is important to emphasize, *Eldred* is not a total defeat **6.14** for those hoping to bring copyright law within the First Amendment fold. Despite the Court's abjuration of First Amendment scrutiny for traditional copyright, the decision leaves room for the First Amendment both to inform copyright jurisprudence and oversee Copyright Act amendments that do alter copyright's traditional contours. Most broadly, in rejecting (or at least qualifying) copyright's categorical immunity, the Court explicitly recognized that, in principle, copyright does implicate the First Amendment. And, in that vein, the Court then suggested some specific ways in which the First Amendment might yet circumscribe copyright holder prerogatives.

We now turn to a closer, critical examination of the *Eldred* decision and what **6.15** it portends for copyright, the First Amendment, and free speech.

(1) Background

Eldred v Ashcroft differs from most previous cases involving copyright and the **6.16** First Amendment. The case arose not as a defence to a particular copyright infringement claim, but as a facial First Amendment challenge to new copyright legislation. The Sony Bono Copyright Term Extension Act of 1998 (CTEA) amended the Copyright Act to extend the copyright term for an additional twenty years. The term extension applied not only prospectively, to works created after the CTEA's effective date, but also retrospectively, to subsisting copyrights in existing works.

6.17 In January 1999, a group of archivists and publishers of public domain material filed a complaint seeking to enjoin the Attorney General from enforcing the CTEA. The complaint posed two constitutional challenges to the CTEA. The first was that the term extension exceeded Congress's enumerated power under the Copyright Clause. The second, the sole ground we will consider here, was that the Act contravened the First Amendment.

6.18 Both the district court and DC Circuit summarily dismissed plaintiffs' First Amendment claims, with the DC Circuit holding explicitly that 'copyrights are categorically immune from challenges under the First Amendment.'[16] In so ruling, the *Eldred* courts went further than any others in immunizing copyright from First Amendment challenge. Other courts have exonerated copyright from First Amendment defences to copyright infringement claims. The DC District and Circuit were the first to hold that the Copyright Act legislation and amendments are immune even from facial attack. In addition, the DC Circuit baldly stated that 'the plaintiffs lack any cognizable first amendment right to exploit the copyrighted works of others.'[17] Most other courts have characterized the copyright–free speech conflict in a more nuanced manner. They have accepted that, in principle, copyright does raise First Amendment concerns, but have held that copyright's internal free speech safeguards adequately address them.

(2) The Eldred *petitioners' First Amendment argument*

6.19 First Amendment doctrine establishes a panoply of standards and tests for determining whether speech-burdening legislation and regulation meets

---

[16] See *Eldred* 74 F Supp 2d 1(DDC, 1999) 3 ('The District of Columbia Circuit has ruled definitively that there are no First Amendment rights to use of the copyrighted works of others'); *Eldred v Reno* 239 F 3d 372 (US Ct of Apps (DC Cir), 2001) 375, *rhrg den* 255 F 3d 849 (US Ct of Apps (DC Cir), 2001).

[17] 239 F 3d 372 (US Ct of Apps (DC Cir), 2001) 376.

First Amendment muster. In particular, 'content based' speech restrictions, generally those in which the government seeks to suppress a particular viewpoint or subject matter, are subject to 'strict scrutiny' and almost never upheld. Examples of content-based speech restrictions include government prohibitions of Communist tracts, hate speech, and flag burning. In contrast, 'content neutral' speech restrictions are those that limit expression without regard to the speech's message or communicative impact. Classic examples include capping decibel levels at music clubs, forbidding sound trucks in residential neighbourhoods, and imposing 'time, place, or manner restrictions' on parades and demonstrations. Content-neutral speech restrictions are subject to a level of judicial scrutiny that, although more rigorous than that applied to regulation that raises no First Amendment (or other special constitutional) concern, is considerably less exacting than the strict scrutiny applied to content-based regulation. Courts and commentators often refer to such scrutiny as 'intermediate scrutiny'.

The *Eldred* petitioners maintained that copyright law is a content-neutral **6.20** speech regulation and thus that the CTEA should be subject to 'intermediate scrutiny' under the standard set forth in a number of prior cases, including, most definitively, in two previous Supreme Court decisions in *Turner Broadcasting Sys Inc v FCC*.[18] *Turner* concerned a First Amendment challenge to a federal law requiring cable television systems to devote a portion of their channels to the transmission of local broadcast television stations. In *Turner I*, the Court characterized those 'must-carry' rules as content-neutral because they 'impose burdens and confer benefits without reference to the content of the speech'.[19] In *Turner II*, the Court restated and applied the standard for intermediate scrutiny: 'A content neutral regulation will be sustained under the First Amendment if it advances important government interests unrelated to the suppression of free speech and does not burden substantially more speech than necessary to further those interests.'[20]

The *Eldred* petitioners trained their First Amendment challenge on the **6.21** CTEA's retrospective extension of copyright duration to copyrights in existing works. Under those provisions, even holders of copyrights in old works about to enter the public domain, like the Mickey Mouse cartoon

---

[18] *Turner Broadcasting Sys Inc v FCC* 512 US 622 (1994) ('*Turner I*'); *Turner Broadcasting Sys Inc v FCC* 520 US 180 (1997) ('*Turner II*').
[19] 512 US at 643.   [20] 520 US at 189.

character, were handed an additional twenty years of exclusive rights. The *Eldred* petitioners argued that the only important governmental interest previously recognized by the Supreme Court as sustaining copyright's speech restrictions—namely, providing incentives to authors to create original works—is irrelevant once a work has been created. As the petitioners put it: 'No matter what we offer Hawthorne or Hemingway or Gershwin, they will not produce anything more.'[21] The petitioners then argued that the other interests that the government advanced in support of the term extension, including providing greater income to authors' heirs, harmonizing US copyright law with that of other countries, and preserving old works, were illegitimate, hypothesized after the fact, or insufficiently substantial to justify the speech burden imposed.

(3) The Supreme Court's ruling

6.22 The Supreme Court did not reach the merits of the petitioners' First Amendment challenge because, like the lower courts, it treated copyright as essentially outside the First Amendment scheme. Indeed, the Court gave short shrift to the conflict between copyright and free speech. Most revealing of the Court's failure to grasp the First Amendment values at stake was its explanation why, in its view, *Turner v FCC* was inapposite to Eldred's challenge.

Distinguishing *Turner*

6.23 *Turner* was the primary case cited by the petitioners in support of their argument that the CTEA should be subject to intermediate scrutiny and should be held to fail to pass First Amendment muster. In rejecting the petitioners' First Amendment claim, the *Eldred* Court summarily dispensed with *Turner*, asserting that that decision 'bears little on copyright'. The Court reasoned that, in contrast to the 'must-carry' provisions at issue in *Turner*, the CTEA 'does not oblige anyone to reproduce another's speech against the carrier's will'. Justice Ginsburg's majority opinion stated that: 'The First Amendment securely protects the freedom to make—or decline to make— one's own speech; it bears less heavily when speakers assert the right to make

---

[21] Petitioners' Brief at 22 (in portion arguing that retrospective extension does not 'Promote the Progress of Science' as required by the Copyright Clause).

other people's speeches.'[22] While that statement stops short of the DC Circuit's blanket rejection of any cognizable First Amendment interest in copying or building upon others' copyrighted works, it runs squarely against established First Amendment precedent and wholly mischaracterizes the First Amendment values that copyright's continuing expansion lays bare.

To begin with, contrary to the Court's crabbed reading, neither *Turner* nor **6.24** other precedent applying intermediate scrutiny is merely about 'forced speech'. *Turner*, rather, stands for the broad proposition that the government may not generally target speech for restriction, even to serve legitimate, speech-enhancing, content-neutral goals, unless the speech restriction meets the test for intermediate scrutiny.[23]

Likewise with respect to the Court's blithe assertion that making 'other **6.25** people's speeches' is of secondary First Amendment import. Speakers often express themselves more fully and effectively when they impart words others have written than when they use words of their own creation. Hence, there are numerous instances in which making other people's speeches stands at the very heart of the First Amendment. Consider the 'Lysistrata Project', when hundreds of simultaneous readings of Aristophanes' play were held nationwide to protest against the Bush Administration's plans to go to war in Iraq. Or consider the public renderings of the Gettysburg Address to commemorate the first anniversary of September 11. Or street corner preachers who hand out copies of the Bible. Or the countless protesters, electoral candidates, and commencement speakers who have quoted liberally from Martin Luther King's ringing 'I Have a Dream.' Outside the copyright context, such choices regarding which of other people's speeches best conveys one's own message enjoy full First Amendment protection, and rightly so. As the Supreme Court has previously held:

---

[22] 537 US 186 (2003) 221. See also JC Ginsburg, 'Recorded Remarks in Panel Discussion: The Constitutionality of Copyright Term Extension: How Long is Too Long?' (2000) 18 Cardozo Arts & Entertainment L J 651, 701 ('The First Amendment is certainly about the freedom to make your own speech. Whether it is about the freedom to make other people's speeches again for them, I have some doubt').

[23] Until *Eldred*, no court viewed *Turner* as limited to forced speech. Indeed, while *Turner* itself involved must-carry, it merely restated the test for intermediate scrutiny enunciated in other cases, and courts have both applied intermediate scrutiny and cited *Turner* to review a variety of speech restrictions, most having nothing to do with forced speech. See NW Netanel, 'Locating Copyright Within the First Amendment Skein' (2001) 54 Stanford L Rev 1, 57.

Nor, under our precedent, does First Amendment protection require a speaker to generate, as an original matter, each item featured in the communication. . . . For that matter, the presentation of an edited compilation of speech generated by other persons is a staple of most newspapers' opinion pages, which, of course, fall squarely within the core of First Amendment security, as does even the simple selection of a paid noncommercial advertisement for inclusion in a daily paper.[24]

6.26 Similarly, and perhaps most disturbingly, the *Eldred* Court's 'right to make other people's speeches' characterization grossly belittles the First Amendment costs that copyright too often imposes.[25] Is the 'right to make other people's speeches' all that was at stake when a court enjoined as copyright infringement Alan Cranston's unexpurgated translation of *Mein Kampf,* designed to expose the official translation as a whitewash?[26] Was copyright infringement defendant Alice Randall merely repeating Margaret Mitchell's speech when Randall took aim at the racist stereotypes and idealized portrait of slavery in *Gone With the Wind* by writing a sequel from the viewpoint of a slave?[27] What about the City Pages newspaper that reprinted a racist fable from a police department newsletter to expose police racism?[28] The Church of Scientology critics who posted Church texts on the Internet to unveil Church foibles?[29] The Worldwide Church of God dissidents who circulated the Church founder's suppressed teachings to engage in their religious practice?[30] The thousands of participants in fan fiction sites who create and exchange sequels to their favourite television series?[31] The creator of the 'mashup', posted on the Internet on the eve of the Iraq war, featuring a recording of the song, *Endless Love,* played over television news images

---

[24] *Hurley v Irish-Am Gay, Lesbian and Bisexual Group* 515 US 557 (1995) 570 (holding that parade organizers have a cognizable First Amendment right to determine which organizations may or may not march in the parade).

[25] The *Eldred* Court said that purported copyright infringers have a weaker First Amendment claim than other speakers, not that they have no First Amendment claim. However, by characterizing that interest as merely one of 'mak[ing] other people's speeches', the Court veered dangerously close to the DC Circuit's blanket rejection of any cognizable First Amendment interest in copying or building upon others' copyrighted works.

[26] *Houghton Mifflin Co v Noram Publ'g Co* 28 F Supp 676 (SD NY, 1939).

[27] *SunTrust Bank v Houghton Mifflin Co* 268 F 3d 1257 (US Ct of Apps (11th Cir), 2001).

[28] *Belmore v City Pages Inc* 880 F Supp 673 (D Minn, 1995).

[29] *Religious Tech Ctr v Netcom On-Line comm Servs Inc* 923 F Supp 1231 (ND Ca, 1995).

[30] *Worldwide Church of God v Phila Church of God Inc* 227 F 3d 1110 (US Ct of Apps (9th Cir), 2000).

[31] On copyright's clash with fan fiction, see Rebecca Tushnet, 'Legal Fictions: Copyright, Fan Fiction, and a New Common Law' (1997) 17 Loy L A Ent L J 651.

carefully selected and edited to create the appearance of President Bush and Prime Minister Blair singing the song to one another? Swiss artist Christian Marclay, whose critically acclaimed *Video Quartet*, a four-channel audiovisual collage commissioned by the San Francisco Museum of Modern Art and the Grand Museum of Luxembourg, combines some 600 sound and film clips from over a hundred classic movies?[32]

From political to cultural to religious to artistic to whimsical, the speech that **6.27** copyright might suppress is as varied, and at times as profound (and creative), as any other speech. Even if the Court were correct that 'the right to make other people's speeches' receives lesser First Amendment protection, copyright often burdens far more than just that right. Contrary to the Court's suggestion that copyright merely prevents infringers from acting as free-riding conduits for other's expression—a suggestion that has, unfortunately, already been repeated in lower courts[33]—today's expanded copyright regularly chills creative and pointed criticism, commentary, artistic insight, and self-expression. Copyright's far-ranging speech burdens implicate the First Amendment no less than does government regulation of speech that stands outside the distended ambit of copyright holders' proprietary control.

Copyright's Constitutional pedigree

As an additional reason for absolving traditional copyright from First **6.28** Amendment review, the *Eldred* Court invoked copyright law's constitutional pedigree: 'The Copyright Clause and First Amendment were adopted close in time. This proximity indicates that, in the Framers' view, copyright's limited monopolies are compatible with free speech principles.' Like the making 'other people's speeches' calculus, that rationale has already been cited by a post-*Eldred* lower court in denying a First Amendment challenge to a provision of the Copyright Act.[34] And it, too, falls apart on even the most cursory examination.[35]

---

[32] G Allen, 'When Fans of Pricey Video Art Can Get It Free', *New York Times*, 17 August 2003, section 2, 25.

[33] See *In re Aimster Copyright Litigation* 334 F 3d 643 (US Ct of Apps (7th Cir), 2003) 656 (quoting Eldred's 'other people's speeches' statement).

[34] *In re Verizon Internet Services Inc* 240 F Supp 2d 24 (DDC, 2003) 42, reversed *Recording Industry Ass'n of America Inc v Verizon Internet Services Inc* 351 F 3d 1229 (US Ct of Apps (DC Cir), 2003).

[35] William Van Alstyne gives a more generous hearing to the argument that copyright

6.29 The Court's Constitutional pedigree argument is right about one thing: the fact of temporal proximity. The Constitution, including the clause empowering Congress to enact a copyright statute, was ratified only two years prior to the First Amendment and the rest of the Bill of Rights.[36] And for that matter, Congress enacted the first copyright statute the very same year it adopted the Bill of Rights.[37]

6.30 But what does that tell us? While it certainly suggests that the Framers could not have intended that copyright is per se unconstitutional, the mere fact of temporal proximity does not mean that whatever copyright statute Congress chooses to enact is immune from First Amendment scrutiny. The essential point of the First Amendment is to impose limits on powers that Congress would otherwise have under the Constitution. Indeed, the First Amendment has been repeatedly held to override legislation enacted by Congress pursuant to other enumerated powers under the Constitution, adopted with the very same temporal proximity to the First Amendment as the Copyright Clause. For example, the Constitution expressly empowers Congress to 'provide for the Punishment of counterfeiting'. But the Supreme Court has held that portions of statutes restricting the use of photographic reproductions of currency run afoul of the First Amendment.[38] Likewise, the Court has struck down on First Amendment grounds legislation, enacted pursuant to Congress' power under the Federal District Clause, prohibiting the public display of any flag, banner, or device on the grounds of the Supreme Court and legislation, enacted pursuant to the Post Office Clause, restricting mailings of communist advocacy.[39] The Court has also subjected to First Amendment scrutiny legislation enacted pursuant to Congress' enumerated power under the Commerce Clause, including, among others, the granting of a special trade mark right in the Olympic symbol and the must-carry rules at issue in

---

law's constitutional pedigree insulates it from First Amendment limitation, but still rejects it. WW Van Alstyne, 'Reconciling What the First Amendment Forbids With What the Copyright Clause Permits: A Summary Explanation and Review' (2003) 66 L & Contemporary Problems 225.

[36] The Constitution was ratified in 1789 and the Bill of Rights in 1791.

[37] The first copyright statute, the Act of 31 May 1790, ch 15, s 1, 1 Stat 124, 124, was enacted in 1790, the same year Congress adopted the Bill of Rights.

[38] *Regan v Time Inc* 468 US 641 (1984).

[39] *United States v Grace* 461 US 171 (1983) (Federal District Clause); *Lamont v Postmaster Gen* 381 US 301 (1965) 307 (Post Office Clause).

Turner.[40] Copyright law enjoys no greater Constitutional pedigree than any of those statutes, and all have been subjected to First Amendment review.

Nor does the Framers' understanding that 'copyright's limited monopolies **6.31** are compatible with free speech principles' tell us anything about whether the current Copyright Act comports with the First Amendment. Today's bloated copyright bears only scant resemblance to the narrowly-tailored short-term entitlement for which the first Congress provided. The 'limited monopolies' enacted by the first Congress entailed only the exclusive right to copy books, maps, and charts. They did not extend to other works and they prevented no one from preparing derivative works or publicly performing or displaying another person's original expression. And even those 'limited monopolies' lasted for at most twenty-eight years, not for well over a century, as typical of today's not-so-limited copyright.[41] The Framers would not recognize today's broad proprietary entitlement as 'copyright'. Whether they would find it compatible with their 'free speech principles' is an entirely open question.

Equally fatal to the Court's temporal proximity argument, First Amendment **6.32** doctrine has also changed radically since the Founding. Our modern First Amendment jurisprudence, largely a product of recent decades, is far more solicitous of free speech interests than were the Framers. It is inconceivable, for example, that the Alien and Sedition Acts or eighteenth-century libel law would today survive First Amendment muster. The Framers' 'free speech principles' bear no more resemblance to today's First Amendment doctrine than does the 1790 copyright statute to its current counterpart.

If brought to the test, the truly 'limited monopolies' that the Framers **6.33** envisioned—the short-term, narrow copyright of their day—would most probably meet current First Amendment strictures. But the First Amendment

---

[40] *San Francisco Arts & Athletics Inc v United States Olympic Committee* 483 US 522 (1987). See also *Thompson v Western States Medical Center* 535 US 357 (2002) (holding that a prohibition on consumer advertising of 'compounded drugs', enacted pursuant to Congress' power under the Commerce Clause, is forbidden by the First Amendment). The Supreme Court has also held that the First Amendment restricts Congress's power to enact legislation under its enumerated spending power. *Legal Servs Corp v Valasquez* 531 US 533 (2001) (striking down under the First Amendment a congressionally mandated restriction on the use of grants provided under the spending power for certain legal services by recipient organizations).

[41] The 1790 copyright statute provided only for an exclusive right to copy books, maps, and charts, lasting for 14 years unless renewed for a second 14 year term. See Act of 31 May 1790, ch 15, § 1, 1 Stat 124, 124.

compatibility of the CTEA and other recent Copyright Act amendments is an entirely different question. And the fact that the Copyright Clause and First Amendment were ratified more or less contemporaneously, at a time in which both copyright and free speech rights were a pale shadow of what they are today, bears not at all on how that question should be answered.

Copyright's free speech benefits

6.34 Following its invocation of the Framers' view of copyright's compatibility with free speech principles, the Court rehearsed another old saw of copyright's First Amendment immunity, the notion that copyright's purported role as 'the engine of free expression' excuses any speech burdens copyright imposes. Like the other rationales for copyright's First Amendment immunity, the copyright-as-engine argument runs aground on the shoals of empirical examination and prevailing First Amendment doctrine. As I have discussed elsewhere, copyright's free speech benefits are considerably more attenuated than is often assumed.[42] One cannot say with confidence that copyright's speech benefits even outweigh its costs. Certainly those benefits are not so overwhelming as to obviate any need for First Amendment scrutiny.

6.35 Moreover, even if copyright does yield important free speech benefits, it does not follow that copyright thus ought to escape First Amendment scrutiny. As Mark Lemley and Eugene Volokh have pointed out, much speech-burdening regulation, ranging from defamation law to campaign finance restrictions to time, place, or manner regulation, may be characterized as speech enhancing.[43] But the fact that speech-burdening regulation might also enhance some speech does not generally absolve the regulation of First Amendment scrutiny. Indeed, the Supreme Court recognized that the must-carry rules at issue in *Turner* aimed to achieve two important free speech objectives: to 'preserve access to free television programming' for those without cable and to promote 'the widespread dissemination of information from a multiplicity of sources'.[44] Yet the *Turner* Court exercised First Amendment review without even considering that the must-carry rules' free speech goals might somehow reduce

---

[42] NW Netanel, *Copyright's Paradox: Property in Expression/Freedom of Expression* (Oxford: OUP, forthcoming).

[43] See MA Lemley and E Volokh, 'Freedom of Speech and Injunctions in Intellectual Property Cases' (1998) 48 Duke L J 147, 187–8.

[44] See *Turner Broad Sys Inc v FCC* 512 US 622 (1994) 646, 662–4.

the need for First Amendment scrutiny. As is routinely the case when courts consider regulation that burdens some speech to enhance other speech or to promote widespread speech benefits, the *Turner* Court asked whether the must-carry rules 'burden substantially more speech than necessary to further those interests'.

So at the very least, the *Eldred* Court's 'engine of free expression' argument is **6.36** sharply out of step with other First Amendment doctrine. The Court's notion that First Amendment scrutiny is less warranted because copyright law broadly aims to promote speech provides yet another example of copyright's peculiarly privileged status.

Copyright's internal free speech safety valves

Finally, the *Eldred* Court emphasized that 'copyright law contains built-in **6.37** First Amendment accommodations', particularly the idea–expression dichotomy and fair use doctrine. The widespread judicial notion that copyright's internal free speech safety valves substitute for First Amendment scrutiny falls apart on two counts.

First, as already noted, given changes in copyright doctrine, copyright's in- **6.38** ternal safety valves have become woefully inadequate to that task. At the very least, the notoriously unpredictable nature of the idea–expression dichotomy and fair use privilege induce considerable speaker self-censorship.

The *Eldred* Court's Panglossian rejoinder that 'every idea, theory, and fact **6.39** in a copyrighted work becomes instantly available for public exploitation at the moment of publication' misses the point so apparent in the Cranston, Randall, and other examples noted in paragraph 6.26. A speaker's ability to copy, convey, quote, or build upon a copyrighted work's particular words and images can be no less critical to the communication of her message than is access to the work's ideas. In other First Amendment jurisprudence, it is axiomatic that speakers must sometimes use particular locution in order to make their point. As the Supreme Court has long recognized, 'we cannot indulge in the facile assumption that one can forbid particular words without running a substantial risk of suppressing ideas in the process.'[45] Neither the idea–expression dichotomy nor fair use privilege were of assistance to Alan

---

[45] *Cohen v California* 403 US 15 (1971) 26.

Cranston or the Worldwide Church of God dissidents. That Alice Randall's sequel was ultimately accorded fair use protection is, as we will shortly see, the exception that proves the need for greater First Amendment intervention. In sum, even if the built-in safeguards of some statutory regimes might sometimes substitute for First Amendment scrutiny, copyright's cannot.

6.40 Secondly, the presence of internal free speech safeguards does not ordinarily obviate the need for First Amendment scrutiny. As we have seen, courts regularly apply the First Amendment to ensure the adequacy of such safeguards in other areas of law. First Amendment doctrine generally recognizes that 'the legal system is imperfect and mandates the formulation of legal rules that reflect our preference for errors made in favor of free speech.'[46] The talisman of copyright's purported 'built-in First Amendment accommodations' cannot justify the failure to do so with respect to copyright. With copyright law no less than with trade mark rights, the right of publicity, defamation, the right of privacy, and other private right regimes that have built-in free speech safety valves, the First Amendment should impose the procedural and substantive constraints required to avoid 'intolerable self-censorship' and the undue suppression of 'speech that matters'.[47]

C. First Amendment Intervention after *Eldred*

6.41 Despite its tepid rejection of copyright's categorical immunity, *Eldred* leaves room for First Amendment intervention in copyright law in two contexts. The first involves copyright legislation that does alter the 'traditional contours of copyright protection'. The second concerns copyright's internal free speech safeguards.

(1) Altering the traditional contours of copyright protection

6.42 *Eldred* holds that no First Amendment scrutiny is necessary when 'Congress has not altered the traditional contours of copyright protection.' That implies that First Amendment scrutiny might be warranted when Congress *does* alter copyright's traditional contours. The decision gives little indication of what

---

[46] See F Schauer, 'Fear, Risk and the First Amendment: Unraveling the "Chilling Effect"' (1978) 58 Boston U L Rev 685, 688 (discussing the 'chilling effect doctrine').
[47] *Gertz v Robert Welch Inc* 418 US 323 (1974) 340–1.

sorts of legislation the Court might view as altering the 'traditional contours of copyright protection'. However, one recent Copyright Act amendment would appear readily to meet that description: the anti-circumvention provisions of the Digital Millennium Copyright Act (or DMCA).

The DMCA's anti-circumvention provisions are designed to secure the effect-   **6.43** iveness of encryption and other technological measures used to prevent unlicensed access to and uses of copyrighted works. The DMCA does this in two ways. First, it contains an access prohibition, which forbids individuals from circumventing technological measures that prevent unlicensed access to a copyrighted work.[48] Secondly, the Act contains device prohibitions, which proscribe the manufacture and trafficking of devices, technology, and services that are primarily designed to assist users in circumventing technological measures that (1) prevent unlicensed access to a copyrighted work,[49] or (2) prevent unlicensed copying or other uses of such content that would infringe the copyright holder's rights.[50] Although the DMCA's ultimate purpose is to assist copyright holders in exerting greater control over their works, the Act focuses on access and copy control technology, not on proscribing or penalizing acts of infringement per se. Accordingly, as the House Committee on Commerce report on the amendment recognized, the DMCA's anti-circumvention provisions 'have little, if anything, to do with copyright law', and 'represent an unprecedented departure into the zone of what might be called paracopyright'.[51]

Indeed, the 'paracopyright' provided for under the DMCA expands content   **6.44** provider control over content significantly beyond that which has traditionally obtained under the Copyright Act. First, the DMCA does not merely secure technological measures designed to prevent copyright infringement. It also enables content providers effectively to control *access* to content, a prerogative not included among copyright holders' exclusive rights.[52] Secondly,

---

[48] See 17 USC 1201(a)(1)(A) (2001).   [49] Ibid, s 1201(a)(1)(E) (2001).
[50] Ibid, s 1201(b) (2001).   [51] HR Rep No 105–551, pt 2, 24 (1998).
[52] In fact, the DMCA does not directly prohibit the act of circumventing technological measures designed to prevent copyright infringement. The rationale for this absence of direct prohibition is that the one who circumvents such controls will be liable for copyright infringement (unless the use is privileged under the Copyright Act). However, the DMCA's trafficking prohibition makes it very difficult for individuals to circumvent technological measures designed to prevent copyright infringement as well as measures that control access because most people can't circumvent without relying on a third-party-provided device or service that enables them to do so.

in many cases, the DMCA's access and device prohibitions effectively apply even to technological measures controlling material that is not protected by copyright. For example, if a content provider deploys a technological measure to control access to an electronic database containing a copyrighted work, the DMCA makes it unlawful to circumvent that technological measure even if the database also contains many public domain works. The same is true where the content provider has appended minimal copyrightable expression to an essentially public domain work (such as adding a new two-paragraph introduction to a Shakespeare play). Finally, the DMCA's access and device prohibitions have been held to apply even when circumvention is needed to use a copyrighted work in a manner, such as fair use, that is permitted under copyright law. The DMCA expressly preserves the fair use privilege to engage in conduct that would infringe traditional copyright.[53] But thus far, courts have universally interpreted the Act to mean that fair use is unavailable as a defence to violation of the access and device prohibitions even when individuals need to circumvent in order to engage in fair use.[54]

6.45 Congress was not unaware that the DMCA's sweeping prohibitions might raise First Amendment concerns by impairing the availability of information and public domain expression and by blocking non-infringing uses of copyrighted works. The House Committee on Commerce report on the DMCA, indeed, warns of the development of a 'legal framework that would inexorably create a pay-per-use society' and refers to testimony that '[t]hese newly created rights will dramatically diminish public access to information.'[55] Yet, as its cursory treatment of fair use illustrates, the DMCA only pays lip service to these concerns.[56]

6.46 As I have argued elsewhere, the anti-circumvention provisions should not survive *Turner* scrutiny (or, for that matter, any other formulation of intermediate scrutiny that might be applied following *Eldred*'s seeming narrowing

---

[53] Section 1201(c)(1) provides that nothing in the anti-circumvention provisions 'shall affect rights, remedies, limitations, or defences to copyright infringement, including fair use, under this title'.

[54] See, eg, *Universal City Studios Inc v Corley* 273 F 3d 429 (US Ct of Apps (2nd Cir), 2001) 443–4.

[55] See HR Rep No 105–551, pt 2, 26 (1998).

[56] The DMCA's tepid protection for free speech concerns is limned in more detail in: NW Netanel, 'Locating Copyright Within the First Amendment Skein' (2001) 54 Stanford L Rev 1.

of *Turner's* applicability to 'forced speech').[57] The DMCA provisions quite
clearly protrude beyond the traditional contours of copyright law. Subjecting
them to heightened scrutiny exposes both their internal contradictions and
their capacious, unduly speech-burdening scope.

(2) Copyright's traditional free speech safeguards

Eldred leaves room for the First Amendment to play a role within copyright's   **6.47**
traditional contours as well. The *Eldred* Court appended what might be a
significant footnote to its statement that First Amendment scrutiny is unnecessary when Congress legislates within copyright's traditional contours.
The footnote proclaims that in both facial challenges to copyright legislation
and First Amendment defences to copyright infringement claims, 'it is appropriate to construe copyright's internal safeguards to accommodate First
Amendment concerns.' In the context of the facial challenge in *Eldred*, the
footnote reiterates a cardinal rule of judicial restraint. Courts should not
reach constitutional issues if they can interpret a statute to eliminate doubts
regarding its constitutionality.[58] But the footnote also says something about
the way in which copyright's internal safeguards should generally be construed. It suggests that courts should interpret and define their scope in a
manner that comports with First Amendment concerns.[59] In other words,
contrary to the prior suggestion of some commentators and lower courts,[60]
copyright's internal safeguards do have constitutional import. Even if the

---

[57] NW Netanel, *Copyright's Paradox: Property in Expression/Freedom of Expression* (Oxford:
OUP, forthcoming).

[58] The footnote quotes from the Court's statement of that rule in an earlier case: 'It is . . .
incumbent upon us to read the statute to eliminate [serious constitutional] doubts so long
as such a reading is not plainly contrary to the intent of Congress', quoting *United States v
X-Citement Video Inc* 513 US 64 (1994) 78.

[59] See *Video Pipeline v Buena Vista Home Entertainment* 342 F 3d 191 (US Ct of Apps
(3rd Cir), 2003) 205 (citing *Eldred* for the proposition that courts' enforcement of copyright
should be guided by First Amendment concerns); cf *New Kids on the Block v New Am Publ'g
Inc* 971 F 2d 302 (US Ct of Apps (9th Cir), 1992) 305 (after district court granted summary
judgment to trade mark and right of publicity defendants on First Amendment grounds, the
9th Circuit construed the relevant statutes to affirm that result in order to avoid reaching a
constitutional issue).

[60] See, eg, *Universal City Studios Inc v Corley* 273 F 3d 429 (US Ct of Apps (2nd Cir),
2001) 458 ('we note that the Supreme Court has never held that fair use is constitutionally
required').

First Amendment imposes no external constraints on copyright, First Amendment principles must animate our understanding and application of copyright law. Indeed, only by employing that First Amendment metric can we take seriously the *Eldred* Court's proposition that copyright's traditional safeguards actually serve to protect First Amendment values.

6.48 The Eleventh Circuit's decision in *The Wind Done Gone* case, issued just over a year before the Supreme Court decided *Eldred*, presents a laudable example of that approach. The Eleventh Circuit reversed the district court's preliminary injunction forbidding distribution of Alice Randall's acerbic *Gone With the Wind* sequel. In so doing, the Eleventh Circuit repeatedly invoked the First Amendment as a lodestar for interpreting copyright law.[61] Copyright law, the court emphasized, must be construed to incorporate First Amendment values and comport with First Amendment strictures. The fair use privilege in particular, the court underscored, has 'constitutional significance as a guarantor to access and use for First Amendment purposes'.[62] Accordingly, in conducting fair use analysis, 'we must remain cognizant of the First Amendment protections interwoven into copyright law.'[63] Applying that First Amendment construction, the Eleventh Circuit concluded that Randall was likely to prevail on her fair use claim and that 'the issuance of the injunction was at odds with the shared principles of the First Amendment and the copyright law, acting as a prior restraint on speech because the public had not had access to Randall's ideas or viewpoint in the form of expression that she chose.'[64]

6.49 The *Eldred* footnote and Eleventh Circuit's ruling regarding *The Wind Done Gone* suggests a number of ways that the First Amendment could and should be brought to bear to revive the fair use doctrine. Here follow three brief examples: the first substantive, the second involving burden of proof, and the third involving remedy.

---

[61] *SunTrust Bank v Houghton Mifflin Co* 268 F 3d 1257 (US Ct of Apps (11th Cir), 2001). The Eleventh initially reversed the district court in a per curiam opinion that applied the First Amendment as an external constraint on copyright. It held that the preliminary injunction was an unconstitutional prior restraint on speech. See *SunTrust Bank v Houghton Mifflin Co* 252 F 3d 1165 (US Ct of Apps (11th Cir), 2001). Subsequently, the Eleventh Circuit vacated its per curiam ruling and substituted a more comprehensive opinion that, rather than relying entirely on First Amendment prior restraint doctrine, interprets copyright law in light of the First Amendment.

[62] Ibid 1260.   [63] Ibid 1265.   [64] Ibid 1277.

First, courts should give renewed weight in fair use analysis to the defendant's **6.50**
critical expression and purpose. Copyright holder control should not extend to
preventing reformulations that serve as highly effective critical commentary
on the original. And this constraint should apply even where, as with Alan
Cranston's unauthorized *Mein Kampf*, the defendant's work competes in the
market for derivative works based on the original work.

Secondly, once the defendant shows a colourable claim of fair use, the burden **6.51**
should pass to the copyright holder to prove that the defendant has copied
more than necessary for effective speech and that the defendant's use is likely
to harm the actual or potential market for the copyright holder's work.
Today's market-centred fair use doctrine places the defendant in the onerous
position of proving a negative: that the allegedly infringing use—and other
possible uses like it—will not harm even a market, including a market for
derivative works, that the copyright holder has no concrete plans to exploit.
That formidable burden unduly chills speech and is inconsistent with First
Amendment goals.[65] It also runs squarely against the well-established rule of
First Amendment doctrine that the burden of proof as to constitutionally
relevant facts—such as the veracity of an allegedly libellous statement—must
be placed on those who would stifle or punish the speaker, not the speaker
herself.[66] In the absence of such a rule, as is sadly the case with today's fair use
doctrine, 'the possibility of mistaken fact finding—inherent in all litigation—will create the danger that the legitimate utterance will be penalized'
and that speakers will engage in broad self-censorship in order to avoid that
risk.[67]

Thirdly, where the defendant presents a colourable but unsuccessful claim of **6.52**
fair use, courts should generally award damages in the amount of a reasonable
licence fee instead of enjoining the use. In that manner, defendants will be
better able to convey their message so long as they pay what is in effect a
compulsory licence fee set by the court.

---

[65] Ibid 1290, n 3, stating that, in contrast to recent precedent, 'fair use should be considered an affirmative *right* under the 1976 Act, rather than merely an affirmative defence,
as it is defined in the Act as a use that is not a violation of copyright.'

[66] See E Volokh, 'Freedom of Speech and Intellectual Property: Some Thoughts After
Eldred, 44 Liquormart, and *Bartnicki*' (2003) 40 Houston L Rev 697.

[67] *Speiser v Randall* 357 US 513 (1958) 526.

6.53 To construe the fair use doctrine 'to accommodate First Amendment concerns' in that fashion need not work a radical change in traditional copyright doctrine. First, the defendant's critical, transformative use, including both modified expression and independent purpose, once weighed heavily in favour of fair use.[68] Only recently, the importance of that factor has been eroded as courts have denied that even works communicating vast new expression or possessing a significant independent purpose are 'transformative'.[69] Secondly, the question of which party has the burden of proof on fair use was unsettled until the relatively recent triumph of the market-centred approach. In fact, even today, some courts hold that when the defendant's use is non-commercial, the copyright holder has the burden of proving market harm, the important fourth fair use factor.[70] Finally, the award of damages rather than injunctive relief also lies well within the parameters of judicial discretion. Indeed, as the Eleventh Circuit noted, the Supreme Court itself has repeatedly suggested that given copyright's paramount goal of stimulating 'the creation and publication of edifying matter',[71] in cases of colourable but failed claims of fair use, courts should award damages rather than grant injunctive relief—in effect, issuing a compulsory licence to further the 'strong public interest in the publication of the secondary work'.[72] Explicitly invoking First Amendment values would simply provide a stronger basis to overcome lower courts' reluctance to follow that suggestion.

6.54 Courts are understandably disinclined to adopt rules that would require them to entertain First Amendment defences to individual copyright infringement actions. As Judge Posner recently interposed, 'Copyright law and the principles of equitable relief are quite complicated enough without the super-

---

[68] See DL Zimmerman, 'The More Things Change, The Less They Seem "Transformed": Some Reflections On Fair Use' (1998) 46 J of the Copyright Society of the USA 251, 254–7 (describing development of 'productive' and 'transformative' use factor).

[69] See, eg, *Castle Rock Entm't Inc v Carol Publ'g Group Inc* 150 F 3d 132 (US Ct of Apps (2nd Cir), 1998) 146 (holding that a multiple choice trivia quiz regarding the television series *Seinfeld* is not a 'transformative use'); see also Zimmerman, ibid 358–60 (discussing current doctrinal incoherence of defining 'transformative use' for purposes of fair use analysis).

[70] See, eg, *Princeton Univ Press v Mich Document Servs Inc* 99 F 3d 1381 (US Ct of Apps (6th Cir), 1996) 1385–6.

[71] *Campbell v Acuff-Rose Music Inc* 510 US 569 (1994) 578 n 10 (quoting PN Leval, 'Toward a Fair Use Standard' (1990) 103 Harv L Rev 1105, 1134). The Supreme Court reiterated this point in *New York Times v Tasini* 429 US 298 (2001).

[72] Ibid (quoting Leval, ibid 1132).

imposition of First Amendment case law on them.'[73] But, as the *Eldred* footnote suggests and the Eleventh Circuit has demonstrated, copyright can be construed to 'accommodate First Amendment concerns' without recognizing First Amendment defences or adding a layer of First Amendment analysis to typical copyright infringement cases. First Amendment principles, to paraphrase the Eleventh Circuit, are already interwoven into the history and framework of copyright law. To remain cognizant of those principles requires only that courts reinvigorate copyright's existing free speech safeguards, not undermine or fundamentally modify traditional copyright doctrine. And, as they have done in other areas courts could bring the First Amendment to bear by implementing specific and tightly focused substantive, evidentiary, and remedial rules designed to protect free speech without requiring a case-by-case adjudication of First Amendment principles.

D. Conclusion

The judicial immunization of traditional copyright from First Amendment **6.55** scrutiny is a peculiar and pernicious anomaly. In *Eldred*, the Supreme Court largely perpetuated that anomaly, at least with respect to imposing external First Amendment constraints on traditional copyright. Nevertheless, *Eldred* leaves open considerable room for First Amendment intervention in copyright law. Copyright Act amendments, such as the DMCA anti-circumvention provisions, that extend copyright holder prerogatives beyond copyright's traditional contours are precisely the type of content-neutral speech regulation that, even following *Eldred*, should be subject to First Amendment scrutiny. As *Eldred* suggests, courts should also 'construe copyright's internal safeguards to accommodate First Amendment concerns'. Today's palsied safety valves too often intolerably exacerbate the dangers of self-censorship. Following the Supreme Court's suggestion, courts should reinvigorate copyright's safeguards in light of First Amendment strictures. Among other possible applications, they should mandate greater leeway for critical uses of copyrighted works. They should also require that copyright holders bear the burden of disproving the elements of fair use and should award damages, rather than injunctive relief, where the user raises a colourable, but unsuccessful claim of fair use.

---

[73] *In re Aimster Copyright Litig* 334 F 3d 643 (7th Cir, 2003) 656.

7

COPYRIGHT, THE PUBLIC INTEREST, AND FREEDOM OF SPEECH: A UK COPYRIGHT LAWYER'S PERSPECTIVE

Gerald Dworkin

The traditional approach of most UK copyright lawyers and courts to the **7.01** relationship between copyright, the public interest, and free speech was simple:[1] copyright confers certain statutory exclusive rights upon the copyright owner, including the right to prevent copying the whole or a substantial part of a work; the only exceptions or limitations to the copyright owners'

---

[1] For further exploration of the relationship, see G Davies, *Copyright and the Public Interest* (2nd edn, London: Sweet & Maxwell, 2002).

rights are specific defences, for example, certain types of 'fair dealing'[2] which are expressly provided for in the Copyright Act; there are no express public interest or freedom of speech or expression defences; ergo there is no issue. Few would have thought that there was any merit in the argument that since some of the specific defences indirectly reflected wider values, such as freedom of speech, there was a wider applicable principle inherent in the Act or in the legal concept of copyright.

7.02 This chapter provides an introductory overview of the relationship between copyright, the public interest, and free speech from the perspective of a UK copyright lawyer.[3]

A. Contrasting Approaches to Copyright

7.03 No copyright system, even of those most favourably disposed to authors, confers absolute rights.[4] It would be against the public interest to do so. Copyright and the public interest are inextricably linked. All copyright systems seek to strike an appropriate balance between the rights of the copyright owner and the public interest. Hence, some copyright provisions are part of the fabric of all copyright codes: the copyright term which is of limited, as opposed to perpetual, duration; the principle that copyright is a right to prevent only unauthorized copying, not independent creation; and the idea–expression dichotomy which ensures that copyright does not result in monopolies over ideas or information. Then, each copyright system tends to contain a set of statutory exceptions and limitations, what may be described as 'internal controls'. These (in particular, private use in many civil law systems and fair use or fair dealing in many common law systems) all strive to achieve the right balance of interests, whether between authors and the public, authors and holders of neighbouring or related rights, producers

---

[2] Copyright, Designs and Patents Act (CDPA) 1988 (UK) ss 29, 30. See also the interesting, but narrow, right in s 58 for journalists and reporters to reproduce notes made of certain types of spoken words.

[3] For more detailed analysis of certain issues raised in this chapter, see chs 8 and 9 below.

[4] There have been those who have argued, unconvincingly, to the contrary. For example, an early commentator on French copyright law advanced the view that 'authors are the absolute owners of their work, both before and after publication. Their property right is, like all other property rights, transmissible, perpetual and inviolable.' See J Ginsburg, 'A Tale of Two Copyrights', in B Sherman and A Strowel (eds), *Of Authors and Origins* (Oxford: OUP, 1994), 148, referring to Renouard, a natural lawyer.

and the public, or copyright producing countries in the developed world and copyright user countries in the developing world, and so on. Their justification is the 'public interest', a term which embraces many different social, economic, cultural, and practical reasons for ensuring that others may use copyright material without necessarily having to seek consent from rightholders or, in some cases, without having to pay for such use.

There are different types of copyright regimes. Their different rationales have **7.04** influenced the slightly different ways in which the major copyright systems have developed. Thus, copyright systems concentrating primarily upon strong and expanding rights for authors tend to express exceptions and limitations to them precisely and narrowly. Those concerned also to ensure that strong and expanding rights do not operate against the public interest tend to provide additional broad exceptions or limitations.

The great civil law codes focused upon the natural personal and property **7.05** rights of authors, the term 'droit d'auteur' carrying strong emotive connotations. So, it is not surprising that the Preamble to the seminal international copyright treaty, the Berne Convention, reflects this emphasis: '[The] countries of the Union, [are] . . . equally animated by the desire to protect, in as effective and uniform a manner as possible, the rights of authors in their literary and artistic works.' The text of the Convention, too, in stressing authors' rights perhaps paid less attention to the necessary balance between authors' and other interests.

US copyright law is quite different. It is clearly based upon the public interest. **7.06** Those responsible for producing the current US copyright code emphasized that the primary objective of copyright law is not to reward the author, but rather to secure for the public the benefits derived from the author's labours. Copyright statutes must serve public, not private, ends. Within limits, the author's interests coincide with those of the public. Where they conflict, the public interest must prevail. The ultimate task of the copyright law is to strike a fair balance between the author's right to control the dissemination of his works and the public interest in fostering their widest dissemination.[5]

---

[5] See *Eldred v Ashcroft* 537 US 186 (2003) per Breyer J, cf per Ginsburg J at n 18. Also see Report of the Register of Copyrights on the General Revision of the US Copyright Law, 87th Congress, 1st Session, July 1961.

7.07 Thus, the Berne Convention, which champions the author, and US copyright law, which puts the public interest first, seem theoretically to be at opposite extremes, although for the most part the systems are similar in practice. In recent times, however, more attention is being paid to this relationship, particularly in international instruments.

7.08 The World Trade Organization Agreement on Trade-Related Aspects of Intellectual Property Rights (TRIPs), which is essentially one part of a multilateral trade agreement, acknowledges a centrist position, albeit rather obscurely: 'The protection and enforcement of intellectual property rights should contribute to the promotion of technological innovation and to the transfer and dissemination of technology, to the mutual advantage of producers and users of technological knowledge and in a manner conducive to social and economic welfare, and to a balance of rights and obligations.'[6]

7.09 Perhaps more significant, however, are the express references to a balance between authors' rights and the public interest in recent copyright conventions. The recitals to the WIPO Copyright Treaty 1996, which, in a sense, is an updating revision of the Berne Convention, reads: 'Desiring to develop and maintain the protection of rights of authors in their literary and artistic works in a manner as effective and uniform as possible. . . . Recognising the need to maintain a balance between the rights of authors and the larger public interest, particularly education, research and access to information, as reflected in the Berne Convention.'[7]

7.10 From time to time, changes are made to copyright law which affect the balance of the relevant interests. Today, there is turmoil in the copyright world. Just as the copyright system was feeling more comfortable in its handling of computer programs, other digital technologies came on the scene; and copyright has been forced to grapple with multimedia, internet, and the countless legal issues created in cyberspace. Stronger and more comprehensive exclusive rights have been created to cover most uses of copyright material. This has led to a copyright backlash; more people are questioning whether the drive for stronger rights is overstepping the mark and weakening important social, economic, and cultural interests; they maintain that the

---

[6] Trade-Related Aspects of Intellectual Property Rights, Art 7.
[7] See also similar provisions in the Preamble to the WIPO Performances and Phonograms Treaty 1996.

public domain is shrinking, and that there should be more, not less, opportunity for the public, in pursuit of education, news, culture, and other expression, to utilize freely the creative works of others.

This, in turn, has led to a somewhat uneven approach to the 'copyright balance' in modern copyright laws: on the one hand, legislative devices have been introduced to protect authors against excessive watering down of their strong exclusive rights by overbroad exceptions or limitations; on the other, judicial developments in some countries have tended to widen judicial discretion which may be exercised against the interests of the copyright owner. **7.11**

B. Protecting Authors: The 'Three-Step Test'

A new factor has been brought into play to ensure that strong authors' rights are not eroded too far by overbroad exceptions or limitations. It is the so-called 'three-step test', which first appeared, in relation to the reproduction right, as Article 9.2 of the 1967 Stockholm Revision of the Berne Convention, but which did not acquire real prominence until its appearance as Article 13 of the TRIPs Agreement and then in other international, regional, and national legislation.[8] **7.12**

Article 13 of the TRIPs Agreement provides that 'Members shall confine limitations or exceptions to exclusive rights to certain special cases which do not conflict with a normal exploitation of the work and do not unreasonably prejudice the legitimate interests of the right holder.' The three steps, against which all exceptions to copyright are to be judged, are first, that exceptions must be confined to 'certain special cases'; secondly, that they must not 'conflict with a normal exploitation' of the work; and, thirdly, that they must not 'unreasonably prejudice the legitimate interests' of the copyright owner. **7.13**

The scope of this provision was examined by a TRIPs panel in 2000 which upheld a complaint by the EC against the USA that a newly introduced exemption[9] from copyright liability for the public performance of music **7.14**

---

[8] See, eg, the EC Directive 2001/29/EC on Copyright and Relative Rights in the Information Society, Art 5.5.

[9] Copyright Act (US) s 110(5).

played from radio and television in certain types of bars and restaurants was incompatible, inter alia, with Article 13. Whatever 'public interest' consideration led to widening the copyright exemption was held wanting in the balancing exercise.

7.15 In spite of the vagueness of its language, the three-step test does permit a flexible approach in seeking an appropriate balance between the property rights of authors and others and the public interest.

C. Strengthening Users' Rights

7.16 Notwithstanding the three-step test and other provisions protecting the rights of authors and owners of copyright, there are other provisions which emphasize the rights of users. For example, there has been considerable judicial and legislative activity concerned with the scope of copyright protection for compilations and databases. Both in the USA and Europe, copyright protection was denied for so-called 'sweat of the brow' databases. In the USA, the Supreme Court decision in *Feist*[10] can be regarded as a clear public policy reason for limiting the scope of copyright protection for non-original databases. In Europe, the Database Directive[11] seemed rather to be a shift in the type of protection for certain 'sweat of the brow' databases from copyright to a *sui generis* database right. Nevertheless, it would appear that there can no longer be copyright protection for non-original databases in any WTO country as an obverse consequence of the declaration in Article 10.2 of the TRIPs Agreement: 'Compilations of data or other material, whether in machine readable or other form, which by reason of the selection or arrangement of their contents constitute intellectual creations shall be protected as such. Such protection, which shall not extend to the data or material itself, shall be without prejudice to any copyright subsisting in the data or material itself.'

---

[10] *Feist v Rural Telephones* 111 S Ct 1282 (1991).
[11] Directive 96/9/EC of the European Parliament and of the Council of 11 March 1996 on the legal protection of databases.

D. Expansion of the Scope of the US S 107 'Fair Use' Defence

Of greater relevance to the current discussion, though, is the 'fair use' de- **7.17**
fence. Many common law countries have a defence which involves essentially a balancing of the exclusive rights of the copyright owner with public
interest considerations. This defence, known as 'fair use' in the USA and 'fair
dealing' in the United Kingdom and other Commonwealth jurisdictions, was
judicially created and developed. It was not put into statutory form until
1911 (United Kingdom) and 1976 (USA) and the approaches are quite
different.

The UK 'fair dealing' provision is narrower and applies in three special cases: **7.18**
for the purposes of 'research or private study', 'criticism or review', and 'reporting current events'.[12] There is no statutory guidance as to what 'fair dealing'
amounts to, but, as in the USA, the courts have developed a rich jurisprudence as to its scope and limitations.

The US 'fair use' provision in s 107 of the Copyright Act, by way of contrast, **7.19**
comprises a very broad exemption accompanied by guidelines:

> the fair use of a copyright work for purposes such as criticism, comment, news
> reporting, teaching . . . scholarship or research is not an infringement of copy-
> right.

> In determining [fair use] the factors to be considered shall include—(1) the
> purpose and character of the use, including whether such use is of a com-
> mercial nature or is for nonprofit educational purposes; (2) the nature of the
> copyrighted work; (3) the amount and substantiality of the portion used in
> relation to the copyrighted work as a whole; and (4) the effect of the use upon
> the potential market for or value of the copyrighted work.

> The fact that a work is not published shall not itself bar a finding of fair use if
> such finding is made upon consideration of all of the above factors.[13]

---

[12] See now, CDPA 1988, ss 29, 30. Curiously, authors are subject to greater fair dealing
encroachments than other right-holders, since research and private study only apply to literary,
dramatic, musical, and artistic works.
[13] This sentence was added in 1992 to clear up uncertainty in relation to the application of
the section to cases involving copying of unpublished works.

When the Act was passed, it was made quite clear that the section was 'intended to restate the [existing] judicial doctrine of fair use, not to change, narrow or enlarge it in any way'.[14] However, it was also acknowledged that there was scope for future development; something which is now the subject of controversy in the digital environment.

7.20 The US fair use defence has been subjected to countless analyses; the law reports and law journals are replete with sophisticated discussions of the nature of the defence and of the application of the various statutory guidelines. Its virtues are constantly trumpeted, and with good reason. In weighing the competing interests of the author and the public, economic factors have always been important, although the weight attached to them has varied from time to time. Clearly, where a defence of fair use would not unduly affect an author's economic interests, the defence is easier to sustain.[15] However, in more recent years there has been a tendency to favour the defence even in situations where the rights affected have economic significance. The development of the so-called 'fifth factor' of transformative use whereby parodies and other derivative works can sometimes be excused, notwithstanding the clear commercialism of the defendant's activities and the economic damage done to the right-holder, illustrates how important the courts regard these activities, notwithstanding their use of protected copyright works.[16] Fair use has been described as having 'evolved to guard against the possibility that the author's right of control over his works could defeat rather than serve the public interest in dissemination'.[17] Although the Report preceding the US Copyright Act stressed that the fair use defence should not tilt the balance

---

[14] HR Report on the Copyright Act No 94 at 66. There was no intention 'to freeze the doctrine in statute, especially during a period of rapid technological change. Beyond a very broad statutory explanation of what fair use is and of some of the criteria applicable to it, the courts must be free to adapt the doctrine to particular situations on a case-by-case basis.' House Report.

[15] 'There are many situations in which copyright restrictions would inhibit dissemination, with little or no benefit to the author. And the interests of authors must yield to the public welfare where they conflict.' Register's Report on the General Revision of US Copyright Law 1961.

[16] P Leval, 'Towards a Fair Use Standard' (1990) 103 Harv L Rev 1105; P Leval, 'Campbell (2-Live Crew) v Acuff Rose Music: Justice Souter's Rescue of Fair Use' (1994) Cardozo Arts and Entertainment L J 19. The 'transformative use' case law is discussed elsewhere in this volume.

[17] W Gordon, 'Fair Use as Market Failure: A Structural and Economic Analysis of the Betamax Case and its Predecessors' (1982) 82 Columbia L Rev 1600.

of interest too far against the interests of the copyright owner,[18] the fact of the matter is that courts do have the power to decide that the public interest outweighs an author's rights over his own work.

This raises the question whether the fair use defence is always compatible **7.21** with the three-step test.

E. Fair Use and the Three-Step Test

An interesting example of the potential conflict arose in Europe when the **7.22** legal rules relating to copyright in computer programs were being harmonized throughout the European Community. There was controversy as to whether and in what circumstances competitors should be entitled to reverse engineer or 'decompile' copyright computer programs. If a reverse engineering exemption were to be allowed, particularly in favour of potential competitors, there were obvious problems with regard to the three-step test set out in Article 9(2) of the Berne Convention. There was no consensus as to whether a decompilation defence was consistent with Article 9(2).

The European compromise solution was to employ a belt and braces approach: **7.23** Article 6 of the Computer Program Directive[19] permitted decompilation of computer programs in limited and carefully circumscribed situations and went on to provide that in 'accordance with . . . the Berne Convention . . . this Article may not be interpreted in such a way as to allow its application to be used in a manner which unreasonably prejudices the right-holder's legitimate interests or conflicts with a normal exploitation of the computer program'. Thus, the defence was tailored to ensure that the three-step test in Article 9.2 of the Berne Convention was complied with.

In the USA, the decompilation issue centred not on the Article 9.2 three- **7.24** step test but on the scope of fair use. In the well-known decision in *Sega*

---

[18] 'While some limitations and conditions on copyright are essential in the public interest, they should not be so burdensome and strict as to deprive authors of their just reward. Authors wishing copyright protection should be able to secure it readily and simply. And their rights should be broad enough to give them a fair share of the revenue to be derived from the market for their works.' *Register's Report on the General Revision of US Copyright Law* (1961).

[19] Council Directive (EEC) No 91/250 of 14 May 1991 on the Legal Protection of Computer Programs.

Enterprises Ltd v Accolade,[20] the court undertook a detailed analysis of the facts of the case and concluded that it was fair use, looking at the particular facts of that case, to disassemble the object code of a computer program if that was necessary to gain access to the ideas and functional concepts of the plaintiff's program in order to produce a product which did not compete directly with the plaintiff's program.

7.25 Thus, the court recognized a decompilation defence, in certain situations, by recourse to the fair use doctrine; but it is not clear whether this approach is consistent with Article 9.2 Berne Convention. In the United Kingdom, when the specific decompilation defence was incorporated into UK copyright law,[21] the fair dealing defence was expressly made inapplicable to those decompiling computer programs.[22]

7.26 Although there appears to be a real issue as to whether there is any inconsistency between the general fair use/dealing defences and the three-step test in Article 9.2 of the Berne Convention and Article 13 of the TRIPs Agreement, the question has not yet been tackled as a mainstream matter. The official US position seems to be that the fair use doctrine does not conflict with the three-step test.[23]

7.27 Others disagree,[24] with good reason, for it is difficult to see how, in many cases, a fair use defence, which normally means a free use defence, cannot conflict with the normal rights of a copyright holder.

---

[20] 977 F 2d 1510 (9th Cir 1992).   [21] Now s 50B of the CDPA 1988 (as amended).

[22] Section 29(4) of the revised UK Act, is as follows:
'It is not fair dealing —
(a) to convert a computer program expressed in a low level language into a version expressed in a higher level language, or
(b) incidentally, in the course of so converting the program, to copy it,
(these acts being permitted if done in accordance with s.50B (decompilation)).'

[23] 'Article 13 of [TRIPs] widens the scope of . . . [Article 9(2) Berne] to all exclusive rights in copyright and related rights, thus narrowly circumscribing the limitations and exceptions that WTO member countries may impose. This approach is consistent with s. 107 of [US Copyright Act] relating to fair use of copyrighted works.' (Uruguay Round Agreements Act, Statements of Administrative Action in Relation to Intellectual Property Rights. H R Doc 103–316, 103 Cong 2d Sess 656).

[24] See Nimmer on Copyright (1996): 'Acting in secrecy and unconstrained by American notions of due process, a future WTO panel could conclude, for example, that the free-wheeling fair use doctrine applied by US courts—the Supreme Court's decision in *Campbell v. Acuff Rose Music Inc.* (114 S.Ct. 1164 (1994)) comes to mind—violates Article 9 of the Berne Convention and hence is impermissible under TRIPS.'

Although the US courts have not yet had the opportunity to address this **7.28** particular question, they have dealt with similar issues involving the fair use defence in 'freedom of expression' cases. Here, the potential conflict is between two Constitutional provisions, the Copyright Clause (protecting the rights of the author) and the First Amendment which, inter alia, protects the right to freedom of expression. In these cases, the courts have come out strongly in support of a broad approach to fair use, some preferring to regard it as a right rather than a mere defence.[25]

Whatever balance is struck in the USA between the copyright clause and **7.29** the First Amendment, it does not follow that such a balance resolves the fair use–three-step test problem.

Sooner or later, it is likely that a TRIPs panel will be called upon to pro- **7.30** nounce whether the fair use defence in US copyright law is consistent with the three-step test. The Panel will have a much easier task were the USA to address the issue now.

F. External Controls: The Common Law 'Public Interest' Defence

The discussion so far has dealt with the way in which internal controls, that **7.31** is controls built in to the copyright system itself, can limit the powers of the copyright owner.

A wider question is whether, in applying national copyright law, it is per- **7.32** missible for a defendant to seek assistance beyond the exceptions and limitations available in the copyright system and simply claim that there is a general

---

[25] 'I believe that fair use should be considered an affirmative right under the 1976 Act, rather than merely an affirmative defense, as it is defined in the Act as a use that is not a violation of copyright . . . [It has a] constitutional significance as a guarantor to access and use for First Amendment purposes . . . However, fair use is commonly referred to as an affirmative defense, see Campbell v. Acuff-Rose Music, Inc., 510 U.S. 569, 590, 114 S. Ct. 1164, 1177 (1994), and, as we are bound by Supreme Court precedent, we will apply it as such . . . Nevertheless, the fact that the fair use right must be procedurally asserted as an affirmative defense does not detract from its constitutional significance as a guarantor to access and use for First Amendment purposes.' *SunTrust Bank v Houghton Mifflin* 60 USPQ 2d 1225 (11th Cir 10/10/01) per Birch J at n 3.

public policy or public interest reason, in particular cases, to deny the copyright owner a remedy.

7.33 The tidy view is that copyright law is a self-contained code of rights and exceptions and limitations which can be amended, from time to time, for policy reasons; but it is not proper to interfere with this balanced package by resort to external principles drawn from other areas. Thus, some judges see the US fair use defence as the internal mechanism by which the public interest can be taken into account and defendants should not be able to call upon further external principles[26].

7.34 Curiously, UK copyright law has developed a public interest defence, which was not specifically referred to in the list of limitations and exceptions to authors' exclusive rights in the Copyright Act, by chance.

7.35 Its development was linked to the action for breach of confidence, which has undergone remarkable change in the last thirty years. In the early days, it was recognized that a defendant might be entitled to raise a defence to a breach of confidence action if he could show that the disclosure of confidential information was to publicize some 'iniquity'. This limited defence was gradually widened to permit the defence to be used to disclose other kinds of misconduct, such as a crime or fraud, and gradually the defence became subsumed under a more general principle: that the defence would be available to any defendant who could establish that there was some 'just cause or excuse' or some public interest justifying the disclosure of confidential information to the recipient.

7.36 There was no equivalent statutory 'public interest' defence in the former UK Copyright Act 1956. This led to a difficult situation in cases where a defendant was sued for both breach of confidence and infringement of copyright. Take, for example, the case of a large organization which improperly put on the market goods which threatened the health of the public. If an

---

[26] 'Because of the First Amendment principles built into copyright law through the idea/expression dichotomy and the doctrine of fair use, courts often need not entertain related First Amendment arguments in a copyright case . . . We have repeatedly rejected First Amendment challenges to injunctions from copyright infringement on the ground that First Amendment concerns are protected by and coextensive with the fair use doctrine.' *Los Angeles News Serv v Tullo* 973 F 2d 791, 795 (9th Cir 1992). ('First Amendment concerns are also addressed in the copyright field through the "fair use" doctrine.') *SunTrust Bank v Houghton Mifflin* 60 USPQ 2d 1225 (11th Cir 10/10/01) per Birch J.

employee of the organization, acting in the public interest, notified the appropriate authorities, in breach of his obligation of confidence to his employers, he could be sued for breach of confidence. The employee could plead that the disclosure was in the 'public interest', and it would be for the court to weigh up and balance the competing obligations and determine whether such a defence should succeed. In this type of case, an employee might find it necessary to copy documents owned by his employers and send these to the authorities. This would now enable the employer to claim not only breach of confidence, but also copyright infringement. If the defendant was unable to set up a public interest defence to the copyright action, the public interest defence to the confidence action would be of limited value. Thus, some English courts accepted that an extra-statutory public interest defence was also available in copyright actions. When the UK Copyright, Designs and Patents Act 1988 was drafted, the status of such a defence was still uncertain. It would have been easy for the legislature, had it been clear that such a defence was necessary, to legislate for the defence expressly. Instead, a rather hesitant saving provision was introduced to the effect that: '[Nothing] affects any rule of law preventing or restricting the enforcement of copyright, on grounds of public interest or otherwise.'[27]

Since then, the assumption has been that such a defence, based upon the **7.37** inherent jurisdiction of the court, is now part of copyright law; although it should not be applied in ways which are inconsistent with, and so undermine, relevant specific fair dealing defences.[28] However, the scope of the defence was at first circumscribed very narrowly to cases in which there has been wrongdoing on the part of the plaintiffs: 'a court would be entitled to refuse to enforce copyright if the work is: (i) immoral, scandalous or contrary to family life; (ii) injurious to public life, public health and safety or the administration of justice; (iii) incites or encourages others to act in a way referred to in (ii).'[29] This view was later rejected by the Court of Appeal in *Ashdown v Daily Telegraph*,[30] who emphasized that 'the circumstances in which public interest may override copyright are not capable of precise categorisation or definition.'[31]

---

[27] CDPA 1988, s 171(3).   [28] *PCR Ltd v Dow Jones Telerate Ltd* [1998] FSR 170.
[29] *Hyde Park Residence Ltd v Yelland* [2000] EMLR 363 per Aldous LJ.
[30] [2001] EMLR 44.   [31] Ibid, para 58.

G. From Public Interest to Freedom of Expression: The US Constitutional Relationship between Copyright and Freedom of Expression

7.38 In *Eldred v Ashcroft*[32] the Supreme Court had occasion to examine again the relationship between copyright and freedom of expression when the argument was put that First Amendment free speech principles could trump copyright, and that even where there was no fair use copyright defence, the rights of a copyright owner could be subordinated to a defendant exercising a constitutional right of free expression. The Supreme Court's reply to this, essentially, was to say that most First Amendment issues could be catered for by applying copyright law: copyright's limited monopolies are compatible with free speech principles; and copyright law contains built-in First Amendment accommodations, for example the fair use defence, affording considerable latitude for scholarship and comment, and even for parody. There might be rare cases where there could be scope for resort to external First Amendment arguments, but in most cases this was unnecessary.[33]

7.39 A similar result has been reached in the United Kingdom but by a different route.

H. Copyright and Freedom of Expression in the United Kingdom and Europe: The Human Rights Act and Article 10 of the European Convention

7.40 The Human Rights Act 1998, which incorporated the European Convention on Human Rights into UK law, brought about a sea-change in the thinking of UK lawyers. No area of the law seemed able to resist the argument that long-established principles had to be reconsidered in the light of the Act.

---

[32] 239 F 3d 372 (2003).
[33] 'We recognize that the D. C. Circuit spoke too broadly when it declared copyrights "categorically immune from challenges under the First Amendment." 239 F. 3d, at 375. But when, as in this case, Congress has not altered the traditional contours of copyright protection, further First Amendment scrutiny is unnecessary. See *Harper & Row*, 471 U. S., at 560; cf. *San Francisco Arts & Athletics, Inc. v. United States Olympic Comm.*, 483 U. S. 522 (1987).'

Copyright was no exception. Article 10 of the Convention provides as follows:

> 10.1. Everyone has the right to freedom of expression. This right shall include freedom to hold opinions and to receive and impart information and ideas without interference by public authority and regardless of frontiers. This Article shall not prevent States from requiring the licensing of broadcasting, television or cinema enterprises.
>
> 10.2. The exercise of these freedoms, since it carries with it duties and responsibilities, may be subject to such formalities, conditions, restrictions or penalties as are prescribed by law and are necessary in a democratic society, in the interests of national security, territorial integrity or public safety, for the prevention of disorder or crime, for the protection of health or morals, for the protection of the reputation or rights of others, for preventing the disclosure of information received in confidence, or for maintaining the authority and impartiality of the judiciary.

How does the Human Rights Act affect the rights of copyright owners, if **7.41** at all? Would the view be taken that the right to freedom of expression is a right which is already reflected in the Copyright Act itself (as enlarged slightly by the public interest defence), which has taken into account all necessary public interest considerations; or can it be said that freedom of expression is broader than this and can be exercised and take priority over copyright when appropriate?

This question was discussed by the English Court of Appeal in *Ashdown v* **7.42** *Telegraph Group Ltd*[34] where the defendant had obtained and published a copy of a confidential minute made by a politician and was sued for breach of confidence and infringement of copyright in the document. Various defences were advanced: first, specific defences available in the Copyright Act, namely fair dealing for the purpose of criticism or review and fair dealing for the purpose of reporting current events;[35] secondly, the common law defence of 'public interest';[36] and, thirdly, the new argument that, when considering whether an actionable breach of copyright has occurred, the court must now have regard to the right of freedom of expression conferred by Article 10, ie the court should examine whether on the facts of the case before it, it was necessary in a democratic society to provide for exceptions, exemptions, and defences over and above those permitted by the copyright legislation,

---

[34] [2002] Ch 149, CA. See paras 8.03–8.29 below.   [35] CDPA 1988, s 30(1) and (2).
[36] As preserved by CDPA 1988, s 171(3) discussed earlier.

however extensive they might be. The Court of Appeal recognized that in most cases Article 10 would not alter the protection conferred by copyright; however, rare circumstances could arise where the right of freedom of expression could come into conflict with the protection afforded by the Copyright Act, notwithstanding the express exceptions to be found in the Act. In those circumstances, the court was bound, insofar as it was able, to apply the Act in a manner which accommodated the right of freedom of expression. That would make it necessary for the court to look closely at the facts of individual cases.

I. Conclusions

7.43 From a UK perspective, the express introduction of freedom of expression issues into the copyright equation has not created, so far, any unacceptable ripples. It is a reserve power to be used by defendants in copyright infringement cases almost as a last resort and the courts will need a lot of persuasion to depart from the Copyright Act (including the public interest defence). But, the Human Rights Act, and those lawyers who now approach copyright questions from that entry point, have given copyright lawyers pause for thought; just as happened when competition law and private international law issues began to impact the discipline of intellectual property and copyright.

7.44 This, together with the sustained onslaught upon copyright law by those who argue that increasingly strong copyright has tilted the balance in a socially unacceptable way, suggests that greater consideration should be given to the question how far the courts should be able to go beyond the copyright legislation itself and limit copyright by resort to the public interest in general, and freedom of expression in particular; or, in place of that, to reconsider the copyright legislation so that these matters are properly incorporated into it. Indeed, it may be possible in minor ways for the copyright systems of the USA and the United Kingdom (as restricted by the governing EU Directives) to learn lessons from each other.

(1) Fair use, fair dealing, and the three-step test

7.45 Could the UK legislation be broadened, to allow freedom of expression to be openly considered by courts in copyright infringement cases, by widening its specific fair dealing defences into an all embracing, general, US style fair use defence? This is unlikely for two reasons. First, there is a potential problem with s 107 of the US Copyright Act itself; since it could be incompatible with the three-step test in Article 13 of the TRIPs Agreement. If the USA were prepared to address the problem, it could amend s 107 and make it expressly subject to the three-step criteria, but this is unlikely. The fair use defence is too deeply embedded into the US copyright system—indeed, in the American psyche.[37] The second reason is that this approach could well be impermissible under EU law since European Directives require all exceptions and limitations to be subject to the three-step test.[38] Further, Article 5 of the Information Society Directive provides for a closed list of exceptions and limitations which can be adopted by Member States, and these do not include anything as general as the US fair use approach.

Even so, the United Kingdom should take advantage of one of the exceptions **7.46** in the EU Directive which is not in the Copyright Act. UK copyright law has no special exception for parody and this type of case is dealt with, rather uncertainly, under general copyright law principles: is the unauthorized parody a substantial part of the copyright work? In furtherance of Article 10 of the Human Rights Act, it would be sensible to take advantage of the special exception available in the EU Directive, namely 'use for the purposes of caricature, parody or pastiche'.[39]

(2) Remedies

A more subtle approach to reconciling copyright legislation, the three-step **7.47** test, and the principle of freedom of expression is by more careful use of the remedies available to copyright owners. The economic rights of copyright owners can be respected and so compliance with the three-step test ensured, but the remedies in particular cases can be tweaked to satisfy the public

---

[37] Notwithstanding that the amendment of s 107 relating to unpublished works demonstrates that the form and wording of s 107 are not inviolate.

[38] Directive on Copyright and Related Rights in the Information Society 2001/29/EC Art 5.5. However, the requirement to comply with the three-step test has not been introduced expressly into UK copyright law, or the copyright laws of most of the other Member States of the EU, the assumption being that all the express exceptions and limitations have been tested against, and are deemed to satisfy, the test.

[39] Directive 2001/29/EC . . . on the harmonization of certain aspects of copyright and related rights in the information society, Art 5.3(k).

interest and freedom of expression where appropriate. In certain cases where a defendant is able to demonstrate a strong public interest underlying the infringing act, the copyright owner's interests may be adequately protected by an award of damages, but no injunction. The infringer will not be stopped from copying or otherwise using the work, but the copyright owner's interests will be protected since he obtains a price for the use of the work. Not free fair use; rather a form of compulsory licence. This approach is now receiving attention in the USA.[40] It has also been taken up in the *Ashdown* decision in the United Kingdom when the court was considering whether to decline the grant of an injunction, which is a discretionary, equitable remedy: 'If a newspaper considers it necessary to copy the exact words created by another, we can see no reason in principle why the newspaper should not indemnify the author for any loss caused to him, or alternatively account to him for any profit made as a result of copying his work. Freedom of expression should not normally carry with it the right to make free use of another's work.'[41]

---

[40] See the influential article by Leval, 'Toward a Fair Use Standard' (1990) 103 Harv L Rev 1105, 1132. See also a comment in the Supreme Court that 'the goals of copyright law, to stimulate the creation and publication of edifying matter, are not always best served by automatically granting injunctive relief when parodists are found to have gone beyond the bounds of fair use.' *Campbell (2-Live Crew) v Acuff Rose Music* 114 S Ct 1164 (1994) at 1171 n 10.

[41] Para 46.

8

THE IMPACT OF THE HUMAN RIGHTS ACT 1998 ON UK COPYRIGHT LAW

Kevin Garnett QC

This chapter examines the relatively narrow question of how the Human **8.01** Rights Act 1998[1] has impacted on UK copyright law and, in particular, the extent to which any pre-existing restraints on freedom of expression under UK copyright law have been altered.

---

[1] The Act received the Royal Assent on 9 November 1998 and the relevant provisions came into force on 2 October 2000. In general terms, it gives statutory force to the European Convention on Human Rights.

A. Copyright and Freedom of Expression in
the United Kingdom

8.02 It is not the intention here to discuss in depth how copyright law in general impinges on freedom of expression. Such discussion can be found elsewhere in this volume. However, it is necessary, briefly, to say something about this issue in the specific context of UK law.

8.03 As is often said, copyright protects the expression of ideas, information, and so on, and so it is inevitable that the exclusive rights of a copyright owner to prevent the dissemination of a work will amount to a fetter on what individuals can say or write. As the Court of Appeal observed in *Ashdown v Telegraph Group Ltd*:[2] 'Copyright is antithetical to freedom of expression. It prevents all, save the owner of the copyright, from expressing information in the form of the literary work protected by the copyright.'[3] Sir Andrew Morritt V-C had put the matter more fully at first instance:

> Copyright does not protect ideas, only the material form in which they are expressed. It is therefore a restriction on the right to freedom of expression to inhibit another from copying the method of expression used by the copyright owner even though there may be open to him a host of other methods of expression of the same idea. It must follow that intellectual property rights in general and copyright in particular constitute a restriction on the exercise of the right to freedom of expression.[4]

8.04 UK copyright law has traditionally dealt with concerns about the proper dividing line between the rights of a copyright owner and the public interest in being able to make use of, or have access to, copyright works and material referred to in them in a number of ways. These can be categorized as follows: (1) the idea–expression dichotomy; (2) the substantial part requirement; (3) the fair dealing or permitted act provisions; (4) the public interest defence; and (5) denial of the discretionary remedy of an injunction.

---

[2] [2001] EWCA (Civ) 1142; [2002] Ch 149, CA, para 30.
[3] Note that this statement was made in the context of a literary work, but should be understood as potentially applying to restrictions on expression by the use of any form of copyright work.
[4] [2001] Ch 685, para 12.

(1) Ideas or mere information v expression

Since, as the statements cited above make clear, ideas and information them- **8.05**
selves are not protected by copyright, it might be thought that copyright does
not in practice operate as an important restraint on freedom of expression.
Indeed there is judicial support for this view:

> It is important to emphasise in the present context that it is only the form of
> the literary work that is protected by copyright. Copyright does not normally
> prevent the publication of the information conveyed by the literary work. Thus
> it is only the freedom to express information using the verbal formula devised
> by another that is prevented by copyright. This will not normally constitute a
> significant encroachment on the freedom of expression. The prime importance
> of freedom of expression is that it enables the citizen freely to express ideas and
> convey information. It is also important that the citizen should be free to
> express the ideas and convey the information in a form of words of his or her
> choice. It is stretching the concept of freedom of expression to postulate that
> it extends to the freedom to convey ideas and information using the form of
> words devised by someone else.[5]

The suggestion being made is that the content of a copyright work can always **8.06**
be extracted and disseminated without infringing copyright. However, as is
often the case with generalizations, it can be dangerous to apply the principle
without further examination.[6] First, it is dangerous to assume that copyright
in a literary work is restricted simply to protection of the author's precise
verbal expression. Protection can extend beyond this to such things as plot
or story lines, even though retold in new words.[7] Secondly, compilations of
information and data may be protected even though the information or data
is reused in a different form.[8] Thirdly, the generalization has little or no application in the case of artistic works, photographs, films, and broadcasts, where
use of the actual visual image may be all-important.

Further, given that protection extends to the expression of ideas, it may in **8.07**
practice be difficult to repeat another person's ideas without reproducing a

---

[5] *Ashdown v Telegraph Group Ltd* [2001] EWCA (Civ) 1142; [2002] Ch 149, CA, para 31.
[6] A point that the Court of Appeal in *Ashdown* went on to recognize.
[7] eg, *Ravenscroft v Herbert* [1980] RPC 193.
[8] This is especially so where the compilation is entitled to database right under the
Copyright and Rights in Database Regulations 1997, SI 1997/3032, implementing Council
Directive No 96/9/EC on the legal protection of databases [1996] OJ L77/20.

substantial part of the expression of those ideas. There is no place in English law for the notion that, if an idea can only be expressed in one way, it cannot be the subject of copyright.[9] So too, is it a dangerous over-simplification to say that there is no copyright in 'mere' information. This may be true in relation to a single piece of data, but in relation to copyright works that consist of collections of information or data it may be difficult to reproduce more than minimal amounts of data without infringing the compilation copyright or database right that will usually subsist in such works under UK law. A good example of such a restraint is to be found in *PCR Ltd v Dow Jones Telerate Ltd*,[10] where the Dow Jones wire service was found to have infringed the copyright in the claimant's cocoa crop reports, because too much information had been reproduced from the reports.

(2) Substantial part

8.08 Tied up with this last issue is the further point that copyright is only infringed if a substantial part of the work is taken.[11] Since the test here relates to the quality of what is taken more than the quantity, the point seldom arises in freedom of expression cases.[12]

(3) Fair dealing

8.09 Since the 1911 Act,[13] the UK Copyright Acts have contained express exceptions to the right of the copyright owner in the public interest, particularly those known as the fair dealing provisions. So far as concerns restraints on freedom of expression, the most important of these are now contained in s 30 of the Copyright, Designs and Patents Act 1988, which provides as follows:

(a) Fair dealing with a work for the purposes of criticism or review, of that or another work or of a performance of a work, does not infringe any

---

[9] *IBCOS Computers Ltd v Barclays Mercantile Highland Finance Ltd* [1994] FSR 275, at 291.

[10] [1998] FSR 170.

[11] Copyright, Designs and Patents Act 1988 (hereafter referred to as the 'CDPA 1988'), s 16(3)(a).

[12] Although, see again *PCR Ltd v Dow Jones Telerate Ltd*, above, where the point was in issue.

[13] Before the 1911 Act, the matter was effectively dealt with as a matter of judge-made law. See Garnett et al (eds), *Copinger and Skone James on Copyright* (15th edn, 2005) para 9–19.

copyright in the work provided it is accompanied by a sufficient acknow-ledgment and provided that the work has been made available to the public.[14]

(b) Fair dealing with a work (other than a photograph) for the purpose of reporting current events does not infringe any copyright in the work provided that it is accompanied by a sufficient acknowledgment (although in the case of reporting current events by means of a sound recording, film or broadcast, no acknowledgment is required if to do so is 'impossible for reasons of practicality or otherwise').[15]

These provisions are to be interpreted generously, especially as to what amounts to 'criticism' of a work or the 'reporting of current events'. Their scope is 'wide and indefinite'.[16] Nevertheless, the requirement of a sufficient acknowledgment[17] is strict and can be something of a trap. It should be noted that the 'current events' exception also excludes photographs.

(4) Public interest

The Court of Appeal decision in *Ashdown* is important not only for the **8.10** discussion of the effect of the Human Rights Act on copyright law but also because it would seem to have laid to rest (at Court of Appeal level at least) a separate although overlapping question of whether there exists a defence of public interest in copyright infringement cases. In holding that such a

---

[14] s 30(1), as amended with effect from 31 October 2003 by the Copyright and Related Rights Regulations 2003, SI 2003/2498, to give effect to Directive 2001/29 on Copyright and Related Rights in the Information Society [2001] OJ L1767/10. A work is to be regarded as having been made available to the public if it has been made available by any means, including (a) the issue of copies to the public; (b) making the work available by means of an electronic retrieval system; (c) the rental or lending of copies of the work to the public; (d) the per-formance, exhibition, playing, or showing of the work in public; (e) the communication to the public of the work, but in determining generally for the purposes of that subsection whether a work has been made available to the public, no account is to be taken of any unauthorized act. See CDPA 1988, s 30(1A). Before amendment, there was no requirement that the work should have been previously made available to the public.

[15] s 30(2), again as amended by the 2003 Regulations. Before amendment, no acknow-ledgment was required in any circumstances where the reporting was by means of a sound recording, film, or broadcast.

[16] *Pro Sieben Media AG v Carlton UK Television Ltd* [1999] 1 WLR 605.

[17] ie, an acknowledgment identifying the work in question by its title or other description, and identifying the author, unless the work had been published anonymously or, if unpub-lished, it was not possible to ascertain his identity by reasonable inquiry. See CDPA 1988, s 178.

defence does exist, and had been expressly preserved by s 171(3) of the 1988 Act, the Court of Appeal held that the earlier decision of the Court of Appeal in *Hyde Park Residence Ltd v Yelland*[18] was wrong.[19] The court in *Ashdown* was careful not to circumscribe the possible limits of the public interest defence, merely saying that the circumstances in which public interest could override copyright were not capable of precise categorization or definition. Nevertheless, one example of the defence is where there is a clear public interest in giving effect to the right of freedom of expression, when this right will trump the rights of copyright.

8.11 Although the public interest defence may now be wider than previously thought, particularly where freedom of expression considerations are in play, the general approach to the public interest defence as it has been developed in confidential information cases shows that it is likely to be applied restrictively. In particular:

(a) The courts have repeatedly stressed that a distinction is to be drawn between cases where publication is in the public interest and cases where publication will merely be of interest to the public.[20]

---

[18] [2001] Ch 143, Mance LJ dissenting. The court had held that the permitted act provisions of the Act provided a complete code striking the balance between the interests of the public and the copyright owner. All that was left was the residual jurisdiction of the courts to decline to allow its process to be used in cases relating to the nature of the work itself and not the particular use intended to be made of it (the reason being that copyright is assignable: per Aldous LJ, at para 66). These were cases where the work was: (i) immoral, scandalous, or contrary to family life; (ii) injurious to public life, public health and safety or the administration of justice; (iii) liable to incite or encourage others to act in a way referred to in (ii). See per Aldous LJ at para 66. The defence was not confined to cases in which the claimant had been guilty of some iniquity or wrongdoing. See *Lion Laboratories v Evans* [1985] QB 526, at 537, 538, 550.

[19] Space does not permit an examination of the relative status of the two conflicting decisions of the Court of Appeal in *Hyde Park* and *Ashdown*. They cannot be reconciled simply on the grounds that *Ashdown* was decided after the Human Rights Act came into force. In *Ashdown* the Court held that in *Lion Laboratories v Evans* [1985] QB 526 (discussed in paras 8.53–8.56 below) the Court of Appeal had decided that such a defence existed. There had been no express reference to the public interest defence in the 1956 Act, and the right which the 1988 Act preserved could only have been the right which the court had identified in *Lion Laboratories*. This approach to *Lion Laboratories* had not been adopted in *Hyde Park*, on the grounds that *Lion Laboratories* was in reality a case wholly about breach of confidence (per Aldous LJ at para 58). It will simply be assumed here that the Court of Appeal's decision in *Ashdown* now represents the law.

[20] See, eg, Lord Wilberforce in *British Steel Corporation v Granada Television Ltd* [1981] AC 1096, 1168; O'Connor LJ in *Lion Laboratories Ltd v Evans* [1958] QB 526, 553.

(b) The courts have always examined closely whether the public interest is in fact best served not by publication by the press but by more limited disclosure to the relevant authorities, such as the police.[21] This is particularly liable to be the case where the material reveals wrongdoing.

(c) The courts will consider whether publication of a substantial part of the copyright work is in truth necessary in order to satisfy a genuine public interest or whether that interest can be adequately satisfied by publishing the information in a way that does not infringe copyright, backed up, if necessary, with publication of short, non-infringing, extracts to demonstrate the authenticity of the information.[22]

What is the status of the public interest defence in the light of the Information Society Directive?[23] Article 5 of the Directive sets out the exceptions and limitations which Member States either must or are permitted to provide to the rights prescribed by the Directive. These rights include the reproduction, communication to the public, and distribution rights in respect of authors' works and related rights subject matter. The list of permitted exceptions to these rights is closed, in the sense that no exceptions are permitted other than those referred to in the Directive.[24] Use in the 'public interest' is not one of the listed exceptions, and is not mentioned in the Directive or its recitals, nor indeed is there any reference to a balancing requirement in the interests of freedom of speech.[25] Nevertheless, certain defences of a public interest type are catered for. Thus, reproduction by the press, communication to the public, or the making available of *published* articles on current economic, political, or religious topics, or of broadcast works or other subject matter of the same character and use of works in connection with the reporting of current events are permitted,[26] as are quotations for purposes such as criticism or review, provided they relate to a work or other subject matter *which has already been lawfully made available to the*   **8.12**

---

[21] See, eg, *Initial Services Ltd v Putterill* [1968] 1 QB 396, 405–6, per Lord Denning MR, and *Francome v Mirror Group Newspapers Ltd* [1984] 1 WLR 892, 898, per Sir John Donaldson MR.

[22] See,eg, *Ashdown v Telegraph Group Ltd* [2001] EWCA (Civ) 1142; [2002] Ch 149, CA, para 81.

[23] Directive 2001/29 on Copyright and Related Rights in the Information Society [2001] OJ L1767/10.

[24] See recital 32 and the opening words of Arts 5(1), (2) and (3).

[25] No less than 15 recitals deal with these exceptions. Recital 31 merely speaks in general terms of safeguarding a fair balance between right-holders and users.

[26] Subject to certain conditions: see Arts 5(3)(c), (5).

public.[27] Admittedly, Article 5(3)(o) enables Member States to continue existing exceptions or limitations of minor importance, but only if they concern
'analogue use' and do not affect the free circulation of goods or services.
The existing UK defence of public interest can no doubt be brought within
this provision in the case of analogue use, but what of digital use? The Directive nowhere makes clear what the distinction between analogue and digital
use is. Presumably digital broadcasting qualifies as digital use, but does the
digital reproduction of a work in the ordinary course of newspaper production count as analogue or digital use? Perhaps the public interest defence can
be brought within the spirit, if not the letter, of Article 9, which contains a
general saving for 'other legal provisions'. Thus, it provides that the Directive
is without prejudice to provisions concerning 'in particular' a number of
specified rights, including laws on trade secrets, security, confidentiality,
data protection, and privacy. If the public interest defence is excluded by
the Directive, it would be a backwards step so far as the law of freedom of
expression is concerned.

(5) Denial of an injunction

8.13 Particularly when considering an application for an interim injunction, the
courts have always taken into account freedom of speech concerns. In particular, where publication of copyright material by newspapers is in issue, courts
have been prepared to take into account, as one of the factors relevant to the
exercise of the discretion, the public interest in being informed of matters of
genuine public concern.[28]

8.14 This highlights an important point in relation to the status of an application
for an interim injunction as opposed to a final injunction at trial. It is in the
nature of freedom of expression cases that the decision on an application for
an interim injunction can be determinative of the dispute. If an injunction
is granted, it may be that the defendant will give up the struggle to publish[29]
or that, by the time that there has been a trial, events will have moved on and

---

[27] Again, subject to certain conditions: see Arts 5(3)(d), (5). The amendment made to the
CDPA 1988, s 30(1) was in response to this Article.
[28] See, eg, *Sec of State for the Home Department v Central Broadcasting Ltd* [1993] EMLR
253.
[29] Not least because the costs of going to trial may be prohibitive.

the information will no longer be of pressing public interest.[30] Alternatively, if no injunction is granted and the information is published, freedom of expression will have triumphed.[31] In these cases, the courts have considered, first, whether the claimant has established an arguable case or, in a case where infringement of copyright is not in issue and the only defence is one of public interest, whether the defendant has demonstrated a serious defence of public interest which *may* succeed at trial.[32] If a claimant can clear this hurdle, which is clearly a lower one than he will face at trial,[33] the court will go on to consider the usual factors for and against granting an interim injunction in the exercise of its discretion.[34] It can thus be seen that these procedural considerations can produce a different result, as between the interim and final stages, so that, in one sense, the law of freedom of expression as a matter of practice has varied depending on the stage at which an application is made for an injunction.

Although the denial of an injunction could therefore be used, in limited **8.15** circumstances, as a means of enabling journalists and the like to report matters in the public interest despite copyright infringement, there have been few reported cases in which such relief has been refused at the interim stage[35] and no reported case in which the courts have gone on to the next stage, namely to consider denial of a final injunction at trial where publication is still threatened.[36] Even if a final injunction is denied at trial on discretionary grounds, there are no such grounds for denying a damages claim.[37] It is obvious that the threat of having to pay damages and possibly legal costs is a 'chilling' factor when deciding whether or not to publish, particularly in the case of a publisher of limited means. Whether, by contrast, the public interest

---

[30] Admittedly, the ability of the court to order a speedy trial can alleviate this problem.

[31] At least temporarily, in the sense that the defendant may still be liable in damages at trial—see paras 8.15 and 8.26 below.

[32] *Lion Laboratories Ltd v Evans* [1985] QB 526, at 538. Presumably the test is the same where the defence is one of fair dealing.

[33] ie, when he will have to prove the case on the balance of probabilities.

[34] ie, applying *American Cyanamid Company v Ethicon Ltd* [1975] AC 396. One of the factors is of course that the refusal or the grant of an injunction may be determinative.

[35] eg, *Lion Laboratories Laboratories v Evans* [1985] QB 526; *Hubbard v Vosper* [1972] 2 QB 84.

[36] The reason being, no doubt, that these cases are usually determined, one way or the other, at the interim stage.

[37] See, eg, *Lion Laboratories v Evans* [1985] QB 526, 538, per Stephenson LJ; *Ashdown v Telegraph Group Ltd* [2001] EWCA (Civ) 1142; [2002] Ch 149, CA.

'defence' is also a defence to a damages claim is unclear. The issue is discussed again later.

B. Does the Human Rights Act Engage UK Copyright Law?

8.16 The background having been set, the provisions of the Human Rights Act and the Convention now need to be examined to see to what extent they potentially engage the 1988 Copyright Act, either, on the one hand, coming into conflict with it or, on the other, lending support to its provisions.

8.17 First, Article 10 is obviously in potential conflict with existing UK copyright law and practice.[38] It provides that the right to freedom of expression shall include: '[The] freedom to hold opinions and to receive and impart information and ideas without interference by public authority and regardless of frontiers.'[39]

8.18 In *Ashdown*, it was expressly confirmed that Article 10 is engaged in relation to intellectual property rights and copyright in particular.[40] Nevertheless, Article 10(2) makes it clear that, since the exercise of these freedoms carries with it duties and responsibilities, it may be subject to such restrictions as are prescribed by law and are necessary in a democratic society, for the protection of rights of others. *Ashdown* establishes[41] that such 'rights' include the rights of copyright owners, these also being rights protected in accordance with Article 1 to the First Protocol, which states that: 'Every person is entitled to the peaceful enjoyment of his possessions. No one shall be deprived of his possessions except in the general public interest and subject to the conditions prescribed by law.'

8.19 The only other provision of the Human Rights Act which needs to be mentioned in this context is Article 8, which guarantees a right to privacy: 'Everyone has the right to respect for his private and family life, his home and his correspondence.' Although this Article has now received extensive consideration by the courts in relation to an individual's right to privacy,[42] it does not appear to have an impact on the right to freedom of expression to any significant extent in the copyright field.

---

[38] The Convention is given statutory force by the Human Rights Act 1998.

[39] Note that the right granted by Art 10 is a right to impart both information *and* ideas: *Ashdown v Telegraph Group Ltd* [2001] EWCA (Civ) 1142; [2002] Ch 149, CA, para 24.

[40] Ibid, para 12.   [41] Ibid, para 8.

[42] See, eg, *Douglas v Hello! Ltd* [2001] QB 967, CA; *A v B plc and C* [2003] QB 195, CA; *Campbell v MGN Limited* [2004] UKHL 22.

What conclusion is be drawn in relation to the Article 10 right and the rights   **8.20**
of copyright owners? The Court of Appeal put it as follows in *Ashdown*:

> The infringement of copyright constitutes interference with 'the peaceful
> enjoyment of possessions'. It is, furthermore, the interference with a right
> arising under a statute which confers rights recognised under international
> convention and harmonised under European law—see the Berne Conventions
> of 1886 and 1971 and EC Council Directive of 29 October 1993. There is
> thus no question but that restriction of the right of freedom of expression can
> be justified where necessary in a democratic society in order to protect copy-
> right. The protection afforded to copyright under the 1988 Act is, however,
> itself subject to exceptions. Thus both the right of freedom of expression and
> copyright are qualified. This appeal raises the question of how the two rights
> fall to be balanced, when they are in conflict.[43]

C. Is the CDPA 1988 in Conflict with the Article 10 Right?

In establishing the extent to which existing UK copyright law satisfies the   **8.21**
Article 10 right, the Courts have concentrated on the fair dealing provisions
of the 1988 Act. Given that, under the Convention, a balance has to be
struck between the right to freedom of expression and the rights of owners of
copyright works, do the existing exceptions and defences in UK law already
strike that balance? The cogently argued view of Sir Andrew Morritt V-C,
at first instance in *Ashdown*, was that the existing permitted act provisions of
the 1988 Act did so:

> In my view the provisions of the Act alone can and do satisfy the third require-
> ment of Article 10(2) . . . The needs of a democratic society include the recog-
> nition and protection of private property. This is confirmed by the provisions
> of Article 1 to the First Protocol. Such property includes copyright. As Aldous
> LJ observed in *Hyde Park Residence Ltd v Yelland* . . . [the] CDPA gives effect to
> the United Kingdom's obligations under the [Berne Conventions of 1886 and
> 1971] as well as pursuant to various EC Directives. Article 9 of the Berne
> Convention 1971 left it to the countries of the Union thereby established to
> provide by their own domestic legislation for the circumstances in which a
> copyright work might be reproduced by others. The terms of s. 30 of the 1988
> Act were evidently intended to implement the latitude afforded by Article 10 of
> the Berne Convention 1971. Likewise the United Kingdom is entitled to a
> margin of appreciation in giving effect to the provisions of Article 10 of ECHR

---

[43] *Ashdown v Telegraph Group Ltd* [2001] EWCA (Civ) 1142; [2002] Ch 149, CA, para 28.

in the field of intellectual property . . . I can see no reason why the provisions of the CDPA should not be sufficient to give effect to the Convention right subject only to such restrictions as are permitted by Article 10(2) . . .

It is not suggested that the provisions of the 1988 Act are any more restrictive of the right of freedom of expression than those of the copyright legislation of all or most other democratic states. I can see no reason why the court should travel outside the provisions of the 1988 Act and recognise on the facts of particular cases further or other exceptions to the restrictions on the exercise of the right to freedom of expression constituted by the 1988 Act. Nor, in my view, do any of the decisions of the European Court of Human Rights on which the Sunday Telegraph relied suggest otherwise . . .

For the reasons I have sought to explain Article 10 cannot be relied on to create defences to the alleged infringement over and above those for which the 1988 Act provides. The balance between the rights of the owner of the copyright and those of the public has been struck by the legislative organ of the democratic state itself in the legislation it has enacted. There is no room for any further defences outside the code which establishes the particular species of intellectual property in question.[44]

8.22 On appeal, however, in the defining decision of the English courts to date, this view was held by the Court of Appeal to be wrong. The steps in the argument were summarized by the court as follows:

(a) The restriction imposed by copyright on the freedom of use of a particular form of expression will not normally amount to a significant encroachment on the freedom of a citizen freely to express ideas and convey information, particularly when he does so using his own form of words. Article 10 does not necessitate a freedom to convey ideas and information using the form of words devised by someone else.[45]

(b) Circumstances can, however, arise in which freedom of expression will only be fully effective if an individual is permitted to reproduce the very words spoken by another. In particular:

---

[44] *Ashdown v Telegraph Group Ltd* [2001] Ch 685, 693–6.

[45] The Court of Appeal's comment on *Jersild v Denmark* Series A No 298, (1994) 19 EHHR 1 (where it was said that: 'Article 10 protects not only the substance of the ideas and information expressed, but also the form in which they are conveyed') was that 'these words do not support a general proposition that freedom of the press includes the freedom to make use of the form of words created by another in order to convey ideas and information. The case was concerned with the right to use insulting language which was the creation of those using the language, not copied from another author.' It should be borne in mind, of course, that the protection conferred by copyright on, for example, literary works, is not limited to prevent the copying of the actual words used.

> [Article 10] leaves it for journalists to decide whether or not it is necessary to reproduce such documents to ensure credibility. It protects journalists' right to divulge information on issues of general interest provided that they are acting in good faith and on an accurate factual basis and provide 'reliable and precise' information in accordance with the ethics of journalism.[46]

There will thus be occasions when it is in the public interest not merely that information should be published, but that the public should be told the very words used by a person.[47]

(c) Section 30(2) of the 1988 Act, which permits fair dealing in works for the purpose of reporting current events, will often permit publication of the words used and thus satisfy the freedom of expression requirements of the Convention. Where there is a dealing for the purposes of reporting current events, the requirement of fairness will normally afford the court all the scope that it needs to reflect properly the public interest in freedom of expression and, in particular, the freedom of the press.

(d) While the principles established by decisions made before the Human Rights Act 1998 came into force as to what amounts to 'fair' dealing are still important, inflexible tests based on precedent should not, however, be applied. Rather, it should be borne in mind that considerations of public interest are paramount. Are the facts of the case such that the importance of freedom of expression outweighs the conventional considerations established by the earlier authorities as to what is 'fair'?

(e) It may not always be possible, however, to bring section 30(2) into play, even giving due weight to the right of freedom of expression. Thus, there may be occasions where there is information of the greatest public interest relating to events in the past and where, therefore, section 30(2) is of no application.[48]

(f) It follows that rare circumstances can arise where the right of freedom of expression will come into conflict with the protection afforded by the

---

[46] *Fressoz and Roire v France* (1999) 31 EHRR 2, 60. Fressoz was the publishing director of the French satirical weekly, *Le Canard enchaîné*. He published an article about the salary rise which the head of Peugeot had awarded himself at a time of industrial unrest. Fressoz illustrated the article by reproducing sections of the head of Peugeot's tax returns. He (and the journalist concerned) were successfully prosecuted in France for making unlawful use of these documents. The Strasbourg Court held that Art 10 had been infringed.

[47] But, again, note that protection for literary works under UK law is not limited to the very words used. The statement should no doubt also be understood as applying to artistic works, films, sound recordings, and broadcasts where there is a public interest in seeing the very images or hearing the very sounds in question.

[48] There may be other circumstances too. See para 8.65 below.

CDPA 1988, notwithstanding the express exceptions to be found in the Act. In these circumstances, a court will be bound, in so far as it is able, to apply the Act in a manner that accommodates the right of freedom of expression. It will be necessary for the court to look closely at the facts of each individual case.

8.23 The Court of Appeal therefore appears to have considered that the Article 10 right to freedom of expression is only ever likely to override the rights of the copyright owner where there is a compelling public interest in the publication of the very expression of an author's ideas or information, and where the rigorous application of the 1988 Act would otherwise prevent this.

D. How is the Accommodation to be Made?

8.24 To say that the requirements of the Human Rights Act 1998 may in certain circumstances override the rights of the copyright owner begs the question of precisely what legal mechanism is to be used to achieve this result. The Court of Appeal suggested three possible ways in which it might be possible to accommodate the right to freedom of expression in such cases.

(1) An adjustment of what has conventionally been the boundary of fair dealing

8.25 As already indicated, the Court of Appeal considered that pre-Human Rights Act decisions on the fair dealing provisions of the 1988 Act should not be regarded as inflexible. Rather, it should be asked whether the facts of the case are such that the importance of freedom of expression outweighs the conventional considerations of what amounts to fair dealing.[49] Presumably, this will involve giving, where appropriate, an even more generous interpretation to such expressions as 'criticism', 'review', and 'reporting current events' and, indeed, as to what constitutes 'fair' dealing.

(2) Discretionary refusal of injunction

8.26 Greater use can be made of the court's discretion to refuse an injunction. What the Court of Appeal clearly had in mind was not merely the refusal of an interim injunction but a final injunction as well. The court recognized, however, that this weapon could not be used to deny a claimant his statutory

---

[49] See para 73.

remedy of damages,[50] which would remain intact. As to this, the Court of Appeal considered that, if a newspaper believes it necessary in such circumstances to publish, there is no reason in principle why it should not compensate the copyright owner for any loss caused or account for any profit made: 'Freedom of expression should not normally carry with it the right to make free use of another's work'.[51]

Nevertheless, the prospect of having to pay damages or account for profits, **8.27** together with the incurring of legal costs, may be a seriously inhibiting factor, particularly in the case of an impecunious defendant. Indeed, the Court of Appeal recognized, when considering the question of fair dealing, that having to pay damages or account for profits might be a 'chilling' factor against publication, and that is why the fair dealing provisions allow use without compensation.[52]

(3) Public interest defence

As already noted, the decision in *Ashdown* was important not merely for the **8.28** discussion of the effect of the Human Rights Act on copyright law, but also because it established that there exists a general defence of public interest in copyright infringement cases. Clearly, this defence was seen by the court as something of a safety valve or a last resort, to be used in those rare cases in which the rights of the copyright owner should not prevail, but where neither of the first two routes, referred to above, could be applied. This is shown by the fact that the court went on to emphasize that where there was a dealing for the purposes of reporting current events within the meaning of s 30(2) the court would normally have all the scope that it needed and therefore that there would be no need to give separate consideration to the availability of the public interest defence. The court's overall conclusion was that it was unlikely that there will be a flood of cases in which freedom of expression is invoked and it will be very rare for the public interest to justify the substantial copying of the expression of a copyright work.

An unresolved issue is the extent to which a public interest defence in a **8.29** freedom of expression case is a defence to a damages claim as well as a defence to a claim for an injunction. As has been seen, the Court of Appeal in *Ashdown* considered that one route to accommodate the Article 10 right is

---

[50] ie, under CDPA 1988, s 96(2).
[51] *Ashdown v Telegraph Group Ltd* [2001] EWCA (Civ) 1142; [2002] Ch 149, CA, para 46.
[52] Ibid, para 69.

to refuse injunctive relief and to leave the copyright owner to his pecuniary remedies. The court did not discuss whether, in the case where the alternative route of a public interest defence is successfully invoked, the court will similarly refuse an injunction and leave the claimant free to pursue the remedy of damages or an account of profits, or will refuse all relief. Although it is often described as a 'defence', s 171(3) itself does not use this term, stating only that nothing in the Act is to affect any rule of law 'preventing or restricting the enforcement of copyright' on grounds of public interest. From this, it would appear that if a case arose where, on the facts, an award of damages or an account of profits would be against the public interest because it would prevent justifiable freedom of expression, the 'defence' might extend to deny a claimant such relief. There is a conceptual difficulty here, however, because the possibility of an award of damages will only arise after publication. Nevertheless, could an impecunious defendant who has published copyright material in the public interest successfully argue that he would not have published had he thought he might have to pay damages?

(4) *Human Rights Act 1998, s 12*

8.30 Section 12 of the Human Rights Act can be regarded as potentially making further adjustments to the law to accommodate the Article 10 right. It makes detailed provision relating to the exercise of the court's power to grant relief of a kind which might affect the Article 10 right. In particular:

(a) No such relief is to be granted so as to restrain publication before trial unless the court is satisfied that the applicant is *likely* to establish that publication should not be allowed (s 12(3)).

(b) In considering whether to grant relief, the court must have particular regard to the importance of the Article 10 right and, where the proceedings relate to material which the defendant claims, or which appears to the court, to be journalistic, literary, or artistic material (or to conduct concerned with such material), have regard to:

    (i) The extent to which (1) the material has, or is about to, become available to the public; or (2) it is, or would be, in the public interest for the material to be published;

    (ii) Any relevant privacy code (s 12(4)).[53]

---

[53] The court is also directed not to grant 'without notice' (ex parte) relief unless satisfied that all practical steps have been taken to notify the respondent or there are compelling reasons why he or she should not be notified (s 12(2)). The subsection is not considered further here.

The most obvious kind of relief being referred to in the context of copyright **8.31** claims is the grant of an injunction, but the section clearly applies to other forms of relief, for example an order for delivery up of infringing copies where such an order could prevent a defendant from disseminating information to the public[54] or even damages or an account of profits if that might affect the right.

An interesting issue is the precise status of s 12 in the context of the Human **8.32** Rights Act. After all, s 1(2) of the Act already gives statutory effect to Article 10. Is s 12 meant merely to reinforce the position or is it intended to do something more, and if so, what? The section was introduced by amendment during the passage of the Bill through Parliament in response to the media's concerns about the potential clash between Article 10 and the right to respect for private and family life under Article 8. As put by the Home Secretary, Mr Jack Straw MP: 'So far as we are able, in a manner consistent with the convention and its jurisprudence, we are saying to the courts that whenever there is a clash between Article 8 rights and Article 10 rights, they must pay particular attention to the Article 10 rights.'[55] It is interesting to note that no mention was made of any potential clash between the Article 10 freedom of expression rights and the rights of property which are preserved by Article 10(2) and Article 1 of the First Protocol. In spite of this, however, the section is drafted widely and is of general application. It thus potentially comes into play whenever the Article 10 rights are involved, including cases where Article 10 and the rights of copyright owners conflict.[56]

It might seem from the above statement of the Home Secretary that the **8.33** Article 10 rights were intended to be given pre-eminence, although whether

---

[54] Although an order for delivery up made under CDPA 1988, s 99 is an exercise of statutory jurisdiction, the remedy is discretionary. There also remains the parallel equitable jurisdiction to make such an order.

[55] HC Debates, 2 July 1998, col 543. A helpful collection of relevant extracts from the debates on 2 July 1998 (Hansard (HC Debates), 6th series, vol 315) can be found in J Wadham and H Mountfield, *Blackstone's Guide to the Human Rights Act 1998* (3rd edn, Oxford: OUP, 2003) App 4.

[56] As will be seen, in *Imutran Ltd v Uncaged Campaigns Ltd* [2001] 2 All ER 385, Sir Andrew Morritt V-C took into account the requirements of section 12 in a copyright infringement claim where Art 10 was also involved.

and the extent to which this is in fact so remains a matter for interpretation by the courts. In fact, it already appears that the courts are unlikely to attach any great significance to the section: 'It seems to us that section 12 does no more than underline the need to have regard to contexts in which [the Strasbourg] jurisprudence has given particular weight to freedom of expression, while at the same time drawing attention to considerations which may nonetheless justify restricting that right.'[57] Is this view correct? To what extent does s 12, perhaps inadvertently, affect an issue which was not referred to in the Parliamentary debates, namely the balance between the Article 10 rights and rights such as those of copyright owners?

8.34 There are three limbs to the directions or restraints imposed by s 12, which, taken in their logical order so far as any proceedings are concerned, are as follows:

(a) relief before trial;
(b) relief at any stage which might affect the Article 10 right;
(c) relief which would affect the Article 10 right and which relates to journalistic material and the like.

8.35 First, no such relief is to be granted so as to restrain publication before trial unless the court is satisfied that the applicant is *likely* to establish that publication should not be allowed (s 12(3)). The section here is clearly talking mainly about the grant of interim injunctive relief. Does the section alter the existing law and practice relating to the grant of interim injunctions? Under normal *Amercian Cyanamid* principles,[58] the court is only concerned at the interim stage to ask whether the applicant has crossed the low threshold of establishing an arguable case. The court has to be satisfied that the claim is not frivolous or vexatious, in other words, that there is a serious question to be tried and a real prospect of success. As already noted, considerations such as the freedom of the press[59] and the respective strengths of the parties' cases[60] have traditionally only come into play at the second stage, where the court

---

[57] See *Ashdown v Telegraph Group Ltd* [2001] EWCA (Civ) 1142; [2002] Ch 149, CA, para 27.
[58] *American Cyanamid Company v Ethicon Ltd* [1975] AC 396.
[59] See paras 8.13–8.15 above, as to consideration of freedom of the press in relation to the grant of interim relief under the pre-Human Rights Act law.
[60] See *Series 5 Software v Clarke* [1996] 1 All ER 853.

has moved on to consider the balance of convenience, or the balance of justice. Again, in cases where the grant or refusal of an interim injunction would have the practical effect of putting an end to the action, the strength or otherwise of the claimant's case must be brought into the balance in weighing the risk of injustice to either party by the grant or refusal of the injunction sought.[61]

Does section 12 mean that applicants for an interim injunction in freedom **8.36** of expression cases now have to establish a stronger case?[62] At first sight, it might seem that the answer is clearly yes, given that the ordinary meaning of the word 'likely' implies a probability of greater than fifty per cent. It was clearly the Government's view that a higher standard was being imposed:

> [W]e believe that the courts should consider the merits of an application when it is made and should not grant an interim injunction simply to preserve the status quo ante between the parties . . . We have already discussed the difficulty of getting interlocutory relief. It will be very difficult to get it unless the applicant can satisfy the court that the applicant is likely to establish that publication should not be allowed. That is a much higher test than that there should simply be a prima facie case to get the matter into court.[63]

> We suggest . . . that the law on granting injunctions is flexible in privacy cases, and we are tightening it to ensure that the applicant will in all cases need to establish a stronger case.[64]

Other authors have thought the same: 'The effect of section 12(3) is to raise the threshold test for the restraint of expression: to require the claimant to establish a stronger *prima facie* case. As a result the standard *American Cyanamid* test for interim injunctions will no longer be applicable in any application to restrain expression.'[65]

---

[61] *NWL Ltd v Woods* [1979] ICR 867.

[62] For example in relation to the claimant's title, or whether a substantial part has been taken, or whether one of the fair dealing defences applies.

[63] The Home Secretary, Mr Jack Straw, *Hansard* HC, 2 July 1998, cols 536–537.

[64] Mr Mike O'Brien MP, Under Secretary of State for the Home Department, *Hansard* HC, 2 July 1998, col 562. Although the statement refers to privacy cases, it is dealing with the effect of section 12(3) and the meaning of 'likely', and is of general application.

[65] R Clayton and H Tomlinson, *The Law of Human Rights* (Oxford: OUP, 2000), para 15.243. Wadham and Mountfield take a similar view (see J Wadham and H Mountfield, *Blackstone's Guide to the Human Rights Act 1998* (3rd edn, Oxford: OUP, 2003) 67–8).

8.37 After a tortuous series of decisions,[66] however, it has now been established by the House of Lords in *Cream Holdings Ltd v Banerjee*,[67] that although the general meaning of 'likely' in s 12(3) is 'more likely than not', the meaning is flexible. This is because the section is of general application and applies to all cases of interim restraint: it must be applied not only in the ordinary case of a decision following a full interim hearing but also where a short-lived injunction may be appropriate to hold the ring, for example, to give a court time to read the papers or consider its judgment, or pending an appeal. Again, the test must be flexible to cope with a case where the claimant's case may be relatively weak but the consequences of publication would be especially grave. The intention of Parliament must therefore have been that 'likely' should have an extended meaning which sets as a normal standard for the grant of an injunction before trial a likelihood of success at the trial *higher* than the commonplace *American Cyanamid* standard of 'real prospect of success' but permits the court to dispense with this higher standard where particular circumstances make this necessary.

8.38 The effect of the decision in *Cream Holdings v Banerjee* is thus that the court should not make an interim restraint order unless satisfied that the applicant's prospects of success at the trial are sufficiently favourable to justify such an order being made in the particular circumstances of the case. As to the degree of likelihood which makes the prospects of success 'sufficiently favourable', courts should be exceedingly slow to make interim restraint orders where the applicant has not satisfied the court that it is more likely than not that he will succeed at the trial. There will be cases, however, where it is necessary for a court to depart from this general approach and a lesser degree of likelihood will be sufficient. This interpretation emphasizes the importance of the applicant's prospects of success as a factor to be taken into account but it provides that the weight to be given to this factor will depend on the circumstances. The conclusion is therefore that this limb of s 12 has altered the previous law, but only in a subtle way. Whether it will make any practical difference in freedom of expression cases must be doubtful.

8.39 The second limb of s 12 is the requirement that, when asked to grant relief which would affect the Article 10 right, the court must have particular regard to the importance of the right. This requirement applies to applications

---

[66] See, eg, *Douglas v Hello! Ltd* [2001] QB 967, CA; *Imutran Ltd v Uncaged Campaigns Ltd* [2001] 2 All ER 385; *Theakston v MGN Ltd* [2002] EMLR 398; *A v B plc and C* [2003] QB 195, CA.
[67] [2004] UKHL 44.

for both interim and final relief, whatever the nature of the relief sought. It is not clear that this requirement affects the pre-existing law in the context of actions for infringement of copyright. It should be noted that the section does not purport to alter the law relating to the parties' substantive rights, but to modify the court's approach to the grant of relief where such rights have been infringed and there is a clash with another right. As already seen, freedom of the press considerations were already a factor in the context of interim relief. As to final relief, the section is consistent with the Court of Appeal's resort in *Ashdown* to the weapon of refusal of an injunction to resolve the clash between the two rights. The status of other relief, such as an award of damages, comes within the ambit of the section. It remains to be seen whether such relief will ever be withheld.

The third limb applies where the court is asked to grant relief which would **8.40** affect the Article 10 right, and where the proceedings relate to material which the defendant claims, or which appears to the court, to be journalistic, literary, or artistic material (or to conduct concerned with such material). In the context of a copyright infringement claim, the copyright work which is the subject of the claim will often be either a literary or artistic work, but may also take the form of a sound recording or film, which, depending on its source, may be described as journalistic. Even if the work is not of that type, the action is likely to be concerned with conduct relating to the publication of such material, so that the subsection will be engaged.

There are in fact three separate branches to this third limb.   **8.41**

(a) The court must have regard to the extent to which the material has, or is about to, become available to the public. The Act does not say what effect such other publicity is to have on the court's decision, whether weakening or strengthening the case for the Article 10 right, but the position becomes clearer once it is remembered that these requirements were introduced primarily to deal with the clash of Article 10 with the Article 8 right to privacy. Thus, in the context of a privacy claim, if what was once private information has been, or is about to be, made public, the arguments for restraining further publication of the information by the defendant become that much weaker. The position was put as follows in Parliamentary debates: 'If the court and the parties to the proceedings know that a story will shortly be published anyway, for example, in another country or on the Internet, that must affect the decision whether it is appropriate to restrain publication by the print or broadcast media in this country.'[68] In a copyright context, however, the position is not always the same, and may even be reversed. If the material has already been made public, or is about to be made public, the public interest argument for further publication by the defendant becomes weaker and the interests of the copyright owner should, it is suggested, normally prevail. Be that as it may, the subsection appears to do little other than to reinforce the kind of considerations which the court would in any event have taken into account.

(b) The court must also have regard to the extent to which it is, or would be, in the public interest for the material to be published. Parliament presumably had in mind the case law on the public interest defence relating to breach of confidence claims. At the date the Act received Royal Assent,[69] the better view as regards a public interest defence to copyright infringement claims was that such a defence existed, although the limits of the defence may have been uncertain.[70] Now that it is established that such a defence exists, it is clearly something s 12 requires to be taken into account in relevant circumstances. Again, however, the Act does not appear to have altered the law in this respect, but simply to have given statutory emphasis to the existing law.

(c) Finally, the court must also have regard to any relevant privacy code.[71] Some consideration has been given to this requirement in the context of privacy or breach of confidence claims. However, it seems to be of little or no application in the context of copyright infringement claims where no privacy claim is involved. For example, where a defendant threatens to publish a private document which has been obtained in breach of confidence, what is the position of the copyright owner? The fact that it was unpublished will now prevent reliance being placed on the defence of fair dealing for the purposes of criticism or review, and it may be a factor in deciding whether the dealing for the purposes of reporting current events was or will be fair. As to the public interest defence, the Press Complaints

---

[68] Mr Jack Straw, The Home Secretary, *Hansard* HC, 2 July 1998, col 537.

[69] 9 November 1998.

[70] See, eg, Garnett et al (eds), *Copinger and Skone James on Copyright* (15th edn, London: Sweet & Maxwell Ltd, 2005) para 22–82; Laddie, Prescott & Vitoria, *The Modern Law of Copyright and Designs* (3rd edn, London: Butterworths, 2000) paras 20.9, 20.10. The decision of the Court of Appeal in *Hyde Park*, in which it was held that only a limited defence existed, was not delivered until 10 February 2000, and *Ashdown*, in which the Court of Appeal held that the decision in *Hyde Park* was wrong, was not decided until 18 July 2001.

[71] The fact that the reference here is to any relevant *privacy* code, rather than *any* relevant code of conduct, again underlines the genesis of s 12.

privacy code already provides an exception if publication can be demonstrated to be in the public interest.

E. Application of the *Ashdown* Ruling

After this general review, it is now possible to look at types of cases in which **8.42** the law may have been altered and, in particular, cases where the Article 10 right may provide a 'new' defence to infringement claims. First, it is necessary to see how the Court of Appeal in *Ashdown* applied the principles to the actual facts of the case before it.

The *Sunday Telegraph* had published substantial extracts from Mr Ashdown's **8.43** confidential and unpublished memorandum of a secret meeting at the Prime Minister's office at which the possibility of a merger between the Labour Party and the Liberal Democrats had been discussed. The contents appeared to contradict statements from 10 Downing Street and, if the meeting had been known about at the time, it might have sparked a Labour revolt. It was too late to prevent publication, but Mr Ashdown applied by way of summary judgment for a final injunction and appropriate financial relief. The case is particularly valuable because although the claim was also for breach of confidence, the application for summary judgment was based wholly on infringement of copyright. It was not therefore necessary to disentangle the copyright and confidential information aspects, a common complexity of such cases.

The *Sunday Telegraph* ran defences of fair dealing for the purposes of criticism **8.44** and review, and for reporting current events, and a separate public interest defence. In relation to criticism and review, the Court of Appeal agreed with Sir Andrew Morritt V-C's rejection of the defence on the ground that the article had not been published for the purpose of criticizing or reviewing the memorandum (or any other work), but for the purpose of criticism or review of the actions of the Prime Minister and Mr Ashdown. It had not been necessary for that purpose to copy the memorandum at all. As to the defence of reporting current events, the Court of Appeal accepted that the article had been published for these purposes, given the liberal interpretation to be applied to these words:

> The meeting between the claimant, the Prime Minister and others in October 1997 was undoubtedly an event, and while it might be said that by November 1999 it was not current solely in the sense of recent in time, it was arguably a

matter of current interest to the public. In a democratic society, information about a meeting between the Prime Minister and an opposition party leader during the then current Parliament to discuss possible close co-operation between those parties is very likely to be of legitimate and continuing public interest. It might impinge upon the way in which the public would vote at the next general election. The 'issues' identified by the Sunday Telegraph may not themselves be 'events', but the existence of those issues may help to demonstrate the continuing public interest in a meeting two years earlier.[72]

It was held, however, that the dealing was not 'fair'. The publication was not only commercially valuable to the *Sunday Telegraph* in terms of its interest to its readers but had also affected the commercial value of the memorandum, which had not previously been published. It had also been unnecessary to publish such large extracts to make the point.

8.45 Going on to take account of the Human Rights Act, and to ask whether the facts of the case were such that the importance of freedom of expression outweighed the conventional fair dealing considerations, the Court held that it was arguable that the *Sunday Telegraph* was justified in making *limited* quotation of Mr Ashdown's own words in order to demonstrate that they had obtained the memorandum, and so were in a position to give an authentic account of the meeting. However, it was not necessary to make such extensive quotation of Mr Ashdown's own words in order to satisfy the reader that the account given of his meeting with Mr Blair was authoritative. A statement that the *Sunday Telegraph* had obtained a copy of the minute, coupled with one or two short extracts from it would have been sufficient. The memorandum had been deployed for reasons that were essentially journalistic in furtherance of the commercial interests of the *Sunday Telegraph*. It was not right that it should be able to profit from use of Mr Ashdown's copyright without paying compensation.

F. Pre-*Ashdown* Decisions

8.46 It is now instructive to look at some of the decisions on the fair dealing defences prior to *Ashdown*, in order to see whether the court's reasoning in those cases provides clues as to how such cases would be decided today. They show, as *Ashdown* itself indicates, that the courts are likely to take a restrictive view.

---

[72] *Ashdown v Telegraph Group Ltd* [2001] EWCA (Civ) 1142; [2002] Ch 149, para 64.

(1) Fraser v Evans[73]

The *Sunday Times* had obtained a copy of a confidential report prepared by **8.47**
the claimant for the Greek Government, and intended to publish extracts as
part of an article, together with further information provided by him during
an interview. An application to restrain publication based on claims for
defamation and breach of confidence failed. The claimant also alleged
infringement of his copyright in the report. As to this, the *Sunday Times*
argued that no interim injunction should be granted since the article had not
yet been published, and it intended to rely on the defence of fair dealing for
the purposes of reporting current events, and also to argue that there was a
public interest in publication.[74] The claimant argued that his copyright
extended to the right to stop publication of the information in the report.

The difficulty which the court faced was that it did not know what the article **8.48**
would contain when published. Lord Denning MR concluded:

> [C]opyright does not subsist in the information contained in the report. It
> exists only in the literary form in which the information is dressed. If The
> Sunday Times were going to print this report in full, thus taking the entire
> literary form, it might well be a case for an injunction to restrain the infringe-
> ment of copyright. But The Sunday Times say that they are going to do no
> such thing. They say that they are only going to print short extracts from it,
> followed up with some of the statements which Mr. Fraser made to them and
> their comments on it. . . .
>
> We have not seen what is going to be published. We cannot pre-judge the
> matter. We cannot say that there is going to be an unfair dealing when The
> Sunday Times say it is to be a fair dealing. So no injunction should be granted
> to prevent them publishing.[75]

The public interest defence was not expressly dealt with, but the point clearly
formed a major part of the court's thinking. As Lord Denning said:

> It all comes back to this. There are some things which are of such public
> concern that the newspapers, the Press, and indeed, everyone is entitled to
> make known the truth and to make fair comment on it. This is an integral part

---

[73] [1969] 1 QB 349.
[74] The report was alleged to reveal that the claimant, who was a public relations consultant,
had been employed by the Greek Government to influence opinion in the UK and among
members of Parliament.
[75] [1969] 1 QB 349, 362–3.

of the right of free speech and expression. It must not be whittled away. The
Sunday Times assert that in this case there is a matter of public concern. They
admit that they are going to injure Mr. Fraser's reputation, but they say that
they can justify it; and that they are only making fair comment on a matter of
public interest; and, therefore, they ought not to be restrained. We cannot
prejudge this defence by granting an injunction against them. I think the
injunction which has been granted should be removed. The Sunday Times
should be allowed to publish the article at their risk. If they are guilty of libel or
breach of confidence, or breach of copyright, that can be determined by an
action hereafter and damages awarded against them. But we should not grant
an interim injunction in advance of an article when we do not know in the least
what it will contain.[76]

Today, the decision would no doubt go the same way. In relation to the copyright claim, the court's hands had in reality been tied by not being able to see
the proposed article.

(2) Hubbard v Vosper[77]

8.49 The defendant published a book which was highly critical of the Church
of Scientology and contained substantial extracts from the published and
unpublished works of its founder, Mr Ron Hubbard. The claimants applied
for an interim injunction, alleging infringement of copyright and breach
of confidential information.[78] The defendant relied on the defence of fair
dealing for criticism and review in relation to the copyright infringement
claim and public interest in respect of the breach of confidence claim. The
Court of Appeal held that the defence of fair dealing could apply where what
was being criticized were the doctrines or philosophy underlying the work,
not merely the work itself, Lord Denning MR adding that the fact that some
of the works were unpublished did not mean that the dealing was not fair,
particularly where there had been some dissemination of the work. There was
therefore a possible defence to the copyright claim. There was also a possible
defence to the breach of confidence claim on the grounds that the practices
of the Church were arguably so dangerous that it was in the public interest

---

[76] [1969] 1 QB 349, 363.

[77] [1972] 2 QB 84.

[78] Mr Vosper had been a member of the Church for many years and had been able to get
access to some unpublished material which was arguably confidential. Some of the material
had been previously published.

that they be made known.[79] As to the grant of an interim injunction. Lord Denning said:

> But here, although Mr Hubbard owns the copyright, nevertheless, Mr Vosper has a defence of fair dealing: and although Mr Hubbard may possess confidential information, nevertheless, Mr Vosper has a defence of public interest. These defences are such that he should be permitted to go ahead with the publication. If what he says is true, it is only right that the dangers of this cult should be exposed. We never restrain a defendant in a libel action who says he is going to justify. So in [a] copyright action, we ought not to restrain a defendant who has a reasonable defence of fair dealing. Nor in an action for breach of confidence, if the defendant has a reasonable defence of public interest. The reason is because the defendant, if he is right, is entitled to publish it: and the law will not intervene to suppress freedom of speech except when it is abused.[80]

The case prompts the interesting question as to how it would be decided today. With the amendment to s 30(1), the defence of fair dealing would not now be available at trial in relation to the material that was unpublished. It does not appear that the defence of fair dealing for the purposes of reporting current events could apply, even as more generously interpreted today. If there was no other way to bring home to the public what were alleged to be the dangers of the cult than by publishing a substantial part of the unpublished material, it may be that Human Rights Act considerations would prevail today.

(3) Beloff v Pressdam[81]

In *Beloff*, the claimant, the Political and Lobby Correspondent of *The* **8.50** *Observer* newspaper, alleged infringement of copyright (and also breach of confidence) by the publication in *Private Eye* of an internal office memorandum. *Private Eye* had been running a series of articles questioning the relationship between Mr Reginald Maudling, then a cabinet minister in the Conservative government, and a Mr Hoffman and his company.[82] *The Observer* had, in turn, attacked *Private Eye* for smearing Mr Maudling.

---

[79] Megaw and Stephenson LJJ merely agreed with Lord Denning on this. Megaw LJ added that it was arguable that the claimants were seeking to protect their secrets by deplorable means and thus had not come to court with clean hands.

[80] [1972] 2 QB 84, 96–7.

[81] [1973] 1 All ER 241.

[82] Hoffman had been convicted on fraud charges in the USA.

The memorandum was published by *Private Eye* as part of its response. The memorandum was not directly concerned with the Maudling–Hoffman affair, but was a note of a private conversation between the claimant and Mr William Whitelaw, also a cabinet minister, in which Mr Whitelaw expressed the view that Mr Maudling was likely to be the next Prime Minister after Mr Edward Heath. It went on to say that, in his view, *Private Eye*'s campaign against Mr Maudling would not affect this, although he thought Mr Maudling would have to sue for libel if it went on.

8.51 As to the defence of public interest, Ungoed Thomas J stated the law in the then restricted terms of its being justified only in cases of disclosing iniquity or misdeeds:

> The defence of public interest clearly covers and, in the authorities does not extend beyond, disclosure, which . . . must be disclosure justified in the public interest, of matters, carried out or contemplated, in breach of the country's security, or in breach of law, including statutory duty, fraud, or otherwise destructive of the country or its people, including matters medically dangerous to the public; and doubtless other misdeeds of similar gravity. Public interest, as a defence in law, operates to override the rights of the individual, (including copyright), which would otherwise prevail and which the law is also concerned to protect. Such public interest, as now recognised by the law, does not extend beyond misdeeds of a serious nature and importance to the country and thus, in my view, clearly recognisable as such.[83]

The defence therefore failed because the memorandum did not disclose any iniquity or misdeeds. It shed no light on allegations which *Private Eye* were making against Mr Maudling:

> [T]he nub of this case is not the verbal quotation of the memorandum at all. As the plaintiff's counsel made quite clear in his reply, it is not even that the names of Mr Whitelaw and Mr Carr were revealed in the memorandum as the two Cabinet Ministers referred to in the plaintiff's article as supporting Mr Maudling as the successor to Mr Heath in the event of his ceasing to be Prime Minister; but the disclosure by the memorandum of Mr Whitelaw as the source of the plaintiff's information. If it were not for that disclosure I am completely satisfied that this action would never have been brought. In that sense it is an action for breach of confidence under the guise of an action for infringement of copyright—an action springing from breach of confidence but framed in breach of copyright.[84]

---

[83] [1973] 1 All ER 241, 260.   [84] Ibid 259.

As to fair dealing, it was conceded in the light of the evidence that publication of the article amounted to dealing both for the purposes of criticism and review and for the purpose of reporting current events. The *Private Eye* article of which the memorandum formed part amounted to criticism or review of the article in *The Observer*, in particular as to its truth, relevance, sources (including how the research for it had been done), and how it came to be written. It was also for the purposes of reporting current events since the fact of *The Observer*'s taking up such an issue in its article was itself news.[85] As to whether the dealing was fair, Ungoed-Thomas J emphasized that the dealing had to be fair for the approved purposes of criticism, review, or the reporting of current events, not fair for some other purpose, or fair in general. This justified his view that: 'public interest as such is outside the purpose of the section and of fair dealing.'[86] He went on to hold that publication by *Private Eye* had not been fair, since the memorandum was an unpublished confidential memorandum which had never been intended to be published and which had been leaked by someone within *The Observer*, none of this being justifiable for any of the approved purposes.[87]

As to how the case would be decided today, the defence of fair dealing for the **8.52** purposes of criticism or review would in any event now fail, whether fair or not, since the memorandum had not been made available to the public.[88] As to fair dealing for the purposes of reporting current events, the fact that the memorandum had not previously been published and had been obtained in breach of confidence was not, as Ungoed-Thomas himself recognized, an absolute bar to publication, but remains an important factor today.[89] The central reason for not granting the claimant an injunction would, however, remain valid today, namely that the memorandum did not go to the allegations being made against Mr Maudling and thus it was not necessary to quote it to make the point. This is despite the fact that: 'the verbatim quotation of the memorandum brought home to the reader that Private Eye had inside information and gave credibility to the rest of the article, or, as Mr. Foot expressed it, it gave "a lift to the whole article".'[90] Even allowing for freedom of expression considerations, therefore, the case would probably be decided the same way today.

---

[85] Ibid 262.   [86] Ibid.   [87] Ibid 63.   [88] CDPA 1988, s 30(1).
[89] See, eg, *Ashdown v Telegraph Group Ltd* [2001] EWCA (Civ) 1142; [2002] Ch 149, CA, discussed in paras 8.42–8.45 above.
[90] [1973] 1 All ER 241, 267–8.

(4) Lion Laboratories Ltd v Evans[91]

8.53 Lion Laboratories manufactured breathalyser kits, the results of which were used as evidence, often the only evidence, in prosecutions for drink driving. The first two defendants worked for Lion Laboratories. They removed confidential memoranda casting doubt on the accuracy of the breathalysers, and thus the safety of convictions, and supplied these to the *Daily Express* (the third defendant), which intended to publish them, in breach of confidence and in infringement of the claimant's copyright.

8.54 An interim injunction was refused, on the grounds that there was an arguable defence of public interest to both the copyright and the breach of confidence claims, such that a final injunction might not be granted at trial.[92] Stephenson LJ's judgment could almost have been written after the Human Rights Act came into force and contains a prophetic discussion of the issues:

> The problem before the judge and before this court is how best to resolve, before trial, a conflict of two competing public interests. The first public interest is the preservation of the right of organisations, as of individuals, to keep secret confidential information. The courts will restrain breaches of confidence, and breaches of copyright, unless there is just cause or excuse for breaking confidence or infringing copyright. The just cause or excuse with which this case is concerned is the public interest in admittedly confidential information. There is confidential information which the public may have a right to receive and others, in particular the press, now extended to the media, may have a right and even a duty to publish, even if the information has been unlawfully obtained in flagrant breach of confidence and irrespective of the motive of the informer. The duty of confidence, the public interest in maintaining it, is a restriction on the freedom of the press which is recognised by our law, as well as by Article 10(2) of the Convention for the Protection of Human Rights and Fundamental Freedoms (1953) (Cmd 8969); the duty to publish, the countervailing interest of the public in being kept informed of matters which are of real public concern, is an inroad on the privacy of confidential matters.[93]

---

[91] [1985] QB 526, CA.

[92] The Court of Appeal considered that the claimant would still have a claim in damages. See Stephenson LJ, ibid 538.

[93] Ibid 536–7, citing the judgments of Lord Denning MR in *Initial Services Ltd v Putterill* [1968] 1 QB 396; *Fraser v Evans* [1969] 1 QB 349; *Hubbard v Vosper* [1972] 2 QB 84; *Woodward v Hutchins* [1977] 1 WLR 760; *Schering Chemicals Ltd v Falkman Ltd* [1982] QB 1 (dissenting) and the speeches of Lord Wilberforce, Lord Salmon and Lord Fraser of Tullybelton in *British Steel Corporation v Granada Television Ltd* [1981] AC 1096.

The court pointed out that the defence will not prevail, however, where it is merely alleged that publication is in the public interest: 'To be allowed to publish confidential information, the defendants must do more than raise a plea of public interest; they must show "a legitimate ground for supposing it is in the public interest for it to be disclosed".'[94] The conclusion of the Court of Appeal was that publication should not be restrained:

> The issue raised by the defendants is a serious question concerning a matter which affects the life, and even the liberty, of an unascertainable number of Her Majesty's subjects, and though there is no proof that any of them has been wrongly convicted on the evidence of the plaintiffs' Intoximeter, and we certainly cannot decide that any has, we must not restrain the defendants from putting before the public this further information as to how the Lion Intoximeter 3000 has worked, and how the plaintiffs regard and discharge their responsibility for it, although the information is confidential and was unlawfully taken in breach of confidence.[95]

Curiously, a defence of fair dealing seems not to have been argued in the Court of Appeal,[96] and if argued today it seems likely that such a defence would succeed. It is likely that the current events would have been regarded as the convictions of motorists using the evidence of the breathalysers which had been introduced about ten months previously, and the controversy about

---

[94] Ibid 538, citing Roskill LJ's judgment in *Khashoggi v Smith* (1980) 124 SJ 149, CA.

[95] Ibid 546.

[96] Partly, no doubt, because the more important and heavily argued of the two causes of action was breach of confidence, rather than infringement of copyright, and in relation to breach of confidence there was established jurisprudence relating to the disclosure in the public interest. See, eg, the judgment of O'Connor LJ at 547: 'The plaintiffs may have causes of action for breach of copyright and conversion, and after publication for libel or slander of goods; but the heart of the matter is the unauthorised use of the confidential information, and that can be protected by the equitable remedy of injunction.' In *Hyde Park Residence Ltd v Yelland* [2001] Ch 143, Mance LJ considered the reason for not taking the point may have been that: 'The fact that the newspaper wished to publish hitherto unpublished internal memoranda may have been viewed as preventing reliance on section 30. Perhaps the full scope of section 30 may not have been appreciated.' A possible fair dealing defence does, however, seem to have been raised at first instance, as appears from the following passage in Stephenson LJ's judgment, at 546: 'If [Leonard J] had had the full argument that we have had on the evidence contained in these documents and their implications, and had had less of his attention directed to questions of copyright *and fair dealing*, he might well have come to the opposite conclusion and found in public interest just cause and excuse for their disclosure' (emphasis added).

such convictions,[97] which the *Daily Express* had been running, even though what the newspaper intended to do was not merely to 'report' these already well known facts but to publish information which questioned what was taking place.

8.55 There are two other interesting and important features about this case to be noted in the present context. First, that the court considered that the publication of the actual documents was required to give the story the necessary impact: publication of the mere facts would not have been enough. Secondly, that the court considered that it was appropriate in this case to give the information to the press, and for the press to publish the information, rather that provide the information to the 'authorities'. At first instance, Leonard J had taken the view that the appropriate course was for the defendants to have passed the information over to the Home Office to take the matter up. This approach was rejected by Stephenson LJ in the Court of Appeal:

> [Leonard J] may, I think, have been influenced also in reaching that decision by giving too much weight to his view that a daily newspaper was not the best forum for investigating technical matters, and a less appropriate forum than the Home Office for the discussion of the Intoximeter's merits and demerits. I have tried to explain that the public interest in the confidential information which the fourth defendants' newspaper wants to publish does not depend on understanding or misunderstanding technical matters, though the result of the publication of that information may well be to apply pressure on the authorities to conduct a scientific investigation and discussion of those matters (such as appears to have been carried on already in The Law Society's Gazette). Furthermore, the Home Office is publicly committed to supporting the machine and its continued use, and however strongly it might make plain its opposition to obtaining unjust convictions by means of which it at present approves, it is associated in the public mind with the machine, and the police use of it, as reliable evidence in courts of law.[98]

Griffiths LJ said much the same:

> But I believe that a campaign to put pressure on the authorities is from time to time an essential function of a free press, and we would all be the worse for it if

---

[97] The public had been exposed to a 'blitz' of testing over the Christmas and New Year period and there seem to have been existing doubts about the Intoximeter (see 539). It also seems that there had already been some press coverage of the controversy by the *Daily Express* and other newspapers and journals (see 542, 544, 545, 549), although the issue may only have come to real prominence after the *Daily Express* published their first article about the Intoximeter, after which further publication of the memoranda had been halted by an ex parte injunction (see 534).

[98] *Lion Laboratories Ltd v Evans* [1985] QB 526, CA, 544.

the press were unduly inhibited in this field or their activity. Nor do I think it any answer to say in this case that the Daily Express should have gone to the Home Office in the first instance, rather than publish.

The public stance of the Home Office is that there is no risk of a false conviction as a result of the use of the machine. The Home Office is an interested and committed party. Of course I do not suggest that the Home Office would deliberately shut their eyes to evidence that the machine, or the manufacturers, might not be as reliable as they thought; but civil servants are human, and beauty lies in the eye of the beholder. I think in all the circumstances that the Daily Express is not to be criticised for thinking that the impact of the revelations in their newspaper would be more likely to galvanise the authorities into action than a discreet behind-doors approach.[99]

Thus the court identified two reasons why publication in the media was appropriate, the most significant of which in the present context was the fact that such publication might lead to public pressure for an investigation.

Clearly today it is likely that the same decision would be reached. Whether **8.56** the defence of fair dealing for the purposes of reporting current events would succeed is a moot point. The fact that the documents were unpublished and obtained in breach of confidence is a highly relevant factor, but in the light of *Ashdown* it is more than likely that this is the route that would be taken to deny the claimant relief, without having to rely on a public interest defence.

(5) Hyde Park Residence Ltd v Yelland[100]

The Sun had published certain stills of Princess Diana and Mr Dodi Fayed **8.57** taken by a security camera. *The Sun* relied on the fair dealing defence but also claimed that it was in the public interest to publish these photographs as they gave the lie to claims being made by Mr Al Fayed that the two had enjoyed a lengthy tryst at his house in Paris and were engaged to be married.

The Court of Appeal held that the publication was for the purpose of **8.58** reporting current events,[101] but had not been fair. The stills were unpublished

---

[99] Ibid 553.   [100] [2001] Ch 143.

[101] Namely, the recent controversy caused by Mr Al Fayed's public statements. Although Princess Diana's and Mr Dodi Fayed's deaths some 12 months previously were still current events, given the ongoing investigation, publication had not been for the purpose of reporting *those* events but for the purposes of vilifying Mr Fayed and exposing the falsity of his statements.

works which had been dishonestly obtained. The extent of the use had been excessive and the point could have been made by reporting the story without publication of the photograph. Aldous and Mance LJJ made the point[102] that the only significant parts of the photograph were the times recorded on them. The information so revealed could have been reported simply as a fact, and in any event did not go to the truth or the falsity of Mr Al Fayed's statement that the couple were engaged to be married. As Aldous LJ observed: 'Nobody has suggested nor could it be suggested that the information recorded on the driveway stills could be the subject of copyright or that use of that information would be an infringement of the copyright which subsists in the film. It follows that the weighing operation is not apt when the information can be published even though the action for infringement of copyright succeeds.'[103] The majority[104] held that there was no general defence of public interest to copyright infringement claims, which were different in this respect from breach of confidence claims.[105] Mance LJ, who was the only member of the Court of Appeal to rule that a general defence of public interest existed in relation to a copyright infringement claim, held that, even so, the defence did not apply: 'If the use made of the stills could not be fair dealing in the context of that section, it is difficult to see scope for a conclusion that it was nonetheless in the public interest that the claimants' copyright should be overridden.'[106]

8.59   Today, the case would probably be decided the same way. Although the case was decided before the Human Rights Act came into force, Mance LJ's analysis of the width of the public interest defence is a good guide. The courts would probably take the same approach to the central issue, namely, whether it was necessary to publish the photograph to make the point.

8.60   It is suggested, however, that, in this respect, the courts have tended to take a very restrictive approach because in almost all cases it is possible to argue that the message can be got across without publication of a substantial part of the copyright work. This approach tends to ignore, however, the very great impact which publication of the very words of a document or an actual picture can have in an era of mass communication, where quick impressions count for much. The effect of such publication will often be very much greater than a statement to the effect that the publisher is in possession of documents or

---

[102] [2001] Ch 143, paras 40 and 77, respectively.   [103] Ibid, para 55.
[104] Stuart Smith and Aldous LJJ.
[105] [2001] Ch 143, para 64 (per Aldous LJ).   [106] Ibid, para 79.

material which establish the truth of the statement but which themselves cannot be published. Indeed, the very absence of the crucial document is often
a negative rather than a neutral factor in a story's credibility. So, in *Lion
Laboratories*, it was publication of the very documents which made the story
credible. It is suggested that there is a good deal of force in Jacob J's views
in *Hyde Park*, held to be wrong on the facts of the case by the Court of Appeal,
that:

> It may well be that in some cases what a defendant publishes is completely
> unnecessary so far as any reporting of public events is concerned. That may
> take the use outside the scope of 'fair dealing'. But it by no means follows that a
> use can only amount to 'fair dealing' where it is necessary.
>
> Besides, in this case I think The Sun was in the position where it was close to
> necessary to publish the photographs to refute what Mr Al Fayed said in The
> Mirror and elsewhere. [Counsel] said The Sun could have said they had inter-
> viewed Mr Murrell and seen the photographs without actually publishing
> them. Or it could have first told Mr Al Fayed that it had the pictures and
> challenged them to withdraw his statement. But the former course would not
> have had anything like the same impact and force as actual publication of the
> stills. A picture says more than a thousand words. The Sun was showing that it
> had convincing evidence of the duration of the visit. The latter course would
> have been to invite pre-emptive legal action.
>
> Further, Mr Al Fayed had clearly put into public debate the question of what
> happened at the Villa Windsor. It was used in part to support a matter which
> was not only interesting to the public but involving as it did the mother of a
> future sovereign was genuinely of public interest. The suggestions being made,
> if true, were of far reaching importance. They even had similar hints of evil. So
> if they were false it was equally important that the falsity be exposed as soon as
> possible. It would have been inadequate for The Sun or Mr Murrell to supply
> the photographs merely to a relevant proper authority such as the investigating
> French Judge. By raising the matter in the public forum, in my judgment, Mr
> Al Fayed made it a 'fair dealing' for The Sun to come back in that very
> forum.[107]

(6) Imutran Ltd v Uncaged Campaigns Ltd[108]

The claimants sought an interim injunction to restrain continued breach of   **8.61**
confidence and infringement of copyright by publication of a large number
of leaked and confidential documents relating to its research activities
into the replacement of human organs with those of animals, mostly pigs

---

[107] [1999] RPC 655, 662.   [108] [2001] 2 All ER 385.

('xenotransplantation'). On one view, the documents raised serious questions concerning, amongst other things, animal welfare, the regulation of the research by the Home Office, Imutran's lack of success, and the accuracy of the information on its research. Most of the documents had been published briefly on a web site which had then quickly been closed down by the service providers. By the time of the hearing, all the relevant documents had, pursuant to court orders, been provided to all interested regulatory authorities. The RSPCA had also called for a report on the situation revealed by the documents from Imutran, and the Home Secretary had set in train an investigation into compliance by Imutran with its operating licences.

8.62 The defendants sought to publish seventy-nine documents, being a small part of those leaked, and disclaimed any reliance on a fair dealing defence.[109] They argued that publication was in the public interest, and that the court was no longer bound by the decision in *Hyde Park* since it had been decided before the Human Rights Act came into force. Immediately before he gave judgment in *Imutran*, Sir Andrew Morritt V-C had handed down his judgment in *Ashdown*, in which he held that *Hyde Park* was binding on him and thus that there was no general public interest defence to the copyright claim. It is hardly surprising therefore that in *Imutran* he accepted that there was no defence to the copyright infringement claim. He still had to deal with the provisions of s 12 of the 1986 Act, however, which he did in the following terms:

> It follows from the foregoing conclusions that the cause of action for infringement of copyright is made out to such an extent that I can say with confidence that on the evidence before me it is likely that Imutran will establish that publication by reproduction should not be allowed (cf s 12(3) of the [Human Rights Act 1998]). Equally, given the interaction between the law of copyright and Article 10 . . . as I consider it to be, the importance of the convention right to freedom of expression to which section 12(4) . . . requires me to pay particular regard does not lead to the conclusion that injunctive or other relief in respect of the copyright claim should be refused.[110]

---

[109] Presumably because of the quantity and confidential nature of the documents, the way they had been leaked, and the fact that disclosure to various authorities had taken place pursuant to earlier court orders.

[110] [2001] 2 All ER 385, 394–5. He had earlier held that 'likely' in s 12 imposed a standard that was slightly higher than a real prospect of success (ie the *American Cyanamid* test) but that the difference between the standards was so small as to be virtually immaterial in practice. The case was, of course, decided before *Cream Holdings Ltd v Banerjee* [2004] UKHL 44, discussed in para 8.37 above.

What would have been the position had the Court of Appeal's decision in *Ashdown* been available to Sir Andrew Morritt V-C in *Imutran*? Assuming that a fair dealing defence would still not run, it seems likely that a public interest defence would not run either. The reason can be found in the court's reasons for granting relief in relation to the parallel claim for breach of confidence. Many of the documents were of a specialist and technical nature and Sir Andrew Morritt V-C considered that they were suitable for consideration by specialists in the field, but not by the public generally. The limited disclosure already allowed meant that there was no restriction on the ability of the defendants to communicate the information to the specialist regulatory bodies and, crucially, the defendants' assertion that the relationship between Imutran and these bodies was too close for the latter to do their job properly was not accepted. The case was therefore of a different type from the *Lion Laboratories* case.

G. Conclusions

As already noted, the Court of Appeal in *Ashdown* considered that the Article **8.63** 10 right to freedom of expression is only ever likely to override the rights of the copyright owner where there is a compelling public interest in the publication of the very expression of an author's ideas or information, and which the rigorous application of the 1988 Act would otherwise prevent. What does this mean in practice?

First, there will be no 'new' Article 10 defence where there has been a dealing **8.64** with a work for the purposes of reporting current events, or for the purposes of criticism or review of a work which has previously been made available to the public, but which is not covered by s 30, ie:

(a) Where the use in question amounts to the reporting of current events, but is not 'fair' within the meaning of s 30, even when this is re-construed in the light of Article 10.

(b) This is also likely to be the case if the dealing is fair but a sufficient acknowledgment is not made. It is hard to think of cases in which the requirement to acknowledge the author will substantially interfere with the freedom of expression.[111]

---

[111] Of course, no acknowledgment is required if the work has been published anonymously or, if unpublished, the name of the author cannot be ascertained by reasonable inquiry. See CDPA 1988, s 178.

(c) The same conclusions apply where the use amounts to criticism or review of a work or of a performance of a publicly available work. If the use is not 'fair', there will be no alternative freedom of expression defence.

8.65 On the other hand, there are clearly cases in which the right to freedom of expression may provide a 'new' defence, there being no available defence under the CDPA 1988. Examples are:

(a) Where the use is for reporting current events, but the s 30(2) defence does not apply because the work is a photograph. The issue will be whether the use of the photograph can be justified in the public interest because the point cannot be made simply by reporting what the photograph reveals.[112]

(b) Where the use is for reporting events which are not current. As the Court of Appeal said in *Ashdown*:

> [I]t is possible to conceive of information of the greatest public interest relating not to a current event, but to a document produced in the past. We are not aware of any provision of the 1988 Act which would permit publication in such circumstances, unless the mere fact of publication, and any controversy created by the disclosure, is sufficient to make them 'current events'. This will often be a 'bootstraps' argument of little merit, but on other occasions (such as disclosure by the Public Record Office under the 30-year rule) it may have a more solid basis.[113]

(c) Where the use is for the purposes of criticism or review of a work or a performance of a work which has not been available to the public. This possibility has only arisen following the amendment made to s 30(1) to implement the Information Society Directive, and the facts of *Hubbard v Vosper* show the kind of case in which it might arise. It brings into sharp focus the potential, and unresolved, clash between the European Convention on Human Rights and the Information Society Directive.

(d) Where the use is for the purposes of criticism or review of something which is not a work or a performance of a work (so that it falls outside s 30(1)) and where such use does not constitute the reporting of current events. An example might be a parody, where the object of the parody is not a particular work but the author's style or perhaps the lifestyle of

---

[112] As has been seen, this was the view taken by Jacob J at first instance in *Hyde Park* (although the case concerned a film, not a photograph). However, his decision on the facts of the case was reversed by the Court of Appeal.

[113] *Ashdown v Telegraph Group Ltd* [2001] EWCA (Civ) 1142; [2002] Ch 149, 166–7.

some other person.[114] Such parodies, however, do not usually reproduce the actual expression of the author, as opposed to his style, and it is also difficult to think of cases where there will be a sufficiently strong freedom of expression argument. Again, decisions such as *Hubbard v Vosper*,[115] *Pro Sieben*,[116] and *Time Warner*[117] have already given a very wide meaning to what is meant by criticism or review 'of a work'.

(e) Where the use is neither for the purposes of reporting an event of any kind nor for the purposes of criticism or review. It is difficult, however, to think of freedom of expression cases in which substantial reference is made to a copyright work but which does not involve reporting of current events, criticism, or review.

---

[114] Note that the CDPA 1988 does not provide an express defence of parody or caricature, even though the Information Society Directive permits Member States to make such an exception.

[115] *Hubbard v Vosper* [1972] 2 QB 84, CA.

[116] *Pro Sieben Media AG v Carlton UK Television Ltd* [1999] 1 WLR 605, CA.

[117] *Time Warner Entertainment Ltd v Channel 4 Television Corp Ltd* [1994] EMLR 1, CA.

9

NOT SUCH A 'TIMID THING': THE UK'S INTEGRITY RIGHT AND FREEDOM OF EXPRESSION

Jonathan Griffiths

A. Introduction

The potential conflict between the proprietary rights of copyright owners **9.01** and the public's right of freedom of expression has now been recognized as a significant issue deserving detailed attention. This collection of essays provides ample evidence of that attention. By contrast, there has been little consideration of the relationship between freedom of expression and the non-proprietary, or moral, right of integrity. In the common law world, such lack of interest ought not to be surprising. Where integrity rights exist, they are not very potent. Nevertheless, in principle, there is a clear possibility of conflict between such rights and free speech. This is illustrated by two well-known cases from France, a jurisdiction in which the integrity right is famously well protected.[1]

9.02 In *Godot*,[2] the representatives of a deceased dramatist succeeded in persuading the court to prevent the staging of one of the dramatist's plays with female actors in roles that he had wished to be played by men. It was held that the changes to the play would breach the author's right to 'respect' for his work.[3] In *Turner Entertainment Company v Huston*,[4] the right was breached by the 'colourization' of John Huston's film, *The Asphalt Jungle*. Such decisions can no doubt be justified if it is accepted that creators have a strong right to determine the way in which works are presented to the public. Nevertheless, in both *Godot* and *Turner Entertainment Company*, the defendants were prevented from placing new interpretations of the original works before the public. As a result, their rights to freedom of expression were affected. This is not to say that those rights were necessarily breached, but simply to indicate that they were relevant to, or 'engaged' in, those disputes.[5]

9.03 In this chapter, the relationship between the integrity right and free speech is explored in one particular context. It is argued that the UK's integrity right, established under ss 80–83 of the Copyright Designs and Patents Act 1988 ('CDPA 1988') and widely derided as a 'timid thing',[6] has the potential to collide uncomfortably with the right of free speech. Suggestions are offered as to how the relevant provisions of the CDPA 1988 can be interpreted in order to minimize the impact of this collision.

---

[1] Intellectual Property Code, Art L 121–1. Under French law, the author enjoys a right to respect for name, qualification and work. For a summary of these provisions in English, see JAL Sterling, *World Copyright Law* (2nd edn, London: Sweet & Maxwell, 2003).

[2] TGI Paris (3rd chamber), 15 October 1992, (1993) 155 RIDA 225.

[3] Note that, under the French integrity right, there is no requirement for an author to establish injury to his or her standing in the eyes of the public.

[4] Cour Cass, 28 May 1991, (1991) 149 RIDA 197; CA Versailles, 10 December 1994, (1995) 164 RIDA 256.

[5] See para 2.02 above.

[6] See WR Cornish, 'Moral Rights under the 1988 Act' [1989] EIPR 449, 449.

B. The UK's Integrity Right

(1) The statutory provision

In the United Kingdom, general protection for moral rights was first intro-   **9.04**
duced in Chapter IV of the CDPA 1988.[7] The provisions contained in that
chapter were enacted to secure compliance with the UK's international
obligations under Article 6*bis* of the Berne Convention for the Protection of
Literary and Artistic Works.[8] In relation to the integrity right, Article 6*bis*
states that: 'Independently of the author's economic rights, and even after the
transfer of the said rights, the author shall have the right to . . . object to any
distortion, mutilation or other modification of, or other derogatory action
in relation to, the said work, which would be prejudicial to his honour or
reputation.'

This obligation is implemented in the CDPA 1988 in the following terms: **9.05**

(1) The author of a copyright literary, dramatic, musical or artistic work, and
the director of a copyright film, has the right in the circumstances
mentioned in this section not to have his work subject to derogatory
treatment.
(2) For the purposes of this section—
    (a) 'treatment' of a work means any addition to, deletion from or altera-
    tion to or adaptation of the work, other than—
        i)   a translation of a literary or dramatic work, or
        ii) an arrangement or transcription of a musical work involving no
             more than a change of key or register; and
    (b) the treatment of a work is derogatory if it amounts to distortion
    or mutilation of the work or is otherwise prejudicial to the honour or
    reputation of the author or director . . .[9]

---

[7] Under Chapter IV, four 'moral rights' are introduced—the right to be identified as author
or director (ss 77–9), the right to object to derogatory treatment of work (ss 80–3), false
attribution of work (s 84) and the right to privacy of certain photographs and films (s 85).
However, the latter two rights are not really true moral rights, since they do not protect the
relationship between a creator and his or her work.
[8] International Convention for the Protection of Literary and Artistic Works of
9 September 1886 (latest version, Paris 1971). For history, see S Ricketson, *The Berne
Convention for the Protection of Literary and Artistic Works* (London: Kluwer & QMW, 1987).
Article 6*bis* was introduced into the Berne Convention at the Rome Conference in 1928.
[9] CDPA 1988, ss 80(1)–(2).

9.06 This right, as required by Berne, is not assignable.[10] It can, however, be transmitted on death[11] or waived.[12] It continues in existence for as long as copyright subsists in the work[13] and is infringed whenever a 'derogatory treatment' of a work, as defined in s 80(2) above, is exposed to the public in any of a number of specified ways—for example, by commercial publication of a literary, dramatic, or musical work or by exhibition of an artistic work in public.[14] The right applies whenever the whole or any part of a protected work is

---

[10] CDPA 1988, s 94.   [11] Ibid, s 95.

[12] CDPA, s 87 provides that:

  (1) It is not an infringement of any of the rights conferred by this Chapter to do any act to which the person entitled to the right has consented.

  (2) Any of those rights may be waived by instrument in writing signed by the person giving up the right.

  (3) A waiver—

    (a) may relate to a specific work, to works of a specified description or to works generally, and may relate to existing or future works, and

    (b) may be conditional or unconditional and may expressed to be subject to revocation;

    and if made in favour of the owner or prospective owner of the copyright in the work or works to which it relates, it shall be presumed to extend to his licensees and successors in title unless a contrary intention is expressed.

  (4) Nothing in this Chapter shall be construed as excluding the operation of the general law of contract or estoppel in relation to an informal waiver or other transaction in relation to any of the rights mentioned in subsection (1).

[13] CDPA s 86(1). For the term of copyright under the CDPA 1988, see ss 12–15A.

[14] The full list of acts that potentially breach the right are set out in s 80(3)–(7). Section 80(3) provides that:

    In the case of a literary, dramatic or musical work the right is infringed by a person who—

    (a) publishes commercially, performs in public or communicates to the public a derogatory treatment of the work; or

    (b) issues to the public copies of a film or sound recording of, or including, a derogatory treatment of the work.

    Section 80(4) provides that:

    In the case of an artistic work the right is infringed by a person who—

    (a) publishes commercially or exhibits in public a derogatory treatment of the work, or communicates to the public a visual image of a derogatory treatment of the work,

    (b) shows in public a film including a visual image of a derogatory treatment of the work or issues to the public copies of such a film, or

    (c) in the case of—

      (i)   a work of architecture in the form of a model for a building,

      (ii)   a sculpture, or

      (iii) a work of artistic craftsmanship,

      issues to the public copies of a graphic work representing, or of a photograph of, a derogatory treatment of the work.

subject to 'derogatory treatment'.[15] 'Secondary' infringements of the right are committed where articles infringing s 80 are possessed or dealt with in certain business contexts.[16]

The CDPA 1988 contains a number of exceptions to,[17] or qualifications of,[18] **9.07** the integrity right. The right does not, for example, apply to a computer program or to a computer-generated work,[19] or to any work made for the purpose of reporting current events.[20] In the case of a work in which copyright originally vested in an author or director's employer by virtue of s 11(2) CDPA 1988, the scope of the right-holder's right to object to derogatory treatments is significantly diminished.[21]

(2) Case law on the integrity right

Despite the fact that the UK's integrity right has been in force for over fifteen **9.08** years,[22] it has generated little case law. In fact, there have been only four reported decisions in which s 80 has been considered.[23] Judgments have followed full trial in only two of these cases[24] and one of those was tried in the County Court.[25] There is no reported case in which a claim for breach of the integrity right has succeeded following full trial.[26] Nevertheless, despite this relative dearth of jurisprudence, the four reported decisions provide

---

Section 80(6) provides that:
    In the case of a film, the right is infringed by a person who—
    (a) shows in public, or communicates to the public a derogatory treatment of the film; or
    (b) issues to the public copies of a derogatory treatment of the film.

[15] CDPA 1988, s 89(2).
[16] CDPA 1988, s 83. In order to commit such secondary infringements, the defendant must know or have reason to believe that the article in question is an infringing article.
[17] CDPA 1988, s 81.
[18] CDPA 1988, s 82.   [19] CDPA 1988, s 81(2).   [20] CDPA 1988, s 81(3).
[21] CDPA 1988, s 82.
[22] The relevant provisions of the Act came into force on 1 August 1989. See Copyright, Designs and Patents Act 1988 (Commencement) Order 1989 (SI 1989/816).
[23] *Morrison Leahy Music Limited v Lightbond Limited* [1993] EMLR 144; *Tidy v Trustees of the Natural History Museum* [1996] EIPR-D 86, 39 IPR 501; *Pasterfield v Denham* [1999] FSR 168; *Confetti Records v Warner Music UK Ltd* [2003] EMLR 35.
[24] *Pasterfield v Denham* [1999] FSR 168; *Confetti Records v Warner Music UK Ltd* [2003] EMLR 35.
[25] *Pasterfield v Denham* [1999] FSR 168 (Plymouth County Ct).
[26] Although, in *Morrison*, the claim was found to be arguable for the purpose of the grant of an interlocutory injunction.

significant indications of the way in which UK courts are likely to interpret s 80. It is therefore worth pausing a moment to look more closely at them.

Morrison Leahy Music Limited v Lightbond Limited[27]

9.09 In *Morrison*, the defendants produced a sound recording consisting of a medley of words and music derived from five compositions by George Michael interspersed with additional music composed by others. George Michael, and the owner of the copyright in his compositions, applied for an interlocutory injunction to prevent alleged infringement of copyright and breach of the integrity right. The defendants claimed to be entitled to use the compositions as a result of a licence granted by the Mechanical Copyright Protection Society (MCPS). On the copyright claim, Morritt J held it to be arguable that the MCPS licence did not cover the activities of the defendants. In relation to s 80, he held that the creation of the medley clearly constituted 'treatment' within s 80(2)(a) and could, arguably, amount to 'distortion or mutilation' within s 80(2)(b). The question of whether or not the work had actually been subject to 'derogatory treatment' was a question of fact to be considered at full trial. Nevertheless, as the balance of convenience favoured the claimants, an injunction was granted.

Tidy v Trustees of the Natural History Museum[28]

9.10 In *Tidy*, the claimant was the author of a series of cartoons of dinosaurs. He had entered into a contract under which the Trustees of the Natural History Museum obtained the right to display the cartoons at an exhibition. The Trustees arranged for the publication of a book, in which the claimant's cartoons were reproduced in reduced size. The claimant argued that, as a result of this arrangement, his right of integrity had been breached. He claimed that the reduction in size either 'distorted' the works, or was 'otherwise prejudicial' to his reputation, because it detracted from the visual impact of the cartoons and was likely to cause readers of the book to think that he had not been bothered to redraw the cartoons for publication in book form.[29] He applied for summary judgment. Rattee J refused the application as he was not satisfied that a reproduction in reduced size distorted the original

---

[27] [1993] EMLR 144.
[28] [1996] EIPR-D 86; 39 IPR 501.
[29] The claimant was credited as the author of the drawings in the book.

drawings. He was also unwilling to hold that the treatment of the cartoons was 'otherwise prejudicial to the honour or reputation' of the cartoonist without evidence demonstrating that Tidy's reputation had been adversely affected.

The claimant had argued that, to some degree, the assessment of whether or **9.11** not the treatment of a work was prejudicial to the honour or reputation of a creator should depend upon the view of the creator himself; that is, that the matter should, at least in part, be assessed subjectively.[30] However, Rattee J held that the question of whether or not a work was 'derogatory' should be assessed objectively. He stated that he would be unwilling to take account of the cartoonist's own view that the 'treatment' of a work had prejudiced honour or reputation unless he could be satisfied that this view was reasonable.

Pasterfield v Denham[31]

In *Pasterfield*, the claimants were commissioned by Plymouth County Council **9.12** to design leaflets advertising the Plymouth Dome, a tourist attraction. The claimants created certain artistic works for the leaflets and brochures. Subsequently, the Council commissioned another designer, D, to update the leaflets. In doing so, D altered one of the artistic works created by the claimants. The claimants sued the Council and D for infringement of copyright, breach of the integrity right, and passing off. The judge concluded that the ownership of the original copyright drawings had passed in equity to the Council and, therefore, that the claim in copyright failed. He also concluded that there had been no passing off because there was no misrepresentation and no likelihood of injury to the claimants.

In claiming breach of the integrity right, the claimants had argued that one **9.13** of their drawings had been subjected to derogatory treatment because, in D's leaflet, certain details had been omitted or altered and colours had been changed. The judge accepted that D's activities amounted to 'treatment' because they had 'cut around' certain aspects of the original drawing. In considering whether this treatment could be regarded as 'distortion' or

---

[30] In this claim, he relied upon the Canadian case of *Snow v Eaton Centre* (1982) 70 CPR (2d) 105, in which, it was argued, the court took into account a 'certain subjective element or judgment'.
[31] [1999] FSR 168.

'mutilation', he referred to the Oxford English Dictionary's definition of 'distortion' as 'the twisting or perversion of words so as to give them a different sense' and of 'mutilation' as 'the fact of rendering a thing imperfect by excision or destruction of one or more of its parts'.[32] He adopted the view of Laddie et al that: 'the presence of the word "otherwise" indicates that the words "prejudicial to the honour or reputation" also govern the first part of the definition, namely distortions and mutilations of the work. If this were not the case, any deletion from a work could be said to render it imperfect and thus a mutilation.'[33] Therefore, in order to succeed under s 80, it was held that an author or director had to prove that: '[T]he treatment accorded to his work is either a distortion or mutilation that prejudices his honour or reputation as an artist. It is not sufficient that the author is himself aggrieved by what has occurred.'[34] In assessing the claim on this basis, the judge held that the claimant's evidence fell far short of establishing the objective prejudice to honour or reputation necessary for success. Overall, the allegedly distorting or mutilating changes and additions were minor. Even the claimant's own expert did not notice a number of them. Comparing the facts of the case before him with those in the French case of *Turner Entertainment Company v Huston*,[35] the judge concluded that the changes in *Pasterfield* did not come anywhere near the 'gross differences between a black and white film and a colourised version of the same film'.[36]

Confetti Records v Warner Music UK Limited[37]

9.14 The conclusion that 'distortion' and 'mutilation' will only amount to 'derogatory treatment' where they result in prejudice to 'honour or reputation' was approved by Lewison J in *Confetti Records*:

---

[32] [1999] FSR 168, 180–1.

[33] Laddie et al, *The Modern Law of Copyright and Designs* (3rd edn, London: Butterworths, 2000) para 13.18.

[34] [1999] FSR 168, 182.

[35] Cour Cass, 28 May 1991, (1991) 149 RIDA 197; CA Versailles, 10 December 1994, (1995) 164 RIDA 256.

[36] [1999] FSR 182. With respect to differences alleged to support a claim under s 80, the judge stated that, 'the differences may be such that the two versions could well be the subject of a Spot the Difference competition in a children's comic. However, it would be wrong to elevate such differences to "derogatory treatment" in my judgment. The evidence simply does not support it' (at 182).

[37] [2003] EMLR 35.

It is clear that in Art 6 *bis* the author can only object to distortion, mutilation or modification of his work if it is prejudicial to his honour or reputation. I do not believe that the framers of the 1988 Act meant to alter the scope of the author's moral rights in this respect. Moreover, in the compressed drafting style of the United Kingdom legislature, the word 'otherwise' itself suggests that the distortion or mutilation is only actionable if it is prejudicial to the author's honour or reputation. HH Judge Overend adopted this construction in *Pasterfield v Denham* [1999] FSR 168, and in my judgment he was correct to do so. I hold that the mere fact that a work has been distorted or mutilated gives rise to no claim, unless the distortion or mutilation prejudices the author's honour or reputation.[38]

Confetti Records concerned a musical track called 'Burnin'. The defendant released a version of the track in which 'Burnin' was interposed with another composition and had a rap superimposed upon it. The claimants, who included the copyright owner and author of 'Burnin', sued for infringement of copyright and breach of s 80. In making the latter claim, the author argued that there had been derogatory treatment because the superimposed rap referred to violence, drug-taking, and lynching and because the superimposition of new material resulted in the loss of the coherence of 'Burnin'. The claim based upon the alleged references to violence and drug-taking failed because the words of the rap were extremely difficult to decipher and their meaning was uncertain. As a result, it could not be demonstrated that the composer's reputation or honour had been prejudiced.

Having considered the claim based upon loss of coherence and the references **9.15** to lynching, the judge concluded that there was no evidence to suggest that the author's honour or reputation had suffered prejudice as a result. Indeed, the author himself had not complained of such prejudice in his witness statement. The judge could not infer prejudice from the fact that the defendant's recording 'rode the rhythm right through' 'Burnin'. The original track had itself been intended as a background for a rap.

In respect of the claim relating to the alleged reference to lynching, the **9.16** judge was sceptical whether the author would in fact be connected with the defendant's recording. He also noted that the group to which the author belonged had itself adopted the style of 1930s gangsters. Accordingly, the claim for breach of the integrity right failed.

---

[38] Ibid, para 150.

9.17 Interestingly, in the context of this chapter's concern with the relationship between that right and freedom of expression, the defendants in *Confetti Records* invited Lewison J to 'read down' s 80 in order to ensure compliance with Article 10 of the ECHR.[39] The judge declined to do so, indicating that, under Article 10(2), States are entitled to curtail the right to freedom of expression in order to protect the 'reputation of others'. As a result, he doubted whether reliance on Article 10 added any force to the defendants overall arguments but expressed 'no concluded view'.

Conclusion on the case law

9.18 There are clearly many aspects of the integrity right that remain unexplored. A number are considered in this chapter. Nevertheless, the four decisions described above allow us to come to certain conclusions on the way in which UK courts have interpreted s 80 and are likely to do so in future. The judiciary appears to have moved away from a position in which 'distortion' and 'mutilation' can be interpreted on their own terms and without reference to prejudice to honour or reputation.[40] Recently, it has been made very clear that there can be no breach of s 80 without evidence of prejudice to honour or reputation. It has also been held that the existence of such prejudice must be objectively demonstrated. In providing objective evidence of prejudice, the following factors have been considered to be of relevance: public association of the author with the treatment complained of,[41] the existing reputation of the author,[42] the author's own intended exploitation of the work,[43] and the public's ability to recognize the allegedly derogatory nature of the treatment of a work.[44]

9.19 It is not surprising that this approach has been taken. Acceptance of alternative readings, in which 'distortion or mutilation' would alone be sufficient

---

[39] Under s 3 of the Human Rights Act 1998:

> So far as it is possible to do so, primary and subordinate legislation must be read and given effect in a way which is compatible with the Convention rights.

[40] *Morrison Leahy Music Limited v Lightbond Limited* [1993] EMLR 144.

[41] *Confetti Records v Warner Music UK Ltd* [2003] EMLR 35, paras 159–60.

[42] Ibid 160.

[43] *Pasterfield v Denham* [1999] FSR 168, 182–3, *Confetti Records v Warner Music UK Ltd* [2003] EMLR 35, para 158.

[44] *Pasterfield v Denham* [1999] FSR 168, 182; *Confetti Records v Warner Music UK Ltd* [2003] EMLR 35, para 153–5.

to establish breach, or in which the creator's own view of prejudice would be persuasive, would cause significant difficulties. In order to assess whether or not a work had been subject to 'distortion' or 'mutilation', courts would be forced to make aesthetic judgments. This would breach an accepted principle of copyright law that such judgments are to be avoided wherever possible.[45] It is also difficult to see how a court in this jurisdiction could accept an author's subjective assessment of prejudice to honour or reputation without objective verification. If it were to do so, the opinion of one individual would be elevated over that of the 'objective' reasonable person and the function of the court as decision-maker would be displaced. Such an interpretation might be acceptable in a jurisdiction which has historically placed a high value on a creator's personal right to determine how his or her work should appear before the public. However, it would be uncomfortable for UK courts which, in other related areas of law such as defamation and passing off, are used to measuring a defendant's actions against (at least notionally) measurable criteria.

(3) Commentary on the integrity right

As has been seen above, courts have not had the opportunity to interpret s 80 **9.20** very extensively. The provision has, however, received attention from commentators. Indeed, it is fair to say that it has been subject to sustained criticism. It has often been argued that the UK's integrity right is flawed and ineffective, particularly by comparison with the protection offered to authors and directors in other jurisdictions. Indeed, the UK's attempt to ensure compliance with its international obligations to provide moral rights has been characterized as grudging and 'cynical'.[46] Where s 80 has been welcomed, it has often been as a small step on the road towards the goal of greater protection for authors.[47]

---

[45] See CDPA 1988, s 4(1)(a); See also *Bleistein v Donaldson* 188 US 239 (1903). For a well-known example of the difficulties that can arise when courts consider whether a work is 'artistic', see *George Hensher v Restawile Upholstery (Lancs)* [1976] AC 64 (HL).

[46] JC Ginsburg, 'Moral Rights in a Common Law System' [1990] Entertainment L Rev 121, 129.

[47] See, eg, WR Cornish, 'Moral Rights under the 1988 Act' [1989] 12 EIPR 449; I Stamatoudi, 'Moral Rights of Authors in England: the Missing Emphasis on the Creators' [1997] IPQ 478, 512–3; A Barron, 'Copyright Law and the Claims of Art' [2002] IPQ 368, 400–1.

9.21 Criticism has focused upon the extensive exceptions and qualifications to the right, the ease with which the right can be waived, and the limited scope of the right as defined in s 80. In this last respect, most attention has been devoted to the argument that the scope of s 80 is more limited than demanded by international treaty. Art 6*bis* of the Berne Convention requires States to provide authors with the right to object to 'any distortion, mutilation or other modification of, or other derogatory action in relation to the . . . work, which would be prejudicial to his honour or reputation.' However, s 80 prohibits only the derogatory '*treatment*' of a work. 'Treatment', as has been seen above, is defined as 'any addition to, deletion from or alteration to or adaptation of the work'. Other derogatory actions 'in relation to' a work are not covered. In general, commentators agree that, as a result, the UK's integrity right can only be breached where the composition or structure of a work (its 'internal structure'[48]) has been changed in some way. It is generally considered that it will not be breached, for example, where a work is placed unchanged in a prejudicial situation or context.[49] In other jurisdictions, the right is defined more extensively.[50]

9.22 Some criticism of s 80 is undoubtedly merited. As is very often the case in copyright law, the UK government's aim in introducing the integrity right appears to have been to avoid breach of its international obligations while disturbing existing legal and commercial structures as little as possible. The ease with which the right can be waived seems particularly questionable, as moral rights are designed to secure the interests of authors and directors against those with superior commercial bargaining power. However, amongst this barrage of criticism, little attention has been paid to the fact that the 'timid' right provided under s 80 may, in certain situations, provide authors and directors with unjustifiably *strong* protection and therefore that it may threaten the freedom of expression of those seeking to make use of protected works. This issue is explored further below.

---

[48] L Bently and B Sherman, *Intellectual Property Law* (Oxford: OUP, 2001) 245–6.

[49] Although, see J Griffiths, 'Simplifying Copyright Law', in A Hudson (ed), *New Perspectives on Property Law, Obligations and Restitution* (London: Cavendish Press, 2004), 315.

[50] See, eg, in France, *EMI Music v Brel* CA Paris, June 25, 1996, (1997) 171 RIDA 337; *Chant du Monde v Fox Europe* Cass 1 civ, December 22 1959, (1960) 28 RIDA 361. In Germany, see *Re Neo-Fascist Slant in Copyright Works* [1996] ECC 375.

C. Not Such a 'Timid Thing':
The Wind Done Gone in the United Kingdom

(1) Absence of statutory defence founded on freedom of expression

The argument that, in certain respects, the UK's integrity right may be **9.23** overprotective of authors and directors is based upon the absence of any free-speech-related defence to a claim brought under s 80. In an action for infringement of copyright, a defendant may, for example, be able to rely on the defences of fair dealing for the purposes of criticism or review, or fair dealing for the purpose of reporting current events.[51] There are no equivalent defences to a claim for infringement of the integrity right. This absence has not gone entirely unnoticed. For example, Laddie et al have commented that, where a work has been subjected to derogatory treatment:

> the motive or purpose for carrying out the prohibited act does not appear to afford any defence. So, for example, if a work has been subject to derogatory treatment, the broadcasting of a news item reporting on, and including the treatment of, the work is itself an infringement of the right. This would also be the case where in an arts review programme, for example, the original work and the derogatory treatment were included and discussed, even in circumstances where the programme presenter shared the outraged feelings of the author.[52]

This legislative failure to take account of the public interest in uninhibited criticism, review, and news reporting seems extraordinary, particularly as the fair dealing defences have come to be regarded as essential in assuring an appropriate balance between the rights of copyright owners and important public interests.[53] How can the omission of a relevant defence to a claim for breach of the integrity right be explained? The record of debates during the passage of the legislation suggests that the proponents of the legislation were concerned that the introduction of a defence to protect justified criticism would render the legislation too complex. It also appears to have been thought

---

[51] CDPA 1988, s 30. See Chapter 8 above.

[52] Laddie et al, *The Modern Law of Copyright and Designs* (3rd edn, London: Butterworths, 2000) para 13.28. Although, it could perhaps be argued that there would be no breach of s 80 in the examples cited. On Laddie et al's interpretation of s 80, however, there would inevitably be a breach. See discussion at paras 9.51–9.58 below.

[53] See, eg, *Pro Sieben Media v Carlton UK Television* [1999] 1 WLR 605, 612 (CA); *Ashdown v Telegraph Group plc* [2002] Ch 149, 172, CA.

that alteration of a work could never be justified where such alteration caused prejudice to the creator. In rejecting a proposed amendment to the legislation in debate, one of its sponsors stated that:

> We are already introducing quite a complex provision, and it will not always be easy to tell whether the modifications of a work amount to derogatory treatment. It would be difficult, if not impossible, then to decide whether the treatment was justly or unjustly prejudicial to the author or film director's reputation . . . The amendment raises the question whether it is possible to have prejudice that is not unjust—surely all prejudice is unjust.[54]

However, the argument that, once a treatment of a work has been demonstrated to be 'derogatory', it cannot possibly be justified is wrong. In many different legal contexts, it is accepted that, while a particular publication may cause harm, such harm can be justified on the grounds of some competing public interest.[55] Indeed, acceptance of this position lies at the very heart of the balancing exercise required by Article 10 of the European Convention on Human Rights. Article 10(2) permits States to introduce laws preventing publications: 'in the interests of national security, territorial integrity or public safety, for the prevention of disorder or crime, for the protection of health or morals, for the protection of the reputation or rights of others, for preventing the disclosure of information received in confidence, or for maintaining the authority and impartiality of the judiciary'. However, States may only do so where 'necessary in a democratic society'. A particular publication may cause prejudice to the reputation of a creator or director but ought nevertheless to be permitted in the interest of free speech.

(2) Comparison with other jurisdictions

9.24 The absence of a defence to a claim for breach of the integrity right in situations supported by the interest in freedom of expression sets the United Kingdom apart from a number of other jurisdictions. For example, when creators' moral rights were introduced in Australia in the Copyright Amendment (Moral Rights) Act 2000, the legislation provided that: 'A person does not, by subjecting a work, or authorising a work to be subjected, to derogatory treat-

---

[54] HC Vol 138 col 186 (Parliamentary Under-Secretary of State, Department of Education and Science, Mr John Butcher).

[55] See, eg, the defences of fair comment and qualified privilege in defamation and the defence of public interest in breach of confidence. See also Contempt of Court Act 1981, s 5 and Obscene Publications Act 1959, s 4.

ment, infringe the author's right of integrity of authorship in respect of the work if the person establishes that it was reasonable in all the circumstances to subject the work to the treatment.'[56]

---

[56] (1) A person does not, by subjecting a work, or authorising a work to be subjected, to derogatory treatment, infringe the author's right of integrity of authorship in respect of the work if the person establishes that it was reasonable in all the circumstances to subject the work to the treatment.

(2) The matters to be taken into account in determining for the purposes of subsection (1) whether it was reasonable in particular circumstances to subject a literary, dramatic, musical or artistic work to derogatory treatment include the following:

(a) the nature of the work;

(b) the purpose for which the work is used;

(c) the manner in which the work is used;

(d) the context in which the work is used;

(e) any practice, in the industry in which the work is used, that is relevant to the work or the use of the work;

(f) any practice contained in a voluntary code of practice, in the industry in which the work is used, that is relevant to the work or the use of the work;

(g) whether the work was made:

(i) in the course of the author's employment; or

(ii) under a contract for the performance by the author of services for another person;

(h) whether the treatment was required by law or was otherwise necessary to avoid a breach of any law;

(i) if the work has 2 or more authors—their views about the treatment.

(3) The matters to be taken into account in determining for the purposes of subsection (1) whether it was reasonable in particular circumstances to subject a cinematograph film to derogatory treatment include the following:

(a) the nature of the film;

(b) whether the primary purpose for which the film was made was for exhibition at cinemas, for broadcasting by television or for some other use;

(c) the purpose for which the film is used;

(d) the manner in which the film is used;

(e) the context in which the film is used;

(f) any practice, in the industry in which the film is used, that is relevant to the film or the use of the film;

(g) any practice contained in a voluntary code of practice, in the industry in which the film is used, that is relevant to the film or the use of the film;

(h) whether the film was made in the course of the employment of the director, producer or screenwriter who alleges that the treatment was derogatory;

(i) whether the treatment was required by law or was otherwise necessary to avoid a breach of any law.

(4) A person who does any act referred to in subsection 195AQ(3), (4) or (5) in respect of a work that has been subjected to derogatory treatment of a kind mentioned in that subsection does not, by doing that act, infringe the author's right of integrity of authorship in respect of the work if the person establishes that it was reasonable in all the circumstances to do that act.

(Copyright Act 1968, s 195AS).

9.25 In the USA, the limited rights provided under the Visual Artists' Rights Act 1990 are subject to the general fair use defence available under s 107 of the 1976 Copyright Act. In Ireland, although the provisions introducing an integrity right generally bear striking similarities to s 80, the right is subject to a defence of fair dealing.[57]

9.26 Many jurisdictions which have longer established and stronger protection for the creator's right of integrity than the United Kingdom also recognize that, in certain circumstances, breach of the integrity right must be excused as a result of compelling competing interests. In Germany, for example, a defendant is entitled to take the benefit of a 'free use' provision that protects derivative works where sufficient 'inner distance' is maintained between the original and derivative work.[58] Even in France, where the creator's right of integrity is notionally 'discretionary', there is a defence for parodies that comply with the 'rules' of the parodic genre.[59]

9.27 The existence of such safeguards is vital. Even though the private rights of creators are important, they should not prevail automatically over fundamental public interests. The danger of allowing s 80 to do so is explored further below. The facts of a well-known recent copyright case from the USA provide a useful test of the provision's scope.

(3) An example of the potential impact of the integrity right on freedom of expression

9.28 In *Suntrust Bank v Houghton Mifflin Company*,[60] the claimant was the Trustee of the Mitchell Trust, which held the copyright in Margaret Mitchell's celebrated novel, *Gone with the Wind*. The defendant was the publisher of *The Wind Done Gone*, a novel written by Alice Randall. *The Wind Done Gone* was a parody of *Gone with the Wind* employing a number of characters and incidents from Mitchell's novel. These characters and incidents were recast in

---

[57] Copyright and Related Rights Act 2000, s 110. Although cf New Zealand, Copyright Act 1994, s 100.

[58] Intellectual Property Code, L 122.5(4).

[59] 268 F 3d 1257 (US Ct of Apps (11th Cir), 2001) See also para 6.48 above.

[60] See '*Alcolix*' BGH, March 11 1993, (1994) 25 IIC 605: 'The question of the infringement of moral rights cannot be dealt with without consideration of the question whether fair use [sic] exists in the sense of s 24 Copyright Act' at 609.

order to expose Mitchell's romantic, idealized portrait of the South of the USA. In particular, Randall's novel was intended as an attack on the depiction of slavery and the relationships between black and white people in the earlier novel. The difficulties of accommodating parody within copyright law have often been discussed.[61] An author wishing to parody a copyright work must inevitably draw substantially on protected elements of the original work in order to make his or her point. A parodist thus risks committing infringement of copyright. However, at the same time, parody is recognized as an important vehicle for social commentary.

The Court of Appeals for the Eleventh Circuit was alive to this dilemma in **9.29** its hearing of Houghton Mifflin's appeal against the grant of a preliminary injunction by the district court. The Court of Appeals found that Randall had made substantial use of *Gone with the Wind* and had, therefore, infringed the copyright in that work. However, it also found that the defendant's use of the work fell within the fair use defence contained in s 107 of the 1976 Copyright Act. Central to the finding of fair use was the fact that *The Wind Done Gone* offered critical commentary on the original work. This conclusion was supported by the demands of free speech: '[T]he issuance of the injunction was at odds with the shared principles of the First Amendment and the copyright law, acting as a prior restraint on speech because the public had not had access to Randall's ideas or viewpoints in the form of the expression that she chose.'[62]

Of course, no claim for infringement of the integrity right could have been **9.30** made in *Suntrust Bank* itself. Notoriously, authors of literary works have no statutory protection for moral rights in US copyright law.[63] Nevertheless, it is interesting to consider how a claim such as that made in the case would fall to be decided in the United Kingdom, where claims for both infringement of copyright and infringement of the integrity right may be available. There seems little doubt that, on the facts of *Suntrust Bank*, a claimant would be able to demonstrate infringement of copyright under the CDPA 1988.

---

[61] See, eg, E Gredley and SM Maniatis, 'Parody: a Fatal Attraction' [1997] EIPR 339; M Spence, 'Intellectual Property and the Problem of Parody' (1998) 114 LQR 595.

[62] *Suntrust Bank v Houghton Mifflin Company* 268 F 3d 1257 (US Ct of Apps (11th Cir), 2001) 1277.

[63] Alternative remedies at common law and under the Lanham Act would have been unavailable to the plaintiff on the facts of this case.

Under the approach currently applied by the courts in this jurisdiction,[64] Randall would be likely to be regarded as having reproduced a 'substantial part' of Mitchell's novel. The defendant would be liable for infringement in the absence of a suitable defence.

9.31 The 'fair dealing' defences under s 30 of the CDPA 1988 are not as broad or as flexible as the US 'fair use' doctrine. Nevertheless, it is possible that a court would hold that the defendant's activities were within the defence of fair dealing for the purpose of criticism or review under s 30(1). Randall's novel could certainly be regarded as a criticism of the protected work. The availability of the defence would depend on whether or not the use of the work could be regarded as 'fair'.[65] The hostility of any commentary is irrelevant in this respect.[66] A court might consider that the parody was not 'fair' because it had taken 'too much' of Mitchell's work[67] or because Randall and her publisher had made a profit out of *The Wind Done Gone*. However, it is to be hoped that it would recognize that s 30(1) should be interpreted in a manner that secures freedom of expression.[68] It has been seen above that the US Court of Appeals viewed *The Wind Done Gone* as protected by the First Amendment. A UK court should similarly recognize that the defendant's claim to be entitled to rely on s 30 is supported by Article 10 of the European Convention. If it were to do so, it seems likely that any claim for infringement of copyright would be covered by the fair dealing defence.

9.32 However, in the UK, the person to whom Mitchell's integrity right had passed on her death would also be entitled to argue that *The Wind Done Gone* breached s 80.[69] Clearly, on the facts of the case, there had been a 'treatment' of the earlier novel. The parody adds to, deletes from, and alters *Gone with the*

---

[64] See *Designers Guild Ltd v Russell Williams (Textiles) Ltd* [2001] 1 All ER 700.

[65] The requirement that 'sufficient acknowledgement' be made has been very liberally interpreted and could certainly be argued to have been satisfied on the facts. See *Pro Sieben Media v Carlton UK Television* [1999] 1 WLR 605 (CA).

[66] See *Hubbard v Vosper* [1972] 2 QB 84; *Pro Sieben Media v Carlton UK Television* [1999] 1 WLR 605 (CA).

[67] See, eg, *Ashdown v Telegraph Group plc* [2002] Ch 149, CA.

[68] At is required to do under the Human Rights Act, see *Ashdown v Telegraph Group plc* [2002] Ch 149, CA.

[69] This would, of course, not necessarily be the same person as the claimant in copyright proceedings, where only the owner of the copyright interest or certain licensees would have standing to bring proceedings.

Wind.[70] In publishing the treatment, Randall's publisher would potentially have committed an infringing act under s 80(3)(a), which prohibits, amongst other things, commercial publication of a derogatory treatment of a protected literary work. Thus, there would be a breach of the integrity right if *The Wind Done Gone* could be regarded as a 'derogatory' treatment of *Gone with the Wind*.

Randall could certainly be argued to have 'distorted' *Gone with the Wind*, **9.33** even if she had not mutilated it. But, as noted above,[71] a claimant would also have to demonstrate that any such distortion was prejudicial to the author's honour or reputation, or that the treatment was otherwise prejudicial to those interests. This issue is to be assessed objectively. Was Mitchell's 'honour or reputation' prejudiced by Randall's work? It certainly seems possible that, as a result of reading Randall's parody, many readers would have been left with a diminished opinion of Mitchell and of her novel.[72]

It would seem plausible to argue that her 'honour or reputation' had suffered **9.34** as a result. In the absence of a suitable defence, a court may therefore be prepared to grant an injunction for breach of s 80 in such a claim.[73] This seems extremely unsatisfactory. The grant of an injunction in such circumstances would, to borrow and adjust the wording of the judgment in *Suntrust Bank* itself, violate the shared principles of Article 10 and the copyright law. Randall's publishers would be likely to be insulated from an action for infringement of copyright by the fair dealing defence and from an action for defamation by the defence of 'fair comment'. However, there would appear to be a strong risk that the 'timid' integrity right under s 80 would present a real obstacle to publication of a work such as *The Wind Done Gone* in the United Kingdom.

---

[70] 'Adaptation' is defined in a particular and limited manner in relation to infringement of the copyright interest (see CDPA, s 21). The definition is stated to apply to the whole of Part I of the statute. It therefore seems unlikely that an 'adaptation' of *Gone with the Wind* would have been made.

[71] See paras 9.18 and 9.19 above.

[72] Although a number may not—perhaps because they are not persuaded by Randall's critique, because they expect such attitudes of an author writing at the time that Mitchell wrote *Gone with the Wind* or because they do not assume that a creative work represents the true opinions of its creator.

[73] Although, given the interest in freedom of expression, a court may be prepared to refuse an injunction, while allowing a claim for damages. In the context of copyright infringement, this approach has been supported by the Court of Appeal in *Ashdown v Telegraph Group plc* [2002] Ch 149, CA, 167.

D. Is it Possible to Interpret Section 80 in a Manner that Minimizes Unjustified Interference with Freedom of Expression?

9.35 Thus, it has been seen how s 80 has the potential to restrict freedom of expression. In such circumstances, it is to be expected that courts will seek to interpret the provision in a manner that does not disproportionately favour the interests of creators. A number of options may be open. It may, for example, be possible to extend the application of the common law defence of 'public interest' to a claim for breach of the integrity right. It may also be possible to restrict the situations in which a claimant will be entitled to establish a claim under s 80. These possibilities are explored further below.

(1) Defences

9.36 In *Ashdown v Telegraph Group Ltd*,[74] the Court of Appeal has confirmed that, where a defendant's acts are not covered by a statutory 'permitted act' under the CDPA 1988, but where the grant of damages to a copyright owner would conflict with the right to freedom of expression as protected under the Human Rights Act 1998, courts are obliged to find that the defendant's acts are covered by the residual common law public interest defence.[75] This common law defence is preserved by s 171(3) of the CDPA 1988, which states that: 'Nothing in this Part affects any rule of law preventing or restricting the enforcement of copyright, on grounds of public interest or otherwise.' Is it possible to apply the same mechanism in the context of a claim for breach of moral rights? That is, can it be said that, where a sanction against a defendant for breach of the integrity right cannot be justified under Article 10 ECHR, it is open to the courts to find that the defendant's publication is protected at common law? If it is, a solution to the problem outlined in this chapter may be available. Faced with a claim such as that in *Suntrust Bank*, a court would be able to find that, despite the absence of express statutory defences, Article 10 justified publication of *The Wind Done Gone* and, accord-

---

[74] [2002] Ch 149.
[75] Ibid 167–71. See paras 8.21–8.22. Note, however, the earlier conflicting decision of the Court of Appeal in *Hyde Park Residence Ltd v Yelland* [2001] Ch 143. See Chapter 8 above.

ingly, that the public interest defence should be applied. However, it is important to recognize that the claim in *Ashdown* was a copyright claim and it is far from certain that this approach can be applied in the context of a claim for breach of the moral right of integrity.

As seen above, s 171(3) expressly preserves 'any rule of law preventing or **9.37** restricting the enforcement of *copyright*, on grounds of public interest or otherwise'.[76] It does not refer to a claim for breach of any of the moral rights. It could perhaps be argued that the moral rights established in Chapter IV of the CDPA 1988 are, in a general sense, part of 'copyright law' broadly defined and, therefore, that s 171(3) applies implicitly to the integrity right. However, there are difficulties with this argument. Throughout the CDPA 1988, a clear distinction is drawn between actions for infringement of copyright and actions for infringement of moral rights. Furthermore, in *Ashdown*, the Court of Appeal's conclusion that s 171(3) preserved a flexible common law public interest defence depended heavily upon its view that this defence pre-dated the CDPA 1988 and was therefore preserved by s 171(3).[77] As there were no statutory moral rights before the coming into force of the CDPA 1988, it is hard to argue that s 171(3) preserves any such rule relating to them.

Perhaps the strongest argument available to a defendant on this point is that **9.38** the common law 'rule' of permitted disclosure in the public interest is a rule of general application and that s 171(3) simply confirms the existence of that rule in the field of copyright law and does not exclude the operation of that doctrine in any other body of law (including moral rights). The common law rule that publication of information can be excused in the public interest certainly extends beyond the field of copyright law.[78] The capacity for flexible development of the rule has, for example, been vital in the establishment of privacy rights under the Human Rights Act.[79] It would seem strange (and undesirable) if a court were entitled to hear arguments on the rule in copyright law (as a result of s 171(3)) and in other neighbouring bodies of information law (as a result of common law developments) but not to

---

[76] Italics added.   [77] [2002] Ch 149, para 170.
[78] See, eg, its application in breach of confidence cases such as *Lion Laboratories v Evans* [1985] QB 526, CA; *Woodward v Hutchins* [1977] 1 WLR 760, CA.
[79] See *A v B plc and C* [2003] QB 195, CA; *Campbell v Mirror Group Newspapers Ltd* [2004] 2 WLR 1232 (HL).

hear such arguments in the context of a claim for breach of the integrity right. It is to be hoped that any court faced with a relevant claim would strive to avoid such an inconsistent and illogical position. However, there are reasons to be pessimistic in this respect. Recent decisions on the public interest rule indicate that courts are unwilling to apply the common law rule of public interest in the context of a recently enacted and detailed legislative scheme making no provision for an appropriate statutory exception.[80] It may be found that the fact that moral rights are not specifically mentioned in s 171(3) provides evidence that Parliament did not intend the public interest rule to apply to these new causes of action.[81] The braver approach, however, would surely be to interpret the CDPA 1988's moral rights regime compatibly with the right to freedom of expression and consistently with other related bodies of law.

(2) Interpreting the scope of s 80

9.39 If a court is unwilling to accept that the common law 'public interest' rule applies to a claim for breach of s 80, is there anything else that it can do to minimize the risk of a claimant's succeeding in an integrity right claim in a case such as *Suntrust Bank*? Would it, for example, be possible to 'read down'[82] s 80 by interpreting the scope of the integrity right in a manner that minimizes any conflict with the right to freedom of expression? As noted above, the limited jurisprudence on the provision to date leaves a number of significant points of interpretation open. Perhaps these can be resolved in a manner that compensates for the absence of relevant statutory exemptions. The cases in which s 80 has been considered demonstrate a paramount concern to confine the integrity right within strict limits.[83] It therefore seems worth exploring two potential interpretations of s 80 that would protect a defendant in a case such as *Suntrust Bank*.

'Honour or reputation'

9.40 In order for a claimant to establish a successful claim for breach of s 80, it has been seen that he or she must demonstrate prejudice to his or her 'honour or

---

[80] See *Mars UK Ltd v Teknowledge Ltd* [2000] ECDR 99.

[81] Indeed, statements made by the proponents of the legislation during its passage through Parliament could be employed in support of this position. See HC Vol 138 col 182–184.

[82] See para 9.17 above.   [83] See paras 9.18–9.19 above.

reputation'. However, it is not entirely clear what is meant by 'honour or reputation'?[84] If this phrase is interpreted narrowly, for example as encompassing only an author or director's 'honour or reputation' *as a creator* (as opposed to his or her 'honour or reputation' more generally as a human being), might it be possible to restrict the potentially injurious effects of s 80? If the phrase can be interpreted in this way, would fears that the right of integrity could prevent the publication of a text such as *The Wind Done Gone* in the United Kingdom prove unfounded? After all, Alice Randall's charge against Margaret Mitchell was not that she was a bad writer, but rather that she wrote from a racist perspective.

In order to evaluate the strength of this argument on the scope of s 80, it is **9.41** necessary to investigate the meaning of 'honour or reputation' a little more closely. 'Reputation' seems a relatively familiar interest. It is surely similar to the interest protected at common law by the tort of defamation, in which a statement is defamatory if it: 'Injures the reputation of another by exposing him to hatred, contempt or ridicule, or tends to lower him in the esteem of right-thinking members of society'.[85] Prejudice to an individual's reputation is, in that context, interpreted as prejudice to his or her standing in the eyes of reasonable members of the public. As has been seen, this is strikingly similar to the way in which s 80 has been interpreted by the courts. However, 'honour' seems to be an altogether less familiar interest.

There is little consensus amongst commentators on the question of the mean- **9.42** ing of 'honour or reputation'. In *The Modern Law of Copyright and Designs*, Laddie et al state that:

> 'Reputation' is likely to mean the reputation which the author or director has chosen to carve out for himself in the exercise of his profession. The addition of the word 'honour' in the section indicates that the author's or director's integrity as a human being may not be attacked through derogatory treatment of his work. The concept the Act appears to be aiming at is akin to libel, but where the harmful act is not the speaking or publishing of untrue words but the derogatory treatment of the author's or director's work.[86]

---

[84] It would appear that the terms were included in Art 6*bis* of the Berne Convention at the behest of the British delegation, which was concerned that the wording of the original proposal which outlawed prejudice to the author's 'moral interests' was too vague.

[85] S Deakin, A Johnston and B Markesinis, *Tort Law* (5th edn, Oxford: OUP, 2003) 645.

[86] Laddie et al, *The Modern Law of Copyright and Designs* (3rd edn, London: Butterworths, 2000) para 13.19 (footnote omitted).

Thus, it is suggested that s 80 will cover treatments of the work that harm an author's honour as a human being or his or her reputation as a creator—although no reason is given for restricting 'reputation' to *professional* standing. In general usage, it is not usually so restricted. By contrast, in *Copinger and Skone James on Copyright*, Garnett et al write that: ' "[R]eputation" has an objective connotation, referring to what is generally said or believed about a person. "Honour", which is associated with both reputation and good name, is more a matter of respect for a person or his position.'[87] This definition of 'reputation' seems less contentious—more akin to the interest protected in defamation and to general usage. However, the difference between this and 'respect for a person or his position' is not altogether clear. Bently and Sherman state that: 'While "reputation" is a familiar concept in British law, the same cannot be said for "honour". If "honour" is taken to refer to what a person thinks of themself . . . it would seem that prejudice to honour might well involve a strong subjective element.'[88]

9.43 'Honour' is clearly a problematic concept. It would appear possible for a court to interpret it objectively or subjectively. The first definition of 'honour' offered in *The Concise Oxford English Dictionary* is 'high respect'. In this sense, there seems to be little distinction between 'honour' and 'reputation'. However, as Bently and Sherman suggest, 'honour' seems also to be capable of referring to a person's sense of self-esteem. Nevertheless, every indication suggests that an interpretation of s 80 in which an author is entitled to object to changes to a work, of which he or she disapproves but which a reasonable person would not consider prejudicial, is unlikely to be adopted by courts in the United Kingdom. As has been demonstrated already, courts have not so far been willing to accept anything other than objectively demonstrated harm to reputation as giving rise to a cause of action under the provision.[89] Indeed, courts seem largely to have avoided the difficulties raised by the meaning of 'honour' by ignoring the term completely, and interpreting 'honour or reputation' as a composite phrase synonymous with 'reputation'. They may have been wise to do so. In the absence of suitable defences, the threat to freedom of expression presented by a subjectively determined in-

---

[87] K Garnett, JR James, and G Davies, *Copinger and Skone James on Copyright* (14th edn, London: Sweet & Maxwell, 1999) para 11–44.

[88] L Bently and B Sherman, *Intellectual Property Law* (Oxford: OUP, 2001) 249.

[89] See paras 9.18–9.19 above.

tegrity right is obvious. Indeed, a sanction that, to any degree, is governed by the subjective views of a work's creator could hardly be described as 'prescribed by law' for the purpose of Article 10.[90]

Thus, it can be concluded that, even though a subjective interpretation of **9.44** the term 'honour' in 'honour or reputation' may be available on the statutory language of s 80, it is, for good reason, unlikely to be adopted. Nevertheless, even if 'honour or reputation' is interpreted objectively, questions of interpretation remain. Clearly, the phrase must cover prejudice to the *creative* reputation (or honour) of an author. It is exactly this form of prejudice—garbled rewritings, clumsy and incompetent reproductions—that the integrity right is designed to prevent. However, to what extent is more general injury to the 'honour or reputation' of a creator *as a human being* covered by s 80? As seen above, the consensus among the authors of the leading texts on copyright law in the United Kingdom seems to be that such general injury is covered.[91] A literal reading of the provision itself would also support this reading. In general usage, a person's 'honour or reputation' is not restricted to purely professional interests. Indeed, it could be argued that 'honour' relates more obviously to a person's human qualities than to his or her esteem within a trade, business, or profession.

On the face of it, the interest in 'honour or reputation' would appear to en- **9.45** compass creative or professional prejudice *and* prejudice to a creator's reputation as a human being. However, difficulties arise if the provision extends this far. Defined objectively, 'honour or reputation' is the same interest as the 'reputation' protected under the law of defamation. Of course, the law of defamation is not only concerned with prejudice arising from the treatment of works. However, within the field of operation of s 80, the two causes of action appear to be aimed at the same form of injury. This overlap is problematic because the law of defamation has been shaped very carefully to prevent it from interfering unduly with the right to freedom of expression.

---

[90] Under Art 10(2), the exercise of the freedoms established under Art 10(1) may be subject to formalities, conditions, restrictions, or penalties. However, these must, in all cases, be 'prescribed by law'. For discussion of this issue in the context of breach of the peace, see *Steel v United Kingdom* (1999) 28 EHRR 603.

[91] In *Confetti Records v Warner Music UK Limited*, the court did not object on this ground to elements of the integrity right claim bearing strongly on personal, rather than creative, reputation. See paras 9.14–9.17 above.

For example, any potential claim for defamation comes to an end on the death of the claimant. Juries have an important role in determining whether a particular statement is defamatory in fact and, in an appropriate case, a defendant also has the benefit of a number of far-reaching defences designed to secure freedom of expression.[92] The House of Lords has confirmed that such mechanisms are essential if the action for defamation is to comply with Article 10.[93] However, as has been demonstrated above, there are no obvious free speech restraints on the integrity right. It may be justifiable to grant authors of creative works a separate statutory means of securing their *creative* reputations. For example, the public interest in securing access to unadulterated versions of a creator's work could perhaps justify the fact that the integrity right endures for the full term of copyright. It could perhaps also be argued that a jury would not necessarily be an appropriate body to assess injury to *creative* honour or integrity and, therefore, that such claims should be covered by a separate form of claim in which the jury pays no part. However, if the integrity right is interpreted as covering prejudice to both the creative and personal reputations of creators, it is hard to see how such significant departures from the common law position can be justified. Why should creators be privileged in this way over any other human being?

9.46 The potential injustice of this situation militates in favour of an interpretation of 'honour or reputation' which is restricted to *creative* honour or reputation. Interpreted thus, a breach of the integrity right would arise, for example, where a licensee publishes poorly reproduced copies of a photographer's work and, as a result, the public comes to regard the photographer as a bad artist. By contrast, there would be no breach where publication of a version of a creator's work causes him or her to be regarded as a bad *person*, for example, where an artist's work is deliberately modified to suggest that he or she is mean or dishonest. In such a case, the creator would retain the right to bring proceedings in defamation, in which the defendant's right to freedom of expression would of course be adequately accommodated.

9.47 Thus, despite the fact that a literal reading of the phrase 'honour or reputation' does not readily support an interpretation restricted to 'creative honour

---

[92] Note also the 'rule against prior restraint'. See *Bonnard v Perryman* [1891] 2 Ch 269 (CA).
[93] *Reynolds v Times Newspapers Ltd* [2001] 2 AC 127, 200–5, 206–8, 223–4, 229.

or reputation', there appear to be compelling reasons of principle for interpreting it in this way. Adoption of such an interpretation would not solve all potential conflicts between s 80 and freedom of expression. Sometimes it must be justifiable even to risk harm to an author's *creative* reputation in pursuit of the important social activities of criticism, commentary, or parody. Nevertheless, if this restrictive interpretation were adopted, the scale of any potential conflict would be reduced. It might be possible, for example, to argue that publication of a work such as *The Wind Done Gone* would not breach s 80 as it would not give rise to prejudice to Margaret Mitchell's reputation *as a creator*.

However, if we pause to consider this apparently promising interpretation **9.48** further, difficulties readily appear. Is it really possible to make the distinction upon which the interpretation is based? Where does an author or a director's *creative* reputation end and where does his or her *personal* reputation begin? There may well be examples where it is, in general terms, possible to distinguish between the two forms of interest. For example, it is unlikely that George Michael's personal reputation would have suffered as a result of the defendant's medley in *Morrison Leahy Music Limited*.[94] By contrast, and as suggested above, any injury to the artist whose work had been modified to suggest that he or she is mean or dishonest would be predominantly to personal rather than creative reputation. However, in many other cases, the distinction may not be easy to discern.

For example, in *Tidy*,[95] one of the cartoonist's claims was that, as a result of **9.49** the defendants' treatment of his works, readers would have formed the impression that he had not been bothered to redraw the cartoons appropriately for the changed format. Is such an allegation of creative laziness a slur on creative or personal reputation? In the French case of *EMI v Brel*, a composer brought proceedings for breach of the integrity right arising from the use of his composition in commercial advertising.[96] Such a claim may not, in any event, fit easily within s 80 because the use of the composition in advertising is unlikely to constitute 'treatment'. However, putting that difficulty aside, it remains difficult to discern whether any resulting prejudice

---

[94] See para 9.09 above.
[95] See paras 9.10–9.11.
[96] *EMI Music v Brel*, CA Paris, June 25 1996, (1997) 171 RIDA 337.

would be to creative or personal reputation?[97] Would the commercial use sully the work or would the public think the worse of the man if it thought that he had licensed the use of his work for this purpose? In the German case, *Re Neo-Fascist Slant in Copyright Works*,[98] the author of a musical composition relied on his integrity right in bringing proceedings complaining of the inclusion of his work in a collection of works by groups with neo-Fascist sympathies.[99] Such a claim clearly raises the possibility of injury to general, personal reputation. However, it also seems possible that, if the public were to consider the creator to have such political views, it would regard his work in a different, and less favourable, light. In the case of *The Wind Done Gone*, the public may not have viewed Margaret Mitchell as a *technically* poorer creator as a result of Randall's critical work. However, literary achievement is not necessarily a question of purely 'technical' merit. Qualities such as perception, insight, and judgement are also relevant. It certainly seems possible that, as a result of Randall's critique, some members of the public might doubt the extent to which Mitchell possessed those qualities and, as a result, think less well of her as a creator.

9.50 Ultimately, then, it may be necessary to concede that the apparently promising interpretation of 'honour or prejudice' as restricted to creative reputation seems unlikely to provide even a partial solution to the difficulty with which this chapter is concerned. It appears too difficult, and indeed perhaps theoretically unsound, to distinguish between an author's 'creative' and 'personal' reputations. If s 80 is to be kept within tolerable boundaries, some other interpretative solution must be found.

How must 'prejudice to honour or reputation' be caused under s 80?

9.51 A further question of interpretation that has not been answered concerns the manner in which prejudice to 'honour or reputation' must arise if a breach is to be established under s 80. Some authors have suggested that liability can only arise if the public believe that the author or director in

---

[97] In the case itself, there was of course no need to prove injury to reputation because, as noted above, under French law it is not necessary to establish such harm in order to succeed in a claim for breach of the integrity right.

[98] OLG Frankfurt-am-Main, December 6 1994, [1996] ECC 375.

[99] Under Art 14 of the German Copyright Law, authors receive the right to prevent degradation of their work. In order to succeed under this provision, it is necessary for an author to establish proof of injury to reputation.

question is responsible for the contested treatment of a work. That is, a treatment of a work can only harm the honour or reputation of an author where the public is under the misapprehension that the treatment in question is his or her own work. In *Copinger and Skone James on Copyright*, Garnett et al write that:

> Assuming that . . . it is necessary in all cases to show that the treatment is prejudicial to the honour or reputation of the author or director, it would seem necessary to adduce evidence that some members of the public at least made a connection between the altered work and the author or director and that as a result his honour or reputation has been adversely affected. Thus if the altered work is published anonymously, and no one is aware that it is the altered work of the plaintiff, it is difficult to see how such treatment could be prejudicial to his honour or reputation. Related to this issue is whether a treatment which would otherwise be derogatory can be saved from being so if, on any use which is made of it, it is made clear that the author has played no part in making the alterations and has objected to them, or as the case may be. Again, it is difficult to see how such treatment could be derogatory if the evidence is that in the particular circumstances no one thought the less of the plaintiff.[100]

This argument seems convincing. If the public does not consider the author to be responsible for the treatment, how can his or her reputation be prejudiced?

Difficult questions may arise in some cases. For example, where a disclaimer **9.52** is applied to a treatment of a work, its effectiveness may be uncertain.[101] Where an altered work is published anonymously, the public may nevertheless associate it with an author or director, perhaps as a result of the work's style or of other clues within it. Questions of fact may also arise in cases in which the public would tend, as a result of the context in which a treatment is presented, to believe that an intermediary, rather than the author or director, is responsible for that treatment. An example is provided by the *Godot* litigation outlined at the beginning of this chapter. Clearly, a case on identical facts would be unlikely to succeed under s 80. First, it would be very

---

[100] K Garnett, JR James, and G Davies, *Copinger and Skone James on Copyright* (14th edn, London: Sweet & Maxwell, 1999) para 11–45.

[101] For similar difficulties in the context of the right to object to false attribution under CDPA 1988, s 84 and the tort of passing off, see *Clark v Associated Newspapers* [1998] 1 All ER 959.

difficult to convince a court that Beckett's honour or reputation would be prejudiced by the use of a female cast. Secondly, it is unlikely that the casting decision would qualify as 'treatment'. However, there may in any event be another obstacle to a successful claim on those facts. The audience for a treatment of *Waiting for Godot* may be well aware that Beckett had died some years prior to the contested performance and may therefore not associate the casting with the dramatist. Alternatively, the audience may think that a dramatist does not generally have responsibility for casting decisions and, therefore, will not, in any event, attribute casting decisions to him or her. At bottom, these questions about the state of the audience's belief are questions of fact and ought to be surmountable.

9.53 However, one leading text challenges this understanding of the way in which prejudice must be established, by suggesting that an infringement under s 80 can arise even where the public does not consider a contested treatment to be the work of a claimant author or director. Laddie et al write that:

> Although the point is not entirely clear from doubt, its seems to us that, in deciding whether a 'treatment' is derogatory the court is directed by s 80 to confine its attention to the 'treatment' and it should not, apart from certain exceptions specified in the Act [ie ss 82(2) & 103(2)], take into account the surrounding circumstances of the way in which the 'treatment' is brought to the attention of the public. The section says that the right is infringed when, for example, a derogatory treatment of the work is published commercially; it does not say that the right is infringed when a 'treatment' of the work is published commercially in a derogatory manner. If this view is correct, it means that it is still an infringement to publish a derogatory treatment even when there can be no room for doubt that the 'treatment' is one to which the author has not consented to and has no responsibility for.[102]

Thus, it is suggested that the question of whether or not a treatment can be regarded as prejudicial to honour or reputation is to be decided solely by looking at the 'addition to, deletion from or alteration to or adaptation of the work' itself. This argument is based upon the structure of s 80, which appears to suggest that the question of whether or not a ' treatment' is derogatory is separate and antecedent to the question of whether any of the infringing acts specified in s 80(3)–(6) has been committed.

---

[102] Laddie et al, *The Modern Law of Copyright and Designs* (3rd edn, London: Butterworths, 2000) para 13.19.

Although this reading is attractively literal, it is flawed and certainly does **9.54** not accord with the way in which claims under s 80 have been approached to date. Courts have sought evidence of *actual* prejudice arising as a result of the contested publication and have not asked whether the treatment of a claimant's work is, in abstract, prejudicial to his or her honour or reputation. There is good reason for them to have approached the provision in this way. If the question of whether or not a particular 'treatment' is 'derogatory' is to be considered outside the context of actual publication, it is difficult to see how courts will be able to assess the prejudicial effect of that treatment. Presumably, if Laddie et al's reading is accepted, a court would have to consider, in abstract, how a particular 'treatment' would be received *if* it were presented to the public and to ignore evidence of the actual manner of presentation.[103]

This method of assessing prejudice would be extremely artificial and seems **9.55** unlikely to be attractive to a court faced with the need to determine whether or not a particular treatment is derogatory. Consider, for example, a case in which the 'treatment' of a work is published anonymously. Assume that, when published, the 'treatment' would not be associated with the author of the original work. If a court were to adopt the interpretation suggested by Laddie et al, it would be necessary to consider whether prejudice would be caused to the author by looking only at the treated work itself and by imagining its likely effect on the public. In doing so, the court would presumably have to assume that the public would know the identity of the author because, in the absence of such knowledge, it is difficult to see how any form of prejudice could actually arise. However, the court would know that, as a matter of fact, the treatment of a work had been published without disclosure of the identity of the work's author.[104]

---

[103] It would then go on to consider separately whether any of the infringing acts within s 80(3)–(6) had been committed.

[104] Laddie et al support their interpretation of s 80 by arguing that, if a disclaimer could be effective in preventing a particular 'treatment' from being 'derogatory', there would be no need for s 103(2), CDPA 1988, which provides that:

> In proceedings for infringement of the right conferred by section 80 . . . the court may, if it thinks it is an adequate remedy in the circumstances, grant an injunction on terms prohibiting the doing of any act unless a disclaimer is made, in such terms and in such manner as may be approved by the court, dissociating the author or director from the treatment of the work.

However, in response, it could be argued that the remedial power granted to the court simply provides an effective means of bringing infringement to an end.

9.56 It seems preferable to strive for a less artificial interpretation. Even if it is accepted that the question of whether or not a particular treatment is deroga- tory is separate and antecedent to the question of whether there has been an infringement under s 80(3)–(6), it does not necessarily follow that the court should not consider evidence that the work will not actually be associated with its creator. Such evidence is surely relevant to the question of whether or not a particular treatment is likely, in its context, to cause prejudice.

9.57 If courts are permitted to consider evidence as to the circumstances in which a work is communicated, or is to be communicated, to the public, there will be less potential for conflict between s 80 and the right to freedom of expres- sion than if Laddie et al's suggested interpretation is adopted. A creator will only be able to object to the publication of a treatment of his or her work where there is *actual*, as opposed to notional or abstract, likelihood of prejudice to honour and reputation. Thus, for example, the director of a reworking of a protected dramatic work will be assured that a prominent disclaimer will insulate him or her from the risk of liability arising as a result of cuts or additions made to the work in the course of reworking or reinterpretation. Adoption of this approach will not, however, solve the prob- lem raised on the facts of *Suntrust Bank*. In such a case, any harm to the creator's reputation arises despite the fact that it is absolutely clear that he or she is not responsible for the 'treatment' in question. The public does not think worse of the author because it believes that he or she has produced the 'treatment'. Prejudice arises in a different way.

9.58 It is perhaps this distinction which finally leads us to an interpretation of s 80 that ensures that it cannot interfere unjustifiably with freedom of expression in a case like *Suntrust Bank*. It will be recalled that, under s 80: 'the treatment of a work is derogatory if it amounts to distortion or mutila- tion of the work or is otherwise prejudicial to the honour or reputation of the author or director.'[105] The author's or director's 'honour or reputation' must be prejudiced by the 'treatment' in question. It must be as a result of the defendant's 'addition to, deletion from or alteration to or adaptation of the work' that the author's 'honour or reputation' suffers prejudice. However, in a case like *Suntrust Bank*, the prejudice does not result directly from this 'treatment', but from the public's reassessment of the original work. Even when confronted with the parody, the public remains fully aware of the

---

[105] CDPA 1988, s 80(2)(b).

existence of the original work as a separate work in its original form. The parodist's use of the original work creates the conditions for public reconsideration of the earlier work. However, the changes made to the work are not the operative cause of any prejudice that may arise. The causative mechanism is different from that which occurs when a licensee's incompetent treatment of a creator's work is placed before the public as though it were the creator's own. It thus seems justifiable to interpret s 80 as limited to cases in which the primary or operative cause of prejudice to reputation is the change that has been made to the work. This reading also avoids the potential dangers that the integrity right may present to the right to freedom of expression in a case like *Suntrust Bank*.

E. Conclusion

This chapter has highlighted some of the surprising difficulties presented by the UK's integrity right. Courts have a responsibility to ensure that this right is not employed to provide authors and directors with unreasonable advantages over those forced to rely only on related causes of action such as defamation. Judges have already taken the first steps in this direction by emphasizing that a claimant must furnish objective evidence of prejudice and by interpreting 'honour or reputation' as synonymous with 'reputation'. Further desirable restraints could be imposed if courts were to confirm that (i) the 'public interest' rule is available in an action for breach of the integrity right, (ii) the scope of s 80 is restricted to cases in which there is a misrepresentation that the author or director in question is responsible for a contested 'treatment' of a work, and (iii) that misrepresentation is the operative cause of any prejudice to an author's or director's reputation. **9.59**

If s 80 is interpreted in this way, a creator would be protected against injury to reputation arising, for example, as a result of bodged editorial amendments or poorly printed photographic reproductions. The success of such a claim would depend upon the creator's ability to present convincing evidence of injury to professional or personal reputation. Claimants in cases such as *Pasterfield* or *Beckett/Godot* would be unlikely to be able to do so. In cases like *Tidy*, *Confetti Records*, and *EMI Records v Brel*, detailed evidence of the public's reaction would be determinative. Thankfully, a claim on the facts of *Suntrust Bank v Houghton Mifflin Company* would inevitably fail. **9.60**

10

CANADIAN COPYRIGHT LAW
AND ITS CHARTERS

Ysolde Gendreau

More often than not, contemporary copyright debates focus on the advent **10.01** of the digital world and on its impact on the evolution of copyright law. Commentary on the digitization of works, multimedia creations, internet transmissions, technical protection measures, and other technological issues abounds in conference papers and publications all over the world. The issues at stake are serious and so much attention is indeed warranted. Arising out of this movement has been a discussion on the effect of the extension of copyright in this new context on fundamental freedoms and rights. Thanks to proverbial hindsight, it seems surprising that such discussion has not been more prominent in the pre-digital age. There is nothing specifically technological about a conflict between copyright law and fundamental rights and freedoms. Once again, it appears that the digital revolution has helped to bring to the fore a strategic component of copyright law.

When this conflict is examined today in Canada, and especially from a **10.02** Quebec perspective, one is immediately confronted with the federal nature of the country. In addition to the federal Canadian Charter of Rights and Freedoms,[1] there is also the Quebec Charter of Human Rights and Freedoms,[2] the only provincial text of such stature.[3] While there are some overlapping provisions, a normal phenomenon given the nature of the texts, both Charters influence the application of the law in slightly different ways. The federal Charter is said to apply only to 'vertical' relationships between the State and its citizens, while most provincial texts, including the Quebec one, are perceived as instruments that apply to the 'horizontal' transactions between citizens. However, despite its vertical nature, the federal Charter can be invoked in a private dispute to challenge the constitutionality of the provision that governs the matter at hand.[4]

10.03 Since copyright law is a federal subject matter, one would expect that the confrontation between copyright law and freedoms protected by a Charter would essentially be a matter for federal law. Such an approach, however, would ignore the private law nature of copyright law.

A. Copyright Law and the Federal Charter

10.04 Compared with the Copyright Act, the Canadian Charter of Human Rights and Freedoms is a recent enactment. Adopted in 1982, it has not spawned the case law and literature that copyright social activists would perhaps like to see. A relatively early case refers to it in a rather unusual way. In criminal proceedings, an accused charged with infringing reproductions of pornographic material argued unsuccessfully that copyright could not exist in obscene works. The court referred to the 'supremacy of God', to which the Charter alludes in its opening provision, in stating that one cannot rely on such supremacy to justify a freedom of expression that manifests itself through the reproduction of grossly immoral pornographic material contrary to the standards of tolerant Canadians.[5] The overwhelming majority of the case law, however, deals more directly with the conflict between copyright

---

[1] RSC 1985, App II, no 44.   [2] RSQ, ch C-12.

[3] The Quebec Charter is not an entrenched constitutional text. However, it must prevail over other statutes unless a special derogation is expressly mentioned (Art 52, Quebec Charter of Human Rights and Freedoms).

[4] G Scoffoni, J Bell, and J Woehrling, '*Chronique: Droit constitutionnel étranger*' (2003) 53 Rev fr dr const 187, 188.

[5] *R v Ghnaim* (1988) 28 CPR (3d) 463.

law and freedom of expression. Two particular problem areas have become apparent in judicial proceedings: Crown copyright material and fair dealing.

(1) Crown copyright material

The advent of the Charter has not led to a questioning of the existence of **10.05** Crown copyright per se. In particular, one could have expected, or even welcomed, a debate on the relevance of Crown copyright and State control over the statutory and judicial materials that are so essential to the working of a democratic justice system.[6] The discussion that has come closest to this issue pertains to access to court judgments.

In *Wilson & Lafleur Ltée v SOQUIJ*,[7] a private publisher of law reports was at **10.06** odds with SOQUIJ, a government agency that collects and publishes court judgments. As far as the collection of judgments is concerned, SOQUIJ operates a State monopoly because it is the only entity entrusted by law to obtain all judgments rendered by courts in Quebec. With such 'raw materials', SOQUIJ publishes various series of law reports. A person who wishes to obtain the judgments as issued by the courts may ask for a copy and pay a charge of CAN$2.00 per page. This fee applies to published as well as unpublished judgments. The publishing arm of SOQUIJ, however, obtains the judgments at cost price. Wilson & Lafleur claimed that the situation was discriminatory and prevented it from doing business on the same grounds as SOQUIJ the publisher. In particular, it claimed non-competitive access at cost price to judgments not published by SOQUIJ.

The freedom of expression argument was used in the following manner. **10.07** Wilson & Lafleur considered itself to be a member of the legal press. Freedom of the press formed an important part of freedom of expression. The high costs charged by SOQUIJ prevented it from running its business on an equal footing with the largest legal publisher of the province. These costs constituted a hindrance to its freedom of expression. The Superior Court of Quebec did not respond favourably to this line of argument. It found that Wilson & Lafleur's expression was not being restrained, but rather that it

---

[6] On this debate, see JAL Sterling, 'Crown Copyright in the United Kingdom and Other Commonwealth Countries' (1996) 10 Intellectual Property J 157; J Frémont, 'Normative State Information, Democracy and Crown Copyright' (1996) 11 Intellectual Property J 19.

[7] [1998] RJQ 2489.

merely suffered economic harm. Access to judgments was not being denied since it could obtain them in the same way as any other person. SOQUIJ's pricing policy did not restrain the right to information, the freedom to gather judgments, access to courts, or the freedom to talk about the functioning of the justice system. In short, it was held that freedom of expression was being trumped up as an excuse for claims of unfair competition. It is nevertheless worth noting that the argument based upon freedom of expression was employed in a context where the contested subject matter was Crown copyright material.

10.08 In fact, the earliest case on the conflict between copyright and freedom of expression was the Federal Court of Appeal decision in *R v James Lorimer & Co Ltd*.[8] The object of contention was a one-volume abridgement of a seven-volume report entitled *Canada's Oil Monopoly*. This report had been prepared by the Director of Investigation and Research under the Combines Investigation Act (the former Competition Act). According to the Copyright Act, such a text was subject to Crown copyright.[9] The defendant raised three separate defences to the infringement action: fair dealing for the purposes of review, public interest, and freedom of expression according to the Charter.

10.09 All three defences were rejected. The court found that the defence of fair dealing did not apply because the use of the original work was not minimal.[10] Likewise, the common law defence of public interest could not come into play because enough free copies of the report were available throughout the country and, therefore, people easily had access to the ideas in the report.[11] The innovative aspect of the decision lies in its recognition that the Charter of Human Rights and Freedoms could form an independent defence to copyright infringement. Despite this openness towards a new type of argument in copyright litigation, the court nevertheless concluded that the Charter was of no avail to the defendant in this particular instance because the

---

8 (1984) 77 CPR (2d) 262.   9 Copyright Act, s 12.

10 It is often said that it is very difficult to rely on the fair dealing defence successfully. Up until this case, there seems to have been only one reported case in which the defendant had prevailed in reliance on this defence: *Allen v Toronto Star Newspapers Ltd* (1997) 78 CPR (3d) 115.

11 Unlike UK copyright law (Copyright, Designs and Patents Act 1988, s 171(3)), the public interest defence in Canada has no statutory connection. On this defence in general, see G Davies, *Copyright and the Public Interest* (2nd edn, London: Sweet & Maxwell, 2002) 63 ff.

abridgement contained so little of its own thoughts, beliefs, opinions, and expression. The defendant's activity had been more akin to an act of appropriation than to one of self-expression. The only freedom of expression protected by the Charter was Lorimer's own expression. The mere abridgement of another's work could not warrant reliance on the Charter.

The *Lorimer* decision has proved to be an illuminating forerunner of the later **10.10** decisions on copyright and freedom of expression under the Canadian Charter. Without stating so openly, the case placed the conflict between contents and form or, to put it in standard copyright parlance, between idea and expression, at centre stage. The Charter tends to protect contents (idea) rather than form (expression). Since copyright does not protect ideas, it is unlikely that the spheres of protection really conflict. A second observation is that the Charter argument, though independent, was made together with arguments based on the public interest defence and on the fair dealing exception. Although the public interest argument is much more difficult to put forward in Canada than in the United Kingdom, fair dealing has been the mainstay of the confrontation between copyright law and freedom of expression.

(2) Fair dealing

Introduction

In the fair dealing cases, one should not expect a fine dissection of the **10.11** relationship between copyright and freedom of expression. Of the five cases referring to the relationship, only one provides substantial reasoning. Moreover, the relatively cursory dismissal of the Charter argument in the *Lorimer* case, an appeal decision, can only have had the effect of curbing what initial enthusiasm there could have been for detailed exploration. Direct references to the Charter have, however, been made in a series of cases arising as a result of labour disputes. These cases concerned corporate logos or trademarks 'distorted' by employees' unions at times of labour unrest. The fact that a Charter argument has been made in that context is perhaps a reflection of the greater familiarity of labour lawyers with this legal instrument. Only one case in this group of five is not labour-related.

In that case, dealing with a pornographic version of the most popular tele- **10.12** vision soap opera in Quebec, the defendant unsuccessfully sought to rely on the exception of fair dealing for the purpose of criticism.[12] In its analysis of the exception, the Quebec Court of Appeal declared that a distinction must be drawn between humorous imitation for criticism or comment and appropriation for commercial opportunism, having regard to 'copyright protection as well as freedom of expression'. The reference to freedom of expression is very general and even independent of the Charter itself. Yet, its mere mention may be regarded as a reflection that the inroads into legal reasoning made in the other cases may be starting to produce a more general effect on the analysis of fair dealing beyond the narrow context of labour disputes.[13]

The labour disputes

10.13 Soon after the *Lorimer* decision, two attempts to invoke the Charter protection of freedom of expression as a defence to alleged infringement by workers' unions through the modification of company logos were made. In both instances, the argument was cursorily dismissed, though the courts paid lip-service to the possibility of its relevance: 'While there may be situations where the guarantee of freedom of expression in para 2(b) of the Canadian Charter of Rights and Freedoms may properly limit the protection otherwise given to the owners of copyright, I do not believe this represents such a situation.'[14] Similarly, the Charter was found to be inapplicable in a case where an injunction was sought to prevent the use of the parodied logo of a roast chicken restaurant chain. In that case, the court considered that the grant of an injunction would not prevent the union from informing the public about its position in the labour dispute; thus, freedom of expression was not violated by the exercise of copyright in the logo.[15]

10.14 Together with the *Lorimer* case, these two decisions seem to indicate a general unwillingness to explore the reasoning required by this line of argument, an argument which forces all parties to rethink the concepts of infringement and the role that defences lying outside the Copyright Act can play. Although it was not mentioned, it is again possible to perceive the tension between

---

[12] *Productions Avanti Ciné-Vidéo Inc v Favreau* (1999) 1 CPR (4th) 129 (Que CA).

[13] The *Avanti* decision is but two years after the more fundamental *Michelin* case. See para 10.15 and n 17 below.

[14] *Canadian Tire Corporation Ltd v Retail Clerk Union, Local 518 of United Food & Commercial Workers Union* (1985) 7 CPR (3d) 415, at 420.

[15] *Rôtisseries St-Hubert Ltée v Le Syndicat des Travailleurs(euses) de la Rôtisserie St-Hubert de Drummondville (CSN)* (1986) 17 CPR (3d) 461, at 476.

contents and form where copyright protection and the Charter might be operating on two different fields. The decisions make no direct reference to the fair dealing defence. However, they are regularly cited when the case considered immediately below is discussed, most probably because of the similarity in the fact patterns.[16]

The *Michelin*[17] case, concerning a parody of the Bibendum man, is indeed **10.15** the most explicit decision on the conflict between copyright protection and freedom of expression as guaranteed by the Charter. Thirteen years after *Lorimer*, an argument combining reliance upon a defence of freedom of expression with a pleading of fair dealing was again advanced. Once again, the fair dealing exception was set aside. The court refused to consider that parody could come within the notion of criticism and insisted on the technical identification requirements of the statute. The analysis of the Charter argument was handled separately as the court wondered whether parodies were protected by the Charter provision on freedom of expression. Its answer was both specific to the case and general; and the outcome was, once again, favourable to the copyright owner.

The first step in the reasoning is a property argument. The court considered **10.16** that it was not possible to use another's private property right (copyright-protected material) to express oneself. If such property is used, the use must be compatible with the function of that good. That function of copyright called into question a second consideration, that is, the general purpose of copyright protection. Framed in a Charter perspective, this led to an interrogation of the nature of copyright law along the following lines: is the object or effect of the Copyright Act to restrict freedom of expression? The answer to that question was negative because the rights granted by the Act are justified in a free and democratic society (language referring directly to the first article of the Charter). The objectives sought by a statute like the Copyright Act were important enough to justify the suppression of a fundamental right, and the means that were used to implement these objectives were in themselves reasonable and justified.

---

[16] See D Vaver, *Copyright Law* (Toronto: Irwin Law, 2000) 193, n 109; JS McKeown, *Fox on Canadian Law of Copyright and Industrial Designs* (3rd edn, Toronto: Carswell, 2000) 585, n 118. One should also appreciate that the fair dealing defence had been almost completely ignored by litigants until the 1990s.

[17] *Cie Générale des Établissements Michelin—Michelin & Cie v CAW Canada* (1996) 71 CPR (3d) 348.

10.17 In comparison with the earlier case law, the *Michelin* decision was more explicit, and articulated its reasoning according to more orthodox Charter language. It also avoided the contents–form discourse. However, the conclusion drawn with respect to the general appreciation of the Copyright Act in light of the Charter seemed to put a brake on any further analysis of the relationship between the two sets of rights.

10.18 The last case in this Canadian survey does indeed indicate that the Charter argument does not lead anywhere in a copyright analysis.[18] It suggests, however, that the argument may become more useful in relation to peripheral or related rights. During interlocutory injunction proceedings concerning alleged copyright infringement by a union, whose web site had similar interface, logos, addresses, and so on as the plaintiff's own, a fair dealing defence was raised. The defence met with the same result as in *Michelin*.[19] The Charter right to freedom of expression was also pleaded by the union, but in a different manner than had been done previously. The union argued that its right to freedom of expression was limited by its inability to appropriate or gain access to the plaintiff's intellectual property rights. The argument was rejected in relation to copyright, but accepted with respect to passing off. The common law was not to be interpreted in a way that unreasonably infringes a person's freedom of expression. Consequently, the injunction sought by the plaintiff was not granted because the balance of convenience favoured the union.

10.19 The relative failure of the federal Charter to influence the interpretation of the Copyright Act may be due to the fact that courts consider that the Act already internalizes the values protected by the Charter.[20] However, when the time comes to determine whether a right guaranteed by a provincial Charter interferes with copyright, the situation may turn out to be different.

---

[18] In its much awaited pronouncement on the fair dealing exception, the Supreme Court of Canada makes no reference to the notion of freedom of expression as a guiding parameter for an understanding of the concept of fair dealing: *CCH Canadian Ltd v Law Society of Upper Canada* 2004 SCC 13.

[19] *British Columbia Automobile Association v Office and Professional Employees' International Union, Local 37* (2001) 10 CPR (4th) 423.

[20] See Y Gendreau, 'Copyright and Freedom of Expression in Canada' in PLC Torremans (ed), *Copyright and Human Rights* (The Hague: Kluwer Law International, 2004), 21–36.

B. Copyright Law and the Quebec Charter

While the federal nature of the Copyright Act makes the federal Charter a **10.20**
normal reference for its interpretation, the private law character of copyright
equally allows reference to the Quebec Charter in copyright disputes between
individuals. Here, however, unlike a defendant's reliance on the fair dealing
defence, the right invoked to counter a copyright claim is not itself another
copyright principle, but a right to be found in the Civil Code of Quebec.
This is indeed what has occurred in relatively recent cases, where defendants
have sought to assert privacy rights in order to prevent the publication of
works. In these cases, reliance upon the right to one's likeness has been much
more successful than reliance on a general right of privacy.

(1) Right to one's likeness

The Quebec Charter of Human Rights and Freedoms does not state cate- **10.21**
gorically that a person has a right to his or her likeness. However, it does
enshrine the right 'to the safeguard of his dignity, honor and reputation' as
well as the right 'to respect for his private life'.[21] It is then through the
implementation of these principles in Article 36 of the Civil Code of Quebec
that the Charter can be said to play a role in the interpretation of the right to
one's likeness. Indeed, Article 36(5) of the Code identifies the use of a person's 'name, image, likeness or voice for a purpose other than the legitimate
information of the public' as an invasion of his or her privacy.

This provision of the Civil Code of Quebec made new law when it **10.22**
was introduced in 1994, on the coming into force of the new Code. The
Charter protection of privacy had existed since 1975, but had not influenced
the development of the right to one's likeness, which was instead based
solely on general principles of civil liability.[22] However, the early case law,
whose beginnings can be dated from 1971,[23] had created the basis for
the 1994 enactment. Subsequent case law has not been much more

---

[21] Arts 4 and 5.
[22] See, in general, L Potvin, *La personne et la protection de son image* (Cowansville: Éditions Yvon Blais Inc, 1991).
[23] *Field v United Amusement Corp Ltd* [1971] CS 283.

activist,[24] but has provided the opportunity to pit the 'new' right to one's likeness against photographers' copyright interests on two occasions.

10.23 The first case is particularly noteworthy because it led to a ground-breaking decision of the Supreme Court of Canada. In *Aubry v Éditions Vice-Versa Inc,*[25] a young woman's photograph, taken without her knowledge, had been used to illustrate a magazine article on loneliness. Her right to her likeness, based on the Civil Code provision, was regarded as a component of the Charter right to privacy. It was also recognized, in the circumstances, as a right that was superior to the photographer's right to make his work known to the public, a right falling within the scope of protected freedom of expression.

10.24 The *Aubry* decision paved the way for consideration of the more complex issues raised by the right to likeness in an overtly commercial setting, that is, the publicity right. Here again, the individual's right to control the use of her image was considered to be so fundamental as to trump the copyright owner's right. In *Malo v Laoun,*[26] a publicity shot for an eyeglasses company, Silhouette, was later used for the advertisement of an optician's store in a commercial directory. The copyright ownership in the photograph by Silhouette was not challenged—Silhouette was not even party to the action—but the actress whose image had been used strongly asserted her personality right. The difficulty, however, lay in the commercial nature of her claim. While it was easier to characterize the use of the *Aubry* photograph as an invasion of privacy through the exploitation of a picture taken without authorization, the *Malo* photograph had been taken for publicity purposes and was again being used in this context. How then could it be characterized as an encroachment upon the actress's right of privacy as protected by the Charter? The court simply bypassed this difficulty by referring to Articles 1 (freedom of the person) and 5 (right of privacy) of the Quebec Charter, to Article 3 of the Civil Code of Quebec (inalienable personality rights *such as* the right

---

[24] See, eg, L Potvin, 'Protection Against the Use of One's Likeness in Quebec Civil Law, Canadian Common Law and Constitutional Law (Part I)' (1996–1997) 11 Intellectual Property J 203; L Potvin, R Howell, and T McMahon, 'Canada' in M Henry (ed), *International Privacy, Publicity and Personality Law* (London: Butterworths, 2001), 73.

[25] [1998] 1 SCR 591. See P Trudel, '*Droit à l'image: La vie privée devient veto privé: Aubry c Éditions Vice-Versa Inc* [1998] 1 RCS 591' (1998) 77 Canadian Bar Rev 456.

[26] [2000] RJQ 458. See N Chalifour, '*Droit à l'image: une amorce de protection de l'identité artistique?*' in Barreau du Québec, Service de la formation permanente (ed), *Développements récents en droit du divertissement (2000)*, vol 133 (Cowansville: Éditions Yvon Blais Inc, 2000) 57.

to the respect of one's name, reputation and privacy) and to the *Aubry* decision, in which the Supreme Court had upheld the award of damages for the reproduction of the photograph in a commercial publication. The combination of all these elements made it possible for the court to declare that the right to one's likeness is independent of the right of privacy and exists autonomously. It therefore seems that this status hovers somewhere between *inalienable* personality rights and Charter freedoms. On appeal, the Quebec Court of Appeal upheld the trial decision, but denied the autonomy of the right to one's likeness. The right to one's likeness was comprised within the right of privacy, even where the likeness was exploited for purely commercial reasons.[27]

The facts of the *Malo* decision were such that there was no direct conflict **10.25** between the publicity right and the copyright right of reproduction. Nevertheless, the decision can be read as a confirmation, after *Aubry*, that both aspects of the right to one's likeness, privacy and publicity, enjoy Charter status. As such, they should always trump the copyright owner's rights of exploitation.

(2) Right of privacy

The right of privacy does not extend only to the right to one's likeness. **10.26** Quebec courts were provided with another occasion to examine a conflict between copyright law and another form of privacy interest in the case of *Michaud v Turgeon*.[28] Here, the defendant Turgeon had been hired to write the biography of Desrosiers; the founder of a chain of hardware stores. In the contract, the plaintiffs reserved the right to decide whether or not the work was to be published and imposed a confidentiality covenant on the author with respect to the information to which he would become privy. Faced with the plaintiffs' refusal to publish, Turgeon intimated to them that he was seeking another publisher. The plaintiffs sought to rely on the confidentiality agreement to prevent the publication.

Each side had a different opinion as to the scope of the same provisions, **10.27** that is, Article 35 of the Civil Code of Quebec on the right of privacy and the corresponding provisions in the Quebec Charter of Human Rights and

---

[27] *Laoun v Malo* [2003] JQ no 80.   [28] (1998) 80 CPR (3d) 416.

Freedoms, Articles 4 and 5. For the plaintiffs, these provisions protected their right to the non-disclosure of personal information. For the defendant, the provisions were subservient to his freedom of expression as an author. The court, however, preferred to disregard arguments based on fundamental rights. According to the judge, the matter was not a stand-off between the right to privacy and the author's freedom of expression, but merely an instance that required the interpretation of a confidentiality agreement in a private contract freely entered into. In this light, the conclusion was that the plaintiffs could prevent the publication of the manuscript.

10.28 Even though the court refused to analyse the situation in light of the Charter argument, the end result remains a vindication of the right to control the use of private information. The mechanics of this reasoning are interesting. Why not use the Charter as an interpretative tool where it is relevant? On the one hand, the legislator has enacted a quasi-constitutional Charter aiming to protect what society considers fundamental rights and, on the other hand, the courts—and litigants—are wary of relying on this text to assert rights. Indeed, this retraction from the Charter was manifest not only in the *Turgeon* case,[29] but also, to a lesser extent, in the *Malo* decisions, where it was obvious, especially in the appeal decision, that the comments on the relationship between the right of privacy and the right to one's likeness were not essential to the determination of the case. It could be that this reluctance to engage in Charter analysis is a reaction to the absolutism of the *Aubry* decision, as a result of which the Charter right to one's likeness has become a 'right to veto' the publication of any work featuring a person's image.[30]

10.29 Indeed, the mistrust of Charter rights whenever the publication of a work is at stake is a feature of both the federal and the provincial Charters. Canadian copyright jurisprudence has not yet successfully integrated the mode of thinking required under the Charter, either as a tool to refine copyright principles or as an explicit counterweight to copyright interests. This development stands in marked contrast to what has happened, say, in the fields of criminal law or of labour law. Canadian copyright law may well be on its way towards becoming an outpost of Charter resistance.

---

[29] This movement finds confirmation in the appeal decision of the case: *Turgeon v Michaud* REJB 2003–43940.

[30] See P Trudel, '*Droit à l'image: La vie privée devient veto privé: Aubry* c *Éditions Vice-Versa Inc* [1998] 1 RCS 591' (1998) 77 Canadian Bar Rev 456.

11

COPYRIGHT AND FREEDOM OF POLITICAL COMMUNICATION IN AUSTRALIA

Robert Burrell and James Stellios

A. Introduction

As in many other jurisdictions, the relationship between copyright and freedom of expression has historically received little attention in Australia. However, as elsewhere, this is beginning to change as commentators who are concerned about the expansion of copyright seek to find a language with general resonance with which to critique the current Australian copyright regime. The position in Australia is complicated, however, by a constitutional framework that guarantees a limited, but still evolving, 'freedom of political communication'. Consequently, when considering the relationship between copyright and freedom of expression in Australia, it is important to distinguish

11.01

between the intersection that exists between copyright and freedom of expression broadly conceived, and the intersection that exists between copyright and the constitutionally entrenched freedom of political communication.

11.02 A consideration of the intersection that exists between copyright and freedom of expression generally leads to a broad focus. It would, for example, require a consideration of the relationship between copyright law and the expressive interests of those who wish to make 'transformative' use of copyright material in cases where the use in question is not overtly political. In contrast, focusing on the relationship between copyright and the constitutionally guaranteed freedom of political communication results in a narrower focus, because it is only communication with a political content that falls within the constitutional freedom.[1] It is this latter, more restricted, starting point that we adopt here. This is not because we are unconcerned about the broader question of the relationship between copyright and freedom of expression. On the contrary, we have argued elsewhere that the intersection between copyright and freedom of expression is much more significant than is normally assumed to be the case.[2] By adopting a narrow focus here, we hope to reinforce this claim by demonstrating that copyright has the capacity to conflict with free speech interests even when such interests are viewed in terms of Australia's relatively narrow and idiosyncratic freedom of political communication.

B. Australia's Constitutional Framework and the Development of the Implied Freedom

11.03 The drafters of the Australian Constitution were influenced by two constitutional traditions: the federal system created by the US Constitution,

---

[1] The simplicity with which this distinction is expressed is misleading. As will be discussed below, Australian courts have struggled to identify the parameters of 'political' communication.

[2] R Burrell and J Stellios, 'Fair Dealing and Freedom of Expression in the United Kingdom' (2003) 14 Australian Intellectual Property J 45. See also R Burrell and A Coleman, *Copyright Exceptions: The Digital Impact* (Cambridge: CUP, 2005), chs 1–3.

and the Westminster system of government. The drafters created a hybrid instrument that took from its US counterpart a federal structure that gave enumerated powers to the central government, leaving the residue with the States and a formal separation of powers at the federal level into legislative, executive and judicial. From the English constitutional tradition, it incorporated the concept of responsible government, whereby government ministers are members of, and responsible to, Parliament. Importantly, the drafters did not incorporate a bill of rights.[3] As Mason CJ explained in *Australian Capital Television v Commonwealth*:[4]

> The adoption by the framers of the Constitution of the principle of responsible government was perhaps the major reason for their disinclination to incorporate in the Constitution comprehensive guarantees of individual rights . . . The framers of the Constitution accepted, in accordance with prevailing English thinking, that the citizen's rights were best left to the protection of the common law in association with the doctrine of parliamentary supremacy.[5]

Constitutionally entrenched rights were therefore foreign to the Australian constitutional landscape for many years.

However, in a series of cases beginning in the mid-1970s, Murphy J in the **11.04** High Court of Australia[6] sought to read into the Constitution a range of rights from the 'nature of our Constitution . . . [as] a Constitution for a free society'[7] including freedom from slavery and serfdom,[8] cruel and unusual punishment,[9] discrimination on the basis of sex,[10] and 'freedom of movement, speech and other communication'.[11] The rest of the Court consistently

---

[3] There are some provisions in the Constitution that are said by many to resemble constitutional rights: s 116 (Commonwealth not to legislate in respect of religion), s 117 (no discrimination on the basis of State residence), s 80 (trial on indictment against a law of the Commonwealth shall be by jury), s 51(xxxi) (acquisition of property on just terms). However, at least some of these provisions can be explained on a basis other than rights protection. For example, s 80 is better understood as a structural or institutional provision that facilitates the exercise of Commonwealth judicial power: see J Stellios, 'The Constitutional Jury—"A Bulwark of Liberty"?' (2005) 27 Sydney L Rev (forthcoming).

[4] (1992) 177 CLR 106.   [5] Ibid 135–6.

[6] Australia's highest court. Hereafter, 'the Court'.

[7] *R v Director-General of Social Welfare (Vic), ex parte Henry* (1975) 133 CLR 369, 388.

[8] Ibid.   [9] *Sillery v The Queen* (1981) 180 CLR 353, 362.

[10] *Ansett Transport Industries (Operations) v Wardley* (1980) 142 CLR 237, 267.

[11] *Miller v TCN Channel Nine Pty Ltd* (1986) 161 CLR 556, 588.

rejected Murphy J's approach, but in the late 1980s and early 1990s, under the leadership of Mason CJ, the Court began to display greater attention to the protection of freedom of expression.[12]

11.05　The revolutionary step was taken in 1992 in two cases, the judgments of which were delivered on the same day: *Australian Capital Television v Commonwealth*[13] and *Nationwide News v Wills*.[14] In these cases, a majority of the Court held that the Constitution creates a system of 'representative government' and that such a system of government requires protection for certain kinds of political communication. On this basis, a majority held that Commonwealth Acts regulating political advertising (in *ACTV*), and making it an offence to bring members of a Commonwealth industrial relations tribunal into disrepute (in *Nationwide News*), were invalid.

11.06　*ACTV* and *Nationwide News* saw an implied freedom of political communication being applied as a limitation on legislative power. Two years later, the Court went further and applied the freedom to the common law of defamation in *Theophanous v Herald & Weekly Times*[15] and *Stephens v West Australian Newspapers*.[16] These cases concerned defamation proceedings instituted by a member of the Commonwealth Parliament (*Theophanous*) and members of a State Parliament (*Stephens*) for statements made about the plaintiffs in relation to the performance of their official duties. In light of the implied freedom, the Court moved away from the traditional Anglo-Australian approach to defamation and seemed to suggest that the freedom provided a constitutional defence to such actions. In 1994, the Court also handed down judgment in *Cunliffe v Commonwealth*,[17] which pushed the boundaries of the implied freedom still further. That case involved a challenge to the validity of federal legislation establishing a registration system for persons who provided immigration assistance. A majority of the Court was prepared to accept that the legislation impacted on freedom of political communication, despite the fact that the provision of advice and services to non-citizens in connection with their applications for entry to Australia would seem to have little direct relevance to the functioning of the system of government.[18]

---

[12]　eg, see *Davis v Commonwealth* (1988) 166 CLR 79.　　[13]　(1992) 177 CLR 106.
[14]　(1992) 177 CLR 1.　　[15]　(1994) 182 CLR 104.　　[16]　(1994) 182 CLR 211.
[17]　(1994) 182 CLR 272.　　[18]　The validity of the legislation was, however, upheld.

The decisions in *ACTV, Nationwide News, Theophanous, Stephens,* and **11.07** *Cunliffe* created a 'political storm'.[19] Despite the controversial nature of the Court's decisions, in a series of cases handed down in 1996 the existence of the implied freedom was reaffirmed by the Court.[20] However, some members of the Court in these cases also signalled their discomfort with the technique of constitutional interpretation employed in the earlier decisions and, in particular, with the way in which the implied freedom had been drawn from a 'free standing' principle of 'representative government'.[21] It was therefore no surprise when the Court decided to revisit the basis of the implied freedom in *Lange v Australian Broadcasting Corporation*.[22] *Lange* was a defamation case involving statements made in a newspaper about a former New Zealand Prime Minister. The Court affirmed unanimously the existence of the freedom, but reconceptualized its foundation. In particular, the Court tied the freedom to particular provisions in the Constitution that create federal governmental institutions and processes: provisions that provide for federal elections, federal referenda, and for the monitoring of the federal executive.[23] In so doing, the Court seemed to retreat from some of the broader statements about the operation of the freedom made in earlier cases. Although not formally overruling the decisions in *Theophanous* and *Stephens,* the Court in *Lange* eschewed the approach of creating a constitutional defence to defamation actions in favour of developing the common law defence of qualified privilege to accord with the constitutional freedom.

Despite the unanimity of the Court in *Lange,* the case left a number of **11.08** important issues unresolved (many of which are considered below). Moreover, although the Court in *Lange* departed from the approach adopted in *Theophanous* and *Stephens,* it did not expressly overrule those decisions, nor did it cast doubt on other pre-*Lange* cases. Consequently, the pre-*Lange* cases remain of more than purely historical interest, but the extent to which it is appropriate to draw conclusions from them about the scope of the implied

---

[19] See H Lee, 'The Implied Freedom of Political Communication', in H Lee and G Winterton, *Australian Constitutional Landmarks* (Port Melbourne: CUP, 2003), and the sources cited therein.

[20] *McGinty v Western Australia* (1996) 186 CLR 140; *Langer v Commonwealth* (1996) 186 CLR 302; *Muldowney v South Australia* (1996) 186 CLR 352.

[21] See *McGinty v Western Australia* (1996) 186 CLR 140, 168–71 (per Brennan CJ); 180–4 (per Dawson J); 231–6 (per McHugh J); 291 (per Gummow J).

[22] (1997) 189 CLR 520.

[23] In particular, ss 7, 24, 64, and 128 of the Constitution.

freedom is unclear. Nor have decisions of the Court subsequent to *Lange* done much to clarify the outstanding issues. Indeed, although such cases have either accepted or assumed the existence of the implied freedom,[24] they have at times added to the uncertainty surrounding its operation. Attempting to delineate the contours of the implied freedom, or to assess how it might intersect with branches of the law other than those already considered by the Court (such as copyright), is therefore a complex matter. This chapter begins by outlining what the authors take to be the fundamental features of the implied freedom. It then turns to consider the ways in which copyright might collide with the freedom, and how the potential conflict between the two interests might be resolved.

C. The Operation of the Freedom

(1) Freedom not a right

11.09 Perhaps the first thing to note about the implied freedom of political communication is that the Court has emphasized on a number of occasions that the freedom is not to be equated with a constitutional right of the type one would expect to find in a constitutionally entrenched bill of rights. Articulating the practical consequences of the distinction that has been drawn between the Australian 'freedom' of political communication and a 'right' of political communication is, however, rather more difficult. The Court in *Lange* indicated that one consequence that flows from conceptualizing the constitutional guarantee as a mere freedom is that it operates in a purely negative fashion. The Court quoted with approval a passage from Brennan J's judgment in *Cunliffe* that, '[t]he implication is negative in nature: it invalidates laws and consequently creates an area of immunity from legal control, particularly from legislative control.'[25] More recently, in *Mulholland v Australian Electoral Commission*,[26] five members of the High

---

[24] See *Levy v Victoria* (1997) 189 CLR 579; *Australian Broadcasting Corporation v Lenah Game Meats* (2001) 208 CLR 199; *Roberts v Bass* (2002) 212 CLR 1; *Coleman v Power* [2004] HCA 39; *Mulholland v Australian Electoral Commission* [2004] HCA 41. Only Callinan J has expressed doubt as to the existence of the implied freedom, see *Australian Broadcasting Corporation v Lenah Game Meats* (2001) 208 CLR 199, 331; *Roberts v Bass* (2002) 212 CLR 1, 101–2; *Coleman v Power* [2004] HCA 39, [289].
[25] (1994) 182 CLR 272, 327.   [26] [2004] HCA 41.

Court emphasized that the freedom does not confer a positive 'freedom *to* communicate'.[27]

Closer observation suggests, however, that to describe the freedom as purely   **11.10** negative in nature does not usefully differentiate it from a constitutionally entrenched right in the traditional model, since such rights are also negative in nature.[28] Indeed, part of the socialist critique of liberal rights is that the majority of the population is not provided with the resources necessary to take advantage of these rights; that, in the words of A J Liebling, 'the only freedom of the press . . . is for those who own one.'[29]

A further potential consequence of defining the constitutional guarantee as a   **11.11** freedom might be thought to be that no question can arise as to who is to be treated as a 'right holder'. Some support for this can be gained from *Cunliffe*, Deane J commenting:

> The implication is not confined to direct communications by or with the individual citizen. It extends to the broad national environment in which the individual citizen exists and in which representative government must operate. In the context of that broad national environment, the implication's confinement of the content of legislative power protects the freedom of communication and discussion of non-citizens, be they corporations or aliens, to the extent necessary to ensure that the freedom of citizens to engage in discussion and obtain information about political matters is preserved and protected.[30]

Again, however, when the claim that the Australian freedom can be distinguished from a constitutional right on the basis that the freedom is not

---

[27] Ibid [107] (per McHugh J); [184] (per Gummow and Hayne JJ); [337] (per Callinan J); [354] (per Heydon J). This idea was originally expressed by McHugh J in *Levy v Victoria* (1997) 189 CLR 579, 622. Also see *McClure v Australian Electoral Commission* (1999) 163 ALR 734, in which Hayne J (sitting alone) rejected an argument that the implied freedom required media organizations to provide greater coverage for the petitioner's candidacy and policy launches. His Honour said, '[t]he short answer . . . is that the *freedom* of communication implied in the Constitution is not an *obligation* to publicize. The freedom is a freedom from governmental action; it is not a right to require others to provide a means of communication' (at 740–1, emphasis in original).

[28] As Stone has recognized, the classification of the freedom as negative in nature is consistent with conventional understandings of liberal constitutional rights: A Stone, 'Rights, Personal Rights and Freedoms: The Nature of the Freedom of Political Communication' (2001) 25 Melbourne U L Rev 374, 401.

[29] Quoted in T Streeter, 'Some Thoughts on Free Speech, Language and the Rule of Law', in D Allen and R Jensen (eds), *Freeing the First Amendment* (New York: New York University Press, 1995).

[30] (1994) 182 CLR 272, 336.

confined to a category of 'right holders' is examined in more detail, this distinction seems unconvincing for at least two reasons: first, other jurisdictions have not in fact confined the enjoyment of constitutional rights to individual citizens;[31] secondly, this distinction suggests that the freedom is broader than most constitutional rights, whereas the Court has consistently suggested that it is of a more limited nature.

11.12 A third potential consequence of defining the constitutional guarantee as a freedom is said to be that it operates in a 'vertical' manner because it 'applies only to actions of the state and does not protect individuals from actions of other private parties'.[32] But again, there are a number of difficulties with this point of differentiation. First, as has been seen in other jurisdictions where rights operate in a vertical manner, this characterization is of little practical consequence as the freedom limits legislative power and shapes the common law and thus operates indirectly in a horizontal fashion. Secondly, and more fundamentally, the fact that it is possible to point to other jurisdictions (including the United Kingdom) where 'rights' operate in a principally vertical fashion demonstrates that this too fails to distinguish the Australian 'freedom' of political communication from the 'rights' that are found elsewhere.

11.13 In summary, it can be seen that although the Court has made much of the fact that the constitutional guarantee operates as a freedom and not a right, when this distinction is examined more closely it seems to occlude more than it reveals. This is not to suggest, however, that the distinction is of no consequence. Rather, it is probably best thought of as a shorthand way of communicating that the interpretive framework within which freedom of communication issues are decided in Australia is different from that elsewhere, and that by insisting that the constitutional guarantee operates as a mere freedom and not a right the Court has signalled the relatively limited nature of the implied freedom. It is this restricted framework that perhaps best explains the outcome in *Mulholland v Australian Electoral Commission*, where the High Court rejected a challenge to Commonwealth provisions

---

[31] See, eg, the protection of corporate speech in the United States: *First National Bank of Boston v Bellotti* 435 US 765, 777–84 (1978); *Austin v Michigan State Chamber of Commerce* 494 US 652, 657 (1989).

[32] A Stone, 'Rights, Personal Rights and Freedoms: The Nature of the Freedom of Political Communication' (2001) 25 Melbourne U L Rev 374, n 27, 400.

requiring minimum political party membership for party endorsement of a candidate on the federal ballot paper. It would appear that a majority of the Court was reluctant to extend the freedom into the administrative process underpinning the electoral system.[33]

(2) Mode of communication

Despite the limited nature of the implied freedom of political communica- **11.14** tion, the Court has accepted that the freedom is not confined to verbal or written forms of communication. The clearest indication of this point came in *Levy*. In that case State legislation restricted entry to hunting areas for reasons of public safety. The plaintiff was charged with breaching the law after he entered a restricted area with the intention of protesting against Victorian hunting laws by displaying dead or injured birds in front of television cameras. Although the point was not finally decided, all the judges seemed to accept that the protection afforded by the implied freedom was not confined to particular forms of communication. For example, Brennan CJ stated: 'In principle . . . non-verbal conduct which is capable of communicating an idea about the government or politics of the Commonwealth and which is intended to do so may be immune from legislative or executive restriction so far as the immunity is needed to preserve the system of representative and responsible government that the Constitution prescribes.'[34] Similarly, McHugh J noted: 'For the purpose of the Constitution, freedom of communication is not limited to verbal utterances. Signs, symbols, gestures and images are perceived by all and used by many to communicate information, ideas and opinions. Indeed, in an appropriate context any form of expressive conduct is capable of communicating a political or government message to those who witness it.'[35] The latter statement is particularly important for present purposes since it provides clear authority to suggest that all art forms will fall within the scope of the implied freedom. It therefore seems safe to conclude that the implied freedom will extend to protect paintings, sculptures, photographs, and other such works, provided they have a political content.

---

[33] Consequently, the emphasis placed by the judges in this case on a distinction between a freedom *from* legal control and a right *to* communicate was misplaced. Rather, it appears their Honours were reluctant to extend the freedom to every corner of the bureaucracy.

[34] (1997) 189 CLR 579, 594–5.

[35] Ibid 622–3. See also ibid 613 (per Toohey and Gummow JJ); 638, 641 (per Kirby J).

(3) Type of protected communication: Defining the political

11.15 In contrast to the expansive approach that has been taken to the form that protected communication can take, it has long been clear that it is only 'political' communication that benefits from the constitutional protection. Distinguishing 'political' from 'non-political' communication is, however, exceptionally difficult. The Court has recognized this problem, but as yet has not come close to providing a definitive test for determining when a communication is to be treated as 'political' in character.

11.16 Early indications were that the Court would take a broad view of the type of communication that would attract the protection of the freedom. Although it was recognized from the outset that the implied freedom could not be equated with the broad right of freedom of expression found in the US Constitution, nevertheless, in *Theophanous*, Mason CJ, Deane, and Gaudron JJ contemplated a broadly defined concept of political communication:

> It is sufficient to say that 'political discussion' includes discussion of the conduct, policies or fitness for office of government, political parties, public bodies, public officers and those seeking public office. The concept also includes discussion of the political views and public conduct of persons who are engaged in activities that have become the subject of political debate, eg, trade union leaders, Aboriginal political leaders, political and economic commentators. Indeed, in our view, the concept is not exhausted by political publications and addresses which are calculated to influence choices.[36]

Cases since *Theophanous*, particularly the unanimous judgment in *Lange*, do not explicitly reject these statements. However, it is clear that the methodology adopted by the Court in *Lange* provides a different framework for identifying what communication is protected by the freedom. The reconceptualization of the freedom in *Lange* requires a sufficient connection between the communication and the constitutional system of government created by the Constitution: that is, federal elections, federal referendums, and the monitoring of the federal executive. To attract the constitutional protection, the communication must 'bear on', 'illuminate', or 'throw light

---

[36] (1994) 182 CLR 104, 124.

on' these federal institutions and processes.[37] The question of what is protected communication is not to be answered in the abstract, removed from the constitutional context.[38]

Unfortunately, however, there is still little guidance as to when communica- **11.17** tion is to be treated as 'bearing on', 'illuminating', or 'throwing light on' the relevant federal institutions and processes. There is a spectrum of communication that might affect these institutions and processes to different extents. This spectrum ranges from direct criticism of the behaviour of a member of Federal Parliament, coupled with a call for that person not to be re-elected, to an abstract work of art that changes our outlook on the world and hence, potentially, our voting behaviour.[39] The difficulty in identifying communication as relevantly political was demonstrated by the recent High Court decision in *Coleman v Power*.[40] In that case the appellant had been convicted of an offence of using insulting words in a public place: the appellant having accused a State police officer of corruption. The members of the High Court reached different conclusions on whether the insult was protected communication. McHugh and Kirby JJ were of the view that the communication was relevantly political: 'Insults are as much a part of communications concerning political and government matters as is irony, humour or acerbic criticism.'[41] Gummow and Hayne JJ also seemed to favour that view, although it

---

[37] Ibid 571.

[38] As the Court said in *Lange* (1997) 189 CLR 520, 657: '[t]o the extent that the requirement of freedom of communication is an implication drawn from ss 7, 24, 64 or 128 and related sections of the Constitution, the implication can validly extend only so far as is necessary to give effect to these sections. Although some statements in the earlier cases might be thought to suggest otherwise, when they are properly understood, they should be seen as purporting to give effect only to what is inherent in the text and structure of the Constitution.'

[39] The latter is clearly an extreme example and one that would unquestionably be treated as falling outside the scope of the implied freedom. However, it is important to emphasize that a vast range of communicative acts can be said to have a political dimension. As has long been recognized in artistic circles, there is a sense (or, more accurately, several senses) in which 'all art is political.'

[40] [2004] HCA 39.

[41] Ibid [81] (per McHugh J). Kirby J also said that the constitutional system of government 'belongs as much to the obsessive, the emotional and the inarticulate as it does to the logical, the cerebral and the restrained' (at [260]). McHugh J had also said in *Levy* (1997)189 CLR 579, 623, that the freedom 'protects false, unreasoned and emotional communications as well as true, reasoned and detached communications'. Toohey and Gummow JJ made a similar point (at 613).

was not necessary for their Honours to decide the point.[42] Gleeson CJ was not as confident, instead seeing it 'operating at the margins of the term "political" '.[43] On the other hand, Callinan and Heydon JJ were of the view that insulting language is beneath constitutional protection as it throws no light on government or political matters.[44]

11.18 Given this uncertainty within the Court itself, it is not surprising that lower courts have had considerable difficulty identifying the protected category of communication. This can be illustrated by reference to two apparently inconsistent cases dealing with political satire. In *Australian Broadcasting Corporation v Hanson*,[45] a controversial member of Federal Parliament was the subject of a musical composition featuring snippets of speeches made by the politician. The snippets were edited in such a way as to give the impression that the politician was making obscene comments. The politician sued for defamation and an interim injunction was ordered by a judge at first instance in the Queensland Supreme Court. In dismissing an appeal, the Court of Appeal held that enjoining the broadcast 'could not possibly be said to infringe against the need for "free and general discussion of public matters" fundamental to our democratic society' as the material contained 'grossly offensive imputations' and constituted a 'fairly mindless effort at cheap denigration'.[46]

11.19 In contrast, in *Brander v Ryan*[47] the Full Court of the South Australian Supreme Court took a more generous view, holding that political satire may be political communication. In that case, the defendant published a newspaper article about the plaintiff who was the chairman of a radical political party and a candidate in a local government election. The article made satirical comments about the plaintiff's political beliefs and views about immigration. In considering whether the defendant could rely upon the *Lange* qualified privilege defence, the Court held that the publication was of political matter, even though it 'was published in a form which may be described as satirical and which invited the reader to hold the plaintiff up to ridicule'.[48]

---

[42] [2004] HCA 39, [197]: 'Insult and invective have been employed in political communication at least since the time of Demosthenes.'

[43] Ibid [28].   [44] Ibid [299] (Callinan J); [332] (per Heydon J).

[45] Judgment of the Queensland Court of Appeal, 28 September 1998.

[46] per De Jersey CJ, with McMurdo P and McPherson JA agreeing.

[47] (2000) 78 SASR 234.   [48] Ibid 248.

The decisions in *Hanson* and *Brander* serve to illustrate the difficulty faced **11.20** by lower courts in identifying the contours of the category of protected communication. Given the various views expressed in *Coleman*, it is clear that the High Court is deeply divided on where the outer limits of the freedom lie.

(4) The level of protection

(i) Are all powers subject to the freedom?

In the early stages of development of the freedom of political communica- **11.21** tion, there was a suggestion that the nature of some Commonwealth legislative powers might override it.[49] In other words, there is authority to indicate that some heads of legislative power are not subject to the implied freedom, although there is little indication as to what those heads of power might be.[50] It is submitted, however, that the claim that some heads of power are beyond the reach of the freedom is not a sustainable proposition. Once it is accepted that the freedom protects the system of government created by the Constitution, it must be recognized that no head of legislative power should be capable of being exercised in a way that threatens that system of government. That is not to say that the nature of the power is unimportant to the question whether legislation breaches the implied freedom, but the starting position must be that all heads of legislative power—including the copyright power— are subject to it.

(ii) Standards of review

Assuming that all legislative power is subject to the implied freedom, it is **11.22** important to emphasize that, even if a law burdens political communication, it will not necessarily be held invalid. Rather, the Court will enquire whether the law imposes an unjustifiable restriction upon the freedom. Again, however, the Court has struggled to identify the standard to be applied when

---

[49] eg, see *ACTV* (1992) 177 CLR 106, 168 (per Deane and Toohey JJ); *Cunliffe* (1994) 182 CLR 272, 338 (per Deane J).

[50] In *Rann v Olsen* (2000) 76 SASR 450, 491 Prior J appeared to treat the Commonwealth's power in relation to parliamentary powers, privileges and immunities as not subject to the implied freedom. The other members of the Court, however, resolved the issue by applying the *Lange* test considered in para 11.23 below.

determining this question. In the pre-*Lange* cases, different judges adopted very different ideas about the test to be applied. On the one hand, some judges seemed to adopt a single-tiered test that closely resembled European style 'proportionality' analysis, whereas, on the other hand, other judges seemed to identify circumstances that required a US style strict scrutiny test.[51]

11.23 It was against that background that the Court in *Lange* turned to consider the standard of review. The Court held that whether federal or State legislation or common law rules infringe the implied freedom depends on two questions:

> First, does the law effectively burden freedom of communication about government or political matters either in its terms, operation or effect? Secondly, if the law effectively burdens that freedom, is the law reasonably appropriate and adapted to serve a legitimate end [in a manner][52] which is compatible with the maintenance of the constitutionally prescribed system of representative government ... If the first question is answered 'yes' and the second is answered 'no', the law is invalid.[53]

There are a number of features of this test that warrant further attention. First, it should be noted that an illegitimate *purpose* is enough to invalidate a law. Plainly, if the law aims to undermine the constitutionally prescribed system of government, it will be deemed invalid. Significantly, however, we have little further guidance as to how the 'end' a law serves it to be determined or as to when a law will be treated as pursuing an illegitimate end. Secondly, even if the law pursues a legitimate purpose, the law will still be invalid if the method chosen to achieve that legitimate purpose does not exhibit a certain fit with that purpose, that is, if it is not 'reasonably appropriate and adapted' to serve that purpose. It was indicated further in *Lange* that this test is more or less equivalent to a proportionality test, but the case does little more to clarify the applicable standard. For example,

---

[51] See further, A Stone, 'The Limits of Constitutional Text and Structure: Standards of Review and the Freedom of Political Communication' (1999) 23 Melbourne U L Rev 669; J Kirk, 'Constitutional Guarantees, Characterisation and the Concept of Proportionality' (1997) 21 Melbourne U L Rev 1; A Glass, 'Freedom of Speech and the Constitution: *Australian Capital Television* and the Application of Constitutional Rights' (1995) 17 Sydney L Rev 29.

[52] This alteration in the wording of the test was accepted by a majority of the Court in *Coleman v Power* [2004] HCA 39, [93] (per McHugh J); [196] (per Gummow and Hayne JJ); [211] (per Kirby J).

[53] *Lange* (1997) 189 CLR 520, 567–8.

it fails to indicate what factors should be taken into account when determining whether a law is reasonably appropriate and adapted to serve a legitimate end. It therefore remains far from clear what standard of review will be applied when determining whether a law breaches the implied freedom.[54]

(5) Summation

It can now be seen that considerable uncertainty surrounds the scope of the **11.24** implied freedom of political communication in Australia. In particular, doubt remains as to the range of communications that fall within the freedom and the test that is to be applied when determining whether a law that restricts freedom of political communication is valid. It is, however, reasonably clear that the constitutional freedom is not confined to prescribed forms of communication such as speech or writing. As has already been indicated, the uncertainty that surrounds the scope of the implied freedom of political communication makes a comprehensive analysis of the intersection that exists between the freedom and copyright almost impossible. Nevertheless, even on a narrow reading of the scope of the implied freedom, it is clear that the current copyright regime comes into conflict with it. In other words, even if one adopts a restricted understanding of 'political' communication, it is still clear that copyright can collide with the constitutional freedom. In the next section, after a brief outline of the current Australian copyright regime, a number of examples are provided of situations in which copyright would come into conflict with freedom of political communication on any reading of the scope of that freedom. It will then be considered how the Court might reconcile copyright and the implied freedom. It is argued that a fundamental reinterpretation of the fair dealing provisions would probably be sufficient to deal with the constitutional objection to the reach of the present copyright regime. While this would still leave Australia with an overly restrictive copyright system, it would nevertheless mark a significant improvement on the current position. Moreover, the Court's intervention in the sphere of copyright exceptions might itself provide a spur to legislative action, particularly if

---

[54] Although the question of the applicable standard of review was raised in the recent High Court cases of *Coleman* and *Mulholland*, the decisions in those cases do not clarify these matters to any significant extent.

the Court accepts the need to move beyond deference to the UK case law and begins to mark out a distinctive Australian position.

D. The Implied Freedom and Copyright Protection in Australia

(1) Overview of copyright in Australia

11.25 For reasons that will become apparent shortly, it is important to appreciate that copyright law in Australia is still very much governed by principles derived from UK law. Prior to Federation in 1901, copyright in the Australian colonies was governed on a colony-by-colony basis. On Federation, power to regulate copyright, patents, and trade marks was vested in the Commonwealth Parliament,[55] the first Commonwealth Copyright Act being passed in 1905. The 1905 Act was superseded by Copyright Act 1912, which declared that the UK Copyright Act 1911 was to apply to Australia.[56] The 1912 Act was in turn superseded in 1968, when a new Act was passed. Although now much amended, it is the Copyright Act 1968 that continues to govern copyright law in Australia. The 1968 Act was to a very large extent modelled on the UK's 1956 Copyright Act—the 1959 Spicer Committee Report that preceded the 1968 Act took the UK legislation as its starting point. One consequence of this history is that Australia has adopted the same approach to the provision of copyright exceptions as the United Kingdom. Thus, like the United Kingdom, rather than providing a small number of generally worded exceptions covering 'fair use' or 'private use', Australia makes provision for users by providing a long, but exhaustive, list of closely defined exceptions. The most generous of these exceptions are the 'fair dealing' provisions, which allow for fair dealing for the purposes of 'research or study',[57] 'criticism or review',[58] 'reporting of news',[59] or the 'giving of

---

[55] Constitution, s 51(xviii).

[56] Copyright Act 1912, s 8. In *The Gramophone Company v Leo Feist Incorporated* (1928) 41 CLR 1 the High Court held that the 1912 Act was an Imperial Act in force in Australia, and not enacted pursuant to an exercise of legislative power under s 51(xviii) of the Constitution.

[57] Copyright Act 1968, ss 40; 103C.

[58] Copyright Act 1968, ss 41; 103A.   [59] Copyright Act 1968, ss 42; 103B.

professional advice' by a legal practitioner.[60] It must be emphasized that, as with the fair dealing provisions in the United Kingdom and elsewhere, these exceptions only apply if the work is used for one of the approved purposes. Other types of use will not fall within the aegis of the fair dealing provisions, irrespective of how 'fair' they appear.

Given that the fair dealing provisions have been the most generous excep- **11.26** tions under Australian law since 1912, it is surprising that they have not generated a much greater body of case law. In fact, cases in which fair dealing defences are raised are rare in Australia. The infrequency with which fair dealing cases have arisen, coupled with the close historical connection between Australian and UK copyright law, has meant that Australian courts have invariably looked to the United Kingdom for guidance as to the principles to be applied when assessing whether a defendant's use amounts to fair dealing. For example, in the recent 'Panel' case, the most authoritative decision to examine the scope of the fair dealing defence in Australia,[61] it was uniformly accepted that UK fair dealing cases such as *Hubbard v Vosper*,[62] *Hyde Park v Yelland*,[63] and *Ashdown v Telegraph Group*[64] establish 'the' principles governing fair dealing. The fair dealing provisions, in particular, fair dealing for the purpose of criticism and review, and fair dealing for the purpose of news reporting, are particularly significant when considering the intersection between copyright and freedom of communication. We will turn shortly to consider specific examples of situations in which these exceptions fail to provide sufficient protection for freedom of communication. Before doing so, however, it is worth drawing attention to some of the general limitations of these provisions.

One limitation that affects both of the relevant fair dealing provisions is that, **11.27** generally speaking, the fair dealing provisions will only apply to published

---

[60] Copyright Act 1968, ss 43(2); 104(c).

[61] *Channel Nine v Network Ten* (2002) 55 Intellectual Property Rep 112 (Fed Ct of Australia—Full Court). The facts of this case are complex. In outline, it concerned twenty separate occasions on which the defendant rebroadcast extracts from the plaintiff's programmes during *The Panel*, a weekly television programme that pokes fun at other television shows. In relation to nineteen of the extracts, the defendant pleaded a fair dealing defence. It was eventually concluded that ten of the uses did not amount to fair dealing. One of these uses (the Prime Minister singing 'Happy Birthday' to Don Bradman) is discussed in detail in para 11.35 below.

[62] [1972] 2 QB 84, CA.   [63] [2001] Ch 143, CA.   [64] [2002] Ch 149, CA.

works. This is because it has been held that any use that results in the publication of a substantial part of a previously unpublished work will not be 'fair'.[65] There is some authority to suggest that even if a work has not been published to the world at large it may have been circulated to a sufficiently wide audience that it becomes fair to publish sections of it. For example, it has been said that it might be enough that a work has been widely distributed within a religious community or has been sent to all of the shareholders of a public company.[66] However, in the United Kingdom, it has recently been reiterated that such examples do not replace the general rule that it will not be fair for the purpose of reporting current events to publish extracts from a previously unpublished work.[67] It should also be noted for present purposes that the question whether a more relaxed approach should be taken to unpublished 'Government documents' has been left open in Australia but there is not any positive support in the cases for the existence of such a rule.[68]

11.28 The exception permitting fair dealing for the purpose of criticism and review is further limited by the fact that it only applies where the criticism or review is 'of that work or another work'.[69] Although there is no Australian authority directly on point, this would seem to exclude cases where the criticism or review is of something other than a work. This would seem to mean, for example, that it would not be possible to rely on this provision in order to quote from the text of a dramatic work when reviewing a performance of a play.[70] More importantly for present purposes, this would also seem to mean that it would not be possible to rely on this provision where the criticism or review is of the behaviour of a politician or other public figure. This latter point can be illustrated by reference to a recent UK case, *Ashdown v Telegraph Group*. In that case, one question that arose was whether the

---

[65] *British Oxygen v Liquid Air* [1925] 1 Ch 383, 393; *Commonwealth v Fairfax* (1980) 147 CLR 39, 55 (High Ct of Australia, per Mason J, sitting as a single judge); *Hyde Park v Yelland* [2001] Ch 143, CA, 158–9.

[66] *Hubbard v Vosper* [1972] 2 QB 84, CA, 94–5; *Commonwealth v Fairfax*, ibid.

[67] *Hyde Park v Yelland* [2001] Ch 143, CA, 158–9.

[68] *Commonwealth of Australia v Fairfax* (1980) 147 CLR 39, 55. The facts of this case are discussed in detail in para 11.31 below.

[69] Copyright Act 1968, s 41. Also see Copyright Act 1968, s 103A.

[70] The position in the United Kingdom is different: s 30(1) of the Copyright, Designs and Patents Act 1988 allows '[f]air dealing with a work for the purpose of criticism or review, of that or another work *or of a performance of a work*' (emphasis added).

defendants' copying of portions of a minute in order to criticize the behaviour of Tony Blair and another senior politician could be said to fall within the exception for fair dealing for the purpose of criticism or review. In rejecting an application of the criticism and review defence, Sir Andrew Morritt VC said at first instance:

> [W]hat is required is that the copying shall take place as part of and for the purpose of criticising and reviewing the work. The work is the minute. But the articles are not criticising or reviewing the minute: they are criticising or reviewing the actions of the Prime Minister and the claimant in October 1997. It was not necessary for that purpose to copy the minute at all. In my judgment the articles do not come within [the criticism and review defence] because the purpose of copying the work was not its criticism or review.[71]

As regards the meaning of the words 'criticism and review' themselves, it should be noted that, in line with UK authority, it has been said that these are 'expressions of wide and indefinite scope'.[72] Thus, it has been accepted in Australia that parody can fall within the notion of 'criticism and review'.[73] However, despite this acceptance of a broad definition of 'criticism and review,' Australian judges have at times proved slow to accept that the defendant's actions in the specific case before them fell within the defence. For example, although in the 'Panel' case the Court accepted that parodies fall within the notion of 'criticism and review', it nevertheless went on to find that the rebroadcast of excerpts from the plaintiff's programmes infringed except in circumstances where there was direct comment on the excerpt.[74]

---

[71] [2001] Ch 685, Ch D, 697–8. This reasoning was endorsed on appeal: [2002] Ch 149, CA, 171.

[72] *Pro Sieben v Carlton* [1999] 1 WLR 605, 620 (per Robert Walker LJ); *Channel Nine v Network Ten* (2002) 55 Intellectual Property Rep 112, 131 (per Hely J).

[73] *Channel Nine v Network Ten*, ibid 132: 'Criticism may involve an element of humour, or "poking fun at" the object of the criticism' (per Hely J). Similarly, in the United Kingdom, see *Williamson Music v The Pearson Partnership Ltd* [1987] FSR 97, 103; but cf *Cie générale des établissements Michelin—Michelin & Cie v CAW Canada* (1996) 71 CPR (3d) 348, para 66 (Fed Ct of Canada—Trial Division): '[C]riticism is not synonymous with parody. Criticism requires analysis and judgment of a work that sheds light on the original' (per Teitelbaum J).

[74] *Channel Nine v Network Ten* (2002) 55 Intellectual Property Rep 112. This aspect of the Court's reasoning has been criticized on the basis that the judges failed to display sensitivity to the ethos of programmes like *The Panel*. See M Handler and D Rolph, ' "A Real Pea Souper": The Panel Case and the Development of the Fair Dealing Defences to Copyright Infringement in Australia' (2003) 27 Melbourne U L Rev 381, 410–13.

11.29 Turning to the news reporting exception, it should be noted that, unlike its UK equivalent, the Australian provision is not confined to the reporting of 'current events', but rather applies to news more generally. It therefore seems that the defence can apply to the reporting of newsworthy matters of history.[75] It has also been indicated that the notion of 'news' is itself to be interpreted fairly broadly. For example, it was said that the reporting of New Year's Eve celebrations was at least arguably 'newsworthy',[76] and the mere fact that news was being reported in a humorous way would not prevent the exception from applying.[77] It is important to emphasize, however, that it is not any news-related use that gains the benefit of the exception —the exception only applies in cases where the use is for the purpose of *reporting* news. The problem is that 'reporting' may well not extend to include commentary on events that are well known or the expression of opinion. If this is so, then newspaper opinion pieces and humorous topical news programmes will fall outside the scope of the exception. Although this point has not been fully developed in Australia,[78] the cases do show a marked reluctance to apply the defence where the defendant's use is not immediately recognizable as news 'reporting'. It is noticeable, for example, that in the 'Panel' case only two of the extracts were held to fall within the exception. Although the reasoning in this case is often difficult to follow, one possible explanation for this outcome is that the judges were reluctant to treat general discussion of newsworthy topics as falling within an exception that allows for news *reporting.*

(2) Copyright's collision with freedom of communication

11.30 Once the limitations that restrict the operation of the fair dealing provisions generally are appreciated, it becomes relatively easy to think of hypothetical examples in which copyright would collide with the implied freedom of

---

[75] *Commonwealth v Fairfax* (1980) 147 CLR 39, 56; *Wigginton v Brisbane TV* (1992) 25 Intellectual Property Rep 58, 62; *Channel Nine v Network Ten* (2002) 55 Intellectual Property Rep 112, 131.

[76] *Nine Network Australia v Australian Broadcasting Corporation* (1999) 48 Intellectual Property Rep 333.

[77] Ibid.

[78] Cf the New Zealand case, *Copyright Licensing Ltd v University of Auckland* (2002) 53 Intellectual Property Rep 618, 626: the work must be used for the purpose of 'reporting current events' and not for editorial or other purposes.

political communication. However, it is perhaps better to illustrate the problems that might arise by reference to three real case studies.

(i) *Commonwealth v Fairfax*

In *Commonwealth v Fairfax*,[79] unpublished documents created by Australian **11.31** public servants were to be published in a book and were to be serialized in the defendant's newspaper. The documents related to matters such as the Government's East Timor–Indonesia policy, US military bases in Australia, and Australia's support for the Shah of Iran. The purpose of the book, as stated in its introduction, was to allow debate about the effectiveness of the Australian public service and the Government's foreign and defence policies. Accompanying comments were designed to contextualize the documents. The Government sought an interlocutory injunction to restrain publication, inter alia, on the basis that publication would be an infringement of copyright. In the High Court, Mason J (sitting alone) granted the injunction, concluding that the defendant was unlikely to be able to establish a fair dealing defence. First, he considered the claim that the publication was for the purpose of criticism or review and concluded that this argument was unlikely to succeed, since in his view any criticism or review of the documents 'was merely a veneer, setting off what is essentially a publication of the plaintiff's documents'.[80] His treatment of the 'reporting of news' was even more brief, but he seemed to doubt whether the plaintiff's actions could be described as news reporting at all[81] and indicated that, in any event, the unpublished nature of the material posed a serious obstacle to the establishment of a fair dealing defence.[82]

As Mason J had to consider only whether the plaintiff had made out a **11.32** sufficient case for interim relief, his conclusions must be approached with some caution. However, it must be emphasized that his conclusions are perfectly consistent with an application of principles derived from UK fair dealing cases: the material was unpublished, the criticism and review was aimed at the actions of the Government, of which the documents provided evidence, and not at the documents themselves, and the use was not immediately recognizable as news 'reporting'. In contrast, it is our view that the material in *Fairfax* clearly constituted political communication that ought

---

[79] (1980) 147 CLR 39.   [80] Ibid 56.   [81] Ibid.   [82] Ibid 54, 55, 56.

now to attract the protection of the implied freedom. The disclosure of that material related directly to the system of representative government established by the Constitution.

(ii) The 'children overboard' story

11.33 On 7 October 2001, shortly before a General Election, a vessel suspected of carrying illegal immigrants was intercepted by an Australian warship. Realizing that the course of the vessel had been altered away from Australia, some passengers began to jump into the water. Later that day, the then Minister for Immigration and Multicultural Affairs, Mr Philip Ruddock, claimed that some of the children on the vessel had been thrown overboard in an attempt to deter the Navy from forcing their vessel to change course. The story was repeated over subsequent days by other senior ministers, including the then Minister for Defence, Mr Peter Reith and the Prime Minister, Mr John Howard. To support these claims, the Government released close-up photographs, taken by Australian defence force personnel, which showed children being rescued from the water. Subsequent inquiries, however, have revealed that the 'children overboard story' was untrue and the photographs were not in fact taken on 7 October, but rather on 8 October when the Navy was forced to rescue passengers from their vessel because it was sinking.[83]

11.34 Significantly, it became apparent later that photographs other than those released by the Government showed that the vessel was sinking at the time the children were being rescued. If those photographs had been leaked to the media, it is unlikely, on current authority, that their publication would have fallen within the fair dealing defences. The photographs were unpublished, any criticism or review would have been of the Government's previous claims rather than of the photographs themselves and it is not entirely certain that publication would have been treated as news 'reporting'. Yet, as the Parliamentary inquiry into the incident concluded, '[t]he peculiar sensitivity associated with the claim that children had been thrown overboard was that it was made at the beginning of and sustained throughout a Federal election campaign, during which "border protection" and national security were key issues.'[84]

---

[83] These facts have been taken from the Report of the Senate Select Committee on a Certain Maritime Incident, 23 October 2002.

[84] Ibid xxi.

(iii) **The 'Panel' case**

Television station Network Ten broadcasts a show called *The Panel* during **11.35**
which a regular panel of well-known television personalities and their guests
comment (often in a humorous fashion) on excerpts of other television
programmes. On one occasion, an excerpt from Channel Nine's variety programme, *Midday*, showed the Prime Minister, John Howard, singing 'Happy
Birthday' to retired Australian cricketer, Sir Donald Bradman, at the request
of the programme's host, Kerri-Anne Kennerley. The panellists made lengthy
comments relating to the appearance of the Prime Minister in the excerpt
and Kennerley's performance as the host of *Midday*. A majority of the Full
Court of the Federal Court in *Channel Nine v Network Ten*[85] held that the
publication did not come within the fair dealing provisions. Sundberg J was
of the view that the segment was shown on *The Panel* for its entertainment
value and not for the purpose of reporting news.[86] Similarly, Hely J concluded that it would be 'an exaggeration or distortion of the facts' to claim
that the segment was shown for the purpose of reporting the news that the
Prime Minister had sung 'Happy Birthday' to Sir Donald Bradman.[87] In
contrast, dissenting on this point, Finkelstein J considered that there had
been fair dealing for the purpose of news reporting because the Prime
Minister behaving in a 'silly' way is 'newsworthy'. He went on to observe that
'all behaviour of a Prime Minister can be regarded as "political" because it
may affect voters' perceptions and it is newsworthy for that reason.'[88] We
agree wholeheartedly with this conclusion, but would also observe that there
is a good argument to be made that the excerpt did not so much show the
Prime Minister behaving in a 'silly' manner as attempting to trade off the
iconic status of Australia's most famous sportsperson, something that goes
even more directly to character.[89]

The above three case studies show that, if the fair dealing provisions are **11.36**
construed in accordance with UK authority, there are circumstances in which
the Copyright Act 1968 would operate to burden political communication,
thereby satisfying the first limb of the *Lange* test. Having reached this
conclusion, it is necessary to consider the ways in which the Court might

---

[85] (2002) 55 Intellectual Property Rep 112.
[86] Ibid 114.   [87] Ibid 136.   [88] Ibid 118.
[89] See M Handler and D Rolph, ' "A Real Pea Souper": The Panel Case and the Development of the Fair Dealing Defences to Copyright Infringement in Australia' (2003) 27
Melbourne U L Rev 381, n 68, 417.

respond. However, before turning to this question, it is perhaps worth pausing to make some broader observations about what the case studies reveal.

11.37 One point worth emphasizing is that copyright subsists in documents such as those at issue in *Commonwealth v Fairfax* largely by accident. More specifically, it needs to be appreciated that copyright will subsist in works such as internal memoranda because copyright has been extended to cover certain types of product irrespective of their form, merit, or purpose. This extension has resulted from an appreciation on the part of the legislature that it is unwise to spell out in too much detail what 'a work' will look like, and from an understandable reluctance on the part of the judiciary to engage in consideration of the aesthetic merits of a work. However, whilst these may provide good practical reasons for extending copyright to these types of work, it can be seen that none of the theories that are usually used to justify copyright really explain why protection should be extended to works of this kind. More specifically, there is no need to provide incentives for the creation of these works, nor in most cases can they truly be said to embody the personality of their creator.

11.38 A second point worth emphasizing is that, in each of the case studies identified, freedom of political communication requires that the public have access to the work itself. Merely describing the contents of the work would not be sufficient in these cases because this would deprive members of the public of the opportunity to see the evidence for themselves. More generally, it can be seen that any claim that the idea–expression dichotomy prevents copyright from conflicting with freedom of political communication is unconvincing. Indeed, the examples have been carefully chosen to refute this very argument: in these cases the form of communication cannot be disentangled from its content. Cases like *Fairfax* are also important because they demonstrate that, although a right to reproduce the work itself is particularly important in the case of photographic material and broadcasts, it is not only in such cases that free speech interests require access to the work itself.[90] The children overboard example also illustrates the danger that the copyright owner will be able to release extracts of documents or other material selectively in order to convey a particular message. In contrast, critics will be restricted to describing any contrary evidence that they have seen.

---

[90] Cf M Nimmer, 'Does Copyright Abridge the First Amendment Guarantees of Free Speech and the Press?' (1970) 17 UCLA L Rev 1180.

E. Options for the High Court

(1) Introduction

Since copyright protection can burden protected communication, the second **11.39**
limb of the *Lange* test requires that the law be reasonably appropriate and
adapted to serve a legitimate end in a manner which is compatible with the
constitutionally prescribed system of government. There is no doubt that
the protection of copyright serves a legitimate end given the existence of
the copyright power—there is no indication from the Court that it would
require more than this. The question, therefore, is whether there is a reasonable proportionality between the protection of copyright and the protection
of political communication. This is a difficult issue and, as yet, the Court has
not even settled the parameters of the enquiry. Nevertheless, a number of
factors that ought to be treated as relevant have already been indicated: first,
copyright now extends to many types of work whose creation is not dependent on the financial incentives that copyright protection offers and which
cannot be said to reflect the personality of their creator; secondly, there are
circumstances in which an ability to reproduce the precise form of the communication is critical to the effective conveyance of political information;
and thirdly, there are less communication-intrusive ways of promoting the
objectives underpinning copyright than the current regime, in particular, a
broader system of exceptions would not undermine the overall aims of the
Australian copyright system. These factors might suggest that elements of the
present Copyright Act do not satisfy the second limb of the *Lange* test. However, a recognition of the conflict between the implied freedom and copyright
protection would not necessitate the Court's declaring central provisions of
the Copyright Act invalid. Rather, we believe that a fundamental reappraisal
of the basis and scope of the fair dealing provisions would probably be
sufficient to resolve copyright's *constitutional* problems in Australia.[91]

---

[91] It should perhaps be noted that we leave aside the possibility that the Court could instead
recognize a common law public interest defence to actions for infringement of copyright. In
the absence of express statutory support for such a defence of the type found in both the
United Kingdom (Copyright, Designs and Patents Act 1988, s 171(3)) and New Zealand
(Copyright Act 1994, s 225(3)), a reinterpretation of the scope of the fair dealing exceptions
is less objectionable on constitutional grounds. Moreover, as a practical matter, it should
be noted that Gummow J (who now sits on the High Court) has long been opposed to the

(2) Reinterpreting the fair dealing provisions

11.40 Handler and Rolph have argued for a 'rigorous and principled reconsideration of the operation and effect of fair dealing defences under the Act'.[92] To this call, we would add that the implied freedom of political communication compels a rejection of the UK authority on fair dealing and requires a reconsideration of the Australian fair dealing provisions to allow greater protection for political communication. This argument rests on two propositions. First, there is no compelling reason to give the Australian fair dealing defences a restrictive meaning. Secondly, the statutory language allows for a construction that is compatible with the implied freedom. We therefore believe that it is both *possible* and *desirable* to reinterpret the fair dealing provisions in a way that is appropriate for the Australian constitutional context.

11.41 In relation to the first proposition, namely, that there is no compelling reason to give the Australian fair dealing defences a restrictive interpretation, it is important to appreciate that the current approach to fair dealing did not result from a conscious legislative decision. Significantly, the first Commonwealth Copyright Act 1905 adopted a very different approach to the provision of copyright exceptions from that found in Australia today. Section 28 of that Act provided that copyright in a book would not be infringed by a person making a copy for private use, or 'by a person making fair extracts from or otherwise fairly dealing with the contents of the book *for the purpose of a new work*, or for the purposes of criticism, review, or refutation, or in the ordinary course of reporting scientific information'.[93] This broad and open-ended provision apparently created or preserved a general fair use defence of the type found in British and American law at the

---

recognition of public interest defences to actions for both infringement of copyright (*Collier Constructions v Foskett* (1990) 97 ALR 460, 473) and breach of confidence (*Corrs Pavey Whiting & Byrne v Collector of Customs* (1987) 14 FCR 434; *Smith Kline & French v Department of Community Services and Health* (1990) 22 FCR 73, 111). For recent support for Gummow J's views, see D Thomas, 'A Public Interest Defence to Copyright Infringement?' (2003) 14 Australian Intellectual Property J 225.

[92] See M Handler and D Rolph, ' "A Real Pea Souper": The Panel Case and the Development of the Fair Dealing Defences to Copyright Infringement in Australia' (2003) 27 Melbourne U L Rev 381, n 68, 383.

[93] Emphasis added.

time. The accompanying Parliamentary debates suggest that this was indeed the intention.[94]

The replacement of the 1905 Act with the Copyright Act 1912 brought with **11.42** it the fair dealing provision of the UK Copyright Act 1911. It has been argued elsewhere that the available evidence suggests that the 1911 Act was not intended to be more restrictive than the old law as regards fair use, rather it was thought that the fair dealing provision and the newly introduced substantial part test would preserve the fair use defence.[95] Some further support for this argument can be gained from the legislative history of the 1912 Copyright Act in Australia. There is no indication in the Parliamentary debates that anyone thought that the 1912 Act would be more restrictive as regards fair use than section 28 of the 1905 Act. In contrast, other significant differences between the 1905 and 1912 Acts were outlined carefully.[96]

The more restrictive approach that developed towards fair use in the post- **11.43** 1911 period resulted from a handful of UK cases decided prior to the 1950s, together with the fact that commentators at the time chose to emphasize the restrictive parts of these judgments, with F E Skone James, then editor of *Copinger*, bearing particular responsibility.[97] By the time the question of copyright reform arose in the 1950s, it was widely accepted that the restrictive interpretation that had been placed on the fair dealing provision of the 1911 Act represented the starting point for any legislative reform. Thus, in the United Kingdom, the Gregory Committee, which reported in 1952, did not revisit the fundamental question whether the 'fair dealing' approach adopted by the courts was appropriate. Rather, working within this general approach, it recommended a limited number of liberalizing measures. In Australia, the Spicer Committee, which reported in 1959, took the Gregory Committee's report and the 1956 UK Copyright Act as its starting

---

[94] Commonwealth of Australia, Parliamentary Debates 1905, vol 27, pp 2912–3 (per Senator Keating, the Minister responsible for the passage of the Bill through the Senate).

[95] R Burrell, 'Reining in Copyright Law: Is Fair Use the Answer?' [2001] Intellectual Property Q 361.

[96] The second reading speech highlights important differences between the 1911 UK Act and the 1905 Commonwealth Act, but the fair dealing provision is not discussed (see Commonwealth of Australia, Parliamentary Debates, 30 October 1912, p 4859).

[97] See R Burrell, 'Reining in Copyright Law: Is Fair Use the Answer?' [2001] Intellectual Property Q 361, n 89.

point.[98] In relation to the exceptions, the Spicer Committee recommended the enactment of fair dealing provisions 'to the same effect as section 6(1), (2) and (3) of the 1956 Act',[99] and it did so without any independent evaluation of the purpose of providing copyright exceptions and despite the fact that, at the time, there had not been a single Australian fair dealing decision.

11.44 A further opportunity to re-examine the correctness of the fair dealing approach was lost in 1968. Unfortunately, the Bill that became the 1968 Act was introduced late in the Parliamentary session and consequently there was no consideration of the effect of individual provisions during the Committee Stage. It is therefore no exaggeration to say that there was no official re-evaluation of the desirability of the fair dealing approach until the report of the Australian Copyright Law Review Committee in 1998. Significantly, that report recommended that the fair dealing provisions be replaced with a broad US style fair use defence.[100] The desirability of the current approach has never been properly debated by the Australian Parliament and cannot even be said to represent the will of the Imperial Parliament in 1911. There is therefore no reason why the Court should not feel free to take a completely fresh look at the fair dealing provisions and reject entirely both the UK fair dealing cases and the Australian cases that have followed them.

11.45 In relation to the second proposition, namely, that the statutory language allows for a construction that is compatible with the implied freedom, it is important to make two further points. First, it should be emphasized that there is nothing in the statutory language that requires unpublished works to be excluded from the scope of the fair dealing defences.[101] The best justification for excluding unpublished works from the scope of fair dealing exceptions is to protect authors from having extracts of their works placed

---

[98] Copyright Law Review Committee, *Report of the Committee appointed by the Attorney-General of the Commonwealth to Consider what Alterations are Desirable in the Copyright Law of the Commonwealth* (Canberra, 1959).

[99] Ibid, para 107.

[100] See Copyright Law Review Committee, *Simplification of the Copyright Act 1968, Part 1: Exceptions to the Exclusive Right of Copyright Owners* (Canberra, 1998), paras 6.07–6.08.

[101] Nor does the Berne Convention compel such a result. Although Article 10(1) restricts the right to make quotations to works which have already been made lawfully available to the public, such a restriction is not to be found in Article 9(2) of Berne (which covers exceptions to the reproduction right generally) or in Article 17 of Berne which allows Members of the Union 'to *permit*, control, or to prohibit' the circulation of a work on public interest grounds (emphasis added).

into the public domain before the work has been completed, because the threat of premature disclosure might seriously undermine the creative process.[102] In contrast, on current authority, the exclusion is not confined to 'unfinished' works, but rather applies to all unpublished works, irrespective of how important the content of the work is for public debate. Thus, whilst we would accept that the unpublished nature of a work is a relevant factor when deciding whether a taking was 'fair', it should be accorded little weight in a case such as *Fairfax*. Secondly, as regards the accepted purposes themselves, the Court needs to emphasize not merely that the purposes are to be construed broadly, but also that lower courts should be slow to dismiss a defendant's argument that the use was for an approved purpose. One possibility left open by the statutory language is that the purpose of the taking should be judged subjectively, such that if a defendant honestly believes that her taking was for an approved purpose the defence will apply.[103] On this approach, it would still be necessary to show that the taking was 'fair'. Consequently, even if the defendant's purpose were to be assessed subjectively, an honest but misguided defendant would not be allowed to reproduce an unlimited amount of copyright material. The Court also needs to signal that, although the statute requires that criticism and review be 'of a work', where there is oblique criticism of an underlying work this should be treated as sufficient even if the main thrust of the criticism is of something other than a work.[104] Finally, the Court needs to give news reporting an expansive interpretation, making it clear that any use for the purpose of conveying or commenting on news should be treated as falling within the scope of the exception.[105]

---

[102] W Fisher, 'Reconstructing the Fair Use Doctrine' (1988) 101 Harv L Rev 1659, 1773–4: arguing forcefully against the disclosure of creative works before their creators deem them finished.

[103] Cf the recent entrenchment of an objective standard in the UK: *Pro Sieben v Carlton* [1999] 1 WLR 605, CA, 620; *Hyde Park v Yelland* [2001] Ch 143, CA, 157; *Newspaper Licensing Agency v Marks and Spencer* [2001] Ch 257, CA, 249.

[104] This would catch cases such as the Prime Minister singing 'Happy Birthday'. On the facts, there was at least 'oblique' criticism of the programme on which John Howard appeared.

[105] General support for a more speech protective interpretation of the copyright provisions may be found in the judgments of Gummow and Hayne JJ, and Kirby J in *Coleman* [2004] HCA 39. In giving a narrow reading to the reach of the legislative prohibition on the use of insulting words, their Honours were guided by a concern to protect common law freedom of expression and the constitutional freedom of political communication: [185], [194] (per Gummow and Hayne JJ); [225] (per Kirby J).

F. Conclusion

11.46 The aim here has been to demonstrate that, even if one adopts a fairly narrow interpretation of the implied freedom of political communication, it is possible to point to circumstances in which copyright would interfere with the sphere of constitutionally protected communication. In light of the resulting constitutional objection to the current Copyright Act, it has been argued that the Court needs to reinterpret the fair dealing provisions. While this would not by itself solve all of the problems with the current copyright regime (for example, it would not provide sufficient protection for certain types of creative reuse of copyright material), it would nevertheless go some way towards improving the current position. It is important, however, to end on a cautious note, since it is far from certain that the Court would be prepared to take a fresh look at the fair dealing provisions. In particular, there is a danger that the Court may find other ways of resolving the tension between the protection of copyright and the protection of political communication. It is possible that it will take the view that the nature of the copyright power overrides, or is not subject to, the implied freedom. Alternatively, it may seek shelter behind the idea–expression dichotomy or may simply assert that the legislature has already struck a 'balance' between the interests of copyright owners and the interests of the wider community. However, we would urge the Court to resist the temptation to sidestep the problem and to think seriously about developing an autochthonous interpretation of the fair dealing provisions.

12

FREEDOM OF EXPRESSION AND COPYRIGHT UNDER CIVIL LAW: OF BALANCE, ADAPTATION, AND ACCESS

Alain Strowel and François Tulkens

European copyright lawyers have not pondered very seriously the impact of **12.01** freedom of expression on their field. All too often, they have failed to consider the requirements that freedom of expression imposes on the contours of copyright, and some copyright scholars still profess, or at least tacitly believe, that copyright should remain immune from free speech concerns.[1]

---

[1] Interestingly, the same opinion is sometimes shared by copyright lawyers as to the relationship between copyright and competition law: some IP purists maintain that IP should remain immune from any claims arising out of competition law concerns. This extreme view is of course as unacceptable as the one that competition law always trumps intellectual property law, a view apparently popular among competition lawyers.

12.02 While highly regrettable, the fact that freedom of expression is not taken seriously by intellectual property lawyers in civil law Europe can be justified to a certain extent by the difficulty of grasping all the complexities of the growing body of case law on freedom of expression. It is definitely not acceptable for copyright to be placed by zealots in a sanctuary where it remains untouchable and out of reach. However, neither should freedom of expression be sanctified, particularly today, when claims of freedom of expression are often made by commercial operators in an attempt to veil more mercenary interests. In addition, some restrictions on speech may be justified, not only in the traditional sense of defamation but also in relation to the spread of hate speech on the Internet and elsewhere.[2] There is no compelling reason for elevating freedom of expression above all other interests and believing that it should always prevail over other rights and civil liberties.

12.03 If neither copyright nor freedom of expression should in principle prevail, the difficult task remains of defining the right balance between the two. Some parameters for conducting this balancing test will be presented. Needless to say, clear criteria will not be developed as to when freedom of expression should prevail over copyright or vice versa but rather ways will be proposed to distinguish between two types of cases that require a slightly different approach: those where copyright appears as a content-related regulation (allowing the prohibition of some derivative forms of expression), and those where copyright functions as a content-neutral regulation that could nonetheless conflict with freedom of speech as it arguably restrains access to works.

12.04 In addition to the analysis of the case law and the attempt to find the right balance between copyright and freedom of speech, an underlying and related issue will be addressed, that is the expansion of the boundaries of copyright. Freedom of expression has been employed by many scholars as a useful tool to limit this expansion. In his 2002 seminal overview of Community case law on the interface between copyright and freedom of expression, Bernt Hugenholtz[3] wondered whether the rising tide of copyright would, or at least

---

² See eg, H Dumont, P Mandoux, A Strowel and F Tulkens (eds), *Pas de liberté pour les ennemis de la liberté? Groupements liberticides et droit* (Bruylant, 2000).

³ PB Hugenholtz, 'Copyright and Freedom of Expression in Europe', in N Elkin-Koren and NW Netanel (eds), *The Commodification of Information* (Kluwer, 2002), 239–63.

could, be stopped by counter-pressure exerted by freedom of expression and information as guaranteed by the constitutional provisions of EU Member States and the European Convention on Human Rights (ECHR). He noted that relevant case law had developed in several European countries, including Austria, France, Germany, the Netherlands, and the United Kingdom. It is worthwhile updating his analysis, as new cases have been decided in the interim, particularly in civil law countries such as France and Belgium. A short review of the legal framework is, however, a useful prerequisite to such a journey through the case law and the more general reflections on the expansion of copyright that this journey triggers.

A. The European and International Legal Framework

(1) Freedom of expression and limits in favour of the 'rights of others'

The need to balance freedom of expression with other interests derives **12.05** from Article 10 of the ECHR, which shapes the entire debate on the balance that must struck between copyright and free speech in the European context:[4]

1. Everyone has the right to freedom of expression. This right shall include freedom to hold opinions and to receive and impart information and ideas without interference by public authority and regardless of frontiers.
2. The exercise of these freedoms, since it carries with it duties and responsibilities, may be subject to such formalities, conditions, restrictions or penalties as are prescribed by law and are necessary in a democratic society, in the interests of national security, territorial integrity of public safety, for the prevention of disorder or crime, for the protection of health or morals, for the protection of the reputation or rights of others, for preventing the disclosure of information received in confidence, or for maintaining the authority and impartiality of the judiciary.

Freedom of expression, as recognized by Article 10 of the ECHR, has two **12.06** facets. The first is the right to hold opinions and impart information and ideas. This is the most widely known aspect of freedom of expression in any democracy. According to the case law of the European Court of Human

---

[4] See eg, T Pinto, 'The Influence of the European Convention on Human Rights on Intellectual Property Rights' [2002] EIPR 209–19.

Rights (ECtHR), this means that 'freedom of expression is applicable not only to "information" or "ideas" that are favourably received or regarded as inoffensive or as a matter of indifference but also to those that offend, shock or disturb the State or any section of the community. In addition, journalistic freedom also covers possible recourse to a degree of exaggeration, or even provocation.'[5] The second aspect of freedom of expression is the right to receive information and ideas. This aspect is less present but not altogether absent from the ECtHR's case law ('not only does the press have the task of imparting such information and ideas: the public has also a right to receive them.')[6]

12.07 Both aspects are fundamental, albeit not absolute. The possibility of reconciling freedom of expression and copyright stems, however, from Article 10(2) of the ECHR, which provides that the 'exercise of these freedoms . . . may be subject to . . . restrictions . . . for the protection of . . . rights of others.' Nothing precludes copyright from being considered as one of the 'rights of others', the protection of which could justify certain limitations on freedom of expression.[7] Even though these restrictions are mostly applied to the first aspect of freedom of expression, this does not mean that they do not apply to the second. As the ECtHR has held, 'freedom to receive information basically prohibits a government from restricting a person from receiving

---

[5] *See* ECtHR, *Jersild v Denmark*, 23 September 1994, (1994) 19 EHRR 1; *Castells v Spain*, 23 April 1992, (1992) 14 EHRR 445, para 42; *Oberschlick v Austria*, 23 May 1991, (1995) 19 EHRR 389, para 57; *Handyside*, 7 December 1976, para 49.

[6] ECtHR, *Worm v Austria*, 29 August 1997, (1998) 25 EHRR 454, para 50; ECtHR, *Handyside v United Kingdom*, 7 December 1976, para 52.

[7] PB Hugenholtz, 'Copyright and Freedom of Expression in Europe', in N Elkin-Koren and NW Netanel (eds), *The Commodification of Information* (Kluwer, 2002), 246, refers to a restrictive opinion of a Dutch commentator (PJ Boukema, *Enkele aspecten van de vrijheid van meningsuiting in de Duitse Bondsrepubliek en in Nederland* (Amsterdam, Polak & Van Gennep, 1966) 258), according to which Article 10(2) only refers to the fundamental rights recognized by the ECHR. However, this view is dated and, as Hugenholtz admits, 'doctrine and case law have never accepted this narrow interpretation. Instead, the "rights of others" are deemed to include a wide range of subjective rights and interests, including the rights protected under copyright.' See *Chappell*, ECtHR 24 February 1989, Publ of the ECtHR, Series A 152A. In a 2003 decision discussed below (Ct of App, 's-Gravenhage, 4 September 2003, *Computerrecht*, 2003/6, 357, note K Koelman; *Auteurs & Media*, 2004/1, 44, note A Strowel and G Gathem), the Court of Appeal of The Hague clearly stated that 'among the rights [referred to in Article 10 ECHR] falls copyright, as this right is provided by a law and intends to protect the right of others.' See also T Pinto, 'The Influence of the European Convention on Human Rights on Intellectual Property Rights' [2002] EIPR 209–19, 217.

information that others wish or may be willing to import to him.'[8] If a country or, a fortiori, a private person, does not wish or is unwilling to impart information, there is no right to receive it or duty to impart it.

As for other restrictions on freedom of expression, any copyright-related limitation must be 'prescribed by law' and 'necessary in a democratic society'. Contracting parties to the ECHR have a limited margin of appreciation in deciding what is 'necessary in a democratic society' and the restrictions must be proportionate to the legitimate goal.[9] The proportionality test is the real standard in assessing whether a limitation on freedom of expression is compatible with Article 10 of the ECHR. In determining whether a restriction is 'necessary in a democratic society', the ECtHR will take into account:[10] **12.08**

(i) the type of speech: 'ordinary' use of speech by a layperson is less protected than freedom of the press;[11]

(ii) the identity of the speaker: a journalist or politician[12] benefits from a greater degree of protection than an ordinary person or a civil servant;[13]

(iii) the identity of the individual targeted by the speech: politicians have a lesser expectation of privacy,[14] while judges have stronger protection because of their professional obligations;

(iv) the form of the speech: a live broadcast[15] is different from, for example, a website or a newspaper article; and

(v) the content of the speech: political speech, speech of general interest, expressions of fact and opinions are not treated the same as one another.[16]

---

[8] ECtHR, *Guerra v Italy*, 19 February 1998, (1998) 26 EHRR 357, para 53; ECtHR, *Leander v Sweden*, 26 March 1987, (1987) 9 EHRR 433, para 74.

[9] Any measure restricting a Convention right must be 'proportionate to the legitimate aim pursued' (*Handyside v United Kingdom* (1976) 1 EHRR 737, at 754, para 49).

[10] For an overview, see S van Drooghenbroeck, *La Convention européenne des droits de l'homme. Trois années de jurisprudence de la Cour européenne des droits de l'Homme 1999–2001* (Larcier, 2003) 163–79.

[11] ECtHR, *Janowski v Poland*, 21 January 1999, (2000) 29 EHRR 705, para 33.

[12] ECtHR, *Jerusalem v Austria*, 21 February 2001.

[13] ECtHR, *Wille v Liechtenstein*, 28 October 1999, (2000) 30 EHRR 558, para 64.

[14] ECtHR, *Feldek v Slovakia*, 12 July 2001, para 74; *Tammer v Estonia*, 6 February 2001, (2003) 37 EHRR 43.

[15] ECtHR, *Fuentes Bobo v Spain*, 29 February 2000, (2001) 31 EHRR 50, para 46.

[16] For the subtleness and lack of coherence of the ECtHR's evaluation, see Van Drooghenbroeck (n 10 above) 170–3.

12.09 All of these elements are taken into consideration by the Court on a case-by-case basis in order to balance the interests at stake and decide if a restriction on freedom of speech is necessary in a democratic society. It is thus a question of proportionality.

12.10 For the sake of completeness, it should also be mentioned that other international instruments have also clearly recognized the predominant value associated with freedom of expression.[17]

(2) Copyright and built-in limits in favour of freedom of expression

12.11 Copyright is occasionally recognized in international instruments for the protection of human rights.[18] Article 27(2) of the Universal Declaration on Human Rights (UDHR), for instance, is quite clear in its inclusion of the protection of the material and moral interests of authors among human rights. According to some French scholars,[19] the position of copyright as a human right is supported by the inclusion, in the first paragraph of Article 27, of the right of everyone to 'participate in the cultural life of the community', what many today would call the right to culture, a new dimension of human rights.[20] Perhaps these two paragraphs of Article 27 of the UDHR should be considered complementary, as the first grants a passive right to culture (a right of enjoyment) while the second grants an active right (the right to become an author).[21]

---

[17] See Article 19 of the International Covenant on Civil and Political Rights. (For further analysis, see U Suthersanen, ch 5 above.) In civil law countries, this provision is less frequently employed than Article 10.

[18] See Article 27(2) of the Universal Declaration on Human Rights and, more importantly, Art 15 of the International Covenant on Economic, Social and Cultural Rights, which is legally binding. In this regard, see U Suthersanen (para 5.16 above) as well as her contribution to the Tenth Annual Conference on International Intellectual Property Law & Policy, April 4 and 5, 2002, 'Public Interest and Fundamental Rights: An Enquiry as to the British Copyright Law Ex-Post the Human Rights Act 1988'.

[19] C Colombet, 'La protection des intérêts moraux et matériels des auteurs (Art 27(2))', in *Droit d'auteur et droits de l'homme*, colloquium of 16 and 17 June 1989, Paris, INPI, 44; A Kéréver, 'Le droit d'auteur, acquis et conditions du développement de la culture juridique européen' (1990) *Droit d'auteur* 146.

[20] The right to benefit from the advancement of culture and to participate in the progress linked to such development is now more often cited as an official human right. For example, since 1993, see Art 23(3)(5) of the Belgian Constitution.

[21] See E Konstantinov, 'Le droit d'auteur et le droit à la culture', in *Droit d'auteur et droits de l'homme*, colloquium of 16 and 17 June 1989, Paris, INPI, 39; A Strowel, *Droit d'auteur et copyright* (Bruylant, 1993) 157ff.

At European and national levels, copyright is more often implicitly protected   **12.12**
by constitutional provisions on property rights (see, for example, Article 14 of
the German GrundGesetz and Article 1 of the First Protocol to the ECHR).[22]
The German Constitutional Court has handed down several decisions con-
firming that the economic prerogatives of authors are protected by constitutional provisions on property. Furthermore, in one decision on intellectual
property the European Commission on Human Rights included patent protection under the aegis of Article 1 of the First Protocol to the ECHR.[23]
Of course, the protection of property is not unlimited and the German
Constitutional Court has held that, although the protection of property
rights

> implies that the economic exploitation of the work in principle vests with the
> author, the constitutional protection of property rights does not extend to all
> such exploitations. It is a matter for the legislature to determine the limits of
> copyright by imposing appropriate criteria, taking into account the nature and
> social function of copyright and ensuring that the author participates fairly in
> the exploitation of his work.[24]

Thus, according to the Constitutional Court, while the legislature is compet-
ent to remove the exclusive aspect of copyright in the case of compilations
of protected works for use in school textbooks, it is obliged nonetheless to
ensure that authors receive fair remuneration for such exempted use.

The most recent development is of course the inclusion of intellectual prop-   **12.13**
erty within the scope of protection of Article II-17(2) of the Charter of
Fundamental Rights as incorporated in the European Constitution ('Intellectual property shall be protected'). The practical consequences of this
provision are not yet clear,[25] but some courts have been quick to refer

---

[22] E Ulmer, *Urheber- und Verlagsrecht* (3rd edn, Springer, 1980) 65.
[23] *Smith Kline and French Laboratories v The Netherlands* Application 12633/87, 66 DR 70
(1990), E Com HR.
[24] Constitutional Court, 7 July 1971, GRUR, 1972, 481 (school book) quoted in the
English translation of C Geinger, 'Fundamental Rights, a Safeguard for the Coherence of
Intellectual Property Rights?' (2004) 35 IIC 271.
[25] See the oral comments of Lord Slynn of Hadley, 'Intellectual Property as Human
Right: What Should Member State Courts Do With This and Other European Charter
Provisions?' at the 2004 Annual Conference on International Intellectual Property Law
and Policy.

to the Charter of Fundamental Rights to confirm the importance of copy-right.[26]

12.14 Finally, copyright, in Germany at least, also falls within the scope of the fundamental right freely to develop one's personality (see Article 1 of the German GrundGesetz).

12.15 While the main provisions on freedom of expression contain an express limitation in favour of the rights of third parties, national copyright laws also integrate certain built-in limitations that are implicitly motivated by the desire to protect free speech. The main safety valve enshrined in copy-right law is the basic distinction between ideas and expressions. The idea–expression dichotomy, according to which only forms of expression, and not underlying ideas, can be subject to copyright protection, in theory guarantees that ideas remain free from copyright control. This built-in limitation has led some traditional continental copyright lawyers to conclude that copyright should be exonerated from further external restrictions (that is, those that originate outside copyright law).[27] Other copyright lawyers do not agree with this conclusion, since prohibiting the use of certain expressions can slow down the diffusion of 'ideas', especially when these expressions take the form of news photographs or other visual materials whose ideas may not be con-veyed unless the expression is copied as well. (How would it be possible to convey the 'idea' for instance of a natural disaster or of a murder without using the pictures made by the photographers who happened to be there when it happened? This explains why some additional safety valves in favour of reporting must be built in.[28]) Freedom of speech will thus play a more prominent role where no substitute can be developed. The balancing test should take into account the element of substitutability and thus the pos-sibility of developing alternate forms of expression. However, there is no

---

[26] Ct of App, Toulouse, 13 June 2002, *J Besset et Société Presse du Midi v Ministère public*, unpublished (quoted in A Lucas and P Sirinelli, 'Droit d'auteur et droits voisins', *Propriétés intellectuelles*, October 2003, 384).

[27] See eg, certain national reports in the ALAI seminar report, *The Boundaries of Copyright—Its Proper Limitations and Exceptions* (Australian Copyright Council, 1999).

[28] Such circumstances are present in a case such as *Time Inc v Bernard Geis Associates* 293 F Supp 130 (SDNY 1968). Cohen Jehoram, 'Copyright and Freedom of Expression, Abuse of Rights and Standard Chicanery: American and Dutch Approaches' [2004] EIPR 275–79, correctly considers that this is one of the rare cases where free speech has to interfere in order to favour the public interest.

'justification [based on freedom of expression] for the copying of expression along with idea simply because the copier lacks the will or the time or energy to create his own independently evolved expression'.[29] The question then focuses on the extent of time/investment that third parties can legitimately be required to expend in producing alternate forms of expression. This is a very difficult question that might require an analysis similar to that which competition lawyers more routinely perform. True defenders of freedom of expression may also be put off by this approach, which seems to subordinate free speech concerns to a market-oriented, cost-benefit analysis, which is quite alien to their body of law. It is nevertheless tempting to suggest that the proportionality test used in the case law of the ECtHR might not be as remote from a 'cost-benefit' analysis as one might at first think.

In addition to this idea–expression dichotomy, copyright has developed **12.16** other internal 'safety valves' that favour free speech, including a range of statutory exceptions and the limited duration of copyright protection. However, these built-in limitations do not guarantee that copyright will not clash with freedom of expression. The conflict between copyright and freedom of expression is not imaginary. The issue rightly attracts academic attention for its genuine interest. Nevertheless, its importance should not be overestimated in practice. Relatively few cases have indeed required a fine balancing between freedom of speech and copyright, which is probably an indication of the real importance of the issue. For example, the ECtHR has yet to rule on this issue.[30]

---

[29] M Nimmer, 'Does Copyright Abridge the First Amendment Guarantees of Free Speech and Press?' 17 UCLA L Rev 1180 (1970), 1203. See also at 1202: 'The point is not that ideas are useful without expression, but rather that while public enlightenment may require the copying of ideas from others, it remains perfectly possible for the speaker (or writer) who copies ideas from another, to supply his own expression of such ideas. True, it would often be easier to copy the expression as well as the idea, but the value of such labor-saving utility is far outweighed by the copyright interest in encouraging creation by protecting expression.' We even believe that the constraints on reusing pre-existing copyright material sometimes encourage the development of more elaborate, varied, and richer forms of expression.

[30] Of course, one could find that the absence of extensive case law is only a sign of the reluctance of courts to recognize the looming conflict between copyright and free speech. See, eg, PB Hugenholtz, 'Copyright and Freedom of Expression in Europe', in N Elkin-Koren and NW Netanel (eds), *The Commodification of Information* (Kluwer, 2002), 241.

B. Articulating and Balancing Copyright and
Free Speech Concerns

12.17 In this section of the chapter, in a review of cases subsequent to Hugenholtz's assessment of this issue, a pragmatic approach is advocated that takes into account the totality of circumstances of each particular case when balancing copyright and freedom of expression. Despite such a fact-based approach, it is thought that some categorical distinctions need to be made, one of which is the distinction between content-neutral and content-related regulation. Netanel has used this distinction to support his view on the appropriate level of scrutiny to apply in cases of copyright infringement. According to Netanel, 'copyright is best categorized as "content-neutral", not as content-based regulation.'[31] While there is no desire to get embroiled in the complex debate as to how these categories are defined under the First Amendment of the US Constitution, this distinction will be used where possible in an attempt to modulate the articulation between copyright and free speech, depending on the issues at stake.

12.18 Rather than considering that all copyright rules fall within the category of 'content-neutral' regulation, it is felt more appropriate to distinguish between two different issues: the issue of parody which raises the issue of content-related regulation (that is, the possibility through copyright to prohibit derivative works and the communicative effect of derivative expression) and the issue of access to works, which arguably involves content-neutral rules. While the parody issue is probably as old as copyright, the issue of control of access has only recently come to the fore with the advent of the Internet and the rise of the digital age. The enquiry is thus divided into two parts: the first part discusses the case law on derivative works or parody, while the second part treats control of access to expression and information. In part one, the copyright prerogative ensuring a modicum of control is the right of adaptation. In part two, it will be seen that different facets of copyright can restrict the availability of works (the right to publication, technological keys to content, and so on).

---

[31] NW Netanel, 'Locating Copyright Within the First Amendment Skein' (2001–2002) 54 Stanford L Rev 1, 6.

(1) Copyright law and the control of derivative uses: parody cases

The parody exception appears as a limitation in favour of free expression. **12.19**
Apart from in a few civil law countries (notably France and Belgium), parody
is usually not listed among the statutory exceptions to copyright, although it
might be included under other headings, such as the free use of existing
materials in Germany.[32] With the entry into force of the 2001 Directive on
Copyright in the Information Society,[33] the parody exception is now clearly
enshrined among the exceptions that EU Member States may implement in
national law (Article 5(3)(k)). Like the idea–expression dichotomy or other
limitations on copyright, this particular restriction, whether imposed by the
courts or the legislature, is a sign that copyright takes into account freedom
of speech.

In general, it seems that the 'courts would probably go beyond literal inter- **12.20**
pretation of the law and be more receptive to a freedom of speech defence in
the context of parody than in other situations.'[34] Such concern for free speech
is obvious, as many parody cases involve the development of truly innovative
expression. More scrutiny should be exercised in these cases to ensure that
freedom of expression is not abridged. The delineation between parasitic
uses, which should be prohibited by the right of adaptation, and speech-
enhancing uses is a content-related problem and a stricter standard should
thus be used before deciding to curtail freedom of expression. The protection
of freedom of expression, as guaranteed by Article 10 of the ECHR, is wide
in scope. As stated above, this protection applies not only to 'information
and ideas' that are favourably received or regarded as inoffensive but also
to those that offend, shock, or disturb the State or any sector of the population.[35] Without a doubt, parodies are protected as a form of expression,

---

[32] A Strowel, 'Some Reflections on the Parody Exception', in the ALAI seminar report, *The Boundaries of Copyright—Its Proper Limitations and Exceptions* (Australian Copyright Council, 1999), 125; L Guibault, 'Limitations Found Outside Copyright Law', in the ALAI seminar report, ibid 44.

[33] Directive 2001/29/EC of the European Parliament and of the Council of 22 May 2001 on the harmonization of certain aspects of copyright and related rights in the information society, OJ No L 167 of 22 June 2001, 10.

[34] L Guibault, 'Limitations Found Outside Copyright Law', in the ALAI seminar report, *The Boundaries of Copyright—Its Proper Limitations and Exceptions* (Australian Copyright Council, 1999), 44.

[35] *Handyside v United Kingdom* (1976) 1 EHRR 737, 754, para 48.

especially if they are critical of the establishment or tend to subvert common ideas. The problem in practice is that certain business interests (particularly in advertising) use the legitimate parody exception for their own ends; the freedom to criticize and use cultural icons can veil commercial interests.

12.21 The tension between freedom of expression and copyright can in principle be presented from two different angles. In other words:

> one can consider copyright and trademark protection as the basic principle. [. . .] From this perspective, parody is an internal exception within copyright or trademark law. [. . .] But one can take freedom of expression as the starting point. [. . .] From this perspective, freedom of expression is the principle, and restrictions based on copyright or trademark protection have to be narrowly interpreted.[36]

It is not felt that the problem should be presented in such a way. A review of the case law tends to show that where there is a parody exception (in copyright law), it is easier for free speech to prevail through application of this exception. In the civil law countries reviewed below, the copyright laws (but not trade mark law) contain such an exception. The tension between freedom of expression and intellectual property is thus tackled from within the framework of copyright law, while trademark law requires a balancing test that often directly uses the provisions of, and test for, limiting freedom of expression.[37]

Belgium

Vers l'avenir v L'avenir vert

12.22 This case involved a political pamphlet published by the Green party (les Verts). The title of this pamphlet, *L'avenir vert*, was a clear allusion to the name of a local newspaper, *Vers l'avenir*, its visual layout also resembled that of the newspaper. The Court of Appeal ruled that neither copyright nor trade mark had been infringed and the Supreme Court upheld this decision.

---

[36] D Voorhoof, 'Freedom of Expression, Parody, Copyright and Trademarks', in Proceedings of the ALAI congress—June 13–17, 2001, ALAI–USA, 2002, p 639. See also J Englebert, 'La liberté d'expression s'impose au droit des marques' [2003] Journal du juriste 22, 1 and 4.

[37] It would not be necessary to refer to Article 10 ECHR in trade mark cases if the courts better understood the limited scope of trademark protection and the requirements of having a use in the course of business and a likelihood of confusion, as distinguished from a mere risk of association.

Applying the former Copyright Act, which contained no express provisions for the exemption of parody, the Court recognized that the law 'does not prohibit the unauthorized reproduction for purposes of parody, to the extent necessary to achieve the desired effect while respecting the rules of parody as a literary genre'.[38] According to the Supreme Court, the Court of Appeal had correctly noted the proportionality in the borrowing. The borrowed elements were just enough to make it clear that an ironic or critical effect was sought. The absence of any possible confusion with regard to the primary work was also advanced by the Court of Appeal in denying any wrongdoing with regard to the newspaper's name. Again, this reasoning was upheld by the Supreme Court. Had the Court of Appeal interpreted the trade mark infringement criteria broadly as requiring only a 'risk of association', as in Benelux before the ECJ's *Sabèl* decision,[39] the holding would have been different because the contested brochure did indeed trigger certain associations with the newspaper's sign and product. In such a case, the need to counterbalance this extensive conception of trade mark infringement would eventually have been challenged through a claim based on freedom of expression.

France

In France, the balancing of intellectual property and freedom of expression **12.23** is well illustrated by three recent cases, *Danone, Esso*, and *Areva*, which are considered to be test cases for the coherence of intellectual property law.[40] However, copyright was not at issue in these cases, which all involved the use of trade marks rather than copyrighted works. Interestingly, it is not easy, if even possible, to find a Belgian or French decision that directly refers to and discusses freedom of expression when the (alleged) parody of a work is involved. This is probably for the reason cited above that parody is an official exception to copyright in these countries. On the contrary, French and Belgian trade mark law contains no such exception. The balancing test is therefore not internalized, but rather requires bringing other bodies of law into play. For a lawyer living in a country where parody is not a statutory

---

[38] Supreme Ct, 5 April 2001, *Auteurs & Media*, 2001, 400, note B Michaux.
[39] Case C-251/95 *Sabèl BV v Puma AG* [1998] ETMR 1.
[40] See C Geiger, 'Fundamental Rights: A Safeguard for the Coherence of Intellectual Property Law' [2004] 35 IIC 268–80.

exception to copyright, this difference (between trade mark and copyright law) is not felt as acutely.

Danone

12.24   In 2001, the worldwide food group Danone announced a massive dismissal pursuant to a restructuring plan. In response, a group of activists, le Réseau Voltaire, called for a boycott of Danone's products and created a website <http://www.jeboycottedanone.com> which reproduced Danone's logo with some modifications to the colour (that is, the red wavy line under the name was changed to black to symbolize mourning).

12.25   At Danone's request, the court ordered the group to stop using the modified logo on the ground that such freedom of expression was not necessary to express the group's ideas since other means were available. The Paris Court of Appeal overturned the verdict in 2003,[41] holding that freedom of expression, which is a constitutional right, had to prevail, as long as the rights of Danone were respected. In this case, the court pointed out that Danone's products were not denigrated, that no confusion was possible in the consumer's mind, and that the use of the words 'je boycotte' could not create any misunderstanding about the nature of the website. The court further added that there was no commercial purpose to the site, which was used solely to express controversial ideas without any link to 'the course of business'.

12.26   As Verbeek and Wybo correctly point out,[42] Article 10 of the ECHR is the legal basis for the parody of a trade mark, notwithstanding the absence of any other provision expressly allowing it. Trade mark laws prevent the use of another's trade mark in the course of business but not other uses, unless harm to the trade mark holder is proven.

12.27   In this case, the clash with freedom of expression was obvious, and the plaintiff sought an injunction. In other cases (such as the access cases reviewed below), the plaintiff mainly seeks compensation, even where an injunction is also requested, and the clash with freedom of expression is less direct because the plaintiff does not wish to block a certain type of speech but rather to ensure a reward, using a court order to exert pressure.

---

[41] Paris, 30 April 2003, *Ubiquité-Rev dr techn inf* [2003/17] 81 and note by J Verbeek and A Wybo.

[42] Verbeek and Wybo, ibid 87.

Esso v Greenpeace

The well-known oil company Esso complained that Greenpeace's website **12.28** undermined its environmental policy by depicting its logo as E$$O and using the slogan STOP E$$O. In the first instance,[43] the court granted a motion for summary judgment to stop Greenpeace from using Esso's logo, even in parody. The Paris Court of Appeal[44] overturned this decision, holding that the rights of Esso were not sufficiently apparent prima facie and that the judgment hindered freedom of speech.

Ruling on the merits, the Paris Court of First Instance[45] dismissed Esso's **12.29** claim on the ground of freedom of expression. In an obvious reference to the appellate court's decision in *Danone*, the court held that, even if parody is not allowed in trade mark law, the fundamental right of freedom of expression requires that Greenpeace may, in writing or on its website, denounce in whatever form it feels appropriate the environmental damage and risk to human health caused by certain industrial activities. Such freedom is not absolute and is subject to restrictions necessary to protect the rights of others. In this case, no confusion could be made with Esso's activities as the logo E$$O and the slogan STOP E$$O were not used to commercialize similar products, but rather to participate in a controversial debate outside 'the course of business'. Greenpeace's activities therefore remained within the limits of freedom of expression, without violating Esso's trade mark rights or creating confusion in the mind of the public. The court further added that there had been no denigration of Esso's products or services, as the oil company itself freely acknowledged.

It is thus not completely correct to view this case as a victory for freedom of **12.30** speech over intellectual property, as the court merely (and correctly) pointed out that there had been no infringement of trade mark law. Again, this case shows that trade mark law partially internalizes free speech concerns, and both copyright and trade mark laws appear, in the end, not so different. (This is not to say that real conflicts cannot arise, but it is a common mistake to think that, say, Coca-Cola could prohibit the reference to its trade marks in a novel.)

---

[43] TGI Paris, 4 July 2001. For comments, see G Haas and O de Tissot, 'Droit des marques et liberté d'expression. Quelques observations sur les affaires *Danone, Esso* et *Areva*', Legalis.net [2002/4], 6–18.

[44] Paris, 26 February 2003.   [45] TGI Paris, 30 January 2004.

Areva v Greenpeace

12.31 As noted above, it is difficult to predict the outcome of a particular case as it depends heavily on the facts. This is confirmed by *Areva v Greenpeace*. Areva is a company that specializes in the treatment of nuclear waste. To protest against Areva's activities, Greenpeace posted certain comments about Areva and a parody of its logo on its website. Areva complained about Greenpeace's transformation of its logo: the 'A' of Areva was represented with a shadow reproducing a skull, and blood was depicted pouring from a dying fish that spelled out Areva's trademark in red letters.

12.32 As in *Esso v Greenpeace*, the Paris Court of Appeal[46] refused, in summary proceedings, to issue a temporary injunction requiring the website to be changed. Ruling on the merits, the Paris Court of First Instance,[47] contrary to its decision in *Esso*, prohibited the use of Areva's logo. The court dismissed the action for trade mark infringement, since there could be no confusion in the mind of the public. Nevertheless, the court found that such use denigrated Areva's products and activities. The court held that the bounds of freedom of expression had been exceeded. The symbols used by Greenpeace suggested that Areva spread death. Greenpeace could have used other means to illustrate its point and to inform the public of the dangers of nuclear waste. The link made by Greenpeace (Areva=death) did not contribute to the public debate, as Areva's ability to control nuclear energy was not discussed. Intellectual property was thus not opposed to freedom of expression here; the issue was rather harm to the plaintiff. The question whether the court's assessment in this regard is correct, which we doubt, falls outside the scope of this chapter.

(2) Copyright law and control of access

12.33 According to Jane Ginsburg, 'in the digital environment, the "exclusive right" that the Constitution authorizes Congress to secure to authors is not only a "copy"-right, but an access right.'[48] In other words, the nature of the

---

[46] Paris, 26 February 2003. For comments, see M Moulla, 'La marque et la liberté d'expression: un rire amer?', <http://www.avocats-publishing.com>, 26 August 2003.

[47] TGI Paris, 9 July 2004.

[48] J Ginsburg, 'From Having Copies to Experiencing Works: The Development of an Access Right in US Copyright Law', Columbia Law School, Public Law & Legal Theory Working Paper Group, Paper No 8; (2003) 50 J of the Copyright Society of the USA 113 (also available at: <http://papers.ssrn.com/sol3/papers.cfm?abstract_id=222493>).

exclusive right known as copyright has evolved towards a right to control access as we move into the digital age. On the other hand, it is considered that access has *always* been a matter of copyright since the end of the eighteenth century. In this sense, the access right that scholars tend to identify in the framework of digital copyright law when they consider the protection afforded to technological measures is not really new. Rather the protection of access indirectly conferred by technological measures reveals the evolving nature of copyright as a form of access control. Much could be said about the control of access which has been afforded for quite some time via the right to distribute, and other rights within copyright, such as the right to reproduce copyrighted works, can also be analysed as forms of access control. The existence of such control has prompted lawmakers to add much-needed exceptions in order to balance the interests of copyright holders with those of the public (for example, the exhaustion rule limits the control of access conferred by the distribution right, and the private copying and time-shifting exceptions, as well as certain exceptions in favour of educational institutions and libraries, limit the scope of the access control linked to the reproduction, communication to the public, and broadcasting rights).

It is, however, true that, in the digital age, the issue of access has come to the **12.34** fore. For instance, the 1996 WIPO Copyright Treaty and the subsequent 2001 Directive on Copyright in the Information Society, provide for a communication right which significantly includes the 'making available to the public of . . . works, in such a way that members of the public may *access* them from a place and at a time individually chosen by them'.[49] A way of controlling on-demand access is thus granted through the right to make available. More importantly for the purposes of this discussion, the preamble to the WIPO Copyright Treaty states that

> [t]he Contracting Parties . . . Recognizing the profound impact of the development and convergence of information and communication technologies on the creation and use of literary and artistic works, Emphasizing the outstanding significance of copyright protection as an incentive for literary and artistic creation, Recognizing the need to maintain a balance between the rights of authors and the larger public interest, particularly education, research and

---

[49] Emphasis added. Article 8 of the WIPO Copyright Treaty; Article 3 of the Directive on Copyright in the Information Society.

access to information, as reflected in the Berne Convention, Have agreed as
follows . . .

In a nutshell, this text sets the whole stage to which we are accustomed:
copyright is a necessary incentive to encourage creation; new digital technologies affect the manner in which works are created and imparted; and
copyright could, but should not, conflict with the public interest, including
the right of access to information, which is clearly recognized for the first
time in a copyright instrument.[50]

12.35 Access *has always been* a matter of copyright law, even though it is now more
important than ever. Access is also definitely of the utmost importance for
at least one aspect of freedom of expression, namely the right to impart ideas
and information. However, while it is not thought that a right *to* (free) access
exists as such,[51] it is clear that freedom of expression guarantees a modicum
of access[52] to at least 'ideas and information' inextricably linked to their copyrightable expression.

12.36 It comes as no surprise that there have been several interesting decisions on
the issue of access where freedom of expression plays a prominent role. A few
recent cases have been selected, most of which were decided by the highest
courts of various (civil law) Member States.

12.37 Control of access has given rise to some debate in France, Germany,
the Netherlands, and, most recently, Belgium. One case (*Utrillo*) concerns

---

[50] On this subject, see A Strowel, 'Droit d'auteur et accès à l'information', in *Copyright:
A Right to Control Access to Works?* (Bruylant, 2000), 5–24. See also, the contributions of
S Dusollier, J Ginsburg, and B Hugenholtz to that volume.

[51] For a short discussion of this issue in the civil law context, see F Jongen, 'Y a-t-il un droit
de savoir?', *Juger*, 1995, no 8/9/10, 17–22. See also M Hanotiau, 'Le droit à l'information',
(1993) *Revue trimestrielle des droits de l'homme* 23–56, distinguishing between the 'right to
information' as an 'alibi' and as 'a fundamental right safeguarding the pluralism of the press'.
(The right to information becomes an alibi when it is used as a synonym for 'access to
information' by unscrupulous journalists and press tycoons in their attempts to justify various
violations of the rights of others.)

[52] Competition law is of course another area which tends to guarantee some form of access
(for instance, to essential facilities). On the issue of access, the tension between copyright
and freedom of expression is thus replicated by the relationship between copyright and competition law, an interesting topic, but one that lies outside the scope of this chapter. (For
an example of an article where the tension between access and copyright is phrased in competition law terms, see U Bath, 'Access to Information v Intellectual Property Rights' [2002]
EIPR 138.)

the right to display protected works of art briefly on television, while the others are related to free access to data and works.

Belgium

Index v Biblo

In this case, the Supreme Court was, for the first time, called upon to rule **12.38** on the validity of the Belgian Copyright Act of 1994 in light of Article 10 of the ECHR.[53]

The dispute concerned Index, a database for tax law, literature, and case law. **12.39** Index was a secondary database based on materials (for example, summaries of judgments) from other sources (namely, two tax journals published by Biblo). In the first instance and on appeal, Biblo obtained an injunction to prohibit Index from using the information contained in its law journals. The Supreme Court confirmed the injunction, holding that Article 10 of the ECHR does not prohibit protection of the original work of an author. Therefore, the Copyright Act was 'not a restriction on freedom of expression'.

This decision, briefly and insufficiently reasoned,[54] can be upheld but on **12.40** different grounds. It is thought that the Copyright Act does constitute a restriction on Article 10 of the ECHR insofar as it limits the right to receive information and ideas. Nevertheless, this restriction is compatible with Article 10(2) of the ECHR as it is created by law in order to protect the rights of others and is proportionate to the goal pursued. In a democratic society, restrictions on the use of a specific database by another without the consent of the owner can be justified. In this case, the restriction on the right to receive information was in keeping with the goal of balancing freedom of expression and other rights.[55]

---

[53] Ct of Cassation, 25 September 2003, *RW*, [2003–2004], 1179; the opinion of Advocate–General Bresseleers; *RABG*, [2004/4], 205; note by F Brison 'Enkele basisbegrippen en dito principes uit het auteursrecht even op en rijtje gezet'.

[54] See Brison, ibid 218.

[55] See also *Microfor v Le Monde*, French Supreme Court (Ct of Cassation), 9 November 1983 and 30 October 1987, comment by A Strowel and J-P Triaille, *Le droit d'auteur, du logiciel au multimedia* (Bruylant, 1997) 236–9 (albeit these decisions did not take into account Art 10 ECHR).

France

Utrillo

12.41 The *Utrillo* case shows how simple facts can lead to completely different decisions. The Paris Court of First Instance[56] initially rejected the Utrillo estate's claim for compensation against France 2, a national broadcasting company, for showing twelve copyrighted paintings in a two-minute news item about a Utrillo exhibition. The court's reasoning was based on Article 10 of the ECHR. In such a case, the right of the public to be informed of cultural events outweighs the interests of the copyright holder. This direct application of Article 10 of the ECHR did not survive scrutiny by the Court of Appeal.[57] According to the appellate court, a healthy balance between copyright law and freedom of expression is implicitly made within the former, as the law recognizes an exception for incidental use of works and provides remedies for abuse. (In the present case, the broadcaster had not made incidental use of the paintings but rather had deliberately filmed them.) The court also stressed that copyright is a fundamental right, enshrined in property law and guaranteed by Article 1 of the First Protocol to the ECHR. In a decision of 13 November 2003, the French Supreme Court upheld the Court of Appeal's decision and rejected the argument that the 'right of the public to information and culture' justifies bypassing the authorization of the copyright holder.[58] No violation of Article 10 of the ECHR was thus established.

12.42 It is thought that the true underlying question in this case is whether it was indispensable for the broadcaster to display the paintings in the manner in which it did in order to inform the public of the exhibition. Such a question requires a fact-intensive analysis for which all of the relevant elements are unavailable here. The opinion of the French court appears quite restrictive, but it is also clear that the broadcaster was invoking the right of the public to avoid payment to the copyright holders. A financial rather than an access issue was thus looming in the background. In a very similar case involving a

---

[56] *Utrillo*, Paris Court of First Instance, 23 February 1999, [2000] RIDA 374, with note A Kerever.

[57] *Utrillo*, Paris Court of Appeal, 30 May 2001, [2001] Dalloz 2504, with note C Caron, 'Les droits de l'homme réconciliés avec le droit d'auteur'.

[58] Supreme Ct, 13 November 2003, JCP, 19 May 2004, no 21–22, 955, note C Geiger, 'Exception de citation et droits fondamentaux, une occasion manquée de faire avancer le discours sur les exceptions aux droit d'auteur?'.

news broadcast by France 2, in which it displayed the frescos of Edouard Vuillard at the theatre on the Champs Elysées, the European Commission of Human Rights[59] found sufficient proportionality by reducing the claim of the collecting society acting on behalf of the heirs of Vuillard to one for unpaid royalties.[60] In such cases, copyright is not used to block access, which had already been granted to the viewers of the program, but rather to obtain compensation a posteriori (for the opposite situation, see the *Church of Scientology* case discussed below).

Germany

CB-Infobank II

The publisher of several well-known newspapers, including the *Frankfurter* **12.43** *Allgemeine Zeitung*, filed a suit against a bank that offered its clients a document delivery service providing full-text copies of newspaper articles (as well as abstracts of the same). In its decision,[61] the federal Supreme Court did not directly discuss the applicability of Article 5 of the German Constitution which protects freedom of expression. Rather, it commented on the general arguments made by the defendant that a 'superior interest for information' would require an extensive interpretation of an exception (the so-called 'copy privilege') provided under the German Copyright Act. The Supreme Court found that 'in the framework of the development of the information society, the general interest of getting access ("Zugang") to sources of information protected by copyright' does not imply that access cannot be prohibited.

This case shows that a request for access (here from a bank) is not necessarily **12.44** based on a claim of freedom of expression[62] and that a request for free access

---

[59] E Com HR, *France 2 v France*, 15 January 1997, case 30262/96, *Informatierecht*, 1999, 115.

[60] We agree with Hugenholtz's analysis on this point, PB Hugenholtz, 'Copyright and Freedom of Expression in Europe', in N Elkin-Koren and NW Netanel (eds), *The Commodification of Information* (Kluwer, 2002), 260.

[61] Bundesgerichtshof (BGH), 16 January 1997—ZR 38/96; GRUR Int, 1997, 464, at 465 (CB-*Infobank* II).

[62] Therefore, we do not feel, unlike Hugenholtz, that the Supreme Court 'refused to apply Article 5 of the Constitution' (PB Hugenholtz, 'Copyright and Freedom of Expression in Europe' in N Elkin-Koren and NW Netanel (eds), *The Commodification of Information* (Kluwer, 2002)). On the contrary, it seems that no link was made between the request for access and the protection of freedom of expression. The other case decided on the same date (BGH, 16 January 1997—I ZR 9/95; GRUR Int, 1997, 459, (CB-*Infobank* I)) did not discuss the balancing of access and copyright control.

is in fact often motivated by the desire to avoid payment. If the request for access is a dressed-up demand for compensation, courts are reluctant to give it precedence over copyright. The fact that the Constitutional Court decided to interpret another exception (the citation exemption) broadly in the context of the reuse of four pages of Berthold Brecht's plays in another original literary work (*Germania 3* of Heiner Müller)[63] simply confirms the view that freedom of expression should receive more weight when there is a transformative use of the copyrighted work.[64] The Constitutional Court correctly held that the freedom of artistic expression enshrined in Article 5(3) of the Constitution was at stake, and therefore a broader interpretation in favour of secondary use was required.

Paperboy

12.45 In a case concerning the legality of hyper-linking to newspaper articles, the German Supreme Court[65] rejected all arguments based on freedom of expression, since access does not fall automatically under the scope of freedom of expression.[66] However, the argument has been made before other courts that prohibiting some forms of linking amounts to an illicit restriction on free speech. Let us recall the well-reasoned decision of the New York District Court in *Universal City Studios v Reimerdes*,[67] which involved the online posting of software (DeCSS) enabling users to circumvent access controls on copyrighted works. The court held that a ban on linking to a site that contains illicit material (DeCSS in this case) 'amidst other content' would threaten 'to restrict communication of this information to an excessive degree'. Recognizing a possible chilling effect, as with remedies sanctioning defamation, the court nevertheless held that anti-linking injunctions are consistent with the First Amendment, provided a strict standard is applied: it is illegal only when those responsible for the link know that the offending material is on the linked-to site, that it is unlawful to offer such material, and

---

[63] Bundesverfassungsgericht (BverfG), 29 June 2000, *Zeitschrift für Urheber- und Medienrecht*, 2000, 867.

[64] See also the parody cases discussed in paras 12.19–12.32 above.

[65] BGH, 17 July 2003—I ZR 259/00; NJW, 2003, 3406 (*Paperboy*).

[66] In this case, it was not necessary to consider arguments drawn from freedom of expression as the application of copyright law does not encompass the provision of access to lawful works through hyperlinks.

[67] 2000 WL 1160678 (SDNY) (decision of 17 August 2000) confirmed by the Court of Appeal for the Second Circuit (273 F. 3d 429; 2001 U.S. App. LEXIS 25330) (decision of 30 May 2001).

that they create or maintain the link for the purpose of disseminating the illicit material. The obligation to tackle such free speech defences in the USA, unlike in Germany, can probably be explained by a more expansive conception of free speech in the USA, out of which stronger access demands can be derived. This is not to say that freedom of expression cannot (and should not) be used to increase access to copyrighted works, as the next case will show.

The Netherlands

Church of Scientology v Dataweb[68]

Ms Spaink had posted extracts of the works of Ron Hubbard, the founder of **12.46** the Church of Scientology, on several web pages. Initially accessible in their entirety, these texts were later replaced by comments written by Ms Spaink and containing short extracts from Scientology reference books. Given that the online posting of these texts infringed the Church's copyright, in particular its publication right under Dutch law, the Church sued Ms Spaink as well as Internet service providers such as XC4All and Dataweb. In the September 2003 decision on the merits of the case, the Hague Court of Appeal upheld the claim of copyright infringement,[69] but stated that the enforcement of copyright 'must give way to the freedom of information in exceptional cases'. The court further asked whether this limitation on freedom of expression corresponded to a pressing social need in a democratic society and was proportionate to the legitimate aim pursued, taking account of the fact that a national court was granted a margin of appreciation in this respect in accordance with the case law of the ECtHR.

After an extensive review of various documents and the statements on the **12.47** Web describing in detail how the Church exerts pressure on its members,

---

[68] Ct of App (Gerechtshof) 's-Gravenhage, 4 September 2003, *Computerrecht*, 2003/6, 357; *Auteurs & Media*, 2004/1, 44, note A Strowel and G Gathem. For the first instance decision, see Arrondissementsrechtbank 's-Gravenhage, 9 June 1999, *Computerrecht*, 1999/4, 200, note PB Hugenholtz; *Mediaforum*, 1999, note Visser; *AMI*, 1999, note K Koelman; *BIE*, 1999, 458, note A Quaedvlieg.
[69] The Dutch publication right (*openbaarmaking recht*) was infringed although the texts had already been made available to a limited public, including following a partial release order by a US district court.

the court held that the borrowings from the Scientology books were used to support Ms Spaink's critical view of the functioning of the Church of Scientology. In addition, the court stressed that the use of these copyrighted extracts did not appear to further a commercial objective. Interestingly, the court employed one of the criteria incorporated in the US 'fair use' test.[70] Finding that (i) the doctrine and organization of the Church of Scientology are contrary to democratic values, (ii) the secrets contained in its copyrighted books help the Church to exert control over its members and to prevent discussion of its practices, (iii) these books had already been made temporarily available to the public in a US court case, and (iv) the Internet service providers' obligation to take down and make this content inaccessible was disproportionate, the court ruled in favour of freedom of expression as there was no demonstrated 'need' within the meaning of Article 10 of the ECHR and the interest of the defendants outweighed those of the copyright holder.

12.48 This well-reasoned decision is just one application of the position adopted by the Dutch Supreme Court in *Dior v Evora*.[71] According to the court, judges may limit copyright in light of interests similar to those underlying the exceptions contained in the Copyright Act, where such exceptions are inapplicable. The *Church of Scientology* decision is apparently the first illustration by a court of appeal of the existence of an implicit 'fair use' test in Dutch copyright law.[72] Where copyright is not used to obtain compensation, but rather to prohibit further access to a copyrighted work (that is, in order to obtain access, it was necessary to become a member of the Church and to pay a disproportionate access fee), freedom of expression must clearly prevail.

---

[70] The criterion of the commercial nature of the use (of Art 107 of the US Copyright Act).

[71] Hoge Raad, 20 October 1995, NJ, 1996, 682.

[72] According to Dutch commentators (K Koelman's note in *Computerrecht*, 2003/6, 357), the possibility of the courts to create ad hoc exceptions based on the balancing of interests was illustrated in a first instance decision in *Fonds Anne Frank*, but this decision favouring freedom of expression over copyright was reversed in appeal (Pres Rb, Amsterdam, 12 November 1998, *Mediaforum*, 1999, 39 (note B Hugenholtz); Hof Amsterdam, 8 July 1999, *Informatierecht/ AMI*, 1999, 116 (note B Hugenholtz)).

C. Conclusion: Is Freedom of Expression the Lifebuoy for Bona Fide Users Drowning in a Sea of Intellectual Property?

In seeking to answer this question, which is borrowed from Hugenholtz's **12.49** seminal work,[73] the moderate view adopted by the US Supreme Court in *Eldred v Ashcroft* is endorsed: 'copyright's built-in free speech safeguards are generally adequate to address' the First Amendment [or, let us add, freedom of expression] concerns, but courts and commentators err in declaring copyright 'categorically immune from challenges under the First Amendment [or under Article 10 of the ECHR]'.[74] A few additional reflections necessitated by the breadth of the topic should be made in this regard.

(1) Different levels of scrutiny and the content-neutrality factor

Questions regarding access are content-neutral. Therefore, the right to receive **12.50** protected ideas or information is less strong if there is a claim to free access and if other means are available to satisfy the alleged right. This evaluation changes if it appears that there are no alternatives to the requested access and that the compensation sought by the copyright holder is obviously disproportionate. (These issues should be examined in light of competition law rather than in the context of freedom of expression.)

Parody issues are content-based as they involve freedom of expression in its **12.51** first, and probably strongest, facet, and restrictions on parody must satisfy strict scrutiny. Therefore, courts in general will vindicate, for example, the right of Greenpeace, or other activist groups which contribute to the public debate, to exaggerate or use provocative expressions, even if this appears to conflict with other rights, such as trade marks. However, use of the same protected item would not be allowed if it were by a competitor or in the course of a business.[75]

---

[73] A similar question is raised by C Geinger, 'Fundamental Rights, a Safeguard for the Coherence of Intellectual Property Rights?' (2004) 35 IIC 267.

[74] *Eldred v Ashcroft* 239 F 3d 372, affirmed, 537 US 186 (2003).

[75] This explains why the same speech critical of a company involved in nuclear energy will or at least should be tolerated if made by Greenpeace but not if made by a windmill producer.

(2) Free expression and free culture

12.52 In his new book *Free Culture* (*How Big Media Uses Technology and the Law to Lock Down Culture and Control Creativity*),[76] Lawrence Lessig argues that copyright often does 'not drive an engine of free expression'. Copyright only favours the development of works which have a 'continuing commercial value', but that part is only 'a tiny fraction' of 'all the creative works produced by humans anywhere'. In Lessig's words, 'for that tiny fraction, copyright creates incentives to produce and distribute the creative work [and for] that tiny fraction acts as an "engine of free expression".'[77] However, most works have a limited commercial life, and '[in] this context, copyright is serving no purpose at all related to the spread of knowledge. In this context, copyright is not an engine of free expression. Copyright is a brake.'[78]

12.53 There is agreement with the core of Lessig's arguments that most creative works, such as the myriad drawings by our children, the essays and poems that so many of us once wrote with the intention of publishing, the improvised music that many bands once played in garages or at school parties, or the photographs taken by amateurs do not depend on copyright. At least one would hope not. Lessig is thus correct in his assumption that copyright plays a relatively modest role in spurring creation. Moreover, it would be undesirable for most creative experience to be governed or driven by copyright. However, there remains a 'tiny fraction' of works for which copyright acts as an incentive for diffusion and sometimes even creation. Does this fraction, however small, not justify the existence of copyright? Free culture can thus coexist with a (robust) copyright law that only applies to that 'tiny fraction'. It is not felt that freedom of expression should be systematically pitted against copyright: commercial production should be distinguished from other domains.

12.54 It is also thought that copyright should take into account the apparently conflicting demands of the public to have better access to productions of the human spirit. It is anticipated that ignorance of these legitimate requests

---

[76] Penguin Press, 2004. This book is available under an on-line creative commons licence at <http://free-culture.org/get-it>.
[77] Ibid 225.
[78] Ibid 227.

based on the right to culture[79] or the reluctance to take them into account, which has in the past been witnessed in relation to claims based on freedom of expression, could produce another backlash against intellectual property. Copyright must not only deal with free speech concerns but also reconcile itself with the right to culture.

---

[79] Since 1994, the Belgian Constitution (Art 23(3)(5)) has granted a right to cultural fulfilment (*le droit à l'épanouissement culturel*).

13

COPYRIGHT AND FREE SPEECH IN TRANSITION: THE RUSSIAN EXPERIENCE

Mira T Sundara Rajan

A. Introduction

Copyright grants authors a monopoly right in their work, while it abruptly **13.01** curtails the right of the general public to enjoy and make use of the fruits of knowledge, an essential aspect of the many-layered right to free speech. The progress of the 'Digital Age', our ongoing revolution in information and communications technology, has further polarized copyright and free speech. The intensification of this conflict largely owes itself to the greatly expanded reach of copyright law in the environment of new technology. In this process of expansion into the technological realm, copyright is increasingly claimed by corporate interests. Highly industrialized countries which are heavily involved in the development of new technologies, like the USA, see technological development as a basis for sustaining their wealth, and in particular, for maintaining their competitive advantage in world trade. For this reason, the growth of technology has been accompanied by the internationalization of copyright standards through the Agreement on Trade-Related Aspects of Intellectual Property Rights (TRIPs) at the World Trade Organization (WTO).

13.02 From the perspective of copyright and free speech, the adoption of the TRIPs Agreement has brought a new international dimension to concerns about freedom of expression. In fact, the strident debate over copyright and freedom of expression masks an interesting new reality: as a result of technological change in the Digital Era, copyright law is itself undergoing a transformation. Traditionally, copyright has developed as a complex and multi-layered branch of the law, as much concerned with matters of culture and society as with economics. However, as copyright law spreads over an ever larger surface area of protected subject matter, discussion of the policy issues implicated in copyright has experienced a corresponding loss of depth. The many layers and complex strands of copyright are increasingly replaced by a monolithic concept of the law, reflected in the internationalization of copyright regulation through the TRIPs Agreement. The post-TRIPs concept of copyright law is as an important area of trade regulation and, therefore, economic policy.

13.03 The commercialization of copyright through the WTO system affects creative work at opposite ends of the social spectrum—at one end, cultural heritage and the arts, and at the other, technology. Concerns about the impact of copyright on free expression are therefore not limited to the debates in the USA and other advanced countries. Rather, they resonate strongly with developing countries as well, including the 'transitional' countries of the post-socialist world which are also 'developing' in the area of intellectual property rights.[1] Reflecting the dual-edged effect of TRIPs, the free speech concerns of developing jurisdictions arise in relation to

---

[1] In the post-TRIPs era, most countries, including the USA and other technologically advanced countries, are engaged in copyright reform. In different ways, they are all 'developing'.

both culture and technology. Developing jurisdictions fear that international copyright regulation will limit their access to new technology by imposing excessive levels of protection on technological products, like computer software, from the industrialized world.[2] Their concerns about culture are subtler, but no less profound. What is likely to be the impact of international copyright regulation on freedom of expression at the cultural or national level? For example, how will the TRIPs Agreement affect traditional knowledge, cultural heritage, or 'folklore', as well as the individual creativity of living artists? Developing countries would like to preserve the freedom of their cultural expression from both corporate and State power. What model of copyright law can address their concerns?

It is clear that the debate about the relationship between copyright and free **13.04** speech must take account of the many layers of interests within copyright law itself: author versus publisher, creator versus right-owner, individual versus corporate entity, private versus public interest. These dichotomies also mask deeper tensions between modern and traditional models of society, keenly felt by developing and 'transitional' countries, where the arcane field of copyright law has somehow become a matter of both economic urgency and intense political drama. Observers of the current scene have often responded to these complex concerns about freedom of expression by advocating a reduced scope for copyright protection. Somewhat ironically, however, their instinctive reaction is itself a product of the prevailing view of commercial copyright, reflected in the structure and content of the TRIPs Agreement. Reducing copyright protection as a whole cannot by itself improve protection for freedom of expression. Instead, it is likely that doing so may actually impede the preservation of free speech values in a global and technological society.

The solution to copyright's current crisis may lie in the development of a **13.05** new understanding of copyright and free speech—one that is not primarily conditioned by the heritage of common law copyright and the technological profile of advanced countries. Instead of subscribing to a monolithic image

---

[2] It should be noted, however, that the success of some developing countries in the technological field makes the dichotomy between advanced and developing countries, in some sense, outdated. A notable example is India, with its internationally competitive information technology industry.

of commercial copyright, the international community now has a rare opportunity to re-examine the many threads which come together in the fabric of copyright law. It may well be that some elements of copyright, far from opposing freedom of expression, may actually contribute to the status of free speech.

13.06 Copyright and freedom of expression share a number of conceptual bases, and it is probably this heritage of common concepts that has led to the inclusion of author's rights in the International Bill of Rights.[3] Notably, human rights instruments recognize that copyright is concerned with both the protection of authors' individual rights and with the dissemination of culture. Traditional copyright parlance approaches these issues as a dichotomy between an author's right to control the reproduction of his work and the public interest in having access to it. In human rights terms, however, this dichotomy is artificial: human rights instruments uniformly identify two components in the rights associated with human creativity, the author's individual right, and the right of the public to enjoy culture.

13.07 For example, in the case of works created by individuals, the prototypical 'authors' of copyright law, copyright is an individual right of creativity. As such, it closely parallels freedom of expression, an equivalent right that is generally available to the public. By protecting an author's creative expression, however, we are also protecting cultural heritage. Protection of creative rights helps to encourage and support individual creativity, and it

---

[3] Rights of authorship, in combination with a public right of access to culture, feature in the Universal Declaration of Human Rights, 10 December 1948; GA Res 217A (III), UN Doc A/810 (1948) at 71; and the International Covenant on Civil and Political Rights, GA Res 2200A (XXI), 21 UN GAOR Supp (No 16) at 52, UN Doc A/6316 (1966), 999 UNTS 171, (entered into force 23 March 1976). However, provisions on intellectual property are not uniformly featured in international human rights documents. Two examples of other approaches are the European Convention on Human Rights, Strasbourg, 20 January 1966, and the African Charter on Human and Peoples' Rights, 27 June 1981, OAU Doc CAB/LEG/ 67/3 rev 5, 21 ILM 58 (1982). The European Convention is highly focused on civil and political rights. In contrast, the African Charter explicitly rejects the distinction between civil and political rights, on the one hand, and economic, social, and cultural rights, on the other. The African Charter includes a number of references to culture, including Art 17.2 on the right of 'every individual . . . [to] take part in the cultural life of his community'; Art 22 on the right of peoples to 'cultural development with due regard to their freedom and identity and equal enjoyment of the common heritage of mankind'; and Art 20 on the right of states-parties to resist 'foreign domination, be it political, economic or cultural'. A right to 'receive information' is protected in Art 9, though rights of creation are not protected at all.

also contributes to the protection of the existing cultural heritage, at least insofar as it is composed of works of individual authorship, and perhaps beyond.[4]

The concept of a right to 'freedom of creativity', built on the twin ideals of **13.08** individual creative rights and a public right of access to culture, is not a purely theoretical construct.[5] In fact, a powerful historical example of how copyright and free expression reinforce one another may be found in the post-socialist world. The socialist and post-socialist experience of copyright provides a unique illustration of the complementary qualities of copyright and free speech. Transitional countries are not usually thought of as a source of ideas in relation to copyright law. Nevertheless, they can make a contribution of unique and lasting value to the international debate on copyright and free speech issues. By an interesting irony, their perspective may even provide a key to resolving the conflicting interests surrounding copyright and free speech in Western democracies.

B. Authorship and Individual Rights in Transitional Countries: The Russian Example

The special relationship between copyright and free speech in transitional **13.09** countries is a product of historical and cultural circumstance. To an extent, it is important to emphasize the shared experience of post-socialist countries in this regard, especially with reference to the socialist, or Soviet, period. In different ways, cultural interests played a major political role throughout

---

[4] For example, countries where authorship takes on many forms—in addition to, or instead of, the model of individual creation—have experimented with copyright protection for anonymous works, works of group or community authorship, and works of unknown authorship. Often, these cultural forms are protected in the name of 'folklore'. In 1967, Tunisia was the first country to introduce protection for folklore into its copyright law, and the WIPO has developed model provisions for dealing with these works. See EW Ploman and LC Hamilton, *Copyright: Intellectual Property in the Information Age* (London: Routledge & Kegan Paul, 1980) 129–31; and World Intellectual Property Organization, *Tunis Model Law on Copyright for Developing Countries* (Geneva: WIPO, 1976).

[5] The term, 'freedom of creativity', was introduced to the author of this article by A Rakhmilovich, 'The Constitutional Court of the Russian Federation: Recent Cases on Protecting the Freedom of Thought and Speech and Related Matters' (1996) 22(2) Rev of Central & East European L 129, 133. Rakhmilovich discusses a decision on freedom of expression by the Russian Constitutional Court.

Central and Eastern Europe, and culture acquired a peculiar significance under the privations of totalitarian government. Through socialist rule, Russian influence also became a common thread uniting Eastern Europe. It is well known that Central and East European countries experienced Soviet expansionism in the political arena. What is less obvious is that they were also subject to a form of Russian imperialism in the legal sphere. Any in-depth study of socialist law inevitably turns towards Russian law. Many copyright laws in the 'Eastern Bloc' were closely based on Soviet copyright statutes. As for free speech, it was conditioned by the physical or psychological presence of the Soviet Union in Eastern Europe, as well as whatever indigenous patterns of repression developed.[6]

13.10 The omnipresence of Russian copyright law in the legal history of Central and Eastern Europe is one reason why the discussion of a post-socialist model of copyright and free speech in this chapter focuses on the Russian experience. An equally important consideration, however, lies in the distinctive characteristics of Russia's historical struggles with freedom of expression. If certain themes in the development of copyright and free speech are common to many Central and East European countries, they often find their most intense and most challenging expression in Russia. Much of Central and Eastern Europe suffered under conditions of cultural oppression during the socialist period. However, the repression of culture was perhaps most thorough and systematic in Soviet Russia.[7] Similarly, many post-socialist countries have experienced different kinds of problems with copyright in the transition period, but these problems seem to be particularly complex and intractable in Russia. An awareness of the relationship between free speech and copyright flowing from socialist history is relevant to all post-socialist countries—and indeed, to many other countries who are experimenting with copyright reform. Yet this model undoubtedly has special significance for Russia, which is experiencing great difficulty in breaking free from its authoritarian past.

---

[6] See M Ficsor, 'The Past, Present and Future of Copyright in the European Socialist Countries' (1983) 118 *Revue internationale du droit d'auteur* 33. This comprehensive article includes a discussion of how the European socialist countries traced their copyright laws to Soviet, and through it, Russian, law.

[7] Of course, this statement is based on the limited information available to the international community. For example, it is still not very well known how the Albanian Communists ruled their country.

In Russia, the development of free speech ideals strongly influenced the **13.11** evolution of copyright law. The impact of freedom of expression on copyright reflects the prominent social status traditionally conferred on culture and the creative professions. Creative people and intellectuals, known as the 'intelligentsia' in pre-socialist days, had long played an important role in Russian political life. As the nineteenth century progressed into the twentieth, however, culture and the arts became increasingly prominent— and indeed, during this period, the Russian government undertook its first detailed study of copyright law, leading to the adoption of a landmark Russian Copyright Act in 1911.[8] In Russia of the late nineteenth century, the cultural arena gradually became a centre of political life, with writers as diverse as Chekhov and Dostoevsky commenting in their different ways on political and social reform.

The relationship between writers and the government in turn of the century **13.12** Russia was balanced on a razor's edge. The government wanted to make use of the skills and abilities of artists and intellectuals for the purpose of national development. Accordingly, the tsarist State was prepared to grant certain freedoms to writers. However, the State simultaneously had to maintain its own viability and, in particular, to avoid any dangerous compromises on the political front. Political reality of the times therefore led to a rather strange situation. The tsar's government tried to exploit the knowledge and skills of intellectuals for its own ends but, in the process, it found itself compelled to recognize and affirm the value of their contribution to society. Virtually in spite of itself, the tsarist State granted certain political concessions to the creative professions.

In the pre-socialist era, the activities of writers and intellectuals had un- **13.13** questionable political implications. They were a voice of political rationality that served to balance the absolutist government of the tsar. While tsarist rule precluded the development of a generally favourable climate for free expression, the situation of writers was far more complex than one of strict repression. Rather, the tsar's dependence on writers, and other makers of Russian culture, for the modernization and development of the country grew in importance throughout the nineteenth century as the concept of Russian

---

[8] Common law copyright lawyers will note that it was a year of great activity for copyright law: a landmark British Copyright Act was also enacted in 1911.

nationhood developed.[9] In a sense, writers were the tsar's wellspring of ideas about successful governance, stability, and legitimacy. They were the conscience of the tsarist State. Indeed, it is fair to say that a degree of political authority, or legitimacy, came to be associated with the 'intelligentsia'. The historian, Geoffrey Hosking, has called this the Russian 'tradition of "alternative government" by writers'.[10]

13.14 For these reasons, writers could be surprisingly influential with the tsar; but they also presented a potential threat to the hegemony of an absolutist government, and as such, they were vulnerable to repression.[11] Their somewhat self-contradictory status is apparent in the influence wielded by writers on copyright law of the time. While freedom of expression was not broadly recognized in Russian society, authors nevertheless enjoyed a certain level of protection for their activities through copyright. Moreover, the influence of authors was directly responsible for improvements to Russian copyright protection on more than one occasion.[12]

13.15 The cultural factors favouring the development of a copyright law based on individual rights were supported by the progress of nineteenth-century legal theory in Russia. For Russian 'liberal' thinkers, legal modernization

---

[9] The role of authorship in nation-building in nineteenth century Russia is emphasized by G Hosking in *Russia: People and Empire 1552–1917* (Cambridge: Harvard University Press, 1997) 286–311.

[10] G Hosking, *A History of the Soviet Union 1917–1991* (final edn, London: Fontana Press, 1992) 408.

[11] Contrasting examples are presented by Pushkin and Dostoevsky. On at least one troublesome occasion, relating to the anonymous publication of a 'blasphemous' poem, Pushkin enjoyed the direct support of the tsar. The incident is discussed by M Hayward in *On Trial: The Soviet State Versus 'Abram Tertz' and 'Nikolai Arzhak'* (New York: Harper & Row, 1967) 31–2. In Dostoevsky's case, his political activities won him a death sentence, which was eventually commuted. See R Pevear, 'Introduction', in F Dostoevsky *The Brothers Karamazov*, trans R Pevear and L Volokhonsky (New York: Vintage Books, 1990).

[12] For example, by Pushkin's efforts, the publication of a translation that appeared alongside an original work was subject to the consent of the original author—a major change to the principle of unrestricted 'freedom of translation', which was well-established in Russian copyright law. Later, Pushkin's widow sued for, and obtained for Russian authors, an improved duration of copyright protection. See LP Rastorgoueff, 'The New Law of Copyright in Russia' (1911) J of the Society of Comparative Legislation 302, 307; V Gsovski, *Soviet Civil Law: Private Rights and Their Background under the Soviet Regime*, HE Yntema (ed), Michigan L Stud Series (Ann Arbor: University of Michigan Law School, 1948) 607; and MA Newcity, *Copyright Law in the Soviet Union* (New York: Praeger Special Studies, 1978) 7.

specifically meant a movement away from tsar-centred legality to the development of a society based on the concept of individual rights.[13] Unsurprisingly, perhaps, in a society built on serfdom where the concept of individual rights had never been encouraged by the rulers, the idea of individual rights was intoxicating to modernizing theorists, and dominated Russian liberal discourse.

Interestingly, the idea of individual rights developed by Russian liberal **13.16** theorists was not limited to Western-style constitutional rights, but went somewhat further. In their view, the Russian legal system should be strongly and directly focused on individual rights, so that 'all individual and social freedoms or rights' should be 'primary rights', in contrast to the residual, 'secondary' nature of rights in Western constitutional democracies.[14] It is also noteworthy that, perhaps in contrast to the more specialized intellectual culture of Western countries, the question of individual rights was widely debated and discussed by intellectuals of all kinds in Russia, from lawyers and philosophers, to novelists. The importance of individual rights for legal modernization and their incompatibility with the Russian autocracy are concisely summarized by Susan Heuman:

> The autocracy dealt with the population as subjects who were granted certain rights and privileges based on their social and economic status. To transform the legal and political system in the Russian Empire would necessitate a change in the relationship between the individual and the state. But the tradition of the French Enlightenment did not have the impact on the Russian Empire that it had in Western Europe, where it produced a sense of natural rights. Natural rights might have given birth to a concept of civil rights that were independent of the bureaucratic state and ideological framework.

When the Bolsheviks seized power in 1917, they initially replaced the tsar as **13.17** an absolute centre of power. However, the political objectives of the Bolsheviks were different from those of the tsar, and much more ambitious. They wanted

---

[13] It should be noted that the 'liberalism' discussed here is 'Russian liberalism', as distinct from Western liberalism. An alternative was presented by the anarchists, who considered that law in Russia had been 'an instrument of ruling class oppression, the antithesis to human freedom'. See SE Heuman, 'Perspectives on Legal Culture in Prerevolutionary Russia', in P Beirne (ed), *Revolution in Law: Contributions to the Development of Soviet Legal Theory, 1917–1938* (Armonk NY: ME Sharpe, 1990) 3, 6–7. In different forms, the same idea inspired thinkers as distinguished and diverse as Mikhail Bakunin, Prince Kropotkin, and Leo Tolstoy.

[14] These ideas are characteristic of Russian 'liberal legal theorist', BA Kistiakovsky, quoted in Heuman, ibid 8.

to remake Russian society in a new mould based on radical political ideal-ism. Like the tsar, the Bolsheviks were intensely ambivalent towards intellec-tuals: they saw creative and intellectual work as a crucial means of social modernization, but they were wary of the moral authority and independence of writers, which presented a potential threat to their political hegemony. As the tsar had wanted to do, the Communists hoped to bring the power of creativity and culture under the yoke of their political control, exploiting creative expression for the consolidation of their own political legitimacy. Indeed, the early Communists were preoccupied with political propagand-izing, and they viewed the written word in its literary incarnation as a natural vehicle for it.[15] Sheila Fitzpatrick aptly identifies this tension between the political leadership and intellectuals in the early years of Communist govern-ment as a fundamental conflict between two competing sources of political legitimacy, representing 'power' and 'culture'.[16]

13.18 In the initial euphoria of Bolshevik success, existing notions of law and legality were abruptly thrust aside. Rather, the Bolsheviks were preoccupied with the political and military challenge of establishing their authority. Marxian social theory made little mention of law and the Bolsheviks were initially satisfied with the assertion that the idealistic society of socialism did not need to resort to the complexities of bourgeois legislation for the pur-poses of resolving conflicts or balancing competing social interests.[17] Later, as the Bolsheviks consolidated power, Soviet jurists became interested in giving some theoretical grounding to this perspective and set about attempting to develop a Communist model of law. The most influential among the early Soviet legal scholars was certainly E B Pashukanis, whose *General Theory of Law and Marxism* became the standard textbook analysis of law from the

---

[15] The peculiar importance of propaganda in the Soviet state is emphasized by P Kenez, *The Birth of the Propaganda State: Soviet Methods of Mass Mobilisation 1917–1929* (New York: Cambridge University Press, 1985) 13. He points out that '[t]he type of propaganda that the Bolsheviks carried out is absolutely central to our understanding of the nature of the regime that they had created. The regime could not have existed without a special brand of propa-ganda, and only a communist system could have developed those methods of mass mobilisa-tion that in fact existed ... From the time of the birth of the regime, Soviet life has been permeated with propaganda to such an extent that it is difficult for an outsider to imagine.'

[16] S Fitzpatrick, *The Cultural Front: Power and Culture in Revolutionary Russia* (Ithaca: Cornell University Press, 1992).

[17] R Sharlet, PB Maggs, and P Beirne, 'PI Stuchka and Soviet Law', in P Beirne (ed), *Revolution in Law: Contributions to the Development of Soviet Legal Theory, 1917–1938* (Armonk NY: ME Sharpe, 1990), 48 n 21.

perspective of 'historical materialism'.[18] However, the writings of Pashukanis, which supported the idealistic view of the socialist State as a society that had no need of law, eventually went out of fashion with the rise of Stalin and new challenges to the Soviet regime in wartime.[19]

As the Communists acknowledged a renewed need for law, they faced the **13.19** difficult problem of how to cope with the legacy of Russian legal development during the tsarist period. In particular, the Russian 'liberals' had irrevocably introduced the idea of individual rights into Russian law. Yet, for the Communists, individual rights sat uneasily with the logic of socialism, as they understood it, which gave predominance to the rights of the public and the collective over individuals. In relation to copyright, both authors and the general public in pre-Soviet times had come to see copyright law as a system of individual rights, and moreover, one that had substantial benefits for society at large. The socialists' instinctive approach to copyright law, however, was to limit its reach, specifically making it subordinate to the requirements of the carefully balanced and highly politicized relationship between the government and the 'intelligentsia'.

At a fundamental level, the development of copyright under the Communists **13.20** was remarkably consistent with the tsarist pattern, and reflected the political view of culture inherited from imperial Russia. As the Soviet Union emerged into a State based on ideology, the importance of securing the cooperation of intellectuals for political purposes became pronounced. If writers and intellectuals could not be made to support Communist society—or at least, to maintain a degree of neutrality towards it—it was very likely that they would become a powerful threat to Soviet ideological hegemony. The social status traditionally enjoyed by cultural figures, and the corresponding sense of social responsibility that was often a deeply held conviction among them, could make them a danger to the regime.

In a deeper sense, the challenges to the Soviet State posed by creative people **13.21** also flowed naturally from the work in which they were engaged. In any other sphere of life, it might be at least theoretically possible to go about one's

---

[18] Excerpts from the *General Theory* may be found in PB Maggs (ed), *Pashukanis: Selected Writings on Marxism and Law* (New York: Academic Press, 1980). Portions are reprinted in WE Butler (ed), *Russian Legal Theory*, The International Library of Essays in Law and Legal Theory Series (New York: New York University Press Reference Collection, 1996) 229–320.

[19] Pashukanis perished in one of Stalin's purges.

daily business without having to confront limitations on one's freedom of expression. For writers, however, this would be an impossibility: their trade demanded certain concessions in relation to freedom of speech and thought. By its very activity, even if it was not explicitly intended, the creative work of writers, artists, and intellectuals tended to generate ideological diversity.[20] The political threat presented by literature in nineteenth-century Russia expanded in Soviet times to include every sign of free thought and freedom of the imagination, which fundamentally threatened the legitimacy of a State based on ideological control.

13.22 It is apparent that post-socialist copyright reform in Russia must confront a complex, dual legacy of concepts inherited from Russian legal culture and transformed through the experience of Soviet rule. Although the precise social objectives of the tsarist State and the Communists may have been different, they shared a common political basis in their desire to maintain hegemonic control. However, the historically important constituency of writers and intellectuals presented a potential challenge to the political aspirations of both regimes. The threat posed by authorship became especially intense in the Soviet period because of the importance of ideology and propaganda to the political establishment. A surprising consequence of the State's historical dependence on the work of intellectuals, combined with the traditional strength of culture as a competing source of political legitimacy, was to effect a *rapprochement* between the 'private' interest of authors in copyright protection and the interest of the public in freedom of speech. Moreover, it is worth noting that this political landscape was, to some extent, shared by many of the countries of Central and Eastern Europe which experienced Communist rule.

13.23 In the final years of tsarist rule, the emphasis of Russian legal reformers on individual rights, especially in the school of Russian 'liberalism', helped to give legal expression to the socially important functions of authorship by linking copyright with the individual's right to freedom of thought and expression. A consideration of socialist copyright legislation shows that

---

[20] This was the underlying problem that Andrei Siniavsky had to confront in his 1966 trial by the Soviet government. He asserted, 'No writer expresses his political views through his writings. An artistic work does not express political views . . . My works reflect my feelings about the world, not politics.' See the examination of Siniavsky in M Hayward, *On Trial: The Soviet State Versus 'Abram Tertz' and 'Nikolai Arzhak'* (New York: Harper & Row, 1967) 94.

socialist law, despite its different premises, was deeply influenced by Russian liberal thought. The development of socialist copyright mirrored the fluctuating status of individual rights in the Soviet Union. As authorship increasingly came to be identified with the dissident movement, socialist copyright law became increasingly restricted in scope. Yet, in its very restrictiveness, the socialist approach to copyright legislation could only reaffirm the importance of copyright as an individual right of authorship, a concept that the Communists inherited from pre-Revolutionary Russia. As dissidents took upon themselves the role of encouraging free thought in Soviet society, the protection of their rights was ever more closely identified with the aspirations—political, cultural, and psychological—of society at large.[21]

C. The Soviet Experience of Copyright

Socialist copyright law in the Soviet Union passed through three major historical phases: the initial period of Bolshevik power, the post-Bolshevik consolidation of the Communist regime, and the period after Stalin's rule. The trajectory of copyright law through Soviet history shows the profound influence of theories of freedom of expression, inherited from pre-socialist society, and in particular, flowing from the activism of social reformers. The Communist experience of cultural manipulation was to transform the significance of copyright law, binding it firmly to the concepts of free thought and speech. **13.24**

(1) Copyright and the public interest: expropriation

When they first came to power, the Bolsheviks attempted to do away with copyright protection in much the same way that they would have liked to destroy every vestige of tsarist society. In fact, in their very attempt to revolutionize Russian culture, the Bolsheviks demonstrated their own susceptibility to the game of power relations in which the tsar had earlier engaged the Russian 'intelligentsia'. **13.25**

The Bolsheviks assumed a bold and interventionist attitude to culture. On the one hand, in keeping with tsarist tradition, they wanted to exploit the **13.26**

---

[21] The psychological impact of terror receives a close and disturbing study in C Merridale, *Night of Stone: Death and Memory in Russia* (London: Granta Books, 2000).

power of Russian culture and creativity for their own political objectives. In this endeavour, they did not suffer from the limitations of the tsar, who did not have the forces of ideology and social theory at his disposal: they intervened wholeheartedly and even recklessly into the cultural sphere to put their policies into action. On the other hand, the Bolsheviks probably had a true, Russian sense of the power and importance of literature, and its capacity to transform the most fundamental revolutionary battlefield, the minds of the people, into something new. It seems that Lenin and other Bolshevik leaders believed that literature's potential contribution to the Revolution would be as much social as political. It is probably fair to say that their desire for radical change, political and social, found some sympathy and support among writers themselves. The support of creative people, however, was to become ambivalent as the renewed precariousness of their own position under the Communist regime gradually became apparent.[22]

13.27 As early as December 1917, the new Bolshevik government embarked on an ambitious programme of nationalizing literary works. Initially, the government took over publication rights in classic works of Russian literature whose authors were no longer living, including those of Pushkin, Tolstoy, Dostoevsky, Gogol, Chekhov, and Turgenev.[23] In November 1918, the nationalizations were extended to the works of living authors, as well.[24]

13.28 The nationalization programme highlights a number of interesting features of the developing relationship between socialism and culture. In this early period of Soviet rule, culture was already perceived to be an area of special importance for revolutionary progress. The rationale behind the nationalizations was presumably to make the wealth of Russian literature available as widely as possible to the Soviet public. The Bolsheviks believed that this literature would have value for the Revolution—value in education and in nation-building, no doubt. The fact that most of the authors whose works were nationalized, with the notable exception of Chekhov, came from upper-class backgrounds was irrelevant. As Sheila Fitzpatrick points out, the

---

[22] This process is described in Boris Pasternak's now classic novel, *Dr Zhivago*, published in 1957: see B Pasternak, *Dr Zhivago*, trans M Hayward and M Harari (London: Vintage, 2002); originally published (London: Collins, 1958).

[23] This was accomplished through a Decree of 29 December 1917. See C Prins, 'Emile Zola Receives an Answer: The Soviet Union Is to Join the Berne Convention' (1991) 13(7) EIPR 238, 239–40.

[24] Decree of 26 November 1918; ibid 240.

'specialist' skills of writers and artists, and their importance for Russian development, were acknowledged by the Bolsheviks. However, from the point of view of Russian intellectuals, the attention of the Bolsheviks had ambiguous consequences. Fitzpatrick observes:

> [T]he complex relationship between the Bolshevik Party and the Russian intelligentsia in the decade after the Revolution is probably best understood as two competing elites, essentially interdependent, jealously jockeying for position, and withal constituting the only possible claimants for leadership in a fragmented and unsettled post-revolutionary society. It was a cliché of the 1920s that the Soviet regime could not survive without the collaboration of 'bourgeois specialists'.[25]

It is not difficult to sympathize with the initial programme of nationaliza- **13.29** tions undertaken by the Bolsheviks, notwithstanding its potentially negative impact on authors' rights. The idea of making classic literature widely available to the public without the hindrance of fees and restrictions arising from copyright is understandable, and suggests an appealing and idealistic notion of democratizing culture. Indeed, a number of writers and intellectuals initially supported the approach of the Bolsheviks. As time went on, however, the support of figures like Blok, Mayakovsky, and Gorky, who had once been strong proponents of the Revolution, would eventually be tested beyond the point where it could be maintained. Others were ambivalent from the start.[26]

If the policy of nationalizing classic works attracts ready sympathy, the sub- **13.30** sequent decision of the Bolshevik government to extend nationalizations to living authors is more difficult to justify, and seems to cross the line separating revolutionary idealism from arbitrary control. It is noteworthy that, in practice, this policy was applied only to the works of two living authors, one of whom also happened to be a foreigner.[27] Indeed, it seems

---

[25] S Fitzpatrick, *The Cultural Front: Power and Culture in Revolutionary Russia* (Ithaca: Cornell University Press, 1992) 6–7.

[26] The position of writers with respect to the 'cultural revolution' initiated by the Bolsheviks is discussed by G Hosking, *A History of the Soviet Union 1917–1991* (final edn, London: Fontana Press, 1992) 178–82.

[27] According to S Levitsky, 'Continuity and Change in Soviet Copyright Law: A Legal Analysis' (1980) 6 Rev of Socialist L 425, 425, Upton Sinclair was the only author whose works were nationalized under the 1918 decree. However, MA Newcity, *Copyright Law in the Soviet Union* (New York: Praeger Special Studies, 1978) 19, notes that both Russian translations of the works of Upton Sinclair and the writings of Georgiy V Plekhanov were nationalized by a third decree, issued on 14 May 1925.

likely that this decree was a way for the Bolsheviks to assert their power over the cultural arena, without, however, antagonizing authors excessively by bringing it fully into play.

13.31 In the case of deceased authors, nationalization would have had two kinds of implications for authors' descendants. First, it would have deprived them of the financial benefits of inherited royalties, a policy that has both negative and positive aspects.[28] Secondly, however, the heirs of the author would lose their ability to claim protection for the author's moral rights. Lack of protection for moral rights means that the maintenance of the author's personal rights of attribution and integrity becomes difficult after his death. The negative consequences of this inability to protect a deceased author's moral interests are not restricted to him and his descendants. Rather, the expiry of moral rights has broader implications for cultural heritage, and, in relation to classic works of literature, presents a potentially serious issue. Maintaining attribution and integrity interests after an author's death would contribute to the preservation of cultural heritage and an accurate historical record, to name but the two most obvious benefits flowing from these rights.[29] Of course, in order for broader cultural benefits to be realized from moral rights protection, it is not necessary that the rights should be vindicated by the author's personal heirs and descendants. They can no doubt be effectively protected through a number of special arrangements, by allowing individuals, organizations, or even State agencies to assert them on behalf of the author. However, it is not certain who would be best placed to protect moral rights.

13.32 The extension of the nationalization programme effectively brought the rights of living authors prematurely into the public domain—before the expiry of the usual duration granted by law—or, more precisely in this case, into the ambit of State control. Where the rights of living authors are not recognized,

---

[28] The example of Pushkin's widow pleading for extended copyright benefits illustrates the problem. The impoverishment of literary families, especially in cases where the poet may have died prematurely, can be an injustice. Madame Pushkin's suit is discussed by LP Rastorgoueff, 'The New Law of Copyright in Russia' (1911) J of the Society of Comparative Legislation 302, 307.

[29] The reach and importance of moral rights for cultural heritage are examined in MT Sundara Rajan, 'Moral Rights and the Protection of Cultural Heritage: *Amar Nath Sehgal v Union of India*' (2001) Intl J of Cultural Property 79, 79–83, 89–90.

the problem of protecting works in the public domain becomes acute. Moreover, it seems likely that the deprivation of a degree of control over the publication process would make authors generally ambivalent about the commercialization of their works. The policy indicates a lack of sensitivity to authors' perceptions of their own interests and needs. The decree reveals the extent to which concepts of individual rights of authorship, whether for reasons of doctrine or practice, were disliked by the socialists.[30]

(2) Authors versus publishers: a socialist copyright

By the early 1920s, faced with enormous economic and political pressures, **13.33** Revolutionary politics were in decline, and new concerns preoccupied the Soviet government. In the mid-1920s, the legal development of authors' rights in ordinary legal instruments, rather than extraordinary decrees, once again became a relevant issue. The shift in cultural policy that had initially taken place with the Bolshevik accession to power now underwent a further process of transformation. The Bolsheviks had been preoccupied with the problem of popular access to knowledge; they were prepared to prioritize accessibility over all other interests, including those of authors and artists. Indeed, the potential cooperation of at least some authors may have strengthened their resolve, though revolutionary zeal would almost certainly have driven them to continue even without the authors' support. As the 1920s progressed, however, the relatively fluid relations between the government and the intelligentsia hardened into a new mould. The government's need for culture was as urgent as ever, but it was combined with other factors that made the situation more complex. First among these was a need, political and ideological in essence, to control the circulation of knowledge and information throughout society. Authors and artists increasingly felt alienated, disillusioned, and victimized by the Revolution, a situation that is tragically symbolized by Mayakovsky's suicide in 1930.[31]

The Soviet government had to make some effort to redress the disenchant- **13.34** ment of intellectuals with the Revolution. In 1925, a new copyright law that

---

[30] See S Levitsky, 'Continuity and Change in Soviet Copyright Law: A Legal Analysis' (1980) 6 Rev of Socialist L 425, 425.

[31] See the discussion of the circumstances surrounding Mayakovsky's death in G Hosking, *A History of the Soviet Union 1917–1991* (final edn, London: Fontana Press, 1992) 181, 183.

reflected the changed circumstances of Russian socialism was drafted, and its provisions were refined in further legislation only three years later. The Copyright Act of 1928 was to govern authors' rights in the Soviet Union for more than three decades, and would establish the defining principles of copyright law under Soviet rule.

13.35 In substance, the law of 1925—and, to an even greater extent, the legislation of 1928—signified a return to the copyright landscape delineated in the landmark legislation of 1911: namely, a copyright law based on individual rights of authorship, which were seen to be beneficial for both authors and the public at large. However, the authorship orientation of the 1911 law was tempered by the requirements of Soviet socialist ideology, reflected in the form in which these copyright principles were expressed. The integration of socialist ideology into the 1925 law was, in many ways, rather crude. The impact of socialism on the 1925 law could be felt in three ways. First, copyright was specified as being a non-property right. Secondly, the protection of an author's right after his death was eliminated from the legislation, reflecting the unacceptability of inheritance to the socialist mind. It is noteworthy, however, that in practice, this provision did not bring the Soviet standard of protection for copyright far below the internationally accepted duration of the times.[32] Thirdly, although the moral rights of authors were protected, the terminology of 'personal' rights was strictly avoided. The collective interests emphasized by socialist ideology sat uneasily with the nomenclature of individual rights.

13.36 The approach of the 1928 law to 'socializing' copyright law was much more refined; as Russian copyright scholar Serge Levitsky observes, the 1925 Act had been a mere 'sketch', whereas the 1928 legislation was a 'broad panorama'.[33] The Copyright Act of 1928 reintroduced some important substantive prin-

---

[32] The 1928 Rome revision of the Berne Convention increased the potential duration of copyright to life plus fifty years. However, it also made provision for a lesser duration of copyright protection, determined by the standard in the country of origin of the work, in the case where all member countries of the Union did not enact the longer term: see Rome Copyright Act 1928, Art 7(2). The provisions show great ambivalence about prolonging the term of copyright protection.

[33] S Levitsky, 'Continuity and Change in Soviet Copyright Law: A Legal Analysis' (1980) 6 Rev of Socialist L 425, 432. It should be noted that Levitsky prefers to deal with the RSFSR Act of 1926, which was, however, bound by law and practice to follow the 'principles' (*osnovy*) of 1925. Levitsky's analysis moves quite freely between the two.

ciples from Russian law into Soviet copyright legislation.[34] In this respect, the legislation of 1928 brought Russian copyright full circle, from the comprehensive and ambitious Act of 1911, through a revolutionary interruption, and back to many of the 1911 principles. It restored the term of protection to the lifetime of the author and an additional fifteen years after his death. In keeping with Marxist ideology, the Copyright Act of 1928 avoided a property-based theory of copyright law. However, it did not return to the *sui generis* formula of 1911. Rather, it followed, and tried to perfect, a trend set in the 1925 legislation, towards distinguishing copyright from property.

The 1928 Act dealt with the problem of property rights in two ways. In the **13.37** first instance, the drafters tried explicitly to eliminate references to property and property concepts from the body of the law.[35] A second approach was to continue to grant limited recognition to the property interests of authors, but to place them within the broader context of a non-property theory of authorship. Interestingly, the theory of choice was the protection of individual authors from the exploitative treatment of publishers—an idea that had already informed the 1911 Act.[36] As expressed in a 1938 commentary on the Russian copyright law:

> In bourgeois society, the author's right is a monopoly, establishing the exclusive right to distribute the products of science, literature and art. . . .
>
> [It] is characteristic that, except for a small group of bourgeois authors, the author's right is the property, in bourgeois society, not of the author, but of the publisher, of a big capitalist, an industrialist. . . . [T]he author's right in capitalist countries is made into a tool of the interests of the monopolist-publisher, a means of exploiting the author and retarding the cultural growth of the masses of the people. . . .

---

[34] USSR Laws 1928, no 246 (16 May 1928). An English translation of a number of the provisions may be found in JN Hazard, *Materials on Soviet Law* (New York: Columbia University, 1947) 35–7.

[35] An example from the 1925 Act, retained in the 1928 revisions, is cited by S Levitsky, 'Continuity and Change in Soviet Copyright Law: A Legal Analysis' (1980) 6 Rev of Socialist L 425, 429, dealing with works of joint authorship. The Act of 1911 had specified that the relationship of joint authors was 'analog[ous] to the rules applicable to *joint property* [emphasis added]'. This was reproduced in the 1925 text such that 'the relations between co-authors were governed by agreement'.

[36] V Gsovski, *Soviet Civil Law: Private Rights and Their Background under the Soviet Regime*, HE Yntema (ed), Michigan L Stud Series (Ann Arbor: University of Michigan Law School, 1948).

> The basic principles of the Soviet author's right are completely different . . . [It] has the objective of protecting to the maximum the personal *and property* interests of the author, coupled with the assurance of the widest distribution of the product of literature, science and the arts among the broad masses of the toilers [emphasis added].[37]

13.38 In many ways, the substantive treatment of authorship in the 1928 Act retained a number of key resemblances to property rights; but they could be justified under a broad theory of authors' rights and, in particular, on the grounds that the author needed to be protected against the interests of his publisher. Again, Soviet law betrayed its ancestry in Russian legal liberalism and the protection of authors' individual rights—and indeed, the adoption of the 1925 and, especially, the 1928 Acts occurred in a period of greater conciliation between the political and cultural elites, partly in response to threats from outside the country.

(3) Authors versus the State: freedom of thought and expression

13.39 The statute of 1928 was to remain the primary source of Soviet copyright law until the 1960s. This copyright legislation saw Soviet authorship through a bitter period of unparalleled repression under Stalin. Like other aspects of law and legality, including the 'beautiful' Soviet Constitution,[38] the legislation was explicitly contravened by Stalin, or expressly disregarded. As a consequence of Stalin's policies, the concept of the rule of law suffered severe degradation, a situation which the post-socialist Russian Federation of today has not yet outgrown. Indeed, if law had any meaning at all in Stalin's Russia, it was as a tool of political power, to be exploited by the State against its own citizens.

13.40 For a brief period in the wake of Stalin's death, it appeared that law and legality might be resurrected from the ashes of his terrorist regime. Khrushchev took the unprecedented step of acknowledging and condemning Stalin's policies in his 'Secret Speech' at the XXth Communist Party Congress in

---

[37] 'A Text Writer's Opinion', *Grazhdanskoe Pravo* (Civil Law), Part I, Moscow 1938, 254–5; translated in JN Hazard, *Materials on Soviet Law* (New York: Columbia University, 1947) 35.

[38] See G Hosking, *A History of the Soviet Union 1917–1991* (final edn, London: Fontana Press, 1992) 416–17. The phrase can be attributed to Aleksandr Esenin-Volpin, a mathematician and son of the poet, Sergei Esenin.

1956.[39] As the unsuspected extent of Stalin's terror and the sufferings of the Soviet public came to be known, the Communist leadership was thrown into disarray. In an attempt to fill this political and cultural void, Khrushchev invoked the idea of 'socialist legality', a way of introducing the concept of law-limited power into Soviet government. He simultaneously initiated a period of leniency towards the publication of literature, which provided a cathartic means for the Soviet public to attempt to come to terms with the unfathomable scale of the sufferings experienced by their country.

Revised Soviet copyright legislation was adopted in 1961.[40] In contrast to the liberal criminal justice reforms of 1960, however, the new copyright provisions of the Fundamentals of Civil Legislation did not reflect the 'Thaw' in author–State relations.[41] The reasons for this are not immediately apparent, though political timing must have been a crucial factor. The new criminal laws were adopted as a direct response to the post-Stalin revelations of persecution. However, the copyright legislation appears to have been the product of earlier reform initiatives, and therefore, may not have been directly implicated in the Stalinist debacle. Alternatively, it is also possible that the reforms were influenced by the growing nervousness of Communist officials as the decade of the 'Thaw' wore on.   **13.41**

At first glance, the approach to copyright reform appears to have been primarily technical in nature. Indeed, the reasons given by scholars of Soviet law for the development of the 1961 legislation are both technical ones, having to do with the technological outdatedness of the 1928 law in the new era of television, on the one hand, and the technical shortcomings of the law   **13.42**

---

[39] The 'secret speech' is discussed by G Hosking, *A History of the Soviet Union 1917–1991* (final edn, London: Fontana Press, 1992), 334–7. The speech dealt primarily with the impact of Stalin's repression on the Party elite, rather than the experience of the population at large, and was delivered before a special 'closed session' following the Twentieth Communist Party Congress of 1956. Although it was not published in the Soviet Union, it immediately became known abroad because of the presence of foreign Communist leaders, who had been invited to the session by Khrushchev.

[40] Fundamentals of Civil Legislation of the USSR and the Republics, *VVS SSSR*, 1961 No 50, Item 525. An English translation of the copyright provisions appears in MA Newcity *Copyright Law in the Soviet Union* (New York: Praeger Special Studies, 1978), Appendix A, 182.

[41] In his extensive 1966 study, Harold Berman points out that the revised criminal legislation was in large measure a reaction against the abuse of criminal law during the Stalinist period: H Berman *Soviet Criminal Law and Procedure: The RSFSR Codes*, trans H Berman and JW Spindler, Russian Research Centre Studies 50 (1st edn, Cambridge: Harvard University Press, 1966). The 'Thaw' gained its name from a novel of the period by Ilya Ehrenburg.

itself, on the other.[42] This second reason for the legislative changes indicated an increasing distance between the letter of the 1928 law and the practices of the mature Soviet State in relation to copyright. In practical terms, the Soviet treatment of copyright had become highly restrictive, far beyond the provisions of the 1928 law. Many of these practical constraints had to do with the rigid bureaucratic structure of Soviet publishing, which allowed the government to maintain close control of the circulation of literature and, except within the most specialized circumstances, virtually deprived the Soviet author of the ability to exercise his copyright.[43]

13.43 While technically superior to the 1928 law, the 1961 copyright provisions introduced two important new restrictions on authors' rights. It removed the idea of copyright as an exclusive right of the author, for the first time in the history of Soviet or Russian copyright legislation, and it also reduced the duration of copyright protection. Article 105 of the Fundamentals provides only that copyright is protected for the lifetime of the author, without specifying any required duration of protection after his death. The movement towards a lifetime-only term of protection was supported by restrictions on the inheritance of copyright, and the assertion of the right by the author's heirs under the 1961 provisions, which was to be 'limit[ed]'.[44]

13.44 The Fundamentals did, however, lead to one puzzling concession to authors' rights, incorporated into the Russian Civil Code reforms of 1964. They introduced the terminology of 'personal rights' for the protection of authors' moral rights into the history of Soviet or Russian copyright legislation for the first time.[45] Within the framework of Soviet publishing, this terminology

---

[42] See MA Newcity *Copyright Law in the Soviet Union* (New York: Praeger Special Studies, 1978) 27, who emphasizes the importance of television, and S Levitsky, 'Continuity and Change in Soviet Copyright Law: A Legal Analysis' (1980) 6 Rev of Socialist L 425, 443.

[43] As Newcity observes, in the environment of Soviet publishing, the right to choose whether or not to publish a work—the right of disclosure—was effectively the only aspect of copyright that an author could expect to exercise.

[44] S Levitsky, 'Continuity and Change in Soviet Copyright Law: A Legal Analysis' (1980) 6 Rev of Socialist L 425, 444. The main purpose of the limitation was to restrict the apparently exorbitant royalties enjoyed by many authors' descendants. However, it should be noted that the possibility of an author's descendants asserting moral rights is also implicated in the provision, and cannot be said to be favoured by the law.

[45] 'Protection of the Personal Non-Property Rights of the Author', Art 499, RSFSR Civil Code of 1964: *VVS RSFSR*, 1964 No 24,406. An English translation may be found in MA Newcity, *Copyright Law in the Soviet Union* (New York: Praeger Special Studies, 1978) 495, and on the current version of the Russian legal database, Garant.

had little practical significance; but it was an ideological concession, and one aimed directly at the authors' association of their own interests and responsibilities with freedom of expression. For the first time in Soviet law, Russian authors were recognized as individuals with special rights—rights associated with their creative role.

In many ways, the copyright provisions of the 1961 Fundamentals reflected **13.45** the ambiguities of the times in relation to creative authorship, codifying the practical limitations of copyright in legislation while giving recognition to the personal rights of authors. The Fundamentals came into effect just as the official attempt at tolerance towards dissent from the creative community was about to peak, with the publication of Alexander Solzhenitsyn's *One Day in the Life of Ivan Denisovich* in 1962. Ironically, the national sensation generated by the publication of Solzhenitsyn's work, widely exposing the realities of Stalinist repression to the Russian public from the personal and intimate perspective of a single victim, aroused the party's fears about the deeper consequences of ideological liberalization. As it became apparent that the maintenance of political control depended anew on the imposition of order, the Soviet leadership once again attempted to tighten its restrictions on creative expression.

However, it proved to be difficult for the government to retrace its steps on the **13.46** path of greater accountability. Rather, the Soviet leadership confronted the difficult challenge of re-establishing control while appearing to maintain consistency with its own, post-Stalin discourse of renewed legality over the course of the previous decade. One of the methods by which it attempted this impossible reconciliation of opposites was to undertake a series of prosecutions, in which the State attempted to make writers criminally responsible for their imaginative work.[46] The most famous of these trials was the Siniavsky–Daniel affair of 1966, involving two writers who had published works of political satire abroad, to great critical acclaim. The prosecution of Siniavsky and Daniel for their writings created a huge political stir. The condemnation of the two writers to punishment in labour camps brought a conclusive end to the notion of 'socialist legality', which became a confirmed contradiction in terms.

---

[46] Details of the landmark prosecution may be found in Y Feofanov and D Barry, 'The Siniavskii–Daniel Trial: A Thirty Year Perspective' (1996) 22(6) Rev of Central & East European L 603. See also, Y Feofanov and D Barry, *Politics and Justice in Russia: Major Trials of the Post-Stalin Era* (Armonk NY: ME Sharpe, 1996) 15–49.

13.47 Following the revelations of the Khrushchev era, and the humiliation and abuse of creative people in the 'show trials' of the 1960s, the break between the Communist Party elite and intellectuals became definitive and irrevocable. What is fascinating, however, is that the experience of 'socialist legality' in the Khrushchev period did not tarnish even slightly the idea of law as a source of protection from injustice. Rather, the experiment with 'socialist legality' only served to strengthen the belief of dissidents in the liberating power of the law. Moreover, their perspective on law became more strongly oriented than ever towards individual rights. In particular, the language of international human rights law was an invaluable resource for the Soviet dissident movement in the late 1960s. For example, they made Article 19 of the Universal Declaration of Human Rights on freedom of expression, opinion, ideas, and information—which the Soviet Union had ratified—their political manifesto.[47] Indeed, the dissident movement came to be known, quite simply, as the human rights movement, on the basis of its primary strategy of 'urging the Soviet government to observe its own constitution'.[48]

(4) Freedom of speech and international copyright: State control

13.48 An author's right to freedom of creative expression became the central issue in a debate over the historic internationalization of Soviet copyright law during the 1970s. Imperial Russia had been among the earliest countries to take an interest in the Berne Convention, though, for a variety of policy reasons, it eventually decided not to join.[49] Since this early decision, Russia had remained aloof from international copyright matters—a position, how-

---

[47] Hosking points out that the first issue of an important dissident journal, the *Chronicle of Current Events*, appeared in 1968 with Art 19 on its cover. The *Chronicle* was a *samizdat* journal, part of the dissident network of 'self-published' works, see *infra* n 51. See G Hosking, *A History of the Soviet Union 1917–1991* (final edn, London: Fontana Press, 1992) 412, 415.

[48] Ibid 419; see Hosking's interesting discussion at 419–22.

[49] Russia's discomfort with the idea of Berne membership had to do with the necessity of abandoning the principle of 'freedom of translation'. Translators continued to have an unrestricted right of access to original works of foreign authorship, even after this right had been made subject to certain limitations with regard to Russian authors. The argument was that Russia would have to pay huge royalties to foreign authors in order to meet the substantial demand for foreign literature in Russia. Russian authors who favoured membership of Berne argued that the sales of Russian literature abroad would more than offset this loss. The issue receives a detailed treatment in C Prins, 'Emile Zola Receives an Answer: The Soviet Union is to Join the Berne Convention' (1991) 13(7) EIPR 238, 239.

ever, that it did not impose on its satellite States in Eastern Europe.[50] By the 1970s, a number of factors compelled it to reconsider its international isolation in copyright matters. The Soviet Union eventually put forward its intention to join, not the Berne Convention, but the less demanding Universal Copyright Convention which had been initiated by the USA.

An important reason for the Communist aversion to international copyright **13.49** was its fear of losing ideological control. Under the Communists, ideological control was a pressing concern of the government. The legitimacy of the Communist Party was closely tied to the maintenance of Communist ideology. The control and manipulation of authors was an essential part of this enterprise. Authors were drawn into a web of State activity—State publishing and broadcasting, ideological censorship of works before they could be published—from which they could not escape as long as they continued to be active in the Soviet Union. The alternative was to 'write for the desk drawer' or, through the 1960s and 1970s, to 'self-publish' works through the risky, private network of *samizdat*.[51] However, publishing outside the Soviet Union might be another method of evading Soviet censorship, and this was one avenue of literary escape that the Soviet government would have liked to eliminate. For the Soviet government, publication abroad meant the loss of ideological control at home. It also had the unpleasant side effects of negative international publicity, and the possibility that anti-Soviet 'propaganda' might reach the ears of the Soviet public by clandestine means.

Initially, the government's concern that, through international copyright conventions, Soviet authors might acquire rights abroad that they did not have within the Soviet Union contributed to its reluctance to participate. When the Soviet Union eventually did decide to join the Universal Copyright Convention in 1973, the decision caused great concern, both within Russia and internationally, about the potential that it gave for the government to repress further the activities of dissidents within the Soviet Union.

---

[50] For example, see the list of socialist countries and each country's membership in the different versions of the two Conventions. See M Ficsor, 'The Past, Present and Future of Copyright in the European Socialist Countries' (1983) 118 *Revue internationale du droit d'auteur* 33, 58. The Soviet Union was not a member of the Berne Convention, and it had adhered only to the 1952 Geneva version of the UCC.

[51] *Samizdat* means 'self-publishing'. The term was intended as a retort to *gosizdat*, State publishing.

13.51 The self-proclaimed objective of the Soviet government in joining the UCC was to secure some economic benefit to the country from membership. In contrast to the situation surrounding the Berne Convention, almost a century earlier, the Soviet Union's place in the world of publishing was quite different. As Newcity, writing in 1978, shortly after the Soviet Union's accession to the UCC, observes: 'Each year the Communist Party-controlled publishing houses of the Soviet Union print and disseminate more books than the publishers of any other country in the world . . . Books in the Soviet Union are published in 89 of the languages spoken in the country, as well as in many foreign languages, and cover the entire gamut of subjects from the sciences to poetry and belles-lettres.'[52]

13.52 However, membership in the UCC carried a genuine risk of increased powers of censorship. This problem was due to certain features of post-Stalin copyright law in the Soviet Union that allowed the government to acquire copyright in works, published or unpublished, by means of compulsory purchase. The relevant provision of the 1961 Fundamentals was Article 106, which stated that, '[c]opyright in the publication, public performance, or other use of a work may be compulsorily purchased by the state from the author or his heirs, in the manner provided for by the legislation of the union republics.'[53]

13.53 According to Soviet convention, copyright would be acquired by the State for a lump-sum fee paid to the author or his heirs, in an amount determined by the government.[54] Since the acquisition of copyright was not a confiscation of rights in the work, in formal terms, it may not have been obviously contrary to international norms. However, the purpose of the provision was generally acknowledged in Soviet jurisprudence to be that of 'compelling recalcitrant authors who showed no enthusiasm for sharing their work with society, and particularly of forcing their stubborn heirs, to do so'.[55]

---

[52] MA Newcity, *Copyright Law in the Soviet Union* (New York: Praeger Special Studies, 1978) v.

[53] As translated in Newcity, ibid, Appendix A, 187. See also, ibid 153–4. It is worth noting that, under this provision, only the governments of the republics, rather than the federal government, could effect a compulsory purchase. This represented a change in the law from 1928 to 1961: see SL Levitsky, 'The State As a Subject of Copyright in Soviet Law' (1980) 1 (2) J of Media L & Practice 137, 143.

[54] SL Levitsky, ibid 141.

[55] Ibid 141, 142.

It is interesting to note that Article 106 provides that only certain 'uses' of **13.54** an author's work could be compulsorily purchased by the State. In effect, according to Soviet copyright doctrine, an author's copyright could not be alienated in its entirety, even by the State. Moral rights of disclosure, attribution, and integrity in the work could probably not be acquired by the State.[56] However, the issue of the extent to which copyright could be alienated by the author in accordance with Soviet doctrine remained unclear. As Levitsky observes:

> [T]he concept of 'alienation of copyright in its entirety' . . . was permitted by the Copyright Act of 1928 but was persistently criticized in Soviet jurisprudence. . . . [A]n 'alienation in part' of the author's copyright . . . had also been permitted by the Copyright Act of 1928, but disappeared as a concept during the reforms of the early 1960s . . . Alas, the legal nature of the 'transfer' would remain in doubt for more than a decade, and is still far from being resolved.[57]

Notwithstanding the limitations of the legal provisions on compulsory pur- **13.55** chase of copyright, both the international community and Soviet authors were deeply concerned about the implications of membership in the UCC. No doubt, their interpretation of events was based both on the vagueness of Soviet legal theory in this area, and on the proven heavy-handedness of the Soviet government in its approach to law and legality. For example, a consideration of international moral rights cases involving Soviet authors shows that the Soviet government was able to act 'on their behalf' by 'obtaining their permission'.[58]

At least in crude terms, if not in doctrinally correct ones, Article 106 could **13.56** therefore allow the Soviet government to exercise copyright, and even moral rights, for the purposes of the UCC. It would thereby be in a position to restrict the publication of a work or its translation in any member country of the UCC, and, twisting the initial logic of the provision, to suppress the publication of an unpublished work that was 'in contradiction to the interests of socialist society'.[59] If the government, relying on ambiguous legal

---

[56] See also ibid 142. Levitsky observes that, even under the earlier Soviet legislation of 1925 and 1928, acquisition of an author's copyright by the State did not include the author's moral rights.

[57] Ibid 141–2.

[58] See discussion below.

[59] According to LV Glebova, this was the main reason underlying the compulsory purchase provisions: Glebova (1972), cited in Levitsky, ibid 144.

provisions, considered its rights over acquired works to include the moral rights of the author, they could prove to be an important and particularly dangerous instrument of censorship. For example, the conformity of internationally publicized works with Soviet norms could be enforced through the integrity right, which the Soviet government could potentially assert in the name of the author.

13.57 The *Shostakovich* case provides a famous illustration of how this kind of situation might arise in practice. This 1948 case involved a film entitled *The Iron Curtain*, which featured the music of four Soviet composers, Shostakovich, Prokofiev, Khatchaturian, and Miashkovsky. The film chronicled the activities of Soviet spies in Canada, and its treatment of the subject matter was distinctly unflattering to the Soviet Union.[60]

13.58 The musical works featured in the film were all in the public domain. As the American court said, they 'enjoy[ed] no copyright protection whatever'.[61] However, the Soviet government brought a suit in the name of the composers against Twentieth-Century Fox, the studio which had produced the film.[62] The legal basis on which the State acted is unclear. In the Soviet law of the time, copyright passed by inheritance to the heirs of the author; the period of protection was relatively short, the lifetime of the author and fifteen years after his death.[63] There was no special provision in the 1928 Act regarding copyright in the public domain, although subsequent legislation did address this issue. Article 502 of the RSFSR Civil Code of 1964, based on the 1961 Fundamentals, provided explicitly that works could be 'declared the property of the state by the decision of the Council of Ministers of the RSFSR'. Arguably, the idea of declaring a public domain work to be State property can be traced back to the nationalization decrees of the Bolsheviks. It seems to have been an informal procedure, justifiable by the State on arbitrary grounds of its choice. When this was the case, presumably, the Soviet government felt

---

[60] *Dmitry Shostakovich v Twentieth Century-Fox Film Corporation* 196 Misc 67; 80 NYS 2d 575, 77 USPQ 647 (Sup Ct of New York, 1948). The circumstances of the case are described by Newcity, see MA Newcity, *Copyright Law in the Soviet Union* (New York: Praeger Special Studies, 1978) 34–5.

[61] *Shostakovich*, ibid.

[62] *Shostakovich*, ibid.

[63] In contrast, the minimum duration of copyright specified in the 1961 Fundamentals was simply the lifetime of the author (Art 105).

at liberty to deal with public domain works as if it were responsible for their moral rights.

In effect, the *Shostakovich* suit was a moral rights claim, although, in keeping **13.59** with US practice in this area, it was brought on the grounds of defamation. The 'composers' argued that the association of their work with an anti-Soviet film was damaging to their reputations, and should be banned. However, the court found that, unless the music itself had been distorted, the claim could not succeed.

Interestingly, the same suit was brought as a moral rights case in France, **13.60** where, based on the natural rights rationale of French copyright law, it was possible at that time for authors of any nationality to expect protection of their rights of authorship in a French court.[64] The French Cour de Cassation decided in 1959 that the authors' moral right of integrity had been violated. They ordered the film to be removed from circulation, and awarded damages to the plaintiffs.

A second, lesser-known case of this kind occurred in 1964, and involved **13.61** a novel by Anatoli Kuznetsov, *The Continuation of a Legend*. When the work was first submitted to the Soviet publisher, the author was told to modify it by 'add[ing] more "optimistic" passages' before it could be published.[65] The modified version of the work eventually appeared in the Soviet Union. However, shortly thereafter, a French translation, based on the original, unedited manuscript, was published. Again, the Soviet government undertook a lawsuit 'on behalf of' the author—in this case, on the basis of a 'denunciation' of the translation obtained from him by the Soviet State. Once again, the 'author's' claim that his right of integrity had been violated was upheld by the French courts, resulting in the withdrawal of the work from circulation and an award of damages. Interestingly, Kuznetsov defected to England in 1969. At that time, he wrote to the French authorities, asking them to reopen the case and affirming his support for the French translation of his original work, which '[captured] the very essence of my novel'.[66] However, the case was never reconsidered in France.[67]

---

[64] This was the case until 1964. See MA Newcity, *Copyright Law in the Soviet Union* (New York: Praeger Special Studies, 1978) 35.

[65] Ibid 155.   [66] Ibid 155–6.

[67] Ibid 156, n 20. Newcity suggests that the case was never reopened because of the expiry of a limitation period. However, this is a peculiar conclusion, since French law recognizes moral rights in perpetuity.

13.62 These two cases of Soviet copyright claims abroad show how the State was able to manipulate international copyright rules for political purposes by donning the mask of the author—interestingly, a technique that somewhat resembles the traditional strategy of publishers in common law countries. In this way, copyright law became directly implicated in issues of freedom of expression under the Soviet regime. The two cases highlight the particularly close relationship between moral rights and free creative expression in the Soviet context. The government of the Soviet Union was prepared to use authorship rights for its political ends, and, in these two important cases, it proved its ability to wield the most characteristic of authorship rights, personal or 'moral' rights, against the authors themselves. Against this background, the fears of Soviet dissidents about the consequences of joining the international copyright community through the UCC seem well-founded.

13.63 The government's own pronouncements on UCC accession were quite contradictory. Its statements ranged from aggressive assertions that it would attempt to suppress further the writings of dissidents, and that 'Western publishers would bear "legal responsibility" ' for publishing their work,[68] to assurances that 'there was no intention whatsoever of applying the [UCC] against dissidents.'[69] This situation suggests that the possibility of wielding copyright law against Soviet writers was, at the very least, a latent reality. For their part, writers and other dissidents believed in the gravity of the danger. One writers' group pointed out: 'Our books will be stifled not only during the lives of their authors, but forever, until the end of publishing on earth. This situation did not exist even in Stalin's time, for the books then ended by coming to the surface, at least posthumously.'[70]

13.64 Newcity, a contemporary observer writing shortly after Soviet accession to the UCC, seems relatively optimistic about the internationalization of Soviet copyright. In particular, he argues that the Soviet government had no need to use copyright law for suppressing dissent. The 'depressing' reality was that other, more effective means of control were available. According to him, criminal charges were among the strongest means of suppression. In particular, he notes the suitability of Article 70 of the Russian Criminal Code

---

[68] See MA Newcity, *Copyright Law in the Soviet Union* (New York: Praeger Special Studies, 1978) 153.

[69] Ibid 153.

[70] *The Times*, 27 March 1973, 8, quoted in Newcity, ibid 152.

on 'anti-Soviet propaganda', which was exploited for this purpose in the notorious Siniavsky–Daniel affair of 1966.[71] However, Newcity's optimism towards copyright and his sense of its relative isolation from free speech concerns are not well-founded. It is evident that Soviet writers and intellectuals lived and worked in an environment where law had come to be used as a powerful means of restraining freedom of expression. Creative expression was proven to be vulnerable to quasi-legal challenges. Soviet copyright law, in particular, had already demonstrated its susceptibility to State manipulation at the international level. It is important to recognize that copyright law was one among the legal instruments that lent themselves to subversion by the Soviet government. Authors' rights were turned against authors. They contributed to their persecution, rather than assuring the protection of their efforts.

D. Copyright and Free Expression after Communism

For a variety of reasons, copyright reform in the post-socialist period has been fraught with difficulty. Russia represents the most extreme example of this situation, although, in different ways, it is also characteristic of other post-socialist countries. Russian reform has been characterized by conflicting priorities at both the domestic and international levels. While copyright is subject to the influence of competing forces at the domestic level, the contrast between domestic priorities and the requirements of the international trade regime dominates Russia's involvement in international copyright discourse. For this reason, the copyright sections of the revised Fundamentals of Civil Legislation, adopted as a series of 'transitional' provisions on copyright in 1991,[72] are in some respects more open about the interdependent relationship of copyright and freedom of expression than the subsequent Copyright Act, adopted by post-Communist Russia in 1993. On the other hand, the 1993 Act has had the benefit of being adopted in conditions of relative normality. As such, in some areas, it develops more fully ideas that were

13.65

---

[71] Newcity, ibid 157.

[72] Fundamentals of Civil Legislation of the USSR and the Republics, *VSND i VS SSSR*, 1991 No 26, Item 773; available in English translation on Garant. Given the fluctuating political circumstances of the country, the provisions were regarded as transitional from the outset.

suggested by the 1991 Fundamentals, but which could not be put into practice at that time.

(1) The author's right as an individual right

13.66 In its first attempt at copyright reform, the government, by its 1991 revisions to the Russian Fundamentals of Civil Legislation, greatly expanded the scope of authorship rights. These changes reflected Gorbachev's reformist policies of *perestroïka* (reconstruction) and *glasnost* (openness).

13.67 The twin themes of reconstruction and openness made the *perestroïka* period an active time of change in Russia's copyright regime. On the one hand, the ideological *timbre* of Soviet copyright law, inherited from the period of 'socialist legality' and 'socialist realism', was perceived to impede economic and social development. On the other hand, the failure to protect works of foreign authorship was a growing area of contention in the Soviet Union's international relations, particularly as copyright gradually came to be viewed as a potential source of protection for new technologies.[73]

13.68 Under Gorbachev, the Soviet administration attempted to revisit its long-standing policy of manipulation and repression towards creative authorship. Greater freedom of expression was the very essence of reconstruction and openness in Gorbachev's new society.[74] In keeping with Soviet, and the earlier Russian tradition, the creative and socially-important expression of writers and other artists had a special significance for Gorbachev. Like other rulers over the centuries of Russian history, Gorbachev perceived literary expression as a vehicle for political and social change. To a greater extent than any previous leader, perhaps, Gorbachev hoped to convince intellectuals and creative people to contribute to the renewal of socialist ideals in a liberalized Soviet Union. The parallels between Gorbachev and Khrushchev, between *perestroïka* and the 'Thaw', are striking. However, Gorbachev's programme of change, coming long after the ambivalent attempts at liberalization in the 1950s and

---

[73] For example, see the discussion of American software companies and their influence in Russia in the 1990s in A Yakovlev, 'Legal Protection of Computer Programs in Russia' (1996) 18(5) EIPR 292, 293–4.

[74] Hosking comments on the new role assumed, at Gorbachev's urging, by writers under *perestroika*. See G Hosking, *A History of the Soviet Union 1917–1991* (final edn, London: Fontana Press, 1992) 458.

1960s, was far-reaching and comprehensive by nature, and therefore, much less predictable than Khrushchev's reforms.[75]

Gorbachev's growing sense of the crisis confronting the Soviet Union led to **13.69** an increasing desire to establish a basis for real cooperation between the government and the dissident community. Indeed, Hosking identifies the hope of help from intellectuals as a crucial feature of *perestroika's* 'second phase'. Hosking observes:

> Symbolic of the new movement was the release of Academician Sakharov from exile in Gorky in December 1986. The letter which he had written to Brezhnev in 1970 . . . may be said to contain the first sketch of what was now emerging as Gorbachev's Perestroika Mark 2, at the centre of which was the notion of an alliance between the party leadership and the country's scientific and cultural intelligentsia, including those who had hitherto been execrated as 'dissidents'.[76]

In these circumstances, the emphasis on individual creativity in the new Fun- **13.70** damentals was hardly surprising. Nevertheless, the extent of the reforms was impressive. The revisions included a return to the exclusivity of the author's right over his work;[77] extensive provisions for the protection of the personal, 'moral' rights of the author that exceeded the internationally-accepted standard set by the Berne Convention;[78] and a right of use that stood in contrast both to the long-established principle of freedom of translation that dominated early Russian copyright, and to the idea of government control that became the accepted norm after Soviet accession to the Universal Copyright Convention in 1973.[79] The Fundamentals were also generous with respect to the inheritability of rights. All of these reforms were aimed at assuring for authors a degree of independence in their work, and as such, the idea of copyright on which they were based was the notion of an author's individual right to 'freedom of creativity'. All of these changes continued to characterize Russian copyright under the 1993 Act.

---

[75] This line of discussion is not intended to underplay Khrushchev's denunciation of Stalin and the personality cult, a watershed moment in Soviet history. However, clear limits on both the acknowledgment of official responsibility and the direction of future change were already apparent in Khrushchev's 'Secret Speech': see Hosking, ibid 334–8.

[76] Hosking, ibid 458–9.

[77] Fundamentals of Civil Legislation of the USSR and the Republics, *VSND i VS SSSR*, 1991 No 26, Item 773; available in English translation on Garant.

[78] Ibid.

[79] Ibid.

(2) The importance of moral rights for free creative expression

13.71 If any single feature of the 1991 revisions emphasized the closeness between authors' rights and freedom of expression, it was probably the importance given to the moral right of the author. Moral rights achieved an unprecedented level of recognition in this legislation. In some important respects, the 1993 Act scaled back the scope of moral rights in this law, although it also brought greater precision to some of the provisions it had proposed.

13.72 The treatment of moral rights in the 1991 Fundamentals came as a direct response to censorship issues. The author's right to the integrity of his work was unlimited by any burden of proof on the author—rather, events leading to an integrity rights claim are considered to be a prima facie violation of the right, while the burden of proving his innocence falls on the defendant in a moral rights claim. The author also had a distinct right to his name, reflecting the Soviet government practice of adopting or, alternatively, abusing the name and reputation of the author. Moral rights could be inherited; additionally, the provisions upheld the sometimes inconvenient, but doctrinally sound, principle of the inalienability of moral rights, which enjoyed perpetual protection under this law. It is telling that the author's general right to use his own work also had an important moral dimension, no doubt, reflecting the Soviet government's history of involvement in works of creative authorship.

13.73 The integrity right was defined in precise and unusually strong terms in the 1991 Fundamentals, and merits special mention. In contrast to international formulae, it was defined simply as the right of the author 'to keep his or her work intact'. This right seems to be even more far-reaching than the idea of a right to the 'inviolability' of a work under Soviet law. Inviolability, though strong, seems a more general concept; on the other hand, the obligation to keep a work 'intact' is an utterly unambiguous indication that any alteration of the work without the author's consent, even where undertaken by a publishing house, is prohibited. The omission of 'prejudice to honour or reputation', an important departure from Article 6*bis* of the Berne Convention, is retained from the Soviet legislation, but given new life in the 1991 Fundamentals. This expression of the right of integrity responds fundamentally to censorship under the Soviet regime and, as such, seems even more significant than in jurisdictions with traditionally strong moral rights protection, such as France.

Finally, the Fundamentals take the unusual step of protecting the moral **13.74** rights of performers—a measure that would bring them into step with the most advanced copyright instruments currently in international law, the WIPO Internet Treaties.[80] Article 141.1 of the Fundamentals provided that performers, actors, stage managers, and conductors would all have a right to the protection of their name, as well as a right to the protection of their 'performance or rendition' from distortion. Performers have traditionally been viewed as 'disseminators' of the works of composers, rather than creators and authors in their own right. The decision to protect performers' moral rights carried the Soviet Union forward into the vanguard of a new development in the area of moral rights.

The extensive protection of moral rights in the 1991 Fundamentals demon- **13.75** strates the perception of Gorbachev's administration that the government needed to make amends for the oppressive treatment of authors and artists under the earlier Soviet regime. In fact, the close overlap between moral rights and principles of freedom of expression made them an ideal vehicle for the government's new policy. The right of integrity reflected a new approach to State censorship, while rights to name, reputation, and use responded to the earlier experience of government manipulation, control, and vilification.

Above all, moral rights were an expression of the individual rights of authors **13.76** —rights that, like fundamental human rights, were inalienable and unlimited by time restrictions. The Gorbachev administration clearly saw this aspect of copyright as being very closely allied to the protection of freedom of expression, and accordingly, gave it emphasis in legal reform.

(3) The public interest in culture and heritage

In the area of moral rights, the 1993 Act greatly restricted the scope of the **13.77** author's right of integrity. In its extensive treatment of this right, the Fundamentals closely followed an emphasis on preserving the state of cultural heritage which had long characterized Soviet jurisprudence, and reflected the traditional closeness between authors' rights and human rights. The new provision is succinctly summarized by Russian lawyer, Igor Pozhitkov: 'The

---

[80] The WIPO Copyright Treaty (WCT) and the WIPO Performances and Phonograms Treaty (WPPT).

right to integrity was rescinded and substituted by the right to protection of an author's reputation [in the 1993 Copyright Act] which permits him to object to any distortion of a work or any derogatory action in relation thereto [that is "liable to prejudice his honour or dignity"]. It remains to be seen how broadly the courts will interpret this provision.'[81] However, the 1993 Act further develops provisions in the 1991 legislation that hinted at the adoption of special measures for preserving the integrity of cultural heritage. This particular issue was intensely felt by the Soviet public, which had been victimized by the distortion of historical truth and the destruction of cultural heritage under a regime that specialized in the creation of 'memory holes', and looked upon the vilification of authors as the legitimate exercise of political power.

13.78 The Russian Copyright Act of 1993 is quite original in addressing the vulnerability of the public domain, which is ultimately the most important repository of cultural heritage in any country. The Act addresses the role of copyright in the protection of the public domain. It is based on the understanding that the importance of moral rights does not evaporate when copyright in creative works expires and they enter the public domain. Rather, moral rights in public domain works assume a broader significance for the preservation of cultural heritage.

13.79 In a country like post-Communist Russia, where the integrity of works as well as the integrity of authorship, attribution, and reputation were historically vulnerable to attack by the State, the continued protection of moral rights in the public domain may have considerable value. Article 28.2 states that the three main moral rights of authorship, name, and reputation must be respected by those using works in the public domain. Article 28.3 sets up a *domaine public payant* scheme for collecting a special royalty from public domain works to be paid into 'an authors' professional fund or to an organization for the collective administration of the economic rights of authors'. The scheme could contribute to the welfare of the post-Soviet creative

---

[81] I Pozhitkov, 'Copyright and Neighbouring Rights Protection in the Russian Federation' (1994) 20(1) Rev of Central & East European L 53, 63. However, he goes on to observe: 'Since in the past there was no concept of monetary compensation for moral damage, authors did not usually submit the issues of violations of their moral rights to courts.' This analysis of the reasons why moral rights claims did not find their way into the Soviet courtrooms is slightly surprising, both from the perspective of moral rights doctrine, and in view of the altruistic reputation of the Soviet dissident community.

community. It also has the symbolic value of representing a benefit flowing from the repression of past writers to future generations of authors. However, details of the plan, including the identity of those who will be entitled to benefit and the manner in which the funds are to be spent, still need to be worked out in greater detail.[82]

One more aspect of the protection of moral rights after the author's death is noteworthy. Article 27.5 provides for the protection of copyright and moral rights in the case of an author who has been 'rehabilitated posthumously after having been the subject of repressive measures'. In effect, this provision attempts to compensate the successors of authors who have not enjoyed the benefit of their rights during their lifetime by providing that the copyright term shall, in their case, begin on January 1 of the year following the rehabilitation decree. Since the repression of authors, leading to the denial of their legal rights, was widespread during Soviet rule, this provision is an important gesture of reconciliation, and may also have practical implications for authors' descendants, and for their reputations. **13.80**

(4) A new knowledge regime

All of these changes emphasize the socialist legacy of cultural oppression, which has led post-socialist reformers to attempt to codify in legislation the close connections between authorship rights and free expression experienced in practice by Soviet society. However, a consideration of the post-socialist relationship between copyright and free speech would not be complete without noting the remarkable penetration of copyright-related issues into almost every layer of Russian society. The breadth of these concerns is reflected in the wide-ranging legal treatment of copyright issues, which permeate the Russian legal system. For example, issues related to copyright can be found in a wide variety of Russian public and private legislation touching on the treatment of information, from criminal law regulations to privacy law. This situation attests to the complex impact of copyright issues on Russian society, and the importance of freedom and individual rights as a common thread running through Russian law reform. However, it has also **13.81**

---

[82] An interesting discussion of a *domaine public payant* scheme recently proposed in Germany may be found in A Dietz, 'Term of Protection in Copyright Law and Paying Public Domain: A New German Initiative' (2000) 22(11) EIPR 506, 508–11.

led to difficult practical problems in locating provisions relating to authorship within the Russian legal structure.

13.82 Russian intellectual property rights confront the peculiar 'transitional' difficulty of moving out of an authoritarian system of government based on ideological control, where the manipulation of knowledge, information, and culture was the chief means of maintaining political power and legitimacy, to a society based on ideals of intellectual and expressive freedom, and ideological diversity. The legal framework for controlling these intangibles may be understood as a 'knowledge regime'. The movement out of an authoritarian system of knowledge management is an important part of the transition process. Russia's new knowledge regime must aspire to compatibility with democratic institutions and values.

13.83 Increasingly, copyright law is a prominent feature of knowledge policy. New copyright laws will have to respond to concerns about the protection of intellectual freedom, the encouragement of creativity and innovation among long-oppressed populations, and appropriate limitations on the power of the State to control information and knowledge.

13.84 The post-socialist treatment of copyright needs to attempt this project on two levels. First, copyright should be part of the framework that protects information from manipulation and abuse, particularly by the State, but also, in the post-socialist era of globalization, by private entities and individuals against one another.[83] Specific concerns that copyright needs to address include rights of privacy, access to information, protection for broadcasting and communications media, and the rehabilitation of creative authors and intellectuals who suffered censure in the authoritarian period. Copyright law has a role to play in all of these areas, especially in relation to the individual rights of authors.

13.85 Secondly, new copyright provisions should reflect the aspirations of post-socialist societies for the future, and ensure that the information policies of post-socialist governments help to further political, social, and economic

---

[83] For example, in Russia, information must be protected from corporate abuse and organized crime. The realities of business and crime in today's Russia are described in 'States within the state' and 'Russia: A reconditioned model', in *The Economist*, Survey on Russia, 19 July 2001.

development. The new laws must demonstrate their practical effectiveness in building an appropriate framework for liberalization, but they must also seek to recover the moral stature that was compromised by the degraded legal practices of authoritarian States. The importance of restoring moral authority to copyright law should not be underestimated. It is perhaps the failure of copyright reform to address this particular issue, to date, that is largely responsible for the resistance of the Russian public to many aspects of modern copyright regulation.[84] Indeed, for a variety of reasons, the failure of moral authority is a serious flaw at the heart of modern approaches to copyright law, a problem that has yet to be adequately explored in its psychological or economic dimensions.

E. Conclusion: A New International Model

Recent discussion of free speech issues in the industrialized world has focused **13.86** on the potential conflict between the rights of authors and those of the public. This debate has largely been fuelled by the intrusion of copyright into the technological sphere. In the hands of corporations, which qualify for copyright protection under the guise of authorship, copyright presents a threat to growth and freedom at both ends of the social spectrum, from technology to culture. This conflict is still more intense in developing countries, where access to technology, on the one hand, and the preservation of culture, on the other, are issues of pressing concern. For developing countries, excessive and inappropriate copyright protection is seen as an obstacle to technological progress. It also presents the disturbing spectacle of corporate interests overtaking culture in all its forms.

The new power of copyright has been condemned by many observers as an **13.87** affront to free speech. However, activists in the cause of freedom of expression have been too quick to discard copyright as a whole. What seems clear and undeniable is that the current model of copyright protection has become unable to meet the needs of society—interestingly, a situation that is equally

---

[84] A blatant example: Russia is a world leader in copyright 'piracy'. See the discussion in C Neigel, 'Piracy in Russia and China: A Different US Reaction' (2000) 63 L & Contemporary Problems 179.

characteristic of both the industrialized and the developing worlds. At the same time, the power of vested interests in the current copyright framework is so great that the discussion of alternative views is not encouraged.

13.88 Given the international stalemate, a consideration of the socialist experience of copyright law is illuminating. As illustrated by the Russian example, the confrontation between a State whose political legitimacy was based on the control of ideas, and authors whose trade lay in the diversity of ideas, led to a different understanding of copyright law. The current international model emphasizes the commercial and corporate faces of copyright. The purpose of this model is to secure the return on investments in innovation, while, usually in the name of the author, corporations reap the benefits of the work of their employees. In contrast, the Soviet experience highlights the exploitation of information and knowledge by the powerful and the unscrupulous, while it also reveals the largely unsung heroism of creative people who attempted to maintain standards of truth and integrity. The history of socialist copyright emphasizes copyright law as a kind of right to 'freedom of creativity' for authors, and the corresponding importance for society as a whole of protecting the activities of authors and, thereby, encouraging ideological diversity and freedom of thought and expression.

13.89 In many ways, the contemporary model of copyright law is now an 'author's right without authors'.[85] The degradation of the concept of creative authorship threatens to impoverish society as a whole. The destruction of authorship —with its privileges and responsibilities, and its ability to expand with technology and culture into new and different forms—lies at the heart of copyright's moral vacuum. The expropriation of copyright from authors is a major factor underlying the breakdown of the relationship between creative people and their public, and it has led to a corresponding, possibly irrevocable, loss of credibility for copyright law. Ironically, at precisely the moment when technological and economic trends pose an unprecedented threat to

---

[85] The phrase is coined by J Ralite, 'Vers un droit d'auteur sans auteurs', *Le Monde diplomatique* (March 1998) 5, 6. An English version of the article is available; see, B Wilson (tr) 'Are authors about to lose their rights?', special issue on 'The Dangers of the Multilateral Agreement on Investment', *Le Monde diplomatique* online: <http://mondediplo.com/1998/03/09maira>.

creativity and culture around the world, the potential role of copyright in strengthening and supporting creative values threatens to disappear.[86]

In contrast to the prevailing view, the complementary nature of copyright **13.90** and creativity are emphasized by the socialist legacy of repression, and find expression in post-socialist copyright reform. However, the overwhelming pressure to satisfy international requirements has had a severe impact on the ability of 'transitional' countries, particularly Russia, to develop this perspective in their copyright law. Nevertheless, the importance given to copyright as an element of freedom of expression, and its role in the development of a new approach to knowledge, represents an important new perspective. In an era where corporate power on a global scale seems largely to have replaced the power of the State over cultural and social affairs, it appears ill-advised to neglect copyright's potential for maintaining the integrity of free speech against corporate interests. This objective serves both authors and the interest of the public, as a whole, in cultural vitality.

In the alternative, will a 'copyright without authors' ultimately reflect a society **13.91** without culture?

---

[86] It should be noted that the absence of suitable regulation also makes it difficult for authors to make use of the unprecedented opportunities for creative expression that form part of the global landscape. Some of these are discussed in MT Sundara Rajan, 'Moral Rights in the Digital Age: New Possibilities for the Democratisation of Culture' (2002) 16(2) Intl Rev of L, Computers & Technology 187.

Part III

THE DIGITAL WORLD

14

FIRST AMENDMENT SPEECH AND THE DIGITAL MILLENNIUM COPYRIGHT ACT: A PROPER MARRIAGE

Raymond T Nimmer

A. Introduction

During the past three decades, our world has experienced the greatest explo- **14.01** sion in innovation and the dissemination of information ever seen. Not coincidentally, this period also involved an expansion of intellectual property and other rights in information. Largely ignoring the connection between these two events, however, a group of academics and members of the public insistently campaign for narrowing property rights in information and retrenchment in areas of law such as copyright. The arguments take many forms, but have one thing in common—an insistence that the creation and enforcement of strong rights in information stifles, rather than supports, innovation and information growth and will continue to do so unless checked by courts, legislatures, governmental agencies, or any other available source.

14.02 This argument has spilled onto many different issues, including the topic that is the focus of this chapter—the anti-circumvention rules of the Digital Millennium Copyright Act (DMCA).[1] These rules make it illegal to circumvent technology that restricts access to copyrighted works and, in some cases, to manufacture or traffic in technology or devices that enable such circumvention. Here, it is asked 'What is the relationship between these aspects of the DMCA and free speech?'

14.03 The answer involves two parts. Most obviously, the DMCA encourages and supports creative work and its dissemination. In most cases, the creation and dissemination of copyrighted works is speech. In this respect, then, the DMCA supports First Amendment norms. Indeed, its core purpose is to promote speech by enhancing options for speakers and supporting their choice of how to make their speech available to others. As shown below, the DMCA rules address a reality created by modern information technology that makes possible rapid copying and dissemination of perfect, unauthorized copies of creative works. That technology shifted the scales that once balanced copyright law. The DMCA seeks to restate the balance and to restore the incentives promoting innovation and creative works. The DMCA does not restrict the availability of creative works, but increases it.

14.04 Secondly, in some circumstances, the DMCA allows private or government action against conduct that might otherwise undermine the incentives historically employed in law to encourage creativity and published speech. It is here that some opponents of property rights ('rights restrictors')[2] focus, arguing that any control stifles speech.[3] But the argument misses the mark unless one accepts that the policy supported by the rights restrictors—lesser rights are better—should be enshrined as mandatory law. In fact, in most

---

[1] 17 USC s 1201.

[2] See PM Schwartz & WM Treanor, '*Eldred* and *Lochner*: Copyright Term Extension and Intellectual Property as Constitutional Property' 112 Yale L J 2331 (2003).

[3] The rights-restrictors' arguments constantly mutate. In effect, they support a policy in search of a means of implementation. Whether discussing copyright term extension, the DMCA, software protection, contract law, First Amendment, fair use, or any other issue, the

cases, DMCA-regulated conduct does not involve speech and, to the extent that it does, it properly focuses on conduct elements in a content-neutral manner despite any incidental (minor) impact on speech.

This chapter proceeds in three parts. The second section briefly examines **14.05** the complex relationship between law and innovation and then discusses what the DMCA actually provides. There has been an amazing amount of disinformation about the scope of the DMCA. However, on examination, the Act is a relatively narrow statute that seeks to reinstate or enhance incentives that intellectual property law has long provided to encourage creative speech in a complex framework of influences on innovation. While a rights-restrictive argument assumes that each right granted to a copyright owner takes from the public, the truth is quite different and enhanced protections under the DMCA are likely to create an increase in both proprietary and public domain information. The third section then turns to First Amendment issues, underscoring that most of the conduct affected by the DMCA is not speech. To the extent that speech is adversely impacted by DMCA rules, the proper constitutional standard treats the DMCA as a content-neutral regulation that can be sustained unless it affects substantially more speech than is necessary to achieve the governmental objective. The final section demonstrates that the DMCA meets that test.

B. The DMCA and Innovation Policy

(1) Innovation and law

Every society has an interest in promoting innovation and the dissemination **14.06** of creative ideas, products, and technology. That societal interest has been heightened in recent years by the increasing emphasis in commerce and elsewhere on the use and distribution of information.

---

premise remains constant. One writer commented that, in this view, in a conflict between copyright and any other social value, the 'other' value prevails. See JV Delong, 'Defending Intellectual Property' in A Thierer and C Wayne Crews Jr (eds), *Copy Fights: The Future of Intellectual Property in the Information Age* (Washington DC: Cato Institute, 2002) 17, 19.

14.07 Despite its social importance, the exact way in which law interacts with private creativity and the availability of information for use in commerce and elsewhere is unclear.[4] How law can support innovation and speech is a complex question that has become controversial. In modern history, however, one part of the overall approach has involved laws recognizing proprietary rights in innovative subject matter. These property rights have varied over the years as technology has changed, but they reflect both the fact that the rights create incentives to create and disseminate, and the fact that the speaker has a right to control uses of its own creative product. Laws of this type also reinforce social norms that informational subject matter is, and has long been, an important, protected part of modern society.

14.08 Nevertheless, the rights restrictors advocate a view that rights should not be increased and, ultimately, that existing rights have gone too far and should be curtailed to enable social development. This literature is sufficiently well published and will not be restated here.[5] However, there are two themes that bear on the subject.

14.09 The first is the observation that proprietary rights often result in transactions that place the rights in the hands of large corporations. These corporations, the argument goes, should not be broadly protected because they have assets, and should not obtain enhanced rights, such as those established under the DMCA.[6] This view resonates in post-modern, populist, anti-big-business ideals. As a policy matter, there is little to be said for this view in a culture where commerce shapes parts of our lives and where the creative artist and speaker receives the benefit of the transactions and even large companies are fuelled by small or individual creators. As a First Amendment matter, the argument has the even greater vice of seeking to lock in an untested and radical viewpoint that rejects markets and market behaviour. Avoiding that lock-in is, in itself, a reason to approach the constitutional law aspect of the rights restrictors' arguments with scepticism.

---

[4] For one effort to explain the interaction, see WM Landes and RA Posner, *The Economic Structure of Intellectual Property Law* (Cambridge: Harvard University Press, 2003).

[5] For a list of articles, see PM Schwartz and WM Treanor, '*Eldred* and *Lochner*: Copyright Term Extension and Intellectual Property as Constitutional Property' (2003) 112 Yale L J 2331.

[6] For example, NW Netanel, 'Locating Copyright Within the First Amendment Skein' (2001) 54 Stanford L Rev 1, 34–5.

The second theme begins with the banal observation that creative works **14.10** build on the prior work of others. The political argument against property rights builds on this observation with a flawed syllogism: creative work depends on the work of others that is freely available for use; the creation of rights reduces what information is freely available; and, therefore, expansion of rights impedes the development of new creativity.[7] The syllogism assumes that publicly available (public domain) and privately owned (proprietary) information form a closed system—each increase in private control takes from the public, while each movement toward the public takes from the private. The assumption is grossly incomplete.

The relationship between law and the production and distribution of creative **14.11** works and information is a dynamic one, in which inputs and outputs are induced by a complex variety of factors. Some inputs will not occur unless an incentive and economic base exists for private parties to make and distribute new works; this incentive depends sometimes on whether an effective method exists to prevent others from copying and altering copies of the works. A not-produced and never-distributed work contributes to neither the public nor the private domain. More importantly, not all information in a proprietary work can be controlled by the rights owner. New *proprietary* works contribute to *both* the wealth of proprietary (controlled) information and to information in the public domain.[8] This is not a zero-sum game. Similarly, on the other side, information continuously passes out of use and into unavailability for most purposes. It does so for numerous reasons, one of which is overuse, another is simple lack of interest by any appreciable group of potential users.

Within this complex system, governmental action to preserve previously effec- **14.12** tive incentives is neither irrational nor clearly wrong. It is a reasonable approach to an important issue. That is what is attempted in the DMCA.

(2) What does the DMCA actually do?

The focus here is on free speech aspects of the DMCA. To deal with that **14.13** issue, it is necessary to understand the statute.

---

[7] See Y Benkler, 'Free as the Air to Common Use: First Amendment Constraints on Enclosure of the Public Domain' (1999) 74 New York U L Rev 354.

[8] See RP Wagner, 'Information Wants to be Free: Intellectual Property and the Mythologies of Control' (2003) 103 Columbia L Rev 995.

14.14 The DMCA proscribes three types of conduct. The core provision makes it illegal to circumvent a technological device that controls access to a copyrighted work.[9] There are several exceptions protecting, among other things, academic research and reverse engineering in some cases.[10]

14.15 This circumvention rule focuses on *conduct* (circumventing a technological device). It applies only to copies of a work that the rights owner has chosen to distribute in access-protected form. It thus lends legal support to a speaker's option that has always existed. No law requires distribution of speech or distribution of copies in a form that can be readily recopied in digital form. By supporting the speaker's options, the DMCA increases his or her incentive to speak by increasing the ability to choose how to distribute the work and also reinforces social norms protecting intellectual property. The existence of alternatives encourages speech.[11] If a potential speaker is limited to two choices, (1) not to disseminate at all, or (2) to disseminate with no effective limits on copying or modification of copies, the willingness to create and to distribute information will be less than if he or she were not so limited. Some of us all the time, and all of us some of the time, create, speak, and distribute information without charge or limitation. But there are many situations where speech will not occur unless control and potential rewards exist. It is in such cases that access controls operate. Whether anyone will acquire or listen to speech in the form the speaker chooses is best left to the marketplace.

14.16 The First Amendment and other civil liberties protect personal autonomy and choice. A balance needs to be struck, however, between the speaker and those who use his or her speech for their own purposes. Digital systems altered the balance in copyright law in a manner adverse to the author by allowing no cost, widespread, immediate, and perfect copying. Protecting access technology may reset the balance.

14.17 However, the DMCA does not give the rights owner control over all uses of his speech. For example, assume that an author distributes a digital book under technology that precludes some access and copying. The restriction limits how the user can access the information. Yet, the book would not be

---

[9] 17 USC s 1201(a).
[10] 17 USC s 1201(d)–(h).
[11] RT Nimmer, 'Licensing in the Contemporary Information Economy' (2002) 8 Washington U J of L and Policy 99.

distributed in this form unless others are willing to acquire it because under some conditions they can read or use the text. The protected restraint focuses only on limited uses. A person is not precluded from using the information learned, from discussing it, or from criticizing or lauding it.

In any case, where the speaker would not create or distribute copies if they **14.18** can be copied or modified, the DMCA produces an increase in both the overall amount of available proprietary information and public domain information. The increase to the public domain lies in the many uses of the information that neither the DMCA nor copyright law preclude.

The second and third types of conduct regulated by the DMCA involve **14.19** trafficking in technology or devices that circumvent technology that controls access to a work or that enforces rights under copyright law. Some argue that broad control over disseminating such technology may improperly stifle speech, but the Act is not broad and the narrowing features of it are important. The rules on access device trafficking[12] state that

1) no person shall *manufacture, import, offer to the public, provide, or otherwise traffic* in,
2) a *technology, product, service, device*, component, or part thereof, that
3) is *primarily designed* or produced for the purpose of circumventing, has *only limited* commercially significant purpose or use other than to circumvent, or *is marketed* for use in circumventing
4) a technological measure that effectively controls access to a work protected under this title.

Factual issues relating to the reasons why a person created or distributed a device will arise in applying these rules. However, such distinctions are the essence of First Amendment jurisprudence.

Because the first three elements contain subparts, the statute is complex **14.20** and may seem to cover more than it does. Yet, the statutory language limits the trafficking rules to manufacturing or trafficking in a 'technology, product, service, device [or] component,' and only if that occurs under stated limited conditions. This concerns products and technologies distributed for the purpose of use in achieving circumvention, not for purpose of academic or other research, nor for purposes of public debate.

---

[12] 17 USC s 1201(a).

C. First Amendment Issues

(1) First Amendment issues generally

14.21 In a world in which technology enables immediate and perfect copies of speech to be made and distributed, protecting exclusive rights in digital information in fact requires a focus not only on copying or other infringement, but also on the means to make, modify, and distribute copies. Speakers and authors of information have an interest in being able to place limited fences around their works to protect their rights and to shape how their speech is communicated to, or withheld from, others if they so choose. But how does this square with rules protecting free speech?

14.22 US First Amendment law engages a variety of balancing tests and themes that constrain regulation of speech in favour of preserving robust political, educational, and similar speech, but that also balance the scope of protection with other important social interests. The closer a regulation reaches in affecting the content of public discourse, the more likely that the regulation will be subject to close, often invalidating, scrutiny. The further removed the law is from that type of impact, the more likely it is to receive validating scrutiny.

14.23 The themes of protected speech and of permitted regulation are both central to free speech law. When applied to the DMCA, it becomes clear that the statute is consistent with First Amendment norms and that some of the abuses that some believe might arise under the DMCA would not be sustainable under *either* the DMCA or the First Amendment.

14.24 Copyright and the First Amendment have long coexisted, even though copyright law restricts what parties can and cannot do with information created by other speakers.[13] That long-term relationship recognizes that rights under copyright law enhance and encourage creative speech, while the restrictions copyright places on the ability of others to express their own ideas are relatively minor restrictions on form as opposed to ideas. The issue is whether the DMCA, which deals with copyrighted works in a manner different from traditional copyright law, wrongfully impinges on protected First Amendment interests. It does not.

---

[13] *Eldred v Ashcroft* 537 US 186 (2003).

(2) Is the subject matter protected speech?

First Amendment doctrine balances governmental power and the restraints **14.25** on that power that preserve fundamental speech rights. One issue that underlies all of this is whether or not a particular law or regulation restricts speech at all. That is where this discussion on the DMCA will begin.

The DMCA enhances options available for speakers and supports their **14.26** choice of how to make their speech available to others. To do so, it creates rights to prevent circumvention and trafficking in circumvention technology. Some of that regulated conduct involves speech, but most of it does not.

Speech and actor's purpose

Speech is *expressive* behaviour. In most cases, the expressive component comes **14.27** in words, sounds, or images. In other cases, speech entails conduct, such as dance, miming, or burning a flag. Speech is behaviour that intends to communicate ideas, emotions, or other content to other persons. This requires that the actor use symbols, sounds, or conduct with the intent to communicate to humans.

Especially for conduct not ordinarily associated with expressive behaviour, **14.28** courts have struggled to establish the appropriate standards to determine whether speech, rather than mere conduct, is present and whether a particular law regulates speech as compared to conduct. There is general agreement, however, that whether the communicative intent required is present depends on the circumstances in which the conduct occurs and the purposes of the actor. A person that takes an axe to a log in the forest to obtain firewood is engaged in functional (non-speech) behaviour (chopping wood), while a person that uses an axe to cut a piece of wood during a stage play on the beauty of physical labour may well be engaged in speech, especially if there is a stylized or emotive aspect attached to the activity. The same conduct can be speech in one context and non-speech in another. Burning a flag may be speech if done as part of a political demonstration, or it may be mere conduct if done solely to dispose of a tattered item.

The leading case on the distinction between speech and conduct in the USA **14.29** is *United States v O'Brien*.[14] In *O'Brien*, the defendant destroyed a selective

---

[14] *United States v O'Brien* 391 US 367 (1968).

service card as a symbolic act of protest. The court rejected the argument that punishment for this conduct offended the First Amendment:

> We cannot accept the view that an apparently limitless variety of conduct can be labeled 'speech' whenever the person engaging in the conduct intends thereby to express an idea. However, even [if] the alleged communicative element in O'Brien's conduct [brings] into play the First Amendment, it does not necessarily follow that the destruction of a registration certificate is constitutionally protected activity. [When] 'speech' and 'non-speech' elements are combined in the same course of conduct, a sufficiently important governmental interest in regulating the non-speech element can justify incidental limitations on First Amendment freedoms.[15]

Not all conduct is speech, even if the actor has a point to make. Conduct with some speech element in it can be regulated pursuant to important governmental goals, even if an incidental impact on speech occurs.

Actual circumvention as conduct

14.30 Is actual circumvention of technology speech? In most cases the answer is no. Circumventing a technological control is a functional act with a functional goal—to obtain access to, or use of, a work by defeating the control technology. That conduct typically entails no expressive purpose or intent. The actor does not intend to express ideas to others by the conduct, but rather to achieve a functional result. Like the axe-wielding person in the forest, the person that circumvents an access control device is not by that conduct automatically engaging in expressive activity. There is typically no communicative intent in the conduct.

14.31 The nature of the conduct does not change simply because the person engaged in the circumvention does so with the intent of using the information accessed to create the person's own speech. That ultimate use of the information may or may not be speech. For example, merely making a back-up copy is not constitutionally protected speech. Even so, the DMCA does not regulate *uses* of works, leaving that to other law. Indeed, the DMCA specifically disavows any intent to alter fair use or to change rights under copyright law.[16] Under copyright law, some copying of a protected work constitutes fair use, while some uses do not engage copyright law at all, but

---

[15] Ibid 376.
[16] 17 USC s 1201(c)(1).

other uses are infringement. The DMCA does not change that calculus. It regulates only the act of circumvention or trafficking in circumvention devices.

In some circumstances, the First Amendment creates a right of access in **14.32** order to allow speech to occur. Most such cases, however, focus on access to physical places or to governmental information, public hearings, trials, or the like. But these are not DMCA issues. The First Amendment does not create a right of access to information held by a private party simply because the accessing person desires to copy or use the information for their own purpose. Interests in personal autonomy, property rights, and a simple right not to speak, foreclose such claims. Indeed, the right not to speak or to do so anonymously is well established.[17]

As discussed later, some have argued that the circumvention rules preclude **14.33** speech because they limit access for fair use of a work. As a constitutional issue, that argument fails. More importantly, since the DMCA encourages distribution of digital works, it actually increases access. DMCA limitations focus only on devices that control limited types of use of a *copy*. The information on the copy is available, unless one visualizes, for example, a motion picture distributed under a technology that precludes *all* access at *all* times by *all* persons—an improbable image.

Trafficking: computer programs as speech

In addition to actual circumvention, the DMCA regulates some manufac- **14.34** turing, trafficking in, or distribution of circumvention *technology* or *devices*.[18] In practice, this will most often entail computer programs or devices containing them. Thus, the regulated conduct is manufacturing, trafficking in, or distributing certain computer programs or devices containing them. It is thus necessary to ask whether (or when) dissemination of computer code is speech before asking whether DMCA rules affecting this conduct are permissible under a First Amendment analysis.

Dissemination of computer programs can occur in many ways and for many **14.35** different purposes, not all of which qualify as speech, but some of which may.

---

[17] *Tattered Cover, Inc v City of Thornton* 44 P 3d 1044 (Colorado Sup Ct, 2002).
[18] 17 USC s 1201(b).

Compare, for example, a public reading of source code to an audience of programmers and the use of code to operate a machine. The reading resonates in speech, but use in the machine by the owner does not if the use is not communicative in nature.

14.36 Most courts facing the issue hold that distribution of programs *can be* speech even if the code is in machine form for direct use in a computer. Deciding whether particular conduct constitutes speech requires asking why the alleged speaker engaged in the conduct. The issue can be illustrated by comparing two decisions of the Court of Appeals of the Second Circuit.

14.37 In *Commodity Futures Trading Commission v Vartuli*,[19] the court held that software (called 'Recurrence') as marketed could be subject to rules requiring prior registration of commodities advisors. The program instructed clients when to trade commodities futures. Arguably, registration could not be required of parties engaged in pure speech, but the software *as marketed* was not exempt because it was to be used in an entirely mechanical way—the user was simply to follow instructions to trade or not trade: 'In other words, the fact that the system used words as triggers and a human being as a conduit, rather than programming commands as triggers and semi-conductors as a conduit, appears to us to be irrelevant for purposes of this analysis.'[20]

14.38 This is questionable jurisprudence, but *Vartuli* emphasizes that method and intent matter in distinguishing speech from mere conduct. One year later, *Universal City Studios, Inc v Corley* came closer to getting the analysis right.[21] *Corley* involved a DMCA injunction against the distribution of circumvention code. The court held that the injunction was enforceable, but that distributing computer code in this case was speech. It is the conveying of information to humans that makes distribution of computer programs 'speech'. The court observed:

> [Programmers] communicating ideas to one another almost inevitably communicate in code . . . Limiting First Amendment protection of programmers to descriptions of computer code (but not the code itself) would impede discourse among computer scholars . . . Instructions that communicate informa-

---

[19] *Commodity Futures Trading Commission v Vartuli* 228 F 3d 94 (US Ct of Apps (2nd Cir), 2000).

[20] Ibid 111–2.

[21] *Universal City Studios, Inc v Corley* 273 F 3d 429 (US Ct of Apps (2nd Cir), 2001).

tion comprehensible to a human qualify as speech whether the instructions are designed for execution by a computer or a human (or both). . . . *Vartuli* considered two ways in which a programmer might be said to communicate through code: to the user of the program (not necessarily protected) and to the computer (never protected). . . . Since *Vartuli* limited its constitutional scrutiny to the code 'as marketed,' *ie*, as an automatic trading system, it did not have occasion to consider a third manner in which a programmer might communicate through code: to another programmer.[22]

Code can communicate to humans for purposes of free speech analysis in many different ways. *Corley* reflects the view of other courts that have considered the issue. Computer code can receive First Amendment protection depending on the purpose in distributing it.[23]

(3) *Content neutrality, function, and regulation*

As has been seen, while much of the conduct affected by the DMCA is not **14.39** speech, some of it may be speech. Even as to affected speech, however, the First Amendment does not necessarily bar regulation. The governmental purpose, the actor's intent, and the nature of the speech all shape the First Amendment analysis.

Content neutrality

If a regulation affects speech, the most significant issue in determining how **14.40** free speech concepts apply is whether the regulation is content-based or content-neutral. A content-based regulation is one in which the government takes sides in a political, social, or similar discussion by discriminating based on the *content* of a speaker's viewpoint.[24] This sides-taking touches the core of the First Amendment. The goal of free speech is to ensure an open marketplace of ideas and speech free of governmental control. Content-based regulations are suspect under US law and invoke what is described as 'strict scrutiny' by courts. This often invalidates the law because validity under

---

[22] Ibid 446.

[23] See *Junger v Daley* 209 F 3d 481 (US Ct of Apps (6th Cir), 2000).

[24] See NW Netanel, 'Locating Copyright Within the First Amendment Skein' (2001) 54 Stanford L Rev 1, 34–5. ('First Amendment jurisprudence posits that, at least when exercising its regulatory power, government ought to serve as a neutral umpire in citizens' public discourse.').

strict scrutiny requires not only that there be a strong policy supporting the regulation, but also that the means used to achieve the policy is the least restrictive of speech. In effect, the court closely reviews both the purpose of the law and its method.

14.41 Content-neutral laws receive far less scrutiny because they do not place the government in support of, or in opposition to, a particular viewpoint in a public discussion. As one court noted: '[if the regulation] does not involve government censorship of the subject matter or governmental favoritism among different viewpoints, it is content-neutral and not subject to strict scrutiny.'[25] Content-neutral regulation is permitted if it serves a substantial governmental interest unrelated to the suppression of speech and is tailored so as not to burden substantially more speech than is necessary to further that interest.[26]

14.42 The question thus becomes whether, to the extent it regulates speech, the DMCA is content-based or content-neutral. The primary factor defining content neutrality is whether the government adopted the regulation without reference to the viewpoint expressed. The government's purpose is the controlling consideration. A regulation is content-based only if the government adopted it 'because of disagreement with [or support for] the message [the speech] conveys'.[27] A regulation that serves purposes unrelated to suppressing viewpoints is neutral even if it has an incidental effect on some speakers or messages but not others.[28]

14.43 Content neutrality, thus, does not mean that no subject matter is singled out, but that regulations operate without reference to the viewpoint expressed. In practice, many cases centre on place, manner, and time regulations, but content neutrality also applies to regulations focusing on conduct even if the conduct has a speech component, so long as the regulatory controls focus on the functional or conduct aspects.[29]

---

[25] *DVD Copy Control Association, Inc v Bunner* 75 P 3d 1 (California Sup Ct, 2003).

[26] *Universal City Studios, Inc v Corley* 273 F 3d 429 (US Ct of Apps (2nd Cir), 2001); *Turner Broadcasting System Inc v FCC* 5123 US 622, 662 (1994).

[27] *Ward v Rock Against Racism* 491 US 781, 791 (1989). See also *Hill v Colorado* 530 US 703, 720 (2000).

[28] *Turner Broadcasting System, Inc v FCC* 512 US 622 (1994).

[29] See NW Netanel, 'Locating Copyright Within the First Amendment Skein' (2001) 54 Stanford L Rev 1, 34–5.

The DMCA is content-neutral. Its restrictions on speech are incidental to **14.44** the statute's primary purpose. The governmental purpose is not to restrict discussion of encryption technology or of any particular viewpoint or approach as compared to others. Its purpose is to protect copyrighted works in order to promote dissemination of speech and the development of creative works. Copyright law creates a property right and a goal of the DMCA is to protect that property, a goal both significant and content-neutral. The goal is not to protect works containing one type of content while leaving other content unprotected, nor is the statute applicable to one type of circumvention technology and not others.

The Act does focus on particular types of technology, but that does not **14.45** characterize it as content-based. The California Supreme Court in *DVD Copy Control Association, Inc v Bunner*,[30] for example, affirmed an injunction under trade secret law against posting decryption code on the Internet, holding that the injunction was content neutral even though it referred to *distribution* of a *particular technology* with *particular content*. It was content-neutral because the purpose of the injunction was to protect a property right (the trade secret), rather than to suppress speech based on viewpoint. The court's analysis provides insights applicable to the DMCA:

> [The] injunction's restrictions on Bunner's speech 'properly are characterized as incidental to the primary' purpose of California's trade secret law—which is to promote and reward innovation and technological development and maintain commercial ethics. . . . [The] specific deprivation to be remedied is the misappropriation of a property interest in *information*. Thus, any injunction remedying this deprivation must refer to the content of that information in order to identify the property interest to be protected. . . . Because the preliminary injunction at issue here does not 'involve government censorship of subject matter or governmental favoritism among different viewpoints', it is content neutral and not subject to strict scrutiny.[31]

Content neutrality does not preclude identifying the informational subject matter addressed. To be content-neutral is not to take a position by hindering or helping expression of a viewpoint in the debate itself.[32]

---

[30] *DVD Copy Control Association, Inc v Bunner* 75 P 3d 1 (California Sup Ct, 2003).
[31] Ibid 878–9.
[32] See NW Netanel, 'Locating Copyright Within the First Amendment Skein' (2001) 54 Stanford L Rev 1, 34–5.

Character of the speech

14.46 In addition to content neutrality, courts look to the nature of the affected speech itself and the extent to which regulation of that speech implicates core First Amendment values. Not all expressive conduct is treated equally. Indeed, some expression is outside all First Amendment protection, such as obscenity and words intertwined in unlawful conduct. Thus, threats made with an immediate likelihood of being carried out are criminal, while a criminal conspiracy is not protected simply because it is made by use of words. Distribution of a computer virus with the intent to harm is criminal conduct, even if computer code may constitute speech in some cases. Some conduct affected by the DMCA, even if expressive, may fall within this type of exclusion from First Amendment protection.

14.47 Other types of expressive activity are recognized as speech, but receive less protection than political and artistic speech because of the subject matter. 'Commercial speech' is an illustration; commercial advertising receives less protection than political speech.[33] The explanation lies in the public interest in preventing misleading, fraudulent, or otherwise harmful *commercial* messages, and in the fact that commercial speech does not entail the political, cultural, or other substantive discourse that First Amendment protections primarily address. A commercial broadcast to tout a new beer is not intended to engage a public policy debate about alcohol, but to sell a product. While not evil, that intent does not receive the same protection as an anti-war speech because the latter lies more within the core of First Amendment concerns and because the commercial motivations for advertising may render it more resilient to regulation.

14.48 In general, courts often recognize distinctions among types of speech by imposing less stringent limitations on governmental action in cases involving what might be viewed as speech that lies less close to the core of First Amendment protection. This is relevant to the DMCA and points toward lesser constitutional restriction for a law focused on the use, manufacture,

---

[33] For example, *Central Hudson Gas & Elec Corp v Public Serv Comm'n* 447 US 557 (1980). What is meant by 'commercial speech' is under reconsideration in a manner that may affect our topic. See, eg, *Kasky v Nike, Inc* 45 P 3d 243 (California Sup Ct, 2003) (on a 4–3 vote, the court held that a public relations campaign by a corporation with respect to labour practices was commercial speech), cert gr 537 US 1099 (2003) and cert dism as improvidently granted, 539 US 654 (2003) (three Justices dissent from dismissal with a written opinion).

and distribution of technology or devices. The Second Circuit in *Corley*, for example, emphasized the functional nature of computer code in affirming a DMCA injunction. The comments of the California Supreme Court in *DVD Copy Control Association, Inc v Bunner*[34] are also relevant. The court upheld an injunction against Internet posting of DeCSS decryption code. The defendant had argued that his disclosure of the code was part of a debate on issues of public interest. Rejecting this argument, the court observed:

> [The] content of the trade secrets neither involves a matter of public concern nor implicates the core purpose of the First Amendment. . . . Plaintiff's] trade secrets in the CSS technology . . . convey *only* technical information about the method used by specific private entities to protect their intellectual property. Bunner posted these secrets . . . on the Internet so Linux users could enjoy and use DVD's and so others could improve the functional capabilities of DeCSS. He did not post them to comment on any public issue or to participate in any public debate. . . . Thus, these trade secrets . . . address matters of purely private concern and not matters of public importance. . . . Disclosure of this highly technical information adds nothing to the public debate over the use of encryption software or the DVD industry's efforts to limit unauthorized copying of movies on DVD's. And the injunction does not hamper Bunner's ability to 'discuss and debate' these issues.[35]

The court differentiates between function and public debate. The distinction is based on the intent of the party and the nature of the material distributed. The functionality of computer code affects the scope of its protection.

D. Standards Applied

(1) Permitted content-neutral regulation

The DMCA, in most cases, regulates pure conduct. Even if the affected **14.49** conduct is arguably communicative, however, the DMCA is content-neutral regulation of speech that is often primarily functional in purpose. In First Amendment parlance, content-neutral regulation receives an 'intermediate' level of scrutiny.[36] The DMCA passes that scrutiny.

---

[34] *DVD Copy Control Ass'n, Inc v Bunner* 75 P 3d 1 (California Sup Ct, 2003).
[35] Ibid 15–16.
[36] 'Intermediate' in the sense that it falls between the strict scrutiny of content-based regulation and the largely unlimited regulation of non-speech conduct or expression that falls outside the First Amendment—eg, obscenity.

14.50 A content-neutral law 1) must serve a substantial governmental interest, 2) the interest must be unrelated to the suppression of free expression, and 3) the restriction must not burden substantially more speech than is necessary to further that interest.[37] Content-neutral regulations are not invalid simply because they affect speech. The regulation is invalid only if it has adverse impact on substantially more speech than necessary to achieve its goals.

14.51 There is no doubt that the DMCA deals with a substantial governmental interest—promoting the creation and distribution of creative speech. It does so by protecting use of technology that allows access-protected copies of works to be distributed, reinforcing incentives for innovation, and supporting decisions of persons engaged in distributing or creating speech to do so under technological limitations. These are pro-speech objectives. None entails a desire to suppress speech. Any one of these objectives suffices as the substantial State interest that supports content-neutral regulation. Taken together, they more than suffice.

14.52 That brings us to the question whether the DMCA affects substantially more speech than necessary to further the governmental interest involved. The DMCA has received an unusually large amount of distorted commentary unrelated to the actual language of the statute. The result is a politically-contrived caricature of the DMCA, creating unwarranted fears. The proper place to turn is the statutory language. Do the actual provisions have an impact upon First Amendment speech, and is that impact substantially more than necessary to achieve the governmental goals involved?

14.53 The reality is that most conduct affected by the DMCA does not involve speech at all. This does not mean that all applications of the DMCA are immune from challenge, but it does suggest that the statute is largely pro-speech from a First Amendment vantage—it targets non-speech conduct in order to promote speech.

(2) Actual circumvention and fair use

14.54 With some exceptions, the DMCA makes it illegal to circumvent an access control technology used in a copy of a copyrighted work. But actually circum-

---

[37] *Turner Broadcasting System, Inc v FCC* 512 US 622 (1994).

venting a technology is most often not speech. It is conduct with a functional goal. That is true even if the goal is to undermine the use of the technology because the actor opposes it politically.

Some have argued that the DMCA forecloses the right of 'fair use' under **14.55** copyright law. But is fair use a right? While the argument that fair use is a right has been popular among rights-restrictors seeking to narrow copyright, no court has ever held that fair use is a *right* that cannot be altered or conveyed away. Fair use doctrine lies in equitable, not constitutional, considerations. But even if fair use were characterized as a right, that does not elevate that right to a constitutional mandate. Clearly, fair use is part of a package of copyright jurisprudence as a matter of policy. It is difficult, however, to find a basis to argue for a constitutional right with respect to many types of 'fair use', such as making a copy or giving a copy to a friend. The statute allows this in some cases, but this is not a constitutionally protected interest. The fact that a DMCA restraint may prevent the convenience of making a digital back-up copy does not override the important interests enhanced by DMCA protections as a constitutional matter.

Even if all 'fair use' is a constitutional right, the DMCA does not preclude **14.56** fair use. It does not address partial copying, commentary, or other conduct ordinarily associated with fair use. DMCA rules apply only if the distributor elects to use access controls and the purchaser acquired a copy subject to those controls. Yet, fair use jurisprudence ordinarily deals with cases in which a copy has been made available under terms that do not restrict use. The rights-restrictors' argument is, in fact, that there should be a right to copy (or modify) works *in digital form* regardless of the terms under which the copies were distributed. *Corley* rejected that policy argument, as did Congress and the US Copyright Office:

> We know of no authority for the proposition that fair use, as protected by the Copyright Act, much less the Constitution, guarantees copying by the optimum method or in the identical format of the original. . . . DMCA does not impose even an arguable limitation on the opportunity to make a variety of traditional fair uses of DVD movies, such as commenting on their content, quoting excerpts from their screenplays, and even recording portions of the video images and sounds on film or tape by pointing a camera . . . at a monitor as it displays the DVD movie. The fact that the resulting copy will not be as perfect or as manipulable as a digital copy obtained by having direct access to the DVD movie in its digital form provides no basis for a claim of unconstitutional limitation of fair use. . . . Fair use has never been held to be a guarantee

of access to copyrighted material in order to copy it by the fair user's preferred technique or in the format of the original.[38]

Technology may limit access to digital copies and preclude copying or modification in digital form, but this does not preclude other uses or means of excerpting or commenting. Fair use is not a right to take material in digital form merely because that is convenient.

14.57 There is no basis to argue that the DMCA enacts a total preclusion of fair use. To the contrary, it expressly preserves it. Indeed, it is likely that, by operation of the market or of courts reviewing cases of harmless conduct, even more flexibility will exist. But access in order to copy, alter, transmit, or display works in digital, as compared to other forms, is not a First Amendment right. Convenience is not a protected interest unless the inconvenient becomes the impossible. Even then, a speaker's right not to speak may outweigh any alleged right of the user to access, recreate, or modify the copy of it.

(3) Trafficking rules and the First Amendment

14.58 Trafficking in circumvention technology or devices may, in some cases, involve speech. But the scope of the DMCA here is narrow. The DMCA applies only to manufacture or distribution of 'technology' or 'devices' that 'circumvent' controls used in copyrighted works. This focuses on devices and technology and affects the expressive only indirectly (if at all). The language does not apply to academic or political discussion of circumvention as a policy or to a discussion of the methods involved.

14.59 In addition, the DMCA trafficking rules set out three limiting conditions that narrow the scope of the Act. Conduct is not covered unless it meets one of these conditions.

Designed primarily for circumvention

14.60 Under the first condition, manufacture, importation, or other trafficking in a technology or device is not within the DMCA unless the technology or device was designed or produced *primarily* to circumvent a control system.

---

[38] *Universal City Studios, Inc v Corley* 273 F 3d 429 (US Ct of Apps (2nd Cir), 2001) 459.

As has been seen, speech protection often turns on the purpose of the actor.   **14.61**
This first condition focuses on circumvention technology designed or produced with a functional purpose as its primary goal. The primary purpose
test clearly distinguishes between conduct and expressive purpose. It excludes
cases where speech is the primary or coequal purpose, covering only cases
where speech elements are incidental to a primary purpose of circumventing
access control technology. Manufacturing or distribution with a primary goal
other than circumvention does not violate the DMCA. For example, distribution of academic research, even if it contains code with a capacity to circumvent, is outside the scope because the research and its result were not done
with the primary purpose of circumventing a technology. The purpose was
research and intellectual advancement.

More difficult cases might arise if the violation involves a person that traffics   **14.62**
in a device or technology that was designed or produced primarily for the purpose of circumvention, but does so with a purpose other than circumvention
in mind. If that other purpose is not speech, no conflict arises. For example,
a person who 'offers to the public' a 'product' primarily designed for circumvention is not engaged in a protected act. Neither is a person who distributes
such a device to further his political goal of undermining circumvention
technology. In some few cases, however, the trafficking will entail protected
speech. In those cases, a balancing issue may arise. One cannot predict specific cases, but application of the DMCA regulation will often prevail as incidental regulation of speech essential to the achievement of the statutory
goals. As courts that have reviewed the DMCA have commented, enforcement of restraints against Internet distribution of circumvention technology
is the only means of implementing the statutory goals because of the immediate broad availability that Internet distribution creates.[39]

Limited other purpose

The second condition brings manufacturing, importation, offering to the   **14.63**
public, providing, and otherwise trafficking in a circumvention technology
or device within the DMCA, if the technology or device 'has only limited
commercially significant purpose or use *other than to circumvent*' a control
system.

---

[39]   *Universal City Studios, Inc v Corley* 273 F 3d 429 (US Ct of Apps (2nd Cir), 2001).

14.64 This rule adapts doctrine associated with contributory copyright infringement. Under that copyright doctrine, a manufacturer or distributor of a product can be held liable for another person's use of the product to infringe only if the product has no substantial non-infringing use. That rule was announced in the *Sony* case, a case grounded in concepts of fair use, rather than free speech.[40] Under it, for example, the manufacturer of a photocopy machine is not liable for contributory infringement if machines that it sells are used by third parties to infringe—the machines have substantial non-infringing uses. The contributory infringement doctrine has never been seriously challenged under the First Amendment because it deals with products (not speech) and because it achieves important goals while having little impact upon protected speech. The DMCA's trafficking rules yield a similar result. The statutory language changes the test, but leaves the policy intact. Distribution of technology or devices whose only realistic purpose is circumvention is precluded, but distribution of technology is not, even though the technology or product may in fact be used to circumvent. In effect, the lack of other significant uses indicates that enabling circumvention is the primary purpose.

14.65 The statute refers to 'commercially significant purpose'. The word 'commercial' creates some uncertainty. Does this require a profit-making purpose? One view is that this condition applies only if the manufacture or distribution had a profit-making purpose to begin with and asks whether there are significant purposes other than circumvention. The better alternative treats the reference to 'commercial' purposes as not being limited to money-making activity.[41] Of the two,[42] this better fits the statute since the three conditions refer to the general list of acts that are not limited to commercial activities. It sensibly creates a rule that asks whether the distributed (or manufactured) technology or device has significant other uses, creating a

---

[40] *Sony Corp of America v Universal City Studios, Inc* 464 US 417 (1984).

[41] See *A&M Records, Inc v Napster, Inc* 239 F 3d 1004 (US Ct of Apps (9th Cir), 2001) (posting works for exchange among private parties is commercial use).

[42] A third possibility is that the condition brings in all circumvention technology and devices, but excludes only those with a significant, non-circumvention, profit-making use. That would largely abrogate the other terms of the statute for all non-commercial technology, creating a result that under normal statutory interpretation rules should be avoided. That can hardly have been the intent.

parallel to the rule in condition one but focused on other objective evidence of intent.

Under either view, condition two focuses on conduct that has the primary **14.66** effect of providing circumvention. While in some cases there may be speech-related purposes involved, impact on that speech is incidental to the statutory purpose of precluding dissemination of devices to defeat circumvention technology in situations where the primary purpose of the technology, or its only significant commercial use (however interpreted), is circumvention of technology protecting copyrighted works.

Marketed for circumvention

The third condition brings manufacture or distribution of a technology or **14.67** device within the DMCA only if it is 'marketed by that person' for use in circumventing a control system.

The focus is on cases in which the actor distributes the technology or device **14.68** with the intent that it be used to circumvent. This brings into the DMCA only those cases where the actor's purpose involves marketing the device for use in circumvention. By its terms, it does not apply to any distribution for academic analysis, artistic interest, or other non-circumvention use. It applies if the purpose for which it is marketed includes circumvention—a prohibited act.

E. Conclusion

The relationship between law and innovation is complex and its balance has **14.69** been altered by digital systems for copying and disseminating information. Protecting the use of circumvention technology is a rational response to re-instating or maintaining the incentives to create and disseminate copyrighted works. The DMCA does that in a focused manner, the impact of which expands the wealth of both proprietary and public domain information.

The creation and dissemination of copyrighted works is typically speech **14.70** activity. Thus, the core purpose of the DMCA is pro-speech. The constitutional test of validity for the DMCA as content-neutral regulation is whether substantially more speech is regulated than is necessary to achieve the governmental purpose. In fact, as has been seen, most of the conduct affected by the DMCA is not speech.

14.71 Given the DMCA goal of protecting property rights and encouraging creative speech by protecting measures that control access, it is difficult to conceive of an effective alternative with a lesser impact on speech. In a world where the tools are digital and can be distributed universally in moments, dealing with both circumvention and distribution of circumvention technology or devices is important. The relationship between this approach and its intended effect was recognized in *Bunner*. The court there stated: 'The First Amendment does not prohibit courts from incidentally enjoining speech in order to protect a legitimate property right. . . . Bunner proffers, and we can think of, no less restrictive way of protecting an owner's constitutionally recognized property interest in its trade secrets.' The *Corley* court also noted the connection:

> Although the prohibition on posting prevents the Appellants from conveying to others the speech component of DeCSS, the Appellants have not suggested, much less shown, any technique for barring them from making this instantaneous worldwide distribution of a decryption code that makes a lesser restriction on the code's speech component. [A] content-neutral regulation need not employ the least restrictive means of accomplishing the governmental objective. It need only avoid burdening 'substantially more speech than is necessary to further the government's legitimate interests'.[43]

14.72 It has been possible for opponents to hypothesize extreme applications of the statute to bar all speech about encryption, all academic research on the issue, or to preclude ordinary uses of digital works by the persons to whom they are provided, but hypotheticals such as these require strained and problematic readings of the statutory language, and ignore both the commercial context and the First Amendment jurisprudence that would prevent such applications if attempted and would lead to interpretations that follow congressional purpose and protect actual speech. Stating that such risks exists is an interesting form of advocacy, but the actual risk of occurrence of such hypotheticals is not demonstrated by threats that are withdrawn or by legal actions that fail. Ultimately, the focus of the statute is clear and quite narrow. If grey areas exist, courts are charged with interpreting a statute to effectuate its purpose within proper constitutional limits.

---

[43] *Universal City Studios, Inc v Corley* 273 F 3d 429 (US Ct of Apps (2nd Cir), 2001).

Overall then, in the DMCA, there is an effort to reinforce incentives for **14.73** the creation and dissemination of creative works. While some might desire a policy that moves in the opposite direction and weakens incentives, the approach in the DMCA is more likely to achieve the goal of enhancing diversity, quality, and quantity of distributed speech in society.

15

CONTRACTING OUT OF COPYRIGHT IN THE INFORMATION SOCIETY: THE IMPACT ON FREEDOM OF EXPRESSION

Thomas Dreier

A. Introduction

Digital and networking technologies have substantially altered the world that **15.01** copyright seeks to regulate in at least two ways. On the one hand, copyright material is much more vulnerable to unauthorized taking, copying, and dissemination than ever before. From the perspective of authors and right-holders, this is very unappealing. However, from the perspective of users, there is a positive side to these developments because new technologies overcome restrictions upon the dissemination of copyright material that existed in an analogue world. On the other hand, the controlling grip of both copyright law and digital technology on both intermediate and end users has the potential to become much tighter in the digital and networked environment. This is because, when obtaining access to copyright material in digital form, a user inevitably undertakes acts of reproduction which are subject to the exclusive rights of the copyright owner. In a purely analogue world, this was of course not the case. The reading of books was a copyright-free activity, as was the viewing of theatrical plays or cinematographic works.

15.02 Digital technology turns the end user into a producer of the copy that he or she consumes. This development started with the advent of the magnetic tape, the video recorder, and the photocopier, and it has come to a logical end in the digital world. It follows that a law which, in an analogue world, largely placed restrictions only on the use of copyright works by commercial producers of copies, as well as those who broadcasted or publicly performed works, has been transformed into a law affecting end users. Hence, the freedom of a much greater number of people is at stake in the digital world. Moreover, digital technology does not only make copying easier. It also allows for technological protection measures (TPMs) which are capable of restricting or blocking access to, and use of, copyright material. These measures protecting copyright, and at times even non-copyright, material can have an impact upon the freedom of expression of users of works.

15.03 How then is it possible to 'contract out of copyright'? Of course, copyright cannot just be contracted away. Copyright is a legal right which applies as soon as a work fulfilling the criteria for legal protection comes into being. Furthermore, by virtue of international conventions in the field of copyright, particularly the prohibition on formalities and the principle of national treatment,[1] a work created by a national of a signatory to these conventions must be accorded protection in all other signatory states.

15.04 Owing to the way in which international copyright conventions have harmonized substantive legal rules, copyright protection in states adhering to these conventions has all the characteristics of a property right—at least in the case of the exploitation rights. Moral rights are, of course, a different matter. An author can use a work in any way he or she likes and can exclude third parties from performing the acts of use which copyright legislation exclusively reserves to him or her. Thus, for authors, there appears to be little chance of truly 'contracting out' of copyright. An author may wish to abandon his or her copyright, in the way in which an owner of tangible property can abandon that property by definitively giving up a claim to

---

[1] See Art 5(1) and (2) of the Revised Berne Convention.

possession and ownership. However, while tangible goods can be disposed of, it would appear that the same cannot be achieved with regard to intangible property. There is simply no object capable of disposal. Moreover, at least in countries within the 'author's right' tradition, the personal or 'moral' tie between an author and a work always remains. In some countries, this tie even remains for a time after the economic exploitation rights have come to an end.

However, for the purpose of this chapter, the concept of 'contracting out of **15.05** copyright' is used to refer to contractual deviations from the default rules of copyright which come into play when parties have not decided otherwise. Understood in this way, the activity of 'contracting out of copyright' is limited only to the extent that the law makes certain rules mandatory in their application. 'Contracting out' in this sense may arise in two different ways. One way of deviating from copyright's default rules is by loosening the grip of copyright's control. Conversely, it is also possible to tighten that grip. Where-as the former strategy could be employed by contracting one's rights away or simply by failing to exercise them, as in the diverse forms of free or open source software distribution and the creative commons model,[2] the latter strat-egy could be pursued through the imposition of contractual use restrictions on the user of a copyright work or through the restriction, or blocking, of use by means of TPMs.

Before the impact of these two strategies on freedom of expression is exam- **15.06** ined further, they must be investigated a little more closely.

B. Loosening the Grip of Copyright

As mentioned above, at least as far as the economic rights are concerned, an **15.07** author or right-holder can forgo much, if not all, of the copyright protection granted by law to his work. This may be achieved either by a traditional 'proprietary' exercise of exclusive rights or by way of a free or open source strategy.

Thus, exercising the 'proprietary' exclusivity of the prerogatives conferred **15.08** by law, an author may opt to grant licences to third parties. If the licence is an

---

[2] <http://creativecommons.org>.

exclusive one, then the powers emanating from copyright are merely transferred to someone else. Of course, the exclusivity attached to the use of a
particular work can be split with regard to different uses. The author may
also opt to grant non-exclusive licences. Such non-exclusive licences can
take the form of duly formulated, and sometimes even written, licensing
agreements between the right-holder and the user. Alternatively, for example,
where an author or right-holder posts works on the Internet without technological protection against access, downloading, and copying, he or she can be
assumed to have given implied consent to certain limited acts, such as downloading, storing, and perhaps even further distribution of the posted work.
In order to create legal security, to facilitate transactions on the Internet, and
to propagate free content, the creative commons model already mentioned
provides the user with a set of pre-formulated licence conditions. In addition, an author may decide not to charge or collect royalties, either from
an exclusive or from a non-exclusive licensee, or not to sue third parties for
the unauthorized use of a copyright work. In practice, such strategies are
often resorted to under business models which aim rapidly to gain a substantial market share by giving a copyright product away free. Moreover, the
strategy of not suing unauthorized users is almost invariably followed to some
extent whenever a digital product protected by copyright is used by a substantial number of unlicensed users and where the right-holder is simply
unable to sue each individual infringer. Of course, besides failure of justici-
ability, business reasons may also play a role in the adoption of a non-suit
strategy, especially when it is hoped that today's unauthorized users will take
a licence of the copyright product—or of its later, enhanced, version—
tomorrow.

15.09 Similarly, although with a different aim, an author may adopt a free or open
source approach.[3] This method has proven particularly successful in the case
of software, where a legal monopoly is combined with the de facto secrecy
of ideas, principles, and algorithms within a program's object code. The
extent to which this model can successfully be transferred to other subject
matter is an issue that is currently much under debate. Conceptually, as long

---

[3] The differences between free and open source software, as well as the differences between
true copyleft licences and licences which permit some form of proprietary exploitation,
are not considered here. For definition of these different types of licences, see, eg, <http://
www.gnu.org/philosophy/free-sw.html>, <http://www.opensource.org/docs/definition.php>,
and <http://www.gnu.org/philosophy/free-software-for-freedom.html>.

as copyright exists, any free and open model has to rely on the copyright interest in order to enforce the obligation upon those making improvements to a work to place those improvements under the public licence and to make sure that no portion of an open source work becomes incorporated within software that is subsequently marketed under a proprietary model.[4]

In legal terms, the decisive question with regard to all such strategies of loosening the grip of copyright is the following: 'To what extent can an author or copyright owner, bind him- or herself for the future?' A user will only be able to be confident that an author or copyright owner will not change his or her mind if the loosening of the grip of copyright is irrevocable. Whether or not the law will require an author or copyright owner to abide by a declaration not to enforce the full ambit of his or her rights ought to depend, at least in part, upon the value attributed to the right of freedom of expression. Therefore, the question of the legal validity of the means used by authors and right owners to loosen their copyright grip over a protected work will be considered below alongside discussion of the impact of that strategy upon freedom of expression. **15.10**

C. Tightening the Grip of Copyright

As in the case of a situation in which the grip of copyright is loosened, a tightening of that grip can also be achieved in two ways: either by way of contractual restrictions going beyond the boundaries of the exclusive rights granted to the author or right-holder by law, or by the application of TPMs restricting acts that are legally beyond the control of the right-holder. One preliminary remark needs to be made before entering into a discussion of these two strategies. Of course, authors or right holders may use contractual means to ensure that they benefit fully from the exclusivity granted to them by law without imposing contractual restrictions going beyond the exclusive rights granted by copyright legislation. Similarly, at least in theory, authors and right-holders may use TPMs only to ensure that their exclusive legal rights are not violated. Such use of contractual or technological protection measures would result in a stronger form of control than that exercised under the strategies of loosening control discussed above. However, such behaviour **15.11**

---

[4] See, eg, § 2(b) of the GNU–Licence (V 2.0).

does not constitute a tightening of the grip of copyright as understood here, since 'tightening' has been defined as a deviation from the rules established by the relevant copyright legislation. As a general rule, the application of contractual or technical restrictions limited to the exclusive powers conferred by law would seem to be universally enforceable, even where they appear in non-negotiated standard agreements, or where they are implemented in such a way that a user does not have the ability to circumvent them.

15.12 The possibilities of extending legal protection through contractual as well as technical means are manifold. Of course, it should be noted that, since contractual clauses only bind the parties to the relevant contract containing the restraining clause, they cannot truly extend exclusive rights because exclusive rights have an effect against all third parties. However, putting this preliminary point aside, it can be noted that a first extension of copyright arises when non-protected subject matter is brought within the control of the author or copyright owner. Subject matter extension of this nature may relate to non-copyrightable subject matter as such or to elements of a copyright work—such as small parts or, more importantly, underlying ideas—that do not, in themselves, enjoy copyright protection. Secondly, the scope of the exclusive rights granted by copyright legislation may be extended. This form of extension, effectively the invention of new exclusive private rights, appears to be less frequent than extensions of the exclusivity through incursions into the free realm of the exceptions and limitations to copyright. These incursions are the focus of most concern. Thirdly, an extension of copyright may be sought with regard to works which are no longer protected, thus withholding them from the public domain after the statutory term of protection has expired.[5] Again, in general, the permissibility, and hence enforceability, of such contractual extensions of the exclusivity of copyright ought to depend upon the value attributed to freedom of expression, and upon the appropriate balance between that right and the interests of the party imposing the contractual terms in question. It is therefore discussed further below when the legal status of freedom of expression in this context is explored.

---

[5] Moreover, it should be noted that an extension of the limits of statutory copyright protection may also be achieved by invoking protection which is not conferred upon a work per se, but upon components of the product in question by other intellectual property rights, such as patents or trade marks.

Technical restrictions can, as a matter of principle, be applied in such a way as   **15.13**
to achieve the same extensions as those that can be achieved by contractual
means. In particular, TPMs can 'fence in' non-copyright material as well as
material which has fallen into the public domain. They can also extend the
scope of exclusive rights by rendering exceptions and limitations to these
exclusive rights ineffective. However, it is important to make a distinction in
this regard. Whereas contractual clauses extending the legal rights granted by
copyright are in most instances targeted at specific extensions, current TPMs
tend to control both acts within and acts outside the realm of copyright. For
example, an effective technical protection against unauthorized copying prevents not only outright piracy, but also the making of legitimate private copies
under statutory private copying exceptions. On the other hand, a TPM which
does not prevent the making of legitimate private copies will also fail to prevent
the making of, at least single, copies of works for non-private purposes. This
is the dilemma faced by national legislators. How can effective protection be
granted to TPMs without interfering with the principles of freedom of
expression that underlie many of the copyright exceptions?

D. The Impact on Freedom of Expression

Having outlined the strategies that an author or right-holder may employ   **15.14**
to contract out of copyright, it is appropriate, first, to evaluate the impact of
copyright on freedom of expression in general and, secondly, to evaluate the
impact which the two opposing strategies of contracting out of copyright
have upon that freedom. In doing so, this section of the chapter will focus
upon the practical effects that copyright has on freedom of expression, while
the following section analyses the normative implications of the relationship
between copyright and freedom of expression in this context.

As defined under Article 10(1) of the European Convention on Human   **15.15**
Rights, the right to freedom of expression includes 'the freedom to hold
opinions and to receive and impart information and ideas without interference by public authority and regardless of frontiers'. As far as the freedom
to hold opinions is concerned, it seems that, at least in the strict sense of
having an opinion in one's own mind without communicating this opinion
to anyone else, that freedom is not affected directly by copyright. The control
which can be exercised by copyright's exclusivity does not extend to acts of

private thought. Of course, it may be argued that the freedom to hold opinions is indirectly affected because copyright restricts the free use of protected material and therefore, as a consequence, restricts the flow of information that is necessary to form personal opinions in the first place. However, such indirect effects upon the holding of opinions would, in any event, be covered by the second element of the right to freedom of expression, that is, the freedom to receive and impart information and ideas.

15.16 At least on a notional level, it could be argued that copyright functions as a general restriction upon freedom of expression because a right-holder is empowered to prohibit third parties from making certain uses of copyright works and, as a result, the possibilities of communication are inevitably curtailed. Hence, one might feel tempted to argue that copyright, by its very existence, acts as a permanent restriction upon the right to freedom of expression. However, this argument appears to be purely formalistic. First, by and large, copyright does not even extend to acts of private reproduction and communication of works. Consequently, it does not conflict with the private expression of ideas. Secondly, as the abundance and flourishing of public speech—both spoken and printed—demonstrates, the public domain does not appear to be much affected by copyright restrictions in that respect. Of course, this is largely because copyright protects only against the taking and using of identical or substantially similar expression of a copyright work, or of derivatives of that work. Copyright does not extend to the ideas or components of copyright material which inspire the creation of further works. In addition, users can often substitute a protected work with another.

15.17 In most cases in which copyright does play a role within the communicative process, it is not used by a right-holder to block access to a work. A publisher, for example, grants exclusive translation rights to a publisher in another country, not because he or she wants to prevent the publication of the translation of the copyright work in that country, but in order to secure the utmost availability of the work. Of course, this may not always be the case but, in most situations, the exclusivity granted by copyright is used to secure access and to achieve a certain price for the work on the market rather than blocking access to and withdrawing a work from the communicative discourse. Hence, an impairment of the freedom of expression is not to be feared. Moreover, it is sometimes insinuated that excessively high prices prohibit access to a particular copyright work and therefore render that work inaccessible. But what is the 'right' price for a work? The legal regime of our market-driven society leaves the question of finding the appropriate price for a product to the market. The mere fact that information is not free does not infringe freedom of expression. Most importantly, however, it would appear that the argument that copyright functions as a constant restriction on the freedom of expression is not a normative argument. In view of the fact that copyright and freedom of expression are themselves both normative concepts, it ought only to be permissible to engage in arguments on a non-normative level when the time comes to define, accommodate, and legislate for the conflicting interests.

However, before returning to this issue in the following section, it is necessary **15.18** briefly to examine the effects of the two strategies of contracting out of copyright on the right to freedom of expression. In this respect, it is easy to see that the strategy of loosening the grip of copyright through the grant of non-exclusive licences, or by following a free or open source philosophy, does not restrict freedom of expression. This is certainly true if the strategy is compared to the full exercise of copyright's exclusivity. If, however, the strategy is compared to a total absence of copyright—as those who see in the mere exercise of copyright an infringement of freedom of expression would have to argue—then any action premised upon copyright protection, including copyleft licences,[6] would have to be seen as a restraint on freedom of expression. Once again, such an argument is, in reality, purely formal. It may likewise be argued that, as copyright enhances creativity, any diminution in the power of copyright will inevitably lead to a diminution in the supply of creative works and will therefore have an effect upon freedom of expression, both with regard to the creation of new expressions and to the availability of expressions for subsequent transformative use. However, even if true, this argument does not apply to the situation discussed in this chapter. In the examples under discussion, the grip of copyright's exclusivity is not loosened by the legislature, but by the creator of the work him- or herself, after the work has been created. In such cases, the prospect of exclusive copyright protection has clearly not been the decisive incentive for the creation to materialize. Hence, the public has not been deprived of anything and the right to freedom of expression has not been infringed.

---

[6] See n 3 above.

15.19 By contrast, however, the strategy of tightening copyright's grip does, almost by definition, infringe the right to freedom of expression, since it goes beyond the boundaries of the exclusive rights granted to the author or right-holder by law. Of course, the extent to which such restrictions will be felt in practice depends on a wide range of factors. In particular, it depends upon the nature of the information in question. Sole source information is more prone to monopolization than information that can be obtained from multiple sources. Also, the substitutability of information, as well as the ease and degree of accessibility of that information, are relevant factors. In practice, with appropriate pricing and easy access, such a strategy may not even be felt as a restraint on freedom of expression.

E. Normative Analysis of the Impact of Contracting Out of Copyright on Freedom of Expression

15.20 At this point, a normative analysis of the impact of the strategies of contracting out of copyright upon freedom of expression has to be undertaken. Again two different sets of questions have to be distinguished. It is first necessary to consider the extent to which the right granted under Article 10 of the European Convention on Human Rights (ECHR) is, already, within its own terms, open to restriction. Secondly, the effect of the scope of the normative claim for freedom of expression upon the different strategies of contracting out of copyright has to be ascertained.

15.21 It must first be noted that this right, as formulated in Article 10(1) of the ECHR, is a right against 'interference by public authority'. Historically, this reflects the initial need for protection of the individual against the State and its monopoly of power.[7] Therefore, as with national constitutional rights, rights under the ECHR do not ab initio appear to protect individuals against the acts of other private parties. However, not only have these rights indirectly influenced the development of rights between private parties, the definition of 'public authority' under the ECHR is now understood to refer not only to the executive body but also to the legislature and judiciary. Legislators are bound not to infringe the rights protected under the ECHR. If they do

---

[7] See, eg, PB Hugenholtz, 'Copyright and Freedom of Expression in Europe', in RC Dreyfuss et al (eds), *Expanding the Boundaries of Intellectual Property* (Oxford: OUP, 2001), 345.

so, the judiciary is obliged to interpret national law in a way that ensures that no conflict with fundamental rights arises. If they, in turn, fail to do so, they will violate those rights.

It must also be noted that, as with other fundamental rights—with the **15.22** exception, perhaps, of the right to life—the right to freedom of expression is not in itself absolute. It cannot be absolute because, in societies in which people interact with one another, it is likely that one person's freedom to act will conflict with another's. However, in democratic societies, based upon the equality of their members, no individual freedom can be absolute. Rather, a balancing of conflicting freedoms is required. In the situation under discussion here, the exclusivity of copyright reserves to the author the freedom to exploit his or her work in the manners defined by law. In many countries, this freedom is protected itself as a constitutional right.[8] At the same time, Article 10 of the ECHR guarantees the right to freedom of expression. Potential conflicts between rights such as this have been foreseen, and are addressed in Article 10(2). In addition to permitting derogations from the protected right in the interests of national security, territorial integrity, or public safety, for the prevention of disorder and crime, and for the protection of health and morals, Article 10(2) allows States to subject the exercise of the freedom established in Article 10(1) to 'restrictions . . . as prescribed by law . . . and . . . necessary . . . for the protection of . . . rights of others'. It follows that the mere grant of copyright by a legislature is not in itself a violation of Article 10. The circumstances under which the operation of copyright law could *in fact* infringe freedom of expression in a manner that could not be justified under Article 10(2) is a difficult issue and will not be addressed here.

It is necessary, however, to turn to consider the extent to which the strategies **15.23** of contracting out of copyright discussed above ought normatively to be limited by the right to freedom of expression. At first sight, the practice of loosening the grip of copyright's protection over a work does not appear to pose a problem. However, the situation may not be as straightforward as it first seems. For example, the author's rights laws of France and Germany place great emphasis upon the protection of the author out of respect for his or her personality, rather than for the utilitarian reason of promoting

---

[8] See also Art II–17(2) of the Draft European Constitution (18 July 2003, CONV 850/ 03); Art 14 of the German *Grundgesetz*.

innovation.[9] The author is protected as a person. For this reason, in addition to moral rights, the laws of both countries grant mandatory rights of remuneration to authors.[10] However, unless it is possible to waive this ostensibly unwaivable entitlement in cases where an author grants a non-exclusive licence,[11] the non-proprietary, non-remuneration schemes of free and open source distribution will inevitably fail. In fact, the question whether promises made by the user of free or open source software with respect to alterations to that software are binding has not been answered by a court. Doubts may arise, in particular, because the contractual restrictions in question appear as standard, pre-formulated terms and conditions in a general open source licence. However, one would have to conclude[12] that an agreement not to exercise copyright with regard to any improvements, alterations, or additions made to the initial free and open code, as well as an agreement not to propertize any part of the open code, including improvements, alterations, or additions would not unduly disadvantage a user and therefore would be likely to be upheld by national courts. After all, the user receives permission freely to use the open code. Moreover, in view of the widespread granting of copyleft licences, the restrictive clauses contained within them will probably not be regarded as surprising and therefore—depending upon the provisions of national law—void.

15.24 Of course, the question of the extent to which *tightening* strategies withstand scrutiny is more interesting. As far as contractual restrictions beyond the exclusivity of copyright are concerned, a distinction must be made between restrictions in contracts individually negotiated at arm's length and restrictions contained in mass market standard terms pre-formulated by a party in a stronger bargaining position. It is important to make this distinction because there may be valid reasons for private parties to agree to a restriction of one party's freedom of expression. Consider, for example, the distribution of an early draft of a manuscript under the express condition that it is not to

---

[9] See, eg, §§ 11, 12 et seq of the German Copyright Act (*Urheberrechtsgesetz*); Art L 121–1 et seq of the French *Code de la propriété intellectuelle*.

[10] §§ 32, 32a of the German Copyright Act; Art L 131–4 of the French *Code de la propriété intellectuelle*.

[11] § 32(3)(3) of the German Copyright Act (so-called 'Open-Source'-or 'Linux'-clause).

[12] It should be noted, however, that the law of standard terms and conditions has not yet been harmonized within the EU. For the strict German approach see § 305 et seq of the German Civil Code (Bürgerliches Gesetzbuch, BGB).

be further circulated or cited. It is difficult to see a reason why such a contractual restriction should not be enforceable. Of course, in some situations, an abuse of a dominant market position by one of the contractual parties may be found, or the motives of one of the parties may give rise to difficulties. The producer of a computer program may, for example, grant a use right to a journalist who agrees to test a beta-version of a new program, subject to the condition that the journalist reviews the program positively. However, contrast this example with a situation in which a company gives a new program to an independent expert for testing and the expert contractually promises to disclose his findings to the public only if the program meets certain expectations. These two examples begin to indicate that there is no clear-cut answer that can be easily applied to all cases in question. Nevertheless, it is almost certain that the right to freedom of expression cannot entirely outlaw contractual agreements extending the exclusive limits of copyright.

However, in all likelihood, the situation will be different when a clause **15.25** extending the scope of copyright is contained in a pre-formulated and non-negotiated agreement. Although not all States bound by the ECHR may have in place laws that control mass-marketed, pre-formulated terms and conditions, the fact that a restriction has not been individually negotiated ought to have major significance in assessing the requirements of the right to freedom of expression in this context. In particular, such clauses may be held to be invalid if they effectively remove the benefit of copyright exceptions designed to support powerful public policy objectives of relevance to the right of freedom of expression, such as the citation right or the exception of fair use for the reporting of news events. Of course, the analysis might be different when the standard clause simply eliminates an exception designed to overcome market failure. Market failure no longer arises where parties manage to conclude a contractual arrangement. It is not the intention to discuss this issue in further detail here. However, it can be concluded that not all contractual restrictions which 'eat into' the realm of copyright are per se null and void as infringements of the right to freedom of expression.

The issue of the normative relationship between TPMs and freedom of **15.26** expression is even more difficult. Undoubtedly, technological protection measures should ideally mirror as closely as possible the limits of exclusive rights as drawn within copyright law. In this respect, it is interesting to note that the relevant legal obligations within the two WIPO Treaties only require contracting parties to grant legal protections to TPMs to this extent.

Signatories are not obliged to grant legal protection against unauthorized circumvention of TPMs that 'fence in' material that does not enjoy copyright protection or is in the public domain. Equally, they are not obliged to extend the obligation to grant legal protection against acts of circumvention undertaken to enable users to benefit from statutory copyright exceptions and limitations.[13] However, TPMs tend to protect both legally protected and legally unprotected material indiscriminately and to prevent illegal or unauthorized uses and uses of a work that are permitted under a statutory exception. Hence, the legislature faces a dilemma. On the one hand, it must avoid underprotection—granting anti-circumvention support only in the case of acts prohibited by law and thus running the risk that access to protected material is enabled in cases where it should not be. On the other hand, it must also avoid over-protection—that is, the granting of anti-circumvention protection that is effective even where a user has a statutory right of access and, as a result, the subversion of its own legislative balancing of copyright and freedom of expression.

15.27 It is well known that the legislature of the European Union has opted for overprotection as a general rule. Only in some instances of off-line technical protection are Member States obliged to provide a form of safety valve. They must take appropriate measures to ensure that right-holders make available to the beneficiaries of certain listed exceptions and limitations the means necessary to benefit from those exceptions and limitations, as long as the beneficiary has legal access to the protected work or other subject matter concerned.[14] In the case of private copying, this safety valve is only optional.[15] In the online environment, exceptions and limitations are completely overridden.[16]

15.28 From a strictly positivist point of view, looking at the law as it stands, this solution legitimizes, to a great extent, contracting out of copyright. Legisla-

---

[13] Art 11 WIPO Copyright Treaty (WCT): 'Contracting Parties shall provide adequate legal protection and effective legal remedies against the circumvention of effective technological measures that are used by authors in connection with the exercise of their rights under this Treaty or the Berne Convention and that restrict acts, in respect of their works, which are not authorised by the authors concerned or permitted by law.' Similarly, Art 18 WIPO Performances and Phonograms Treaty (WPPT).

[14] Art 6(4), Directive (EC) 2001/29 on the harmonization of certain aspects of copyright and related rights in the information society [2001] OJ L 167/10.

[15] Ibid.

[16] Ibid.

tion renders illegitimate any attempt by the user to resort to self-help, even in cases where he or she could claim the benefit of a copyright limitation or exception but where a right-holder has employed a TPM protected by law against circumvention. What may, at first sight, appear to be a contradiction can only be justified if one understands copyright law and legal anticircumvention protection as two legal rules of equal stature. This means that if national legislatures choose to grant certain copyright limitations and exceptions, they can take them away in whole, or in part, at a later date. This is true, of course, only as long as doing so does not offend a higher ranking norm. As a result of the balancing exercise required by Article 10(2), the extent to which Article 10 will serve as such a higher norm will depend upon the circumstances of a particular case. It will also depend upon whether or not Article 10 forms part of national law and the rank which the right contained in Article 10(1) has in a Member State's national law.

F. Some Conclusions

This attempt to describe the legal framework within which 'contracting out **15.29** of copyright' must be viewed has found that, although the exclusive rights established by copyright law can enter into conflict with the right of freedom of expression in certain ways, the right to freedom of expression does not outlaw all contractual agreements extending the exclusive limits of copyright. Not all contractual restrictions that 'eat into' the realm of copyright limitations are per se null and void as a result of this conflict. Rather, the extent to which contracting out of copyright ought to be permissible should depend on a variety of factors including, but not limited to, the extent to which a particular restriction has been individually negotiated at arm's length and the nature and accessibility of the information in question.

As far as TPMs, and the legal protection against their circumvention, are **15.30** concerned, the European legislature and, as a result, all Member States of the EU, have largely legalized strategies from deviating from copyright by technical means. Whether they are permitted to do so under Article 10 is another matter, as is the question where a proper balance between the conflicting values of copyright and freedom of speech should lie. Mounting criticism of a balance that has probably been struck too much in favour of the proprietary interest has certainly contributed to the development of TPMs that are better capable of taking account of existing copyright limitations and exceptions, some of which even grant the user greater freedom than would be available under the exceptions and limitations alone.[17] It may well be that, again, the 'answer to the machine will be in the machine'.[18]

---

[17] Most notably, this strategy has been adopted by Apple with its I-tune music download-service, where the user is permitted to make a number of copies which in most jurisdictions would probably exceed the number allowed under a private use exception.

[18] C Clark, 'The Answer to the Machine is in the Machine', in PB Hugenholtz (ed), *The Future of Copyright in A Digital Society* (The Hague: Kluwer Law International, 1996), 139 et seq.

16

DATABASES, THE HUMAN RIGHTS ACT AND EU LAW

*Jeremy Phillips**

A. Where Is the Historical Introduction?

There isn't one. Database right is divided into two rights, a copyright in the **16.01** creative scheme for the arrangement or selection of data and the *sui generis* right in collated data. Neither of these rights can be said to have evolved

---

* This chapter consists mainly of issues requiring serious thought and patient treatment and should be treated at this stage only as a platform for further research and discussion.

through the development of legal doctrine: both are synthetic rights, created in the laboratory of 1990s European legal science and, so far as English lawyers are concerned, without a meaningful history of their own within the context of copyright law. Since these rights are so new and since so little is still known, from a lawyer's perspective, of the operation of either of these rights, it may be safe to say that the past and present of database rights, in general, have no meaningful existence independent of each other. In the text which follows, some historical observations have been made. Those observations should not be taken as having any wider context than that in which they are made.

B. The Subject That Does Not Exist

16.02   This chapter is based upon a paper prepared for a symposium entitled 'Freedom of Expression and Copyright', a title which does not obviously embrace database rights. Yet there is no other area of intellectual property to which database is as closely aligned as copyright and, since general surveys of the human rights–intellectual property interface do not include database right,[1] it is perhaps appropriate that it be discussed within the context of this chapter.

16.03   The omission from the current literature of any serious analysis of the human rights–database right interface leads to the question: is database right the dog that did not bark (or, given the scant importance which many lawyers place upon database right both in theory and in practice, should we say, the mouse that did not squeak)? This discussion therefore commences by listing some hypotheses as to why the database right has been so far neglected in this analysis:

(i)   *No point of contact has been identified which links database right with human rights issues.* This proposition can be firmly rejected. Even if one wished to take a narrow view as to what were the proper subject matter of database right and human rights respectively, one would still be forced to accept that database right regulates the ownership, control, use, and

---

[1] See, eg, T Pinto, 'The Influence of the European Convention on Human Rights on Intellectual Property Rights' [2002] EIPR 209–19, which makes no specific mention of database rights.

extraction of information, and that human rights protect access to information and the freedom to provide information. There is therefore nothing in the one body of law which inherently precludes the application of the other to the same subject matter.

(ii) *The database right–human rights interface is not a proper subject of study in its own right since the issues raised by database right are precisely those which have already been considered in the context of traditional copyright.* This view too can be firmly dismissed since the premise upon which it is built is false: the subject matter of copyright no longer extends to compilations of data. Such concepts as 'extraction of data' are not analogous to the infringing acts recognized by copyright law. Further, copyright law offers a wide range of defences to an action for infringement, some of which are based on economic grounds and others upon political or social grounds, while there are very limited defences to an action for infringement of a database right.

(iii) *The database right–human rights interface is an area in which study is speculative and premature until the European Court of Justice establishes the parameters within which database right functions.* Uncertainty as to the scope of legal rights has never before been considered a valid basis for refusing to study their impact, particularly by academics. Indeed, it is a good idea to study their impact in advance when the results of such a study can make an impact on the future development of those rights.

(iv) *The database right–human rights interface is not studied simply because it is not studied.* The theory of morphic resonance[2] dictates that, the more people say a particular word or perform a task, the easier it is for others to do likewise because there is a morphic resonance between them. This phenomenon may be illustrated by a theatre audience which, when faced with two exits at the end of a play, will not divide evenly between them but will prefer one over the other; the same phenomenon is displayed by postgraduate law students who, even without having any knowledge of each other's existence, begin more or less simultaneously to select the same subject for their theses and dissertations (the topic 'Copyright on the Internet' is a case in point). If no one studies the

---

[2] R Sheldrake, *Morphic Resonance and the Presence of the Past: the Habits of Nature* (Park Street Press, 1988, 1995).

database right–human rights interface, there is no one to transmit morphic resonance to others—but once one person begins to do so, the very fact of his deed stimulates its emulation by others.

v)   *A straight study of the database right–human rights interface is meaningless unless it also includes the interface of both of those subjects with other bodies of relevant law such as competition law and data protection law.* If this were the ground upon which scholars have so far avoided the subject of this chapter, it should be accorded serious consideration. This is because database right is a creature of the European Union's competition policy and the storage, retrieval, and transmission of data has a schizophrenic personality—living both under the blazing sunlight of human rights law and in the misty shades of information technology law. Without the four disciplines, therefore, of human rights, intellectual property, competition, and information technology law, the value of a direct consideration of database right–human rights issues must be open to question.

C. Four Laws, Three Interlinking Disciplines

16.04 Limitations of time and space mean that consideration of information technology law in this chapter (including issues of data protection) will be omitted and the following analysis will consider just intellectual property, human rights, and the European Union's competition policy.

16.05 Intellectual property rights in databases exist to protect both intellectual activity and the effort and investment involved in their creation. The human rights enshrined in Schedule I to the Human Rights Act 1998 (derived from the European Convention on Human Rights) exist to protect a number of fundamental political freedoms, including the freedom both to impart and to receive expression. European Union law, through the establishment of ground rules for trade, exists for the purpose of conferring economic benefits upon its subjects. Each of these bodies of law has the potential to conflict with the others. For example:

(i)   *Database protection v freedom of expression.* To the extent that a database right prevents a third party extracting or reutilizing data, or arranging or selecting it in a particular manner, it limits the ability of a third party to express himself.

(ii) *Database protection v European Competition law.* To the extent that the control of a database gives a person a dominant position in a market, which may be abused, the commercial exploitation of that database may fall foul of European competition law.[3]

(iii) *Freedom of expression v European Competition law.* An advertisement in which price and product data relating to competing products is assembled in tabular format may be protected under the *sui generis* database right. Where comparative advertisements are regarded as unfair or misleading, they will be contrary to the EU's Directive concerning Misleading and Comparative Advertising.[4]

Since the protection of databases by means of a stand-alone right rather than as a subset of ordinary copyright law is a relatively new legal subject, speculation as to the juridical bases for its copyright-based and *sui generis* features has not yet generated much academic writing on its interface with other areas of law. This chapter will look briefly at the nature of database right and freedom of expression and will then consider some of the issues which the two database rights have raised, or may raise, in the context of their interface with human rights and European law. **16.06**

D. Database Rights: What Are They?

'A database' is defined as: 'a collection of independent works, data or other materials which (a) are arranged in a systematic or methodical way, and (b) are individually accessible by electronic or other means'.[5] This definition exists for the purpose of conferring legal rights and does not necessarily accord with reality. Thus a collection of independent works, data, or other materials which is not arranged in a systematic or methodical way (for example the vast body of manuscript and typed notes accumulated by an academic lawyer over the years and stuffed into files and cardboard boxes in his office) would fall outside the legal definition reproduced above but nonetheless be a working database. The fact that the definition does not **16.07**

---

[3] *RTE and ITP v Commission (Magill)* Joined Cases C-241/91 P and C-242/91 P [1995] ECR I-74.
[4] Council Directive 84/450, as amended by Council Directive 97/55.
[5] CDPA 1998, s 3A(1), transposing Art 1 of Directive 96/9.

accord with reality should not be taken as a criticism of the law, though; it is more a reflection of the fact that the law is concerned with the protection of databases which result from intellectual creativity or the direction of effort and expense, rather than at the protection of data which has evolved into an *ex post facto* functional database.

16.08 There are three types of right which protect databases:

(i) where the database is original if, and only if, 'by reason of the selection or arrangement of the contents of the database, the database constitutes the author's own intellectual creation',[6] it is protected by normal copyright in a literary work.' It is widely assumed that the subject matter of this protection is the structure or scheme of arrangement of a database, but the words of the definition are not so limitative. The criterion of the selection of the contents of a database leaves it open to the argument that those contents may themselves be protected, so long as it is by virtue of their selection that the author has demonstrated his intellectual creativity, at least where the data selected by the author has been created by him for the purpose of its selection. This right may be said to address encouragement of authors to exercise their creative abilities and to provide protection for that creativity once it has been exercised.

(ii) where the database is not original in that sense, the *sui generis* database right will nonetheless protect it against unauthorized extraction or reutilization of its contents, so long as there has been a 'substantial investment in obtaining, verifying or presenting the contents of the database'.[7] This right, in contrast with the right described under (i) above, does not address the author's creativity at all—instead it addresses the protection of investment in a data-rich product, where the cost of assembling the data would otherwise make a database vulnerable to copyright-free replication of its contents by others.

(iii) where the database is not sufficiently original to be protected under (i), and regardless of whether it is protected by (ii), it may still qualify for protection as an original literary work in that it is 'any work . . . which is written' or a 'table or compilation [other than a database]'.[8] In such a

---

[6] CDPA 1998, s 3A(2), Directive 96/9, Art 3(1).
[7] Copyright and Rights in Databases Regulations 1997, r 13(1).
[8] CDPA 1998, s 3(1).

case the protection of the author's original act of creation is the objective which that legal right seeks to achieve; such protection will be accorded even to a table or compilation which, while it contains data and may thus be said colloquially to be a database, does not fulfil the legal definition of a database cited above.

The sentient observer will recognize these three rights in databases as having **16.09** a cultural analogue in the world of fairy tales: two are the Ugly Sisters of literary copyright, while the *sui generis* right is the Cinderella. The niceties of definition are important from an intellectual property perspective, since the category of protection into which a database falls will determine issues such as the nature of infringing acts, the availability of defences, the existence of evidential presumptions, the duration of the rights, and the scope of remedies. This in turn makes it unsafe to generalize about databases, since what is true of one type of database may not be true of another.

E. Do the Origins of Database Right Teach Us about Their Present Nature?

When considering the juridical nature of database rights, it is now seen how **16.10** widely-drafted the definition of a database is and how potentially powerful its grip on the dissemination of information.

The database right was originally intended to protect commercially valuable **16.11** lists and compilations of factual material. Its inspiration was the Nordic Catalogue rule,[9] which provided a ten-year span of protection for lists and catalogues which fell beneath the minimum level of originality for protection in the Scandinavian countries as a work of literary copyright. The definition of 'database' as found in the Directive is potentially extremely wide and is arguably capable of hosting not only catalogues and lists such as telephone directories but also highly-focused collections of intellectual product such as

---

[9] The Nordic Catalogue rule goes back to the 1960s: see eg, Upphovsrättslagen 729/1060, para 49 (Sweden), Tekijänoikeuslaki 8 July 1961/404, para 49 (Finland), Ophavsretslaven 12 May 1961/2, para 43 (Norway). For a helpful review, see G Karnell, 'The Nordic Catalogue Rule', in EJ Dommering and PB Hugenholtz (eds), *Protecting Works of Fact: Copyright, Freedom of Expression and Information Law* (Kluwer, 1991), 67–73.

Lexis and the FTSE financial indices and even entire newspapers, libraries, and supermarkets.

16.12 Database right was not something demanded by industry. Its prime mover was the Commission itself. The perceived imbalance between different types of protection under different national laws was not so much a concern to the Commission as the fact that, in the mid-1990s, something like fifty per cent of the commercially exploited databases in the European Union were based in the United Kingdom, where copyright was conferred on works of low authorship, and was protected for (at that time) life plus fifty years. It was felt that, if all countries had the same normative laws for the protection of databases, then the database industries would in the course of time distribute themselves randomly through the EU, conferring employment and prosperity in their wake.

16.13 Even in the mid-1990s, before database right was instituted, issues of freedom of information arose. In particular:

(i)   Most commercial databases which were supplied in machine-readable format for use with a computer were protected *in personam* by the law of contract, through the terms of licences which often prohibited or restricted the extraction or reutilization of data as well as other uses which would otherwise be regarded as 'fair dealing' and therefore, in the absence of the licence, permissible. Licensees, for the most part, signed these contracts without reading them. There is no record to suggest that licensees and individual employees of a licensee who breached the licence terms were ever sued. This may be because (a) there were no such breaches, (b) breaches occurred but were never detected, (c) breaches occurred and were detected but weren't commercially significant enough to sue over, or (d) the breaches were big enough to sue over but the licensor didn't want to alienate licensees.

(ii)   Databases which were issued to the public in printed format were protected by copyright in original literary works even though the copyright work consisted almost entirely of information which existed within the public domain such as the names, addresses, and contact details of lawyers.[10]

---

[10]   See, eg, *Waterlow Ltd v Rose* [1995] FSR 207.

F. Freedom of Expression under the ECHR

Article 10 of the European Convention on Human Rights (ECHR) is in- **16.14**
cluded in Schedule I to the UK Human Rights Act 1998. It reads:

  1.   Everyone has the right to freedom of expression. This right shall include
       freedom to hold opinions and to receive and impart information and ideas
       without interference by public authorities and regardless of frontiers. . . .
  2.   The exercise of these freedoms, since it carries with it duties and respon-
       sibilities, may be subject to such formalities, conditions, restrictions or
       penalties as are prescribed by law and are necessary for a democratic
       society, in the interests of national security . . . public safety . . . for the
       protection of health or morals, for the protection of the reputation or
       rights of others, for preventing the disclosure of information received in
       confidence.

The Convention text was agreed in 1950 and came into force following the **16.15**
tenth ratification on 3 September 1953, a little under three years before the
coming into force of the Copyright Act 1956 in the United Kingdom. In
1950 there was no concept of database right. This should not surprise anyone: the word 'database' was still more than two decades from entering into
common English parlance. Bearing this chronology in mind, it can be stated
with confidence that the authors and signatories of the ECHR, when drafting Article 10, did not contemplate the specific phenomenon of database
protection, either for copyright or for *sui generis* rights. It must be accepted
that the ECHR is interpreted dynamically as a living document, but also that
the terminology of the ECHR gives no clear indication as to the direction
which that dynamic interpretation will take.

G. Other ECHR Provisions Which Address
Freedom of Expression

Article 10 is specifically aimed at protecting freedom of expression, in **16.16**
terms of both communicating information and receiving it. But it does not
operate in a legal vacuum. Other provisions of the ECHR have a claim on the
same patch of legal territory in which freedom of expression and database
protection come into conflict. They include the following: 'Everyone has

the right to respect for his private and family life, his home and his correspondence.'[11]

16.17 The relevance of this provision is at least twofold. First, personal correspondence may recognizably be a database (particularly where it is stored on email or webmail software) and, secondly, its contents may be such as to create a conflict between competing private and public interests in its suppression or disclosure, in much the same way as Article 10 conflicts exist.

16.18 Another provision is: 'Every natural or legal person is entitled to the peaceful enjoyment of his possessions. No one shall be deprived of his possessions except in the public interest and subject to the conditions provided for by law and by the general principles of international law.'[12] Whether this applies to peaceful enjoyment of one's intellectual possessions and, if so, whether it extends to a right such as database right, which subsists at the very fringes of IP law and is not recognized by TRIPs, is open to debate.[13]

H. Database Right and Freedom of Access to Information

16.19 In the USA, there has been a degree of debate in recent years over the right of access to copyright-protected works. Some of this debate has addressed the issue of encryption and whether the decryption of limited access works is permitted where the copying or other acts done in relation to the target work would themselves be permitted under US copyright law. There has also been substantial discussion as to whether the right to furnish links to another's work which is posted on the Internet is a subset of the right of freedom of speech.[14]

---

[11] ECHR, Art 8 (Right to respect for private and family life).

[12] ECHR, The First Protocol, Art 1 (Protection of property).

[13] The Agreement on Trade-related Aspects of Intellectual Property Rights (1994).

[14] See, eg, the reference to the USA in S de Schrijver and A Goulette, 'Information Location Tools—Liability Issues Raised in Belgian Law' [2003] CTLR 4–10, especially p 9; IJ Garrote, 'Linking and Framing: a Comparative Law Approach' [2002] EIPR 184–98, especially at p 197; R Massey, 'Anti Copying Technology—Freedom of Speech or IPR Infringement' [2002] EntLR 128–30, PL Loughlin, 'Looking at the Matrix: IP and Expressive Freedom' [2002] EIPR 30–9.

I. What Does the Drafting of European Database Right Law Tell Us about Human Rights?

The Database Directive[15] may have only sixteen Articles but it is amply **16.20** endowed with recitals, having sixty of them. But neither the Articles nor the recitals suggest any point of intersection between the narrow issue of protecting databases and the broad policy of freedom of expression. The ECHR does get a mention, but only—along with the Data Protection Directive[16]— in the context of Article 8, which protects the right of privacy.[17] The effect of this mention is to confirm that the protection of databases under the Database Directive is without prejudice to the higher norm of the protection of privacy.

Perusal of the Database Directive, particularly the cumulative effect of the **16.21** first twelve recitals, confirms that the policy behind it was purely economic: by providing a level playing field in the form of harmonized norms of protection for databases throughout the single market, competition would be enhanced, investment protected, and the dawn would break on a new world in which an enriched, invigorated European data provision industry would take on the might of competitors from 'the world's largest data-producing third countries'[18] (such as the USA).

J. Can Article 10 Justify the Appropriation of a Commercial Database by a Competitor of the Database's Owner?

This question was considered by the Cour d'appel de Paris in *Reed v Tigest*.[19] **16.22** The claimant, a company that ran trade fairs and exhibitions, sold directories

---

[15] Directive of the European Parliament and of the Council of 11 March 1996 on the legal protection of databases.

[16] Directive 95/46/EC of the European Parliament and of the Council of 24 October 1995 on the protection of individuals with regard to the processing of personal data and on the free movement of such data.

[17] Recital 48.

[18] Recital 11.

[19] *Société Reed Expositions France (formerly Groupe Miller Freeman) v Société Tigest Sarl* [2003] ECDR 206.

which listed the identity of exhibitors together with other significant data concerning them. The directories were supplied under a contractual stipulation that they were only to be used for the purchaser's own purposes. The defendant obtained the claimant's directories and then offered the data contained in them to third parties, informing them that the data could be used for direct marketing purposes. The claimant sued for, inter alia, infringement of database right under the French Database Law 1998. The defendant maintained that the use of the claimant's directories for the purpose of providing information was protected by Article 10 of the ECHR. The Tribunal de Grande Instance rejected this defence and the defendant appealed.

16.23 The court, rejecting the defendant's appeal in forthright terms, drew upon the distinction between freedom of information and the protection of commercial speech:

> the appellant cannot properly claim that the stipulation in question is contrary to Art.10 of the European Convention on Human Rights. The commercial utilisation of a file belonging to another person is not a prerogative of the freedom of expression, which refers to the communication of opinions, ideas or information of any kind whatever but not, as in the present case, to the use of parts of a third party's file for purely commercial purposes and not for information.[20]

K. Can a Restriction on Even Obtaining Data for the Creation of a Database Breach Article 10?

16.24 In *R v Department of Health ex p Source Informatics Ltd*,[21] a Divisional Court of the Queen's Bench was asked to consider an issue which was tangential to the protection of databases but which was fundamental to the existence of protectible databases. Could the operation of Article 10 of the ECHR be invoked so as to prevent a party from even obtaining data for the creation of a database which it proposed to use for commercial purposes?

---

[20] *Société Reed Expositions France (formerly Groupe Miller Freeman) v Société Tigest Sarl* (n 19 above), at para 19.
[21] [2000] 1 All ER 786; [1999] 4 All ER 185 (Latham J).

In July 1997, the Department of Health issued a policy document to the **16.25** various Health Authorities. This policy document appears to have been provoked by the fact that a data collecting company had sought the consent of general practitioners to its obtaining certain information relating to the treatment which they provided for their patients. This information was sought in a form which would ensure the anonymity of those patients. The Department of Health's policy document was couched in the form of advice which discouraged all such disclosures. Source Informatics, a data gathering business, had itself tried to persuade GPs and pharmacists to let it collect data as to the prescribing habits of GPs, but most GPs who had been canvassed refused to cooperate. This data was commercially valuable, since it informed pharmaceutical companies as to the most current trends in prescription practices. Source Informatics sought a declaration that the Department of Health policy document was, among other things, contrary to Article 10 of the ECHR.

In this application Latham J considered two issues: (i) did the disclosure by **16.26** doctors or pharmacists of anonymous information to a third party constitute a breach of confidentiality, and (ii) did the policy advice of the Department of Health interfere with Source Informatics' right to receive and impart information in breach of Article 10 of the ECHR?

Latham J refused the application. It was not disputed that the information in **16.27** prescriptions handed to pharmacists had the necessary quality of confidence; nor was it disputed that, in receiving the information, each pharmacist was under a duty of confidence in relation to it. But would a pharmacist be making unauthorized use of the information if he acceded to Source Informatics' proposal? The judge considered that their cooperation would result in a clear breach of confidence unless the patient gave consent (which was not the case since the obtaining of actual consent did not form part of Source Informatics' proposal and patients could not be said to have given their implied consent). Since there was a public interest in ensuring that confidences were kept in situations such as this, and Source Informatics' proposal involved a breach of confidence which was capable of founding an action, the Department of Health was entitled to give the guidance contained in its policy document. The Department of Health's interference accordingly consisted of guidance which was a correct statement of the law relating to the disclosure of information received in confidence and could not therefore be in breach of Article 10.

16.28 The Court of Appeal allowed Source Informatics' appeal.[22] In its view, the central issue was not the issue of public interest in relation to Source Informatics' proposed scheme but the question whether a pharmacist breached his duty of confidentiality to a patient if, having dispensed the medicine prescribed, he then used the prescription form as the means of selling anonymized information to Source Informatics.

16.29 After reviewing the usual authorities on confidentiality, the court asked whether a reasonable pharmacist's conscience would be troubled by the proposed use to be made of a patient's prescriptions. Because (i) the concern of the law here was to protect the confider's personal privacy, (ii) the patient had no proprietorial claim to the prescription form or to the information it contained, and (iii) in any case involving personal confidences, no confidence was breached where the confider's identity was protected, the pharmacists' consciences ought not reasonably to have been troubled by cooperation with Source Informatics' proposed scheme: patients' privacy would have been safeguarded, not invaded, and the pharmacist's duty of confidence would not have been breached. The court's conclusion was that participation in Source Informatics' scheme by doctors and pharmacists would not expose them to any serious risk of successful breach of confidence proceedings by a patient. If the Department viewed such schemes as operating against the public interest, then it would have to take further legal steps to control or limit their effect, but the law of confidence could not be distorted for that purpose. The Court of Appeal did not consider the human rights issue further, though the ECHR was mentioned in an oblique aside in the context of the court's reference to the first recital to the Data Protection Directive.[23]

16.30 Without having seen the Source Informatics database, it would not be possible to tell if the database it sought to compile was protected by copyright, by *sui generis* right, or by both. The outcome of this case did not in any event depend on the nature of the proposed database. Perhaps the same can be said of *Imutran*, a copyright case considered below.

---

[22] [2000] 1 All ER 786; [2000] 2 WLR 940.
[23] Council Directive 95/46.

L. The *Imutran* Case: What Does It Teach Us about Freedom of Expression and Database Right?

In *Imutran*[24] the claimant company, which conducted research into xenotrans- **16.31**
plantation, sought to restrain alleged infringements of copyright and breaches
of confidence by the defendants, who campaigned against the replacement
of human organs by those of animals. The allegations related to documents,
being laboratory reports, minutes of meetings, and correspondence. Imutran
obtained interim injunctive relief which it succeeded in extending.

The defendants argued that they were entitled to rely on the defence of fair **16.32**
dealing for the purposes of criticism, review, and news reporting.[25] This
defence failed. What is notable is that Imutran did not allege infringement of
database right in the laboratory records. The law report does not describe
their format, but it is commonly the case that laboratory reports in which
data is compiled on the basis of repeated and compared experiments would
be protected by database right. If that were the case here, Imutran could have
pressed for injunctive relief without concern that the 'fair dealing' defence
would be raised. This is because no 'fair dealing' defence exists under the
1997 Database Regulations and the 'fair dealing' defence under the Copyright, Designs and Patents Act 1988 is not imported into the law on database
right.[26]

M. The Competition Law Dimension

The competition law dimension of database protection has been slow to **16.33**
develop its own jurisprudence. One noteworthy case has however come
before the European Court of Justice's Court of First Instance: the *IMS*

---

[24] *Imutran Ltd v Uncaged Campaigns Ltd and Daniel Louis Lyons* [2001] ECDR 191. See
paras 8.61–8.62 above.
[25] CDPA 1988, s 30(1).
[26] Copyright and Rights in Databases Regulations 1997, r 23. Fair dealing does exist as a
defence in respect to the infringement of the copyright-based database right, but it is difficult
to conceive of a set of factual circumstances in which it may be applicable.

case.[27] This case provided an opportunity for reconsideration of the *Magill* case,[28] in which the ECJ controversially ruled that a refusal of a licence to reproduce a (pre-database right) copyright-protected television programme list—a good example of a modern *sui generis* database right—constituted an abuse of a dominant position under what is now Article 82 EC.

16.34 IMS, a market research company, provided regional wholesaler data report services to interested pharmaceutical companies in respect of sales of pharmaceutical products by pharmacies throughout Germany. Those services were based on a 'brick' structure which divided Germany into 1,860 geographical zones ('bricks') within which sales of individual pharmaceutical products were recorded. In January 2000, IMS suspected that two competitors, Pharma and AzyX, were providing information services based on the same 1,860 brick structure. Both Pharma and AzyX were staffed by former senior members of IMS' staff. IMS successfully brought copyright infringement proceedings against Pharma, obtaining an injunction against the use of any brick structure derived from IMS' 1,860-brick structure.

16.35 In October 2000 NDC, which acquired Pharma in August 2000, asked IMS for a licence to use the 1,860-brick structure in return for an annual fee of DM 10,000. IMS refused to enter into licence negotiations, arguing that NDC could compete against it on the German market without using the structure. NDC then lodged a complaint with the European Commission, alleging that IMS' refusal to license the structure constituted an abuse of its dominant position under Article 82 EC. The Commission alleged that access to the structure amounted to an essential facility for IMS' competitors and that IMS' refusal to license was a prima facie abuse of its dominant position in Germany.

16.36 Following a hearing in April 2001, the Commission adopted a decision in which it found that IMS' refusal of access to the structure was likely to eliminate all competition in the relevant market since, without it, it was

---

[27] *IMS Health Inc v Commission of the European Communities* Case T-184/01 R [2002] ECDR 166. After this chapter was completed, the ECJ ruled on the abuse of monopoly issue on a reference from the original German copyright infringement proceedings: *IMS Health GmbH & Co OHG v NDC Health GmbH & Co KG* Case C-418/01 [2004] ECDR 239. Nothing in the subsequent ruling affects the submissions in this chapter.

[28] *RTE and ITP v Commission* (*Magill*), Joined Cases C-241/91 P and C-242/91 P [1995] ECR I-74.

not possible to compete. This finding was based on the conclusion that the structure constituted a de facto industry standard and that there was good reason to suppose that, unless NDC was granted a licence to the structure, its German operation would go out of business, causing intolerable damage to the public interest. The Commission's decision also expressed its concern for the continued presence of AzyX in the market.

IMS applied to the Court of First Instance for the annulment of the decision **16.37** or the suspension of its operation until the Court rendered judgment in the main action. The President, in a decision subsequently confirmed by the Court, ordered that the operation of the Commission Decision be suspended. He considered that the Commission had misapplied the pre-database right decision of the ECJ in *Magill*. Further, even if the Commission was right to say that the potential incompatibility of IMS' refusal to license the use of its copyright with the objectives of Article 82 EC could not be ruled out, that conclusion could not justify the far-reaching interim measures it adopted in this case. Finally, IMS had also made out a not unconvincing case that the interim measures adopted by the Commission exceeded the scope of its powers to adopt interim measures. Far from preserving the *status quo ante*, the Commission required IMS to license its competitors to perform activities which a national court had found to be copyright infringements.

As in *Imutran* the Court did not indicate precisely what the nature of the **16.38** copyright work was. However, from the fact that it is repeatedly described as a 'structure' the impression is clearly given that the work was a copyright-protected database. This case is unlike *Magill* in that (i) IMS was refusing to permit the use of the structure itself: there was no suggestion that its data had to be licensed, and (ii) IMS was principally trading in the same market as its competitors while, in *Magill*, the television companies were treated as being television companies whose provision of programme data was needed for the development of a market in which they did not compete—a market for magazines providing long-term comparative data on forthcoming programmes.

In *Magill* the ECJ conveyed the message that it was anticompetitive to with- **16.39** hold information which others needed for the purpose of communicating it to third parties, an objective which appears to fall within the broad scope of Article 10(1) of the ECHR and which, so far as the ECJ was concerned, was not subject to the exceptions found in Article 10(2). Now that *IMS* has restored the primacy of copyright in a database structure over the interests of others in using it and in communicating it to third parties, it will be necessary to look to the ECHR rather than to competition law for checks upon the use of unique but commercially valuable properties of this nature.

16.40 If the rights provided by the ECHR, presumably including freedom of speech, apply to companies and other non-natural entities, it must be asked whether a meaningful distinction may be drawn between Article 10 free speech and the principle of free competition (at least where the act of competition is dependent upon the exercise of the right of freedom of speech). The analysis of this question, however, lies outside the scope of this chapter.

N. Closing Comments

16.41 This chapter has sought to alert readers to the fact that the issues at stake with regard to freedom of expression and database right are not simply a matter of balancing the one with the other: the focal area of study is an area of intersection between four sets of rules: (i) database right; (ii) ECHR, Article 10; (iii) competition law and, though it was accorded no more than a fleeting mention in this chapter, (iv) data protection right. The first of these is grounded in private property, the second in personal and corporate freedom, while the third and fourth are grounded in both the integrity of private property and the protection of the public interest. There is scope for a great deal more thought and research on the interplay of these laws and it is hoped that this chapter will have offered at least a couple of directions in which that research may be pursued.

INDEX